Readings
in Educational
Psychology

GEORGE J. MOULY
University of Miami, Coral Gables, Florida

Holt, Rinehart and Winston, Inc.
NEW YORK   CHICAGO   SAN FRANCISCO   ATLANTA
DALLAS   MONTREAL   TORONTO   LONDON   SYDNEY

Library of Congress Catalog Card Number: 76-153752
SBN: 03-083002-8
Printed in the United States of America
1 2 3 4   090   9 8 7 6 5 4 3 2 1

Preface

College professors are fully aware of the need to have their students examine the primary literature. Unfortunately, they are also acutely aware of the extent to which this need is frustrated by the overwhelming discrepancy between the single copy of most professional journals in the average college library and the number of potential student "customers" enrolled in our multisectioned undergraduate courses. Current enrollments have simply made obsolete the older practice of having a selected list of readings. On the other hand, having students hunt helter-skelter through journals to locate meaningful articles is more likely to result in excessive wear and tear on both the students and the journals than in efficient and productive learning.

A book of readings designed to provide convenient access to some of the more profitable and relevant articles in the literature is recognized as at least a partial solution to the problem. Such a compilation is particularly crucial to the effectiveness of a course in educational psychology, where the content is so comprehensive as to require considerable guidance of the neophyte's energies if the operation is not to result in frustration, fragmentation, and wasted effort.

Two problems exist, however. First, there is a limit to the number of papers that can be included in a book of reasonable size. Second, and perhaps more pertinent, is the fact that the undergraduate student cannot always make effective use of the articles published in the professional journals; the more technically adequate and sophisticated the report, the less he can grasp its import. A book of readings that simply "lifts" articles from journals does very little beyond increasing the circulation of a very limited number of articles and relieving the congestion at the library. The solution seems to be to condense as well as to simplify the articles to the level of the students.

Condensing articles permits both the use of a greater number of selections and their adaptation to the level of sophistication, not of the mature scholar for whom the article is typically written, but rather of the undergraduate student whose willingness to consult the professional literature is certainly not independent of his ability to understand it. This provides every member of the class with a minimal coverage of a larger number of significant articles to serve as a common basis for classroom discussion. It is expected that at least a few students will become sufficiently interested in one or more of the articles to consult the original for some of the details to bring to the classroom discussion.

Nearly all the papers in the present collection have been abridged with a view to shortening as well as simplifying the presentation. The adaptations have taken several forms: the omission of secondary findings not vital to the main theme of the paper, the deletion of "expendable" discussion of background literature, the elimination of complex statistical data, and the deletion of the suggestions for further research and the references. While condensing may possibly have reduced the full impact of a given article, it is hoped that the sharper focus on its basic theme and the coverage of a larger number and diversity of selections will compensate for any loss in comprehensiveness.

In each adaptation, the editor has made a conscientious effort to retain the flavor and the style of the original report by using the author's wording wherever possible, with transitional sections to maintain the central unity and developmental sequence of the original exposition. Needless to say, the editor assumes full responsibility for any distortion of meaning that may have inadvertently crept into the adapted reports; he hopes that such distortion has been kept to a minimum.

In order to have the student focus on the key ideas, editorial comments have been included both as a brief introduction adding perspective to the different units and as specific reactions to individual papers; the latter has involved listing implications, placing ideas in context, pointing to related sources, encouraging students to weigh the evidence or to consider its possible classroom application, and so on. The student is strongly urged to add comments of his own as evidence of involvement and a means of ensuring a better grasp of what he has read.

The purpose of the "readings" section is two-fold: (a) to promote in students skill and interest in reading the professional literature, and (b) to provide an introduction to the type of primary data that underlie psychological principles of importance to the educative and pedagogical enterprise and to the scholars whose ideas constitute the substance of educational psychology. Besides supplementing the basic text, this volume brings the student in direct contact with actual source material in the hope that he will become more sensitive to the diversity of data, the viewpoints, and the interpretations which bear on educational issues. It should point out to him, for example, that generalizations do not always warrant the dogmatic finality in which they are sometimes couched, that such generalizations are often gross oversimplifications of the truth. Secondary benefits include adding to the scope and interest of classroom discussions and, no less important, ensuring the student a higher rate of return in educational benefits from his investment of time and energy.

A number of criteria were used in the actual selection of the papers: overall significance as a contribution to educational psychology, scholarliness, timeliness, suitability to undergraduates, and so on. The articles were selected from well over 1000 references to be relatively representative of the field, with emphasis on some of the more recent developments in the areas of early experiences, learning, motivation, etc. They represent a diversity of viewpoints and are expected to have appeal to students of different background and interest as well as level of professional development. An attempt was made to emphasize recency of the articles on the premise that, although significance and relevance are undoubtedly more important criteria than recency per se, recent articles are more likely to present an accurate statement of educational psychology as we know it today. Many selections were omitted because of length, because they involved too high a level of abstraction and/or sophistication for the student to whom this volume is addressed, or perhaps because they did not permit easy synthesis. Since a major consideration was to have the present volume serve as a companion-piece to the author's *Psychology for Effective Teaching,* a number of articles were omitted simply because they did not fit into the pattern of the topics covered in the basic text. Some papers were excluded because they are so well known that they have no further novelty appeal. Finally, selection is always a matter of judgment, frequently made to support the compiler's personal biases; undoubtedly, other criteria could have been given priority and different selections made. Nevertheless, it is believed that the present compilation provides a fair sample of what educational psychology is all about and gives some indication of the ways in which educational psychologists can be helpful to those responsible for educational programs.

Also included are a number of short quotations, selected for their succinct and cogent statement of an important point of view. In addition, the author has added a good number of multiple-choice test items covering the content of each chapter of *Psychology for Effective Teaching.* These can be used by the student to evaluate his grasp of the contents of the various chapters; it is hoped that they will be of special help in refining his understanding of the major ideas in the field. The present volume is more a student's handbook than simply a book of readings; together with the basic text, it offers a "package" of basic materials for a relatively self-contained course in educational psychology.

The editor is obviously deeply indebted to the many authors and publishers who so graciously granted permission to draw from their materials. Their willingness to grant such permission has allowed for a much wider dissemination of the significant literature in educational psychology and, hopefully, will lead to a wider use of the journals themselves. Whatever contribution the present compilation may make to the better understanding of the field must be credited to these original writers; the publication of the present volume simply makes their writings more readily available.

Coral Gables, Florida   G. J. M.
March 1970

Contents

PART II

The Child as a Developing Organism   101

8
Social Development

9
Intellectual Development

10
Individual Differences

PART III
The Process of Learning

11
General Nature of Learning

12
Guiding the Learning Process

PART V

Synthesis

20

The Modern Classroom—A Psychological Reorientation

APPENDIX

Autoinstructional Devices

PART I

Psychology: *The Science of Behavior*

CHAPTER 1

Psychology
and the Teacher

Educational psychology is concerned with the application of the principles of psychology to the understanding of educational processes as they occur in a school setting. Broadly speaking, the major principles relevant to education come from such areas as developmental, social, and clinical psychology, the psychology of learning, mental hygiene, anthropology, biology, physiology, genetics—with, of course, support from the broad field of educational research, statistics, and tests and measurements. Unfortunately, the direct contribution of psychology as a science to educational practice has been disappointingly small. Whereas in the days of Thorndike, psychology was *educational psychology,* shortly thereafter psychologists withdrew to their laboratories where they devoted the bulk of their energies to the various aspects of rodentology, or at best, to the investigation of the acquisition and retention of nonsense syllables and other simple forms of learning—all of which has only indirect bearing on what really goes on in the classroom. Teachers meanwhile went on their merry way, teaching as they had been taught, without benefit of the many insights psychology might have been expected to provide. Rarely did the psychologist visit the classroom to discover the real problems the teacher faces or to understand the processes involved in learning meaningful material in a real-life setting.

Fortunately, there has been a movement of psychology toward education—with Skinner, Bruner, and Ausubel, outstanding examples of

3

psychologists who have turned their attention to education and contributed their knowledge and energies to the improvement of classroom operation. Other psychologists—e.g., Hunt and Guilford—have also made significant, though less direct, contributions. The recent increased availability of research monies for the improvement of educational practices in our country has accelerated this movement, with current emphasis on theories of teaching, early childhood development, and computer-assisted instruction. Meanwhile, there has also been a corresponding increase in the psychological sophistication of teachers as a consequence of the overall improvement in the caliber of training of the teaching profession.

We need to recognize the dynamic nature of educational psychology; what was appropriate even 10 years ago is no longer acceptable, as new knowledge, new insights, as well as new demands emerge. New approaches and new premises have presented new possibilities for more adequate and more meaningful answers to old questions and, what is more important, new probabilities of success—and, of course, also new complications and new problems. Recent developments have provided us with a new sophistication; they have particularly provided us with a new positive outlook and enabled us to leave behind the old fixed-maturation position that so stymied educational practice over the past decades. Equally pertinent, however, is the fact that much of what is currently accepted will, in turn, not be accepted 10 years from now. Teachers need to approach the task of teaching with a thorough appreciation of the transitory nature of knowledge and the crucial need to gear themselves for the on-going task of seeking new and better answers. We cannot just sit and wait for the final answer to be derived; although our answers are not final answers, we nevertheless need to make the best of today's knowledge as the basis for greater sophistication tomorrow—meanwhile relying on the child's natural resilience and capacity for growth, self-direction, and self-repair.

The prospective teacher must not expect to find in a collection of this kind the specific answers to all the questions he will encounter in the classroom. Although these papers present important principles, having definite educational relevance, they do not spell out the particulars in the individual case. This is the work, not of the scientist but of an enlightened and informed teacher who is sensitive to the complexity of educational phenomena and the various interpretations and implications suggested by the primary data.

Education is a matter of the interaction among learner, teacher, method, and materials. We cannot say which method will be best for a given teacher or a particular student. It might be nice if teaching could be reduced to a series of prescriptions of what to do and when but, fortunately, teaching does not lend itself to this type of mechanization. The successful teacher is one who has a good grasp of both theoretical and empirical psychology from which an enlightened craftsmanship can be developed for judicious application to the many problems that teaching typically entails. Equally important, he needs pedagogical skill in the application of these principles to the task of teaching children.

The articles that follow present views on a variety of subjects of professional interest to the prospective teacher. Beery, for example, presents evidence that professional training does indeed make a difference in the effectiveness of beginning teachers. Brickman's article concerns the relative lack of professional reading done by teachers, while Scandura evaluates the "scientific" status of today's teaching. Rogers, on the other hand, addresses himself to the more fundamental question of human freedom and human dignity in the new world of the behavioral sciences. Finally, Wesley takes a slap at the chronic critics of American public education; there is, no doubt, cause for dissatisfaction and we ought to welcome responsible and constructive criticism of our efforts as the basis for self-improvement but it behooves our critics to check their assumptions and their facts as much as it behooves us to recognize our shortcomings.

John R. Beery

Does Professional Preparation Make a Difference? *

The problem of teacher recruitment is one of both quantity and quality: Not only are more teachers needed but teachers are needed who have the best possible preparation for the job. The present study is concerned with the contribution of professional education courses toward the effectiveness of beginning teachers.

The Sample

The sample consisted of 76 pairs of white beginning teachers in three counties in southeastern Florida. One member of each pair was teaching on a provisional certificate because of the lack of all or part of the prescribed sequence of professional education courses; 34 had had no professional education courses at all, 42 had had at least one education course but none had had student teaching. They met all other requirements for certification. Each of the 76 was paired with the best match that could be found from a pool of 343 fully certified beginning teachers from the same counties. Where exact matching was not possible in a given pair because of the large number of matching dimensions in relation to the relatively small number of teachers in the "no professional preparation" or "partial professional preparation" categories, differences were counterbalanced from pair to pair so as to cancel individual pair discrepancies within each subgrouping.

The Ratings

Teacher effectiveness was appraised on the basis of a modified version of Ryans' *Classroom Observation Record*. To the three major clusters or patterns of teacher behavior measured by the Ryans scale (X_o: Understanding, friendly vs. aloof, egocentric, restricted; Y_o: Responsible, businesslike, systematic vs. evading, unplanned, slip-shod; and Z_o: Stimulating, imaginative, surgent or enthusiastic vs. dull, routine), a subsection

* Adapted and abridged from *J. teach. Educ.*, 13: 386–395, 1962. By permission of author and publisher.

M was added to focus on teacher behavior more specifically related to the objectives of professional education courses. A summary rating of overall teaching effectiveness was also obtained.

Three types of observers were used in the study: (a) A group of educators ($n = 11$), none of whom was affiliated in any way with the school system involved or acquainted with the teachers he observed; (b) another group of professionals ($n = 6$) selected from fields other than teaching; and (c) one general observer, a former school superintendent, who observed every teacher in order to provide continuity of observation.

Each teacher was observed five times during the course of his first year of teaching, twice by professional educators, twice by other professionals, and once by the general observer. Visits lasted from 1½ to 2 hours in the elementary school and for two 50-minute periods in the secondary school. Each observer observed a relatively equal number of provisionally and fully certified teachers but was not aware of the certification status of the teachers he was rating.

A two-day training session in the use of the *Classroom Observation Record* was held before the start of the observations in the fall semester and a half-day refresher session was provided before the start of the spring observations. The general purpose of the study was explained to the participating teachers; it was emphasized that the visits were in no way connected with the supervisory program of the school system and that none of the information about a given teacher obtained in the study would be used for any purpose other than group comparison as called for in the design of the study. These assurances were repeated at the time of each observation. Observers and principals were instructed not to discuss the teacher either as to certification status or teaching performance.

Analysis of the Data

Since the basic data, i.e., the ratings obtained from the five classroom observations involved different observers operating from different points of reference, each observer's ratings had to be converted into scaled scores before the ratings of the items in each of the four classifications, X_o, Y_o, Z_o, and M, could be averaged. Since each teacher was observed five times, each subscore represented the average of five ratings. The correlations between the two ratings by educators and the two ratings by other professionals were of the order of .70; these were considered adequate as indices of subscore reliability for the type of group analysis with which the study is concerned.

Results

A comparison of the 15 provisionally certified elementary teachers with no professional education and their fully certified counterparts showed the latter superior on all scales and superior at the 1 percent level of significance on Z_o and S. An overall test of the data for the five scales proved significant at the 1 percent level. This type of analysis was made for the 9 possible comparisons of fully and provisionally certified groups on each of the 5 subscores. As shown in Table 1, in each of the 45 resulting comparisons, the differences favored the teachers with full certification; 25 of the comparisons were statistically significant.

Similar analyses were made using combinations of ratings other than all five at once. Of 105 mean differences, every one favored the fully certified teachers, 40 to a degree significant at the 1 percent level and 30 at the 5 percent level. Although these individual comparisons are not independent, since the same pairs were involved in several comparisons and the ratings of a given observer featured in more than one combination of ratings, the statistical evidence is nevertheless overwhelmingly in favor of the fully prepared teachers.

Although the groups were fairly well equated with respect to most

TABLE 1

Significance Ratios of Mean Differences on Effectiveness
Subscores Seventy-six Beginning Elementary and
Secondary Teacher Pairs by Teaching Level
and Professional Preparation

Teaching Level and Professional Preparation		Significance Level of Subscore Means					t-ratios for Mean Pair Differences on Five Subscores		
	N	X	Y	Z	M	S	M	SE	t
Elementary									
None	15	+	+	**	+	**	+2.29	0.42	+ 5.44**
Some	21	**	*	**	**	**	+2.99	0.15	+19.89**
None or Some	36	**	**	**	**	**	+3.77	0.35	+10.69**
Secondary									
None	19	+	+	*	+	+	+0.97	0.40	+ 2.42
Some	21	+	+	+	+	+	+1.11	0.30	+ 3.68*
None or Some	40	+	+	+	*	+	+1.45	0.37	+ 3.97*
Elementary and Secondary									
None	34	+	+	**	**	*	+2.18	0.47	+ 4.61**
Some	42	*	*	*	**	**	+2.84	0.26	+10.99**
None or Some	76	*	**	**	**	**	+3.57	0.39	+ 9.07**

Legend: + Difference in favor of the fully prepared teachers.
* Difference in favor of the fully prepared teachers and significant at the 5 percent level of confidence.
** Difference in favor of the fully prepared teachers and significant at the 1 percent level of confidence.

relevant variables, there was a definite tendency for the provisionally certified teachers to be older and further removed from college graduation than
their fully certified controls. In order to eliminate the possibility that this
factor of age and recency of graduation, rather than professional education, might have been responsible for the greater effectiveness of the fully
certified group, a separate analysis was made of a subgroup of teachers
born in 1936 and 1937 and graduated from college in 1958 and 1959.
The statistical analysis shows that, with age and recency of graduation held
constant, the differences in ratings of teacher effectiveness are still significant and in favor of the fully certified group. This is further corroborated
by correlational analysis and analysis of covariance.

In summary, the fully certified beginning teachers were rated by competent observers consistently and significantly more effective than their
provisionally certified counterparts, this by both educators and professionals outside the field of education and to about the same degree. On the
other hand, there was overlapping between the distributions of the ratings,
with some of the provisionally certified teachers rated higher than some of
the fully certified.

Limitations

A number of relatively obvious limitations are present in the study.
These range from the subjectivity of the ratings to the fact that the teachers were not matched on personality variables and commitment to teaching
(except as might be reflected in the interview ratings). Furthermore, the
study is restricted to effectiveness in the first year of teaching.

Conclusions

The question asked at the beginning of this study was rather simple
and direct: "Do education courses make a difference?" The answer is
equally simple and direct: "Yes." Within the framework of the above limitations, the general conclusion that completion of the professional education sequence of courses is reflected in more effective first-year teaching
seems warranted.

Comments

1. The study fills a gap in that, despite the existence of
schools of education and certification requirements for many decades, no
evidence of effectiveness has previously (or has subsequently) been shown.
The results are interesting in light of the fact that no other factor of
teacher preparation seems to have an effect: A companion study (Hall,
1962) yielded nonsignificant differences between the achievement of the

pupils of the fully certified and provisionally certified teachers of the present study. A parallel study of the effectiveness of graduate training in education (Moretz, 1963) also showed that possession of an M.Ed. degree is not reflected in higher observer ratings or in greater pupil achievement.

      2. As the author points out, it would be of interest to determine the longevity of the superiority of the fully certified teachers. It would also be of interest to determine the extent to which the superiority of the fully certified group revolves around practice teaching (as separate from the other education courses).

References

Hall, Harry O. "Effectiveness of fully certified and provisionally certified first-year teachers in teaching certain fundamental skills," unpublished dissertation, University of Florida, 1962.

Moretz, Elmo. "A study of the comparative effectiveness of fifth-grade teachers with and without a master's degree," *Diss. Abstr.,* 26: 907, 1965. (University of Miami, 1963).

William W. Brickman

Obstacles Impeding Professional Reading *

Certainly, the professional education of a teacher cannot end with the receipt of his certificate. Unfortunately, too frequently it does. One becomes painfully aware of this fact in discussions with educational personnel, in reading their reports, and in examining subscription lists of pedagogical periodicals and the sale of education books; anyone talking with teachers and other school officials is impressed with their lack of post-scholastic professional knowledge and sophistication. There are, of course, exceptions; furthermore, these remarks deal with readings in pedagogy and do not consider readings in their academic fields of specialization.

A number of factors operate against the teacher's expanding familiarity with pedagogical principles, teaching methods, curriculum problems, research, current educational issues, etc.

(a) We must first consider personal problems. Teaching is energy-consuming; there are papers to be corrected, preparations to be made. Many teachers are working on a part-time basis on an advanced degree in order to qualify for salary increments and promotion. Many hold down a second job. An administrator confined to a desk all day or traveling from one meeting to another is not typically in a suitable frame of mind to struggle with pedagogical ideas in the evenings or week-ends. Then there is community service, family responsibilities, and other personal obligations. A few may be lazy, or simply see their responsibilities totally met when they leave the school in the afternoon.

(b) A second category of obstacles is related to the profession itself: Some teachers look upon their position as just another job, a way of earning a living in a socially respectable way. They have no interest in professional growth, no ambition for advancement. They may have security of tenure and see no way of advancement in salary or position. An ambitious young teacher may actually be resented. Many teachers perceive themselves as subject-matter experts and do not see knowledge of pedagogy as essential to their effectiveness as teachers.

(c) A third class of impediments lies in the very nature of the educational literature: Much of the writings involves vocabulary and style

* Adapted and abridged from *Phi Delta Kappan,* 38: 369–373, 1957. By permission of author and publisher.

of writing that frightens the prospective reader. There is need for a reduction in verbiage, for deletion of the obvious, for precision in expression, etc. Many teachers have difficulty with the statistical concepts and the experimental designs and shy away from the more erudite reports. Another source of difficulty is the "embarrassment of riches"; the very flood of printed matter is enough to discourage many teachers.

  (d) Another important impediment is the cost and availability of the professional literature. Many teachers do not have ready access to the library, especially in suburban and rural areas. The situation is clearly one that needs attention; unless the teacher actually buys (or borrows) books and periodicals which he can examine in the comfort of his home, he is not likely to read widely. Perhaps some foundation could benefit the cause of education by subsidizing educational publications so as to place them within the reach of teachers; the government might also contribute.

  Publication itself will have to be improved in order to avoid repetitiousness of content, to present all sides of an educational issue synthesized into perspective to minimize the danger of misinterpretation, etc. There is need for critical surveys of the literature, for guides to the professional literature on given topics, etc. There is also need for suitable incentives for teachers and administrators to engage in professional reading, writing, and research.

  If professional reading is at all an important activity for educators, it follows that the leaders in the field must do all they can to remove as many of the obstacles as possible. The individual, of course, must exert himself to gain familiarity with pedagogical literature, but he must get some help. A profession that can read critically the most significant writings on principles, procedures, and other phases of pedagogy will be in better position to render effective service to the pupils, parents, community, and much wider geographical spheres.

Comments

  1. In a parallel article, Lauwerys (1957) (a) is concerned as to whether teachers actually read the books, articles, etc. that are written and whether they get the message: Does it produce a change in attitude or lead to the adoption of more effective methods in the classroom? (b) suspects that the writings by the leaders in the field actually strengthen the faith and the enthusiasm of those already converted and raises the morale of a group dedicated to reform, but that there is no great interest in the great books, except when prescribed for a given course; (c) comes to the sad conclusion that teachers and administrators do not read nearly as much as their colleagues in other professions. It seems that while the doctor, the dentist, the engineer read the professional literature because it contains accounts of

discoveries, etc. that are crucial to their professional functioning, it is not as clear that the teacher will become a better practitioner or a more far-sighted thinker by reading some of the "stuff" accumulating in our libraries.

2.   It is also possible that undergraduate teacher education has not placed sufficient emphasis on the systematic use of the library; students who have not had occasion to look at the professional literature in their undergraduate work are not going to begin to do so when they go out in the field.

3.   It is also possible that we attract to the field of education people who have no genuine interest in scholarship as such. It sometimes seems easier to generate enthusiasm for opposition to merit pay, the National Teacher Examinations, innovation, or research, than to find support for professional improvement. It can be argued that we are apparently not recruiting scholars, nor are we making scholars out of the students we recruit.

4.   It may also be that teaching attracts people who are security-oriented rather than advancement-oriented. We lose a number of our more ambitious teachers to other fields or to college teaching where there may be greater recognition of competence. Perhaps this is all part of the mediocrity syndrome which tends to characterize the teaching profession (see Bruner, 1961; Griffiths, 1967; Halpin, 1966; Jensen, 1962).

5.   If the profession considers professional readings important, it will probably have to exert more positive leadership, e.g., providing release time, devoting meetings to improvement, and perhaps making professional growth a more critical factor in promotion and salary considerations.

References

Bruner, Jerome S. "The act of discovery," *Harv. educ. Rev.*, 31: 21–32, 1961.

Griffiths, Daniel E. "An interdisciplinary staffing plan for schools of education," in David L. Clark and Blaine R. Worthen (eds.), *Preparing Research Personnel for Education*. Bloomington: Phi Delta Kappa, 1967. Pp. 22–26.

Halpin, Andrew. "A rationale for training research workers," in Jack A. Culbertson and Stephen P. Hencley (eds.), *Educational Research: New Perspectives*. Danville: Interstate, 1963. Pp. 311–324.

Jensen, Arthur. "The improvement of educational research," *T. C. Rec.*, 64: 20–27, 1962.

Lauwerys, J. A. "Definition and goals of professional reading," *Phi Delta Kappan,* 38: 365–368, 1957.

Joseph M. Scandura

Teaching—Technology or Theory *

The choice suggested in the title, "Teaching—Technology or Theory," does not exist. The practical art of teaching is clearly not theory; in its current state of development it is also clearly more an art than a technology. There are, however, currently underway a number of significant attempts to develop teaching as a technology based on an underlying science and theory. This is important if improvement is to be made in the instructional process, for only science and related technology are cumulative with time. The present paper contrasts teaching as a technology based on a science of learning and as a technology based on an as-yet-to-be-developed theory of teaching; its basic premise is that theories of teaching are opposed to and relatively independent of theories of learning.

Much of the current research on teaching is seen in the perspective of the science of learning. Skinner's model of operant conditioning for a theory of learning provides the scientific basis for programed instruction, for example. Although there has been a trend away from the earlier Skinnerian dominance, the implication is that the psychology of learning will eventually provide a sufficient basis for educational technologies. In contrast, increasing consideration has been given in recent years to the need to develop significant theories of teaching, if instruction is to become something more than an art transmitted solely by emulation, with a number of writers emphasizing the need to consider teaching at a level distinct from learning. Gage (1964), for example, points to the possible value of treating teaching as the *independent* variable with student learning explained on the basis of what the teacher does. This is not going to be a complete solution, of course; what the student learns depends not only on what the teacher says or does but also on what the student himself brings to the situation.

Both the proponents of the learning theory approach to teaching and those advocating separate theories of teaching make assumptions. The former postulate that principles found applicable to the laboratory situation are equally critical in the classroom setting. They realize that existing

* Adapted and abridged from J. M. Scandura, "Teaching—technology or theory," *Amer. educ. Res. J.*, 3: 139–146, 1966. Copyright by American Educational Research Association.

learning theories are not sufficient to act as the basis for classroom teaching without the addition of further principles but they are not willing to forego what is already known about learning. They claim that teaching is reducible to the laws of learning but they also recognize the necessity of developing new teaching technologies; it is impossible to provide immediate reinforcement for each student in the class, for example.

Teaching theorists, on the other hand, postulate that many learning principles may be of only incidental importance to the theory of teaching. They contend that the relevance of the various laws of learning to the act of teaching has not been convincingly demonstrated and, further, that there are teaching concepts and to-be-discovered laws that have no direct counterparts in learning theory. They also point out that, conversely, certain technologies having well-defined theoretical bases (e.g., task analysis, assessment of knowledge, and sequencing) are not covered by learning theories.

The issue is the extent to which theories of teaching need to be coincident with theories of learning. Learning theories have been devised more or less independently of neurological principles, for example; physics and chemistry provide another example of how two sciences can proceed at distinct levels for a long time before reduction becomes possible. Teaching theorists believe that theories of teaching are independent, at least to some degree, of theories of learning. The teacher must concern himself with establishing educational objectives, with systematic methods of presenting subject matter, with assessing *what* the student knows; the teaching theorist's foremost problem is not so much to determine how basic learning principles of learning fit into his theory as it is to integrate precisely those factors with which the learning theorist is not concerned. He is not so much concerned with *how* learning takes place but only with *what* learning did take place.

By way of summary, learning theories have been concerned with *how* learning occurs but say nothing about the categorization and sequencing of information and say little about the relationships between past behavior in one situation and present behavior in another. Although any complete theory of teaching and learning will of necessity consider learning as well as teaching variables, it seems reasonable to suspect that teaching theories may evolve that will be largely independent of traditional learning theories.

Comments

1.   Educators have fluctuated in their relative emphasis on the *teaching* as distinct from the *learning* component of the teaching–learning process. The Herbartian steps, popular at the turn of the century, focused on teaching. Then as the pendulum swung in response to advances in the

psychology of learning, teaching was given a very secondary role. It now appears that the psychology of learning does not provide a sufficient basis for instruction.

2.   The extent to which theories of teaching can be developed apart from theories of learning is a crucial issue to be resolved. There might, nevertheless, be room for the two approaches, at the intersection of which the teaching–learning process might be seen in clearer perspective. Perhaps the issue finds a parallel in the producer–consumer interaction in merchandising.

Reference

Gage, N. L. "Theories of teaching," in E. R. Hilgard (ed.), *Theories of Learning and Instruction.* 63d Yearbook, National Society for the Study of Education, Pt. I. Chicago: University of Chicago Press, 1964. Pp. 268–285.

Carl R. Rogers

The Place of the Person in the New World
of the Behavioral Sciences *

The science of psychology is rapidly increasing the number of situations in which it has established that if certain describable, measurable conditions are introduced, then predictable, definable behaviors will result. First, let us review a few selected examples of what I mean by the increased ability of psychology to understand, predict, and control behavior:

We know how to set up the conditions under which individuals will report as true, judgments which are contrary to the evidence of their senses.

We know how to change the opinions of an individual in a selected direction, without his ever becoming aware of the stimuli which caused him to change.

We can predict, from the way an individual perceives the movement of a spot of light in a dark room, whether he tends to be prejudiced.

We know the attitudes which, if provided by a counselor, will be predictably followed by certain constructive personality and behavior changes in the client.

We know how to provide animals with a most satisfying experience consisting entirely of electrical stimulation.

We know how to provide psychological conditions which will produce vivid hallucinations and other abnormal reactions in a thoroughly normal individual in the waking state.

We know how to select individuals who will exhibit certain behaviors; to establish conditions which will lead to various predictable group behaviors; to establish conditions which, in an individual, will lead to specified behavioral results. In animals, our ability to understand, predict, and control goes even further, possibly foreshadowing future steps in relation to man.

However, the prospect has frightening, as well as strongly positive, aspects. It seems to me that we have not given adequate consideration to the profound social, political, ethical, and philosophical problems this power of control which science is making available to us will present.

* Adapted and abridged from Carl R. Rogers, "The place of the person in the new world of the behavioral sciences," *Pers. and Guid. J.,* 39: 442–451, 1961.

While behavioral scientists seem to have taken for granted that the findings of science will be used in the prediction and control of human behavior, they seem to have given little thought to what this will actually mean.

Let us look at some of the elements involved in the concept of the control of human behavior which scientific knowledge will provide.

(a)   First comes the selection of goals. Skinner, for example, suggests that one possible goal to be assigned to behavioral technology is: "Let man be happy, informed, skillful, well-behaved, and productive." In *Walden Two,* using the guise of fiction to express his views, he has his hero say: "Give me the specifications, and I'll give you the man!"

(b)   The second element in this process is to discover the means for attaining the ends we have selected.

(c)   The third element involves the question of power: There has been too little recognition of the fact that someone will have and will use this power. To hope that it will be exercised by the scientists or by a benevolent group seems to me a hope little supported by either recent or distant history. German rocket scientists, for example, worked devotedly for Hitler to destroy Russia and the United States. Now depending who captured them, they are working devotedly for Russia in the interest of destroying the United States, or devotedly for the United States in the interest of destroying Russia.

(d)   The fourth step is the exposure of the individual to the methods and conditions mentioned so that men become productive, or submissive, or whatever it has been decided to make them. Skinner has his hero in *Walden Two* emphasize: We can achieve a sort of control under which the controlled, though they are following a code much more scrupulously than was ever the case under the old system, nevertheless *feel free.* They are doing what they want to do, not what they are forced to do. That's the source of the tremendous power of positive reinforcement—there's no restraint and no revolt. By a careful cultural design, we control not the final behavior, but the *inclination* to behave—the motives, the desires, the wishes. The curious thing is that in that case the *question of freedom never arises.*

The Picture and Its Implications

The increasing power for control which the behavioral sciences will provide will be held by someone who will choose purposes or goals to be achieved. Most of us will then be increasingly controlled by means so subtle that we will not even be aware of them as controls. Thus, if this line of reasoning is correct, it appears that some form of completely controlled society—a *Walden Two* or a *1984*—is coming. Man and his behavior would become a planned product of a scientific society. Concerning individual freedom and democratic rights, Skinner is quite specific: The hypothesis that man is not free is essential to the application of scientific method to the study of human behavior. The free inner man who is held responsible for his behavior is only a prescientific substitute for the kinds of causes which are discovered in the course of scientific analysis. All these alternative causes lie *outside* the individual.

I have strong personal reactions to the kind of world I have been describing, for it would destroy the human person that I have come to know in the deepest moments of psychotherapy. That all of this is an illusion and that spontaneity, freedom, responsibility, and choice have no real existence would be impossible for me to believe. If the results of my efforts and those of others is that man becomes a robot, created and controlled by a science of his own making, then I am very unhappy indeed. If good life of the future consists in so conditioning individuals through the control of their environment and of the rewards they receive that they will be inexorably productive, well-behaved, happy, or whatever, I want none of it. To me this is a pseudo-form of the good life which includes everything save that which makes it good.

Ends and Values in Relation to Science

It seems to me that the view I have presented rests on a faulty perception of goals and values in their relationship to science, in that it grossly underestimates the significance of the purpose of a scientific undertaking. In any scientific endeavor, not only is there a prior personal choice of the purpose or value which that scientific work is to serve, but further this subjective value choice which brings the scientific endeavor into being always and necessarily lies outside of that endeavor. It can never become part of the science involved in that endeavor.

When Skinner suggests that the task of the behavioral science is to make man productive, well-behaved, etc., he is making a choice. He could just as easily have chosen to make men submissive, dependent, etc. Yet, in his scientific picture of man, Skinner denies the existence of man's "capacity to choose," his freedom to select his course of action and to initiate appropriate steps. Here is, I believe, the deepseated contradiction or paradox. Science rests on the assumption that behavior is caused, that a specified event is followed by a consequent event. But we must not forget that science itself, that each specific scientific endeavor, rests on a personal subjective choice. A personal, subjective choice made by man sets in motion the operation of science, which in time proclaims that there can be no such thing as a personal subjective choice.

Each of these choices is a value choice. The scientist investigates this rather than that because he feels the first has more value for him. He interprets his results in a way that is closer to the criterion which he values.

Both these value choices are never part of the scientific venture itself. This does not mean that values cannot be included as the subject for scientific investigation. If I value knowledge of the "three R's" as a goal of education, science will give me increasingly accurate information as to how this goal can be achieved. If I wish to determine whether problem solving ability is "better" than knowledge of the three R's, then the scientific method can also study these two values but *only* in terms of some other value, e.g., college success, which I have subjectively chosen.

It can be argued that a continuing scientific endeavor will evolve its own goals, that initial findings will alter the direction and subsequent findings will alter them further; that the science somehow develops its own purpose. This view, apparently implicitly held by many scientists, appears a reasonable description but it overlooks one element in this continuing development, namely, that subjective personal choice enters at every point at which the direction changes. In other words, science derives its meaning from the objective pursuit of a purpose which has been subjectively chosen by someone. This purpose or value can never be investigated by the particular scientific investigation to which it has given birth and meaning. Consequently, any discussion of the control of human beings must first and most deeply concern itself with the subjectively chosen purposes which such an application of science is intended to implement.

An Alternative Set of Values

This line of reasoning, if valid, opens new doors to us: The fact that science takes off from a subjectively chosen set of values means that we are free to select the value we wish to pursue. We are no longer limited to producing a controlled state of happiness, productivity, etc. Instead, we might value:

Man as a process of becoming; as a process of achieving worth and dignity through the development of his potentialities.

The individual human being as a self-actualizing process, moving on to more challenging and enriching experiences.

The process by which the individual creatively adapts to an ever new and changing world.

The process by which knowledge transcends itself.

We can turn to our science and technology of behavior with a very different set of questions: Can science help us in the discovery of new modes of richly rewarding living? More meaningful and satisfying modes of interpersonal relationships? In short, can science discover the methods by which man can most readily become a continually developing and self-transcending process in his behavior, his thinking, his knowledge? Can science predict and release an essentially "unpredictable" freedom?

A Possible Concept of the Control of Human Behavior

This point of view is in sharp contrast to the usual conception of the relationship of the behavioral sciences to the control of human behavior as previously described. Specifically, it postulates that: (a) It is possible for us to choose to value man as a self-actualizing process of becoming; to value creativity and the process by which knowledge becomes self-transcending. (b) We can proceed by the methods of science to discover the conditions which necessarily precede these processes, and through continuing experimentation to discover better means of achieving these purposes. (c) It is possible for an individual to set these conditions with a minimum of power or control. (d) Exposed to these conditions, individuals become more self-responsible, more self-actualizing, flexible, more unique and varied, and more creatively adaptive. (e) Such an initial choice would inaugurate the beginnings of a social system in which values, knowledge, adaptive skills, and even the concept of science would be continually changing and self-transcending. The emphasis would be on man as a process of becoming; it would be on process, not on end states of being. It would mean moving toward the "open society," at the opposite pole of the closed society represented by *Walden Two*.

The Choice

It is my hope that I have helped to clarify the range of choice which will lie before us and our children in regard to the behavioral sciences. We can choose to use our growing knowledge to enslave people, in ways never dreamed of before, depersonalizing them, controlling them by means so carefully selected that they will perhaps never be aware of their loss of personhood. We can choose to utilize our scientific knowledge to make men necessarily happy, self-behaved, and productive. We can, if we wish, choose to make man submissive, conforming, docile. Or at the other end of the spectrum of choice, we can choose to use the behavioral sciences in ways which will free, not control; which will bring about constructive variability, not conformity; which will develop creativity, not contentment; which will facilitate each person in his self-directed process of becoming; which will aid individuals, groups, and even the concept of science to become self-transcending in freshly adaptive ways of meeting life and its problems.

Comments

1.   This most timely and significant article calls for a clear-cut policy on the use of the results of the behavioral sciences. We need to define our goals and decide how we want to use the power that has been

made available to us. Science can help man achieve his goals; he needs to be sure his goals are worth achieving. In a parallel article, Rogers (1956) emphasizes that there is no problem holding greater potentialities for human growth or human destruction than that of learning how to live with this increased power.

2.   The differences in the Rogerian and the Skinnerian points of view are best presented in a debate between Rogers and Skinner (1956); the articles should be consulted for details.

Reference

Rogers, Carl R., and B. F. Skinner. "Some issues concerning the control of human behavior," *Sci.*, 124: 1057–1066, 1956.

Edgar B. Wesley

The Critic's Creed *

I believe in the failure of American education, in the superiority of foreign schools, the inferiority of American teachers, the frivolity of our curriculum, the superficiality of education requirements, and the degradation of teacher training. I believe that the typical American child cannot read, write, spell, cipher, or think; whereas his counterpart in Russia and Switzerland is a walking phenomenon of achievement. This scandalous condition was achieved deliberately in order to provide students for the culturally benighted professors of education and to restrict teaching positions to the low-ability, miseducated horde of American teachers. Furthermore, I believe that scientists and scholars of all kinds should be given teaching certificates and licenses to practice engineering, architecture, or any chosen profession.

I renounce the doctrines of motivation, progressiveness, life-adjustment, permissiveness, and the whole child. These afflictions descended upon American teachers like murrain upon the cattle of ancient Egypt. In contrast to these delusions I assert my faith in discipline, drill, the transfer of training, phonetics, the segregation of the gifted, and the power of positive teaching. Educational salvation for America can be achieved by abandoning social, emotional, artistic, physical, and vocational aims, by concentrating upon mental development, and by chanting incessantly the wonder-working phrases "basic education," "higher standards," and "excellence."

* From *Phi Delta Kappan,* 46: backcover, 1964. By permission of author and publisher. Originally part of a talk, "Twice Told Wails," made at a PDK-sponsored principals' meeting.

That's What They Said

"Psychology is our chief hope for clarifying man's aims and for discovering the means for achieving them."

> Gordon W. Allport. *Becoming*. New Haven: Yale University Press, 1955. [4]

"One aim of education is to make available the wisdom of the past and present so that youth will be equipped to solve the problems of the future."

> Gordon W. Allport. "Values and our youth," *T. C. Rec.*, 63: 211–219, 1961. [211]

"The teacher is fully successful, however, when his student has become as thoroughly emancipated, self-motivated, and self-directed as to be no longer in need of a teacher. This, I admit, seldom happens; it is merely an ideal. The ideal teacher is so successful at making himself unnecessary that he teaches himself out of a job."

> Robert B. MacLeod. "The teaching of psychology and the psychology we teach," *Amer. Psychol.*, 20: 344–352, 1965. [352]

"It is simply not true that the demands of teaching many people require us to teach badly."

> Arthur W. Combs. *Perceiving, Behaving, Becoming*. 1962 Yearbook. Washington, D.C.: Association for Supervision and Curriculum Development, 1962. [108]

"Although a teacher cannot teach what he does not know, he can sure enough inspire students to learn what he does not know. A great teacher has always been measured by the number of his students who have surpassed him."

> Don Robinson. "Scraps from a teacher's notebook," *Phi Delta Kappan*, 45: 316, 1964.

"The concept of a 'good' teacher as usually defined has led to the encouragement of impersonal criteria; a broader, more comprehensive notion is that of determining a 'better teacher,' which has a personal referent. *'Good' connotes a singular condition and implies some degree of universality in its reference (i.e., good teachers are the same everywhere), whereas*

the dimension of 'better' fits the uniqueness of the person to which it is ap-
plied. Consequently, to become a 'better' teacher suggests diversity; to ap-
proach 'good' implies sameness. Saying all teachers can become better
states something quite different from urging all teachers to be good; 'bet-
ter' suggests an emerging condition emphasizing the process and growth of
becoming rather than an established state, a finished stability of being."

Robert D. Strom and Charles Galloway. "Becoming a better teacher,"
J. teach. Educ., 18: 285–292, 1967. [286]

"We do not select young men just graduated from engineering school
to teach engineering or young men fresh from medical school to teach
medicine. But we do select young people just emerging from college to be
the academic teachers of the young. These young teachers can impart very
little wisdom derived from their own experience, since they have had so
little. The limitations imposed by their lack of experience practically force
young people to teach what they were taught—which is fine if they were
well taught."

Don Robinson. "Scraps from a teacher's notebook," *Phi Delta Kappan,*
47: 279, 1966.

"How many of your social studies faculty have ever held public office
or served a political party? How many of your English teachers have ever
edited or written anything for publication? Have your science teachers
worked in industry or in research laboratories? Have they done anything
to create or operate the scientific side of our culture? Have the art teachers
ever created anything artistically significant?

"In short, have your teachers been successful practitioners of the arts
and science they teach? If not, how can they successfully teach them?"

Don Robinson. "Scraps from a teacher's notebook," *Phi Delta Kappan,*
42: 40, 1961.

"Part of the failure of educational psychology was its failure to grasp
the full scope of its mission. It has too readily assumed that its central task
was the application of personality theory or of group dynamics or what
not. In fact, none of these efforts produced a major contribution to educational practice largely because the task was not really one of application in
any obvious sense, but of formulation. Learning theory, for example, is
distilled from descriptions of behavior in situations where the environment
has been arranged either for the convenience of observing learning behavior or out of theoretical interest in some special aspect of learning—
reinforcement, cue distinctiveness, or whatever."

Jerome S. Bruner. *Toward a Theory of Instruction.* Cambridge: Harvard University Press, 1966. [37]

"Unfortunately, most elementary school teachers have great difficulty in translating global statements of objectives defined in terms of the qualities of the 'educated adult,' the 'good democratic citizen,' or 'areas of competency,' into specific learning opportunities for students. There is no logical way that one can be derived from the other."

> Donald A. Myers and M. Frances Klein. "Educational programs— Elementary schools," in Robert L. Ebel (ed.), *Encyclopedia of Educational Research*. Washington: American Educational Research Association, 1969. Pp. 395–410. [396]

". . . we should not expect the conclusions and principles derived from . . . research to find their way into educational practice unless we make the translation ourselves or develop a systematic technology through which such translation may be effected."

> A. A. Lumsdaine. "Instruments and media of instruction," in N. L. Gage (ed.), *Handbook of Research on Teaching*. Skokie, Ill.: Rand McNally & Company, 1963. Pp. 583–682. [670]

"Nothing revealed by a close study of institutions designated as 'teachers colleges,' as compared to those designated as 'liberal arts' colleges, justifies a sweeping assertion that one *type* of institution consistently gives the student a better education than the other. The belief that 'liberal arts' colleges provide more 'breadth and depth' than teachers colleges rests essentially on the notion that courses in education in teachers college displace general requirements, subject specializations, or both. My investigators have convinced me that this is simply not the case."

> James B. Conant. *The Education of American Teachers*. New York: McGraw-Hill, Inc., 1963. [77]

"It is often assumed, at least by noneducationists, that if prospective teachers were not required to take 'so many education courses' to qualify for licenses, more young people would choose to teach. Without denying the weakness of some such courses, this just could be the greatest fantasy of all."

> Lindley J. Stiles. "Unique tutorial program wins applause," *Phi Delta Kappan*, 50: 108, 1968.

". . . the present condition of research on teacher effectiveness holds little promise of yielding results commensurate with the needs of American education. . . . after 40 years of research on teacher effectiveness . . . one can point to few outcomes that a superintendent of schools can safely employ in hiring a teacher or granting him tenure."

> Committee on the Criteria of Teacher Effectiveness, A.E.R.A. Washington: American Educational Research Association, 1953. [657]

"But knowing little more now than was known then, retaining its place as the most unchanging institution in our society, with the possible exception of the church, feeling its inadequacies but generally ignoring them, education is still here dealing with all the children of all the people 'by guess and by gosh.' "

> David L. Clark. "Educational research: A national perspective," in Jack A. Culbertson and Stephen P. Hencley (eds.), *Educational Research: New Perspectives.* Danville: Interstate, 1963. [8]

"As more than one observer has noted, the planners of some large-scale curriculum projects seem to assume simultaneously (1) that any subject can be taught to children at any age, and (2) that the teachers who will do this teaching are an ineducable lot of dunderheads who are the main barrier to innovation."

> M. B. Miles. *Innovations in Education.* New York: Teachers College, Columbia University, 1964. [11]

"By 2000, or before, 'teaching' as it is now commonly accepted will be dead, and the job of an educator will be transformed into that of a facilitator—one who creates a rich, responsive environment that will elicit the most learning and change from the student. There won't be any compulsory education, but educators will have to make their material relevant to students' needs or they won't get any students.

By 2020, we will have discovered that all learning is joyful, and will realize that solving an elegant mathematical problem and making love are only different classes of the same order of things, sharing common ecstasy. Advanced learning . . . will be like pursuing a pretty girl."

> George B. Leonard and John Poppy. Cited in *Phi Delta Kappan,* 49: 268, 1968. (*Look Magazine.*)

"The story of education is the story of mankind. It is the saga of wisdom and folly, achievement and regression, creativity and lethargy, enlightenment and superstition. The aims of education represent the bases of social advancement. In every generation, great educators like Socrates, Epicurus, Comenius, Pestalozzi, Froebel, and James, have been in the vanguard of humanitarian causes and have made progress possible in man's relationship to himself and to society."

> Frederick Mayer. "The bases of social advancement," *Phi Delta Kappan,* 42: 202–206, 1961. [202]

References

Beck, Robert H., et al. *Perspective on the Conant Report.* Minneapolis: University of Minnesota Press, 1960.

Benne, Kenneth B. "The philosopher and the scientific research in the study of education," *J. soc. Issues,* 21: 71–84, 1965.

Burton, William H. "Basic principles in a good teaching-learning situation," *Phi Delta Kappan,* 39: 242–248, 1958.

Cartwright, William H. "The teacher in 2065," *T. C. Rec.,* 66: 295–304, 1965.

Gage, N. L. "An analytical approach to research on instructional methods," *Phi Delta Kappan,* 49: 601–606, 1968.

Leonard, George B. "Education and Ecstasy. 1. How school stunts your child; 2. Visiting day, 2001 A.D.; 3. The future now," *Look,* 32, No. 19: 31–43, Sept. 17, 1968; No. 20: 37–48, Oct. 1, 1968; No. 21: 57–68, Oct. 15, 1968. Also in paperback: *Education and Ecstasy.* New York: Delacorte Press, 1968.

CHAPTER 1

Test Items

1. Psychology contributes to educational practice by
   a. clarifying the goals toward which education is oriented
   b. clarifying the nature of the interaction among learner, teacher, and learning process
   c. determining the relative effectiveness of various teaching methods
   d. placing human behavior under scientific control
   e. promoting an understanding of human nature

2. The boundaries of educational psychology are best described as
   a. fixed
   b. flexible
   c. indeterminate
   d. a matter of personal preference
   e. unlimited

3. The primary purpose of a control group in an experiment is
   a. to equate the groups on relevant variables
   b. to increase the number of subjects on which the results are based
   c. to neutralize the operation of chance
   d. to permit the comparison of two (or more) experimental programs
   e. to provide a basis for interpreting the effects of the experimental factor

4. In an experimental study of the relative effectiveness of teaching methods, the most difficult factor to control is
   a. the bias due to personal preference
   b. the extra practice between learning session
   c. the interaction among teacher, learner, and method
   d. the operation of chance
   e. student motivation due to novelty (the Hawthorne effect)

5. For their raw data, educational psychologists rely on
   a. deductions from theoretical premises
   b. experimentation almost exclusively
   c. observation and common sense
   d. a variety of research methods
   e. the viewpoints of experts in the psychology of learning

6. Educational psychology is primarily concerned with
    a. clarifying the goals toward which the school is to strive
    b. determining the attainability of the various educational objectives
    c. developing a taxonomy of sound educational objectives
    d. facilitating the process whereby educational goals can be achieved
    e. providing a foundation for developing theories of effective teaching

7. A course in educational psychology is designed to
    a. promote an understanding of the nature of the child
    b. provide the scientific basis for curriculum development
    c. provide rules for effective teaching
    d. provide the scientific basis for educational practice
    e. to serve as the basis for evaluating teaching methods

8. Teaching is best defined as
    a. the art of presenting subject matter
    b. the process of imparting knowledge
    c. the process of promoting pupil growth
    d. the process of structuring knowledge for effective assimilation
    e. the task of promoting pupil learning

9. Probably the most critical criterion of "who should teach" is
    a. a high level of scholarship and intellectual ability
    b. knowledge of subject matter
    c. personal warmth and a mature liking for children
    d. a sense of personal integrity and professional commitment
    e. skill in the use of effective teaching methods

10. Probably the greatest stumbling block in the study of teacher effective-
     ness is
     a. the diversity of tasks in which teachers are involved
     b. the homogeneity of teachers with respect to teaching skills
     c. the relative unimportance of the teacher's contribution to pupil
         growth
     d. the screening already done by teacher-training institutions
     e. the unavailability of a suitable criterion

11. The relative unproductivity of teacher-effectiveness research is mostly
     due to
     a. the complexity of the teaching process
     b. the fact that teaching and learning are essentially independent
         processes
     c. the nonamenability of teacher behavior to scientific appraisal
     d. our failure to devise meaningful theories of teaching
     e. the unwarrantedly global conception of "teacher effectiveness"

12. The major contribution of Project Higher Horizons to educational practice is probably
    a. its demonstration of the effectiveness of compensatory education
    b. its demonstration of the relative futility of special programs undertaken late in the child's development
    c. its development of curriculum materials for lower-class children
    d. its development of a blueprint for similar programs elsewhere
    e. its demonstration of the importance of community involvement

13. The various educational projects for the culturally disadvantaged, e.g., Project Higher Horizons, are predicated on the premise that
    a. the culturally disadvantaged cannot profit from the school's standard academic programs
    b. the fight against crime begins in the school
    c. human potential develops through suitable experiences
    d. we need to do all we can for children of the lower classes
    e. potential dropouts can be reclaimed by suitable education

14. The McGill studies have given support to the view that
    a. the academic and intellectual inadequacies of children of the lower classes are the results of early environmental deprivation
    b. a high level of stimulation is necessary for both the well-being and the development of the organism
    c. human motivation is governed by the principle of homeostasis
    d. maturation is both necessary and sufficient for the development of early behavior
    e. the organism seeks an optimal level of stimulation

15. The current emphasis on Head Start is predicated on the premise that
    a. all American children are entitled to a free education
    b. early sensory deprivation can result in irretrievable intellectual losses
    c. extended schooling is essential if future citizens are to cope with the knowledge explosion
    d. formal preschool experiences are essential to success in first grade
    e. the intellectual inferiority of the lower classes must be overcome by massive compensatory education

16. Moore's success in teaching three-year-olds to read would find support in the writings of all of the following except (choose one)
    a. Ausubel
    b. Bruner
    c. Durkin
    d. Gates
    e. Gesell

17. According to modern psychologists, the years from two to four are of
     greatest significance from the standpoint of the development of
     a. adequate socialization
     b. effective speech and linguistic patterns
     c. emotional security
     d. frustration tolerance
     e. intellectual (cognitive) competence

18. Development of affection in monkey infants is best explained on the
     basis of
     a. the maturational process
     b. operant conditioning
     c. a process closely akin to imprinting
     d. secondary reinforcement associated with the hunger drive
     e. secondary reinforcement associated with contact comfort

19. Harlow's study of the development of affection in young monkeys
     would seem to challenge current emphasis on
     a. the alleged detrimental effects of maternal deprivation
     b. mother–child relationships
     c. peer-group contacts
     d. the primacy of the so-called primary drives
     e. the validity of the drive-reduction theory of motivation

20. Modern psychologists would attribute the ill-effects of extended insti-
     tutionalization of infants and young children to
     a. emotional deprivation
     b. the impersonal atmosphere of institutions
     c. inadequate physical care
     d. initial hereditary limitations
     e. sensory deprivation

21. Ryans found clear-cut differences in teacher effectiveness between
     a. elementary and secondary teachers
     b. experienced and beginning teachers
     c. male and female teachers
     d. physical sciences and social sciences teachers
     e. none of the above classifications showed clear-cut differences

22. Ryans found that, by contrast to their counterparts,
     a. effective teachers were more narrowly focussed in their intellec-
         tual and social interests
     b. experienced teachers were high on "warm, understanding" and
         "stimulating, imaginative"

c. female teachers were more emotionally stable
d. male teachers of English were high on "responsible, business-like"
e. secondary teachers were more permissive

CHAPTER 2

Psychology as a Science

Educational psychology is concerned with the modification of behavior primarily as it occurs in the classroom. The fact that there is no consensus as to just how this modification takes place is evident from the different, if not conflicting, viewpoints represented by current theories of learning. This is not necessarily cause for alarm and despair: To the extent that a theory is simply a way of structuring empirical data into conceptual perspective, postulating one theory as a model does not preclude the possibility of other useful, although different, models. This is especially understandable in dealing with a subject of the complexity of learning. Any attempt to devise, or to telescope existing theories into, a single theory of learning that will encompass the whole field of learning does not, at least for now, appear feasible, or even logical.

A common criticism of our current psychological orientation, particularly that based on associationistic premises, is that it is too directly concerned with simple behavior in simple laboratory settings on the part of relatively uncomplicated subjects and, consequently, unnecessarily divorced from the problems of real life—whether in school learning, community mental health, or social unrest. Educators have been particularly critical of how little psychology has had to offer the classroom teacher. It would seem difficult, for example, to derive much insight into the nature of emotions or of values by studying the behavior of planeria. Nor, in fact, do the generalizations regarding the reinforcement of the rat's bar-pressing behavior with food pellets provide the teacher with ready-made systems of motivational strategies helpful in having children learn algebra. While such findings generated out of the laboratory context are not devoid of educational implications, the extent of their applicability to classroom practice is not particularly obvious, nor pervasive.

An even greater degree of disenchantment prevails with respect to formal theories of learning. While most psychologists readily acknowledge the contribution of current theories of learning to the development of psychology as a science, a growing number of educational psychologists are questioning the relevance of current theories of learning as the foundation for effective pedagogical strategies. In this, they are apparently joining teachers, who, since the days of their last foray into the theory market when they were badly misled into an overuse of drill, for example, have taught—well or badly—with only the vaguest notion of theoretical issues. Reassured that, despite their outward differences, the various theories supported essentially the same educational practices, teachers have maintained that with all of their conflicts and confusion, learning theories are of little help in deciding how to deal with the typical teaching–learning situation. As a consequence, much of today's teaching is based on trial and error or on experience and tradition rather than on well-defined theoretical premises.

In a sense, the issue divides psychologists into two overlapping camps. Some are convinced that psychology has much to offer education, that, even though the transfer may not be direct, the methodologies and concepts of psychology can profitably be brought to bear on educational problems. They feel that psychologists acquainted with the learning literature and experimental methodology can approach real-life learning situations with the ability to develop procedures for more effective classroom operation. Others—e.g., Scandura (Chapter 1)—feel that psychology to date has been relatively unproductive in its contribution to classroom practice and suggest the need for an entirely different approach centering around the psychology of *teaching*.

More specifically, a growing dissatisfaction with theories of learning has led to a corresponding recognition of the need to conceptualize into psychologically meaningful terms complex human learnings as they occur in the complex setting of the classroom, to sketch out the beginnings of a series of instructional theories, and to develop perceptual and psychological generalizations relevant to such matters as curriculum development. So far these efforts have been spasmodic and hardly equal to the complexity of the task. It is recognized, for example, that we must not look for *a* theory of instruction, but rather a number of theories corresponding to the various subaspects of teaching. Before this is done, there is need to define basic premises and dimensions. This is not going to be an easy task and, according to Travers (1966), we ought not to expect "immediate delivery."

Meanwhile, inasmuch as learning theory and research findings do not interpret themselves as to specific applications, there appears to be a definite need for a middleman operating between the psychologist as a scientist and the practitioner in the field.

In the articles in this chapter, Skinner discusses the present status of teaching as a scientific enterprise. Bruner, on the other hand, voices the increasing demand for theories of *teaching,* while Buswell addresses himself to the more fundamental question of the need to synchronize educational practice to current educational theory.

Reference

Travers, Robert M. W. "Towards taking the fun out of building a theory of instruction," *T. C. Rec.,* 68: 48–60, 1966.

B. F. Skinner

The Science of Learning
and the Art of Teaching *

Some promising advances have recently been made in the field of learning. Special techniques have been designed to arrange what are called "contingencies of reinforcement"—the relations which prevail between behavior on the one hand and the consequences of that behavior on the other —with the result that a much more effective control of behavior has been achieved. It has long been argued that an organism learns mainly by producing changes in its environment, but it is only recently that these changes have been carefully manipulated.

Recent improvements in the conditions which control . . . learning are of two principal sorts. The Law of Effect has been taken seriously; we have made sure that effects *do* occur and that they occur under conditions which are optimal for producing the changes called learning. Once we have arranged the particular type of consequence called a reinforcement, our techniques permit us to shape up the behavior of an organism almost at will. . . . Simply by presenting food to a hungry pigeon at the right time, it is possible to shape up three or four well-defined responses in a single demonstration period. . . . Extremely complex performances may be reached through successive stages in the shaping process, the contingencies of reinforcement being changed progressively in the direction of the required behavior. The results are often quite dramatic. In such a demonstration one can *see* learning take place. . . .

A second important advance in technique permits us to maintain behavior in given states of strength for long periods of time. Reinforcements continue to be important, of course, long after an organism has learned *how* to do something. . . . They are necessary to maintain the behavior in strength. Of special interest is the effect of various schedules of intermittent reinforcement. . . . On the practical side we have learned how to maintain any given level of activity for daily periods limited only by the physical exhaustion of the organism and from day to day without substantial change throughout its life. Many of these effects would be traditionally

* Excerpts from B. F. Skinner, "The science of learning and the art of teaching," *Harvard educ. Rev.,* 24: 86–97, Spring 1954. Copyright © 1954 by President and Fellows of Harvard College.

assigned to the field of motivation, although the principal operation is simply the arrangement of contingencies of reinforcement.

. . .

In all this work, the species of the organism has made surprisingly little difference. It is true that the organisms studied have all been vertebrates, but they still cover a wide range. Comparable results have been obtained with pigeons, rats, monkeys, human children, and most recently . . . human psychotic subjects. In spite of great phylogenetic differences, all these organisms show amazingly similar properties of the learning process. It should be emphasized that this has been achieved by analyzing the effects of reinforcement and by designing techniques which manipulate reinforcement with considerable precision. Only in this way can the behavior of the individual organism be brought under such precise control. It is also important to note that through a gradual advance to complex interrelations among responses, the same degree of rigor is being extended to behavior which would usually be assigned to such fields as perception, thinking, and personality dynamics.

From this exciting prospect of an advancing science of learning, it is a great shock to return to that branch of technology which is most directly concerned with the learning process—education. Let us consider, for example, the teaching of arithmetic in the lower grades. The school is concerned with imparting to the child a large number of responses of a special sort. The responses are all verbal. They consist of speaking and writing certain words, figures, and signs which, to put it roughly, refer to numbers and to arithmetic operations. The first task is to shape up these responses —to get the child to pronounce and to write responses correctly, but the principal task is to bring this behavior under many sorts of stimulus control. . . . Over and above this elaborate repertoire of numerical behavior . . . the teaching of arithmetic looks forward to those complex serial arrangements of responses involved in original methematical thinking. The child must acquire responses of transposing, clearing fractions, and so on, which modify the order or pattern of the original material so that the response called a solution is eventually made possible.

Now, how is this extremely complicated verbal repertoire set up? In the first place, what reinforcements are used? Fifty years ago the answer would have been clear. At that time educational control was still frankly aversive. The child read numbers, copied numbers, memorized tables, and performed operations upon numbers to escape the threat of the birch rod or cane. Some positive reinforcements were perhaps eventually derived from the increased efficiency of the child in the field of arithmetic and in rare cases some automatic reinforcement may have resulted . . . from the solution of problems or the discovery of the intricacies of the number system. But for the immediate purposes of education the child acted to avoid or escape punishment. It was part of the reform movement known as progressive education to make the positive consequences more immediately effective, but any one who visits the lower grades of the average school today will observe that a change has been made, not from aversive to positive control, but from one form of aversive stimulation to another. The child at his desk, filling in his workbook, is behaving primarily to escape from the threat of a series of minor aversive events—the teacher's displeasure, the criticism or ridicule of his classmates, an ignominious showing in a competition, low marks, a trip to the office "to be talked to" by the principal, or a word to the parent who may still resort to the birch rod. In this welter of aversive consequences, getting the right answer is in itself an insignificant event, any effect of which is lost amid the anxieties, the boredom, and the aggressions which are the inevitable by-products of aversive control.

Secondly, we have to ask how the contingencies of reinforcement are arranged. When is a numerical operation reinforced as "right"? Eventually, of course, the pupil may be able to check his own answers and achieve some sort of automatic reinforcement, but in the early stages the reinforcement of being right is usually accorded by the teacher. The contingencies she provides are far from optimal. It can easily be demonstrated that, unless explicit mediating behavior has been set up, the lapse of only a few seconds between response and reinforcement destroys most of the effect. In a typical classroom, nevertheless, long periods of time customarily elapse . . . between the child's response and the teacher's reinforcement. In many cases . . . as much as 24 hours may intervene. It is surprising that this system has any effect whatsoever.

A third notable shortcoming is the lack of a skillful program which moves forward through a series of progressive approximations to the final complex behavior desired. A long series of contingencies is necessary to bring the organism into the possession of mathematical behavior most efficiently. But the teacher is seldom able to reinforce at each step in such a series because she cannot deal with the pupil's responses one at a time. It is usually necessary to reinforce the behavior in blocks of responses—as in correcting a work sheet or page from a workbook. . . . Even the most modern workbook in beginning arithmetic is far from exemplifying an efficient program for shaping up mathematical behavior.

Perhaps the most serious criticism of the current classroom is the relative infrequency of reinforcement. Since the pupil is usually dependent upon the teacher for being right, and since many students are dependent upon the same teacher, the total number of contingencies which may be arranged during, say, the first four years, is of the order of only a few thousand. But a very rough estimate suggests that efficient mathematical behavior at this level requires something of the order of 25,000 contingencies.

. . . Perhaps 50,000 contingencies is more conservative an estimate. In this frame of reference the daily assignment in arithmetic seems pitifully meager.

The result of all this is, of course, well known. Even our best schools are under criticism for their inefficiency in the teaching of drill subjects such as arithmetic. The condition in the average school is a matter of widespread national concern. Modern children simply do not learn arithmetic quickly or well. Nor is the result simply incompetence. The very subjects in which modern techniques are weakest are those in which failure is most conspicuous, and in the wake of an ever-growing incompetence come the anxieties, uncertainties, and aggressions which in their turn present other problems to the school. Most pupils soon claim the asylum of not being "ready" for arithmetic at a given level or, eventually, of not having a mathematical mind. . . . Few pupils ever reach the stage at which automatic reinforcements follow as the natural consequences of mathematical behavior. On the contrary, the figures and symbols of mathematics have become standard emotional stimuli. The glimpse of a column of figures, not to say an algebraic symbol or an integral sign, is likely to set off —not mathematical behavior—but a reaction of anxiety, guilt, or fear.

The teacher is usually no happier about this than the pupil. Denied the opportunity to control via the birch rod, quite at sea as the mode of operation of the few techniques at her disposal, she spends as little time as possible on drill subjects and eagerly subscribes to philosophies of education which emphasize material of greater inherent interest. . . . Eventually, weakness of technique emerges in the disguise of reformulation of the aims of education. Skills are minimized in favor of vague achievements— educating for democracy, educating the whole child, educating for life, and so on. And there the matter ends; for, unfortunately, these philosophies . . . offer little or no help in the design of better classroom practices.

There would be no point in urging these objections if improvement were impossible. But the advances which have recently been made in our control of the learning process suggest a thorough revision of classroom practices and, fortunately, they tell us how the revision can be brought about. This is not, of course, the first time that the results of an experimental science have been brought to bear upon the practical problems of education. The modern classroom does not, however, offer much evidence that research in the field of learning has been respected or used. This condition is no doubt partly due to the limitations of earlier research. But it has been encouraged by a too hasty conclusion that the laboratory study of learning is inherently limited because it cannot take into account the realities of the classroom. In the light of our increasing knowledge of the learning process we should, instead, insist upon dealing with those realities and forcing a substantial change in them. Education is perhaps the most important branch of scientific technology. It deeply affects the lives of all of us. We can no longer allow the exigencies of a practical situation to suppress the tremendous improvements which are within reach. The practical situation must be changed.

. . . Children play for hours with mechanical toys, paints, scissors and paper, noise-makers, puzzles—in short, with almost anything which feeds back significant changes in the environment and is reasonably free of aversive properties. The sheer control of nature is itself reinforcing. This effect is not evident in the modern school because it is masked by the emotional responses generated by aversive control. It is true that automatic reinforcement from the manipulation of the environment is probably only a mild reinforcer and may need to be carefully husbanded, but one of the most striking principles to emerge from recent research is that the *net* amount of reinforcement is of little significance. A very slight reinforcement may be tremendously effective in controlling behavior if it is wisely used.

. . .

. . . These requirements are not excessive, but they are probably incompatible with the current realities of the classroom. In the experimental study of learning it has been found that the contingencies of reinforcement which are most efficient in controlling the organism cannot be arranged through the personal mediation of the experimenter. An organism is affected by subtle details of contingencies which are beyond the capacity of the human organism to arrange. . . . We have every reason to expect, therefore, that the most effective control of human learning will require instrumental aid. The simple fact is that, as a mere reinforcing mechanism, the teacher is out of date. This would be true even if a single teacher devoted all her time to a single child. . . . If the teacher is to take advantage of recent advances in the study of learning, she must have the help of mechanical devices.

. . .

Of course, the teacher has a more important function than to say right or wrong. The changes proposed would free her for the effective exercise of that function. Marking a set of papers in arithmetic—"Yes, nine and six *are* fifteen; no, nine and seven *are not* eighteen"—is beneath the dignity of any intelligent individual. There is more important work to be done—in which the teacher's relations to the pupil cannot be duplicated by a mechanical device. Instrumental help would merely improve these relations. One might say that the main trouble with education in the lower grades today is that the teacher is unable to do anything about it and *knows that too*. If the advances which have recently been made in our control of behavior can give the child a genuine competence in reading, writing, spelling, and arithmetic, then the teacher may begin to function, not in lieu of a cheap machine, but through intellectual, cultural, and emotional contacts of that distinctive sort which testify to her status as a human being.

.   .   .

There is a simple job to be done. . . . The necessary techniques are known. The equipment needed can easily be provided. Nothing stands in the way but cultural inertia. . . . We are on the threshold of an exciting and revolutionary period, in which the scientific study of man will be put to work in man's best interests. Education must play its part. It must accept the fact that a sweeping revision of educational practices is possible and inevitable. When it has done this, we may look forward with confidence to a school system which is aware of the nature of its tasks, secure in its methods, and generously supported by the informed and effective citizens whom education itself will create.

Comments

1.   By serving as the groundwork for the introduction of automated instruction and calling for the reconsideration of all aspects of educational operations, the present article has had and will continue to have a tremendous impact on educational practice. It is also of interest in that it relates laboratory experimentation to classroom practice.

2.   The preceding are excerpts from Skinner's classical article; the original source should be consulted for a more complete picture. See also Skinner (1958) and Skinner (1961).

References

Skinner, B. F. "Teaching machines," *Sci.*, 128: 969–977, 1958.
Skinner, B. F. "Why we need teaching machines," *Harv. educ. Rev.*, 31: 377–398, 1961.

Jerome S. Bruner

Needed: *A Theory of Instruction* *

Over the past several years, it has become increasingly clear to me, as to any thinking person today, that both psychology and the field of curriculum suffer jointly from the lack of a theory of instruction. This article attempts to set forth some possible theorems underlying such an instructional theory.

A theory of instruction is prescriptive; it is not a description of what has happened when learning has taken place, but rather something which is normative, which states something about what you do when you put instruction together in the form of a course. Now this is not a very surprising thing, and yet I am struck by the fact that many persons in the field of education have assumed that we could depend on theories other than theories of instruction to guide us in this enterprise. For example, I find the educator's dependence on learning theory as touching as it is shocking. The fact of the matter is that a theory of learning is not a theory of instruction; it is a theory that describes what takes place when learning is going on and after learning has taken place.

A theory of instruction must be prescriptive in the sense that it is before the fact; it is before learning has taken place and not while or after it has taken place. For example, programed instruction relies on small steps —because learning apparently takes place in small increments, but there is no evidence that says that simply because learning takes place in small steps that the environment should be arranged in small steps. In doing so, we fail to take into account the fact that man operates by taking large packets of information and breaking these down to his own bite-size and that, unless he has the opportunity to do that, learning becomes stereotyped. At least, it is a worthy hypothesis about instruction.

There are four aspects to a theory of instruction: (a) It should concern itself with the factors that predispose the child to learn effectively. (b) It should concern itself with the structuring of knowledge in such a way that the diversity of information can be simplified through a structure so

* Adapted and abridged from Jerome S. Bruner, "Needed: a theory of instruction," *Educ. Lead.,* 20 (8): 523–532; May 1963. Reprinted with permission of the Association for Supervision and Curriculum Development and Jerome S. Bruner. Copyright © 1963 by the ASCD.

that this case is a sub-case of something else. We must recognize that structure is relative to the learner and that it does not do to simply say that, because physics has great economy, productiveness, and great power for the scientist, this structure has the same meaning for the child. You take the child where you find him and give the structure that is economical, productive, and powerful for him. (c) It should be concerned with the optimal sequence that is required for learning. And, finally, (d) it should concern itself with the nature and the pacing of rewards and punishments, successes and failures.[1]

I should warn you, in conclusion, to beware of the likes of us. We do not have a tested theory of instruction to offer you. What is quite plain is that one is needed and I would propose that we work together in its forging. I warn you for a good reason. Educators are a curiously doctrinal or ideological kind of people. You are given to slogans and fight and believe in their behalf. You have looked to psychology for help and have often been misled into accepting mere hypotheses as the proven word. It is so partly because it is hard to test the adequacy of ideas in an educational setting.

We are now living through a great revolution in education. Our survival may depend on its successful outcome—our survival as the human race. I know no group in our society more devoted to the commonweal than our educators. In this era of new curriculum, new teaching assignments, new automated devices, your best rudder is a healthy sense of experimentation backed by a skepticism toward educational slogans.

Comments

1.   Psychologists have become concerned over the inadequacies of the learning model as the basis for teaching prescriptions. A number of writers have attempted to define the teaching implications of the various theories of learning, but it is clear that the correspondence does not fall in a one-to-one relationship. Hence, the more recent emphasis on the development of theories of *teaching*.

2.   A number of writers have raised significant issues concerning the development of theories of teaching. Gage (1964), for example, cautions against what he sees as an inevitably futile attempt at developing a single theory to encompass all the phenomena that go under the single name of *teaching;* this is precisely the hang-up that has beset theories of learning. He presents a convincing argument that *teaching* is too broad, vague, and unwieldy to be covered by a single theory, that if we are to avoid chasing ourselves into a dead-end of unproductivity, we need to recognize the multidimensionality of the teaching function and begin by ana-

[1] The article discusses each of these four components in considerable detail.

lyzing teaching into its basic procedures or elements, e.g., the type of teacher activity (information-giver; motivator, advisor, etc.); the type of educational objective (cognitive, affective, and psychomotor); etc. It might be noted in passing that failure to recognize the multidimensionality of teaching was probably responsible in large part for the relative unproductivity of research into teacher effectiveness.

      3.   We must also recognize that developing theories of teaching is no easy matter; in penetrating discussions, Ausubel (1963) and Travers (1966) point to a number of shortcomings in our current attempts in this direction.

References

Ausubel, David P. *The Psychology of Meaningful Verbal Learning*. New York: Grune & Stratton, Inc., 1963.

Gage, N. L. "Toward a cognitive theory of teaching," *T. C. Rec.*, 65: 408–412, 1964.

Travers, Robert M. W. "Towards taking the fun out of building a theory of instruction," *T. C. Rec.*, 68: 48–60, 1966.

Guy T. Buswell

Educational Theory
and the Psychology of Learning *

"Any educational situation involves a purpose or objectives, a content to be learned (a curriculum), and a process of learning. The overall purpose . . . is expressed as theory of education. The *process* of changing behavior in accordance with educational theory is expressed as the psychology of learning. Between these two is the content to be learned, whether substantive subject-matter or behavior traits. The thesis of this paper is that if the psychology of learning is to be effective in the schools, it must focus its interests and design its experiments with awareness of the theory of education that is currently accepted by the society in which the schools operate. As theory of education is modified, the direction of psychological study must be changed if its results are to influence educational practice. . . . In the 1920's, research on drill in arithmetic was in harmony with educational theory; in 1955, such studies would have far less significance because the purpose and theory of teaching arithmetic have undergone marked changes. The ultimate objective, of course, is not merely to relate research to currently accepted educational theory, but rather, to do the kind of research that will help to formulate an educational theory that is valid" [p. 177].

During the last century, the theory of education as the acquisition of knowledge was reflected in such inscriptions as *knowledge is power*. Prior to the Civil War, the amount of knowledge was such that its accumulation did not constitute an insurmountable burden to the learner. But, the situation has changed, particularly in the field of science; the manifold increase in the amount of knowledge raised the problem of what knowledge is of most worth and resulted in a fight for time among the different branches of the curriculum. The problem was met by devising the elective system—at first with a relatively large group of common requirements and a few electives and gradually toward a larger number of electives and a correspondingly smaller group of required subjects. By the 1920's, this was recognized as inadequate and a new orientation toward survey courses was

* Adapted and abridged from Guy T. Buswell, "Educational theory and the psychology of learning," *J. educ. Psychol.*, 47: 175–184, 1956. Copyright © 1956 by the American Psychological Association and reproduced by permission.

tried. This too has been found inadequate. "The elective program was characterized as a specialization in depth in a few areas, with chasms of ignorance between. After the thirty years of experimenting with survey courses, they are often subject to the charge of . . . specialization in superficialities" [p. 178].

If, in theory, we define a good education in terms of the acquisition of knowledge and skill, our research efforts are likely to be oriented toward the psychology of retention, with the major concern centering on the subject-matter to be learned. We can, on the other hand, subscribe to a theory in which education is defined in terms of changes to be brought about in the learner—i.e., in increased abilities "to respond successfully to the diverse and unpredictable situations that life will bring. Advocates of such a view would readily admit the necessity of a fairly large amount of basic knowledge and skill. Certainly, they would not make a virtue of ignorance. But rather than conceive of education as an encyclopedic coverage of knowledge, they would deal with the heritage of knowledge in a highly selective way. They would probably agree on the necessity of certain knowledge and skill, for example, ability to read. . . . However, they would stress such general outcomes as learning how to think, learning how to use a library, . . . , how to adjust to frustrations. However, if a person holding such a theory of education were asked to epitomize it, he might answer somewhat as follows: The expanding body of knowledge has already reached such proportions that an attempt by an individual to cover it is hopeless. Therefore, a better procedure might be to select . . . a basic body of knowledge and skill that will serve as tools and background for whatever kinds of learning one might need to acquire. Using this carefully selected body of facts, concepts, skills, experiences, which would probably constitute the main load of early education, the learner would then test and enlarge his abilities through a rather thorough learning of some sample fields. The essence of such a theory of education is that it is the function of the school to help the pupil learn how to learn; that, beyond the acquiring of basic knowledge and concepts, the purpose of the school is to provide some excellent samples of learning experience in a number of fields and extending over the usual number of years devoted to general education. On completion of such a period of education, the graduate might say, 'There are many things I do not know and many skills I do not have, but I know how to get them, I know how to learn what needs to be learned.' This concept is the opposite of blueprinting or stereotyping the education of a child. It aims at giving him versatility and independence" [pp. 179–180].

Subscribing to such an educational theory would make transfer the crucial psychological factor. But the main concern would not be with the carry-over of one academic subject to another but rather transfer of a general nature as might be embodied in Harlow's "learning how to learn." Three major fields of research suggest themselves: (a) research on teaching students how to think. "There is plenty of evidence that students can learn to think within the area of the subject-matter being taught, but the real issue is whether or not they can transfer the ability to other areas" [p. 182]; (b) research related to the learning of personality characteristics. The school's task of promoting personal responsibility, critical judgment, social relations again revolves around the problem of transfer of training; and (c) research concerning human motivation. A major contribution of the school under this theory of learning would be to modify the motivation operating within the learner. "If, for example, the school could succeed in making students intellectually curious, the operation of such a motive might have a broader effect than the mastery of any specific segment of subject-matter" [p. 183]. These three problems are of relatively little importance in the theoretical structure of "Knowledge is Power"; they are at the heart of the concept of education whose essence is in learning how to learn.

Comments

1.   Buswell points to the most significant question of the direction in which the school's efforts are to be applied. There can be no denying the need for coordination of the psychology of learning and our views on the nature and purpose of education.

2.   This is even more important today with the knowledge explosion and the rapidly changing world for which youngsters are to be educated. At one time, a scholar could be expected to master a substantial fraction of man's total knowledge. This is now patently impossible—and even if it were possible, it would mean educating children for a world that would no longer exist by the time "they got there." Under these conditions, learning how to learn is the only approach to education that makes sense.

3.   Buswell's use of the term *theory* to represent purpose or objective may be bothersome to some people, particularly when used in parallel with theories of learning. Perhaps, *philosophy* of education would be more appropriate.

4.   Buswell's emphasis on transfer as a logical means of dealing with today's superabundance of knowledge also points to a need to structure this knowledge into functional organization. To the extent that broad general principles cut across subject-matter disciplines, such an orientation might make it possible for a person to operate somewhat more effectively in a number of related fields. It now seems that specialization is becoming progressively more necessary while survey courses are becoming progressively more superficial. It behooves the school to make a continuous appraisal of its offerings in a constant search for marginal studies that can profitably make room for what is more meaningful in the light of today's and tomorrow's world.

That's What They Said

"All educational programs presumably rest upon some sort of psychological theory, but, in the case of recent reform movements, the theory is implied more often than stated. Many of the new programs being tried, and the changes being urged, are planned and sponsored by individuals or groups who give scant attention to theories of learning and are concerned primarily with the security of the nation and with the continuity and advancement of the culture."

> Paul Woodring. "Reform movements from the point of view of psychological theory," in E. R. Hilgard (ed.), *Theories of Learning.* 63d Yearbook, National Society for the Study of Education, Part I. Chicago: University of Chicago Press, 1964. Pp. 286–305. [286]

"In reality, preference for understanding-level over memory-level teaching means belief in the proposition that *the only way to make teaching genuinely practical is to make it basically theoretical.*"

> Ernest E. Bayles. *Democratic Educational Theory.* New York: Harper & Row, Publishers, 1960. [194]

"Better theories are achieved by those who do not worship old ones."

> Wendell Johnson. *People in Quandaries.* New York: Harper & Row, Publishers, 1946. [70]

"There is no reason for us to continue to conduct the affairs of education in this country in the knowledge vacuum which now exists."

> David L. Clark. "Educational research: A national perspective," in Jack A. Culbertson and Stephen P. Hencley (eds.), *Educational Research: New Perspectives.* Danville: Interstate, 1963. [18]

"Everything a teacher does is colored by the psychological theory he holds. Consequently, the teacher who does not make use of a systematic body of theory in his day-by-day decisions is behaving blindly."

> Morris L. Bigge. *Learning Theories for Teachers.* New York: Harper & Row, Publishers, 1964. [6]

"One of the distinguishing features of science is that it strives for maximal simplicity, parsimony, and consistency in its basic assumptions, whereas common sense is content with complexity, multiplicity, and inconsistency."

> O. H. Mowrer. "On the dual nature of learning—A reinterpretation of conditioning and problem solving," *Harv. educ. Rev.,* 17: 102–148, 1947. [102]

"It is a necessary assumption of any science that its subject-matter is regular and lawful. If this assumption could not be made, there could, of course, be no science."

> Arthur W. Combs and Donald Snygg. *Individual Behavior.* New York: Harper & Row, Publishers, 1959. [18]

"The pathways of all sciences are littered with discarded theories, and psychology does not differ in this respect."

> Howard Kingsley and Ralph Garry. *The Nature and Conditions of Learning.* Englewood Cliffs: Prentice-Hall, Inc., 1957. [125]

"Relativists do not assert or deny absolute existence. Rather they define *psychological reality* as that which we make of what comes to us. They then deal with reality, so defined, in achieving truth and designing behavior."

> Morris L. Bigge and Maurice P. Hunt. *Psychological Foundations of Education.* New York: Harper & Row, Publishers, 1962. [271]

"One may say broadly that all the animals that have been carefully observed have behaved so as to confirm the philosophy in which the observer believed before his observations began. Nay, more, they have all displayed the national characteristics of the observer. Animals studied by Americans rush about frantically, with an incredible display of hustle and pep, and at last achieve the desired results by chance. Animals observed by Germans sit still and think, and at last evolve the solution out of their inner consciousness. To the plain man, such as the present writer, this situation is discouraging. I observe, however, that the type of problem which a man naturally sets to an animal depends upon his own philosophy, and this probably accounts for the differences in the results."

> Bertrand Russell. *Philosophy.* New York: W. W. Norton & Co., Inc., 1927. [29–30]

"You may recall Procrustes, that legendary highwayman of Attica, who tied his victims on an iron bed, and either stretched or cut off their legs to adapt them to its length. Since man is fallible and finite, every theorist perpetrates some Procrustean adjustment in order to develop his theory. What interests us at this point is how damaging to intellect's prime claim on the curriculum have the amputations and stretchings of theories been."

Arthur R. King and John A. Brownell. *The Curriculum and the Disciplines of Knowledge.* New York: John Wiley & Sons, Inc., 1966. Pp. 99–105. [99]

"Finally, there is admittedly insufficient evidence of how well the concepts derived in psychological theory or the laboratory apply in the classroom. The risks of overgeneralization are great; but they may be reduced somewhat if extensions of psychological concepts of teaching are proposed, not as fact, but as hypotheses that merit further tryout in classrooms. This is what we have advised. With this proviso, we suggest that any remaining risk in the use of learning theories is preferable to the alternative hazards of dependence on hunches, uncritical imitation, or habit."

Robert C. Craig. *The Psychology of Learning in the Classroom.* New York: The Macmillan Company, 1966. [82]

References

Köhler, W. "Gestalt psychology today," *Amer. Psychol.,* 14: 727–734, 1959.
Meierhenry, W. C. "Implications of learning theory for instructional technology," *Phi Delta Kappan,* 46: 435–438, 1965.
Skinner, B. F. "Reinforcement today," *Amer. Psychol.,* 13: 94–99, 1958.

CHAPTER 2

Test Items

1. The ultimate purpose of psychology as a science is
   a. to derive valid empirical antecedent–consequent relationships
   b. to devise effective learning–teaching procedures
   c. to formulate theories of behavior
   d. to promote the relatively complete understanding, prediction, and control of behavior
   e. to test the effectiveness of teaching–learning procedures

2. Which of the following would least qualify as a "hypothetical construct"?
   a. behavior
   b. genes
   c. learning
   d. learning sets
   e. motivation

3. Which of the following is not a major class of hypothetical constructs?
   a. experiential factors
   b. intervening variables
   c. mediating factors
   d. perceptual factors
   e. transfer variables

4. In interpreting an individual's response to a given situation, psychologists would focus on the _____ operating in the situation.
   a. background factors
   b. hypothetical constructs
   c. intervening variables
   d. mediating factors
   e. transfer variables

5. At the extremes of the objectivity–subjectivity continuum are
   a. associationism–functionalism
   b. behaviorism–phenomenology
   c. connectionism–operant conditioning
   d. sign gestalt–psychoanalysis
   e. classical conditioning–operant conditioning

6. Which of the following parts is an *incorrect* association?
   a. Guthrie (classical conditioning)–contiguous association
   b. Hull (classical conditioning)–reinforcement
   c. Skinner (operant conditioning)–motivation
   d. Thorndike (connectionism)–law of effect
   e. Wertheimer (gestalt)–perception

7. Which of the following is an *incorrect* association?
   a. Combs and Snygg–phenomenological reality
   b. Freud–functionalism
   c. Lewin–life space (group dynamics)
   d. Skinner–differential reinforcement
   e. Tolman–means-end expectancies

8. The general consensus as to the contribution of learning theories to educational practice is one of
   a. annoyance: They detract from more productive paths for deriving empirical data.
   b. endorsement: They provide the basis for deriving effective teaching procedures.
   c. general endorsement: They provide insight into the teaching–learning process.
   d. indifference: They are of scientific rather than of pedagogical interest.
   e. strong endorsement: They are vital as the foundation to educational practice.

9. All major theories of learning agree on the importance of _____ in the learning process.
   a. motivation
   b. part–whole relationships
   c. previous experience
   d. reinforcement
   e. none of the above; none has complete acceptance in all theories

10. Disagreement among theories of learning stems primarily from differences in
   a. the empirical data from which they spring
   b. the interpretation they give to the empirical evidence
   c. the kind of learning to which they apply
   d. the terminology they use to describe empirical events
   e. their willingness to sacrifice scientific precision to gain pedagogical relevance

11. The present status of theories of learning suggests
    a. the need for unification of current theories
    b. the need for greater emphasis on critical experiments designed to resolve differences
    c. their irrelevance to learning as it occurs in the classroom
    d. the possible need for scrapping current theories on the ground that they can't all be right
    e. the relative wisdom of an eclectic position as a basis for class-room practice

12. "Shaping behavior" is a term generally associated with
    a. Hull
    b. Lewin
    c. Pavlov
    d. Skinner
    e. Thorndike

13. A curriculum based on operant conditioning principles would be primarily
    a. global and insight-producing
    b. mechanistic
    c. sequential and systematic
    d. specific and definitive
    e. structured and meaningful

14. A curriculum devised according to cognitive specifications would emphasize
    a. the framework that gives material meaning
    b. the motivational bases of all learnings
    c. the phenomenological nature of perception
    d. the setting in which learning takes place
    e. the unity of the parts

15. The major objection to the phenomenological theory of learning is that
    a. its applications are largely in the area of adjustment and psychotherapy
    b. its emphasis on the setting in which learning takes place introduces additional variables difficult to control
    c. it is more appropriate to the complex learnings of the college than to the more basic knowledge of the elementary school
    d. it rests too heavily on the nature of the learner and not enough on the nature of the learning process
    e. it is subjective and lacking in scientific precision

16. In operant conditioning, the initiating force comes from
    a. the apparatus (e.g., shocks)
    b. the incentive
    c. the organism itself
    d. the reinforcing agent
    e. the stimulus

17. What is the status of the phenomenological frame of reference?
    a. It is based on basic Freudian concepts.
    b. It is a common-sense (rather than scientific) approach to behavior.
    c. It is of clinical rather than academic interest and relevance.
    d. It is the only school of psychology which owes its origin to Aristotle.
    e. It is totally speculative and philosophical.

18. Cell assemblies and phase sequences (as per Hebb) are examples of
    a. basic concepts
    b. hypothetical constructs
    c. physiological theories
    d. scientific principles
    e. verbalisms

19. According to the contiguity principle, a student learns through
    a. actual doing
    b. continued help from classmates
    c. a process of successive approximations
    d. a series of simple steps
    e. systematic practice

20. A teacher guided by cognitive theories would emphasize
    a. examples to clarify important points
    b. the lawfulness of underlying phenomena
    c. learner–participation in the learning process
    d. the natural structure of subject matter
    e. a step-by-step presentation of basic details

21. A pigeon pecking at the signal of a green light is an example of
    a. classical conditioning
    b. discriminative learning
    c. instrumental conditioning
    d. selective reinforcement
    e. stimulus–response sequences

CHAPTER 3

Determinants
of Human Behavior

The question of why we behave as we do—i.e., the question of motivation—has been one of man's continuing interests; it is of special concern to teachers. Unfortunately, as a scientific concept, motivation leaves much to be desired: the whole concept is unavoidably circular and, as Keislar points out in Chapter 13, not particularly helpful, at least with respect to certain types of situation. Much of the psychological evidence accumulated to date centers around the manipulation of physiological needs, or the use of electric shocks, a type of motivation not easily harnessed in the service of education. Teachers have had to rely on secondary needs, which are not always as dependable; whereas the average child has a need for social recognition, this need is not necessarily subject to the positive influence of the teacher's approval. To be effective in promoting both productive learning and wholesome personality development on the part of his pupils, the teacher must have a thorough understanding of the dynamics of human behavior; it is important, for example, that the school make every effort to see that each child get at least minimal satisfaction for his dominant needs within the context of the school's program. The newer stimulation theories of motivation may have something especially important for us to hear: It is fair to suggest that teachers have placed far too little emphasis on the attractiveness of the environment, the simple need for the eyes to see, the ears to hear, the brain to learn and to master, for the child to grow and *become*. Hunt's paper on the newer concepts of motivation constitutes an important contribution to the field.

Of primary interest here is the crucial role of early child-rearing practices in determining almost all aspects of the child's later status— personality, aspirations, socialization, etc. This places parents in a particularly sensitive position and suggests an urgent need for serious parent education and for systematic early preschool training of their children. The point is nicely brought out in separate papers by Bronfenbrenner and Loevinger on the effects upon the child's personality development of various child-rearing strategies. The articles by Hess and Shipman and by Hunt on the parental role in cognitive development presented in Chapter 5 are also of immediate relevance in this connection.

J. McV. Hunt

Experience and the Development of Motivation: *Some Reinterpretations* *

If one examines the accruing evidence relevant to what has been the dominant conception of the experiential sources of motivation, one can hardly escape the conclusion that this conceptual scheme needs some revisions. If we based our child-rearing entirely on our dominant theory of motivational development, we would probably goof as often and as badly as run-of-the-mill parents. The present article presents three propositions shared by psychoanalysts and behavioral scientists, cites evidence which calls these propositions into question, and suggests three new interpretative principles which seem more congruent with the evidence.

The Dominant Theory

Drive

The drive-reduction theory, which until a few years ago dominated, if not monopolized, the motivational picture postulate that "All behavior is motivated," and that "The aim or function of every instinct, defense action, or habit is to reduce or eliminate stimulation or excitation within the nervous system." It conceives the organism as driven first by the so-called primary inner stimuli arising from homeostatic imbalance and, secondly, by various forms of painful external stimulation. It has been assumed that these two forms of stimulation arouse an inner stage of excitement which has usually been called "drive." This view implies that the organism would be inactive unless driven by some drive. But, since animals and people are sometimes active even when it is hard to see how homeostatic or external stimulation could be operative, it had to be assumed that some weak innocuous stimulus currently present must have been previously associated with either of these two sets of needs and now has the capacity to arouse the drive. These are known as acquired or conditioned drives or anxiety.

Habit

The fact that the organism acts one way rather than another is likewise explained on the basis of habit; the organism behaves in ways which have served to reduce drive in the past. Changing behavior then is a matter of getting the organism, through either punishment or homeostatic need, to make the desired response which can then be reinforced by arranging for it to reduce the drive aroused by the punishment or the need.

This dominant theory has been a conceptual edifice of large dimensions and of considerable detail. It has provided a plausible account of both personality development and social motives. The experimental facts of homeostasis and of conditioned drive and fear are sound. Nevertheless, it has become more and more evident in the past 10 years that some of the basic assumptions of this dominant theoretical scheme and some of the explanatory extrapolations contradict facts and call for reinterpretation.

Reinterpretation

Is All Behavior Motivated?

A variety of observations contradict the assumption that all behavior is motivated; not only is playful activity most likely to occur when young children or animals are homeostatically satisfied, but the very occurrence of homeostatic need or external stimulation stops play. Evidence of varied spontaneous behavior—unmotivated in the traditional sense—has led to the identification of a number of new motives, curiosity drive (Berlyne), exploratory drive (Montgomery), etc. Rather than compile a long list of such drives to account for a variety of "unmotivated" behavior, let us simply note that such observations do contradict the assumption that the organism will become inactive unless driven by inner or external stimulation. Rather than subscribe to the ancient Greek notion of living tissues as inert matter to which motion must be imparted, we can more profitably embrace the far more dynamic conception of living things as open systems of energy exchange which exhibit activity intrinsically and upon which stimuli have a modulating, but not an initiating, effect.

Reinforcement

To the extent that activity is intrinsic in living organisms, it becomes unnecessary to perceive all activity as an attempt at reducing or avoiding stimulation as implied in the traditional model. There is still a place for drive reduction: Organisms do learn in response to inner or external stimulation; they learn strategies leading to gratification or reduction in external stimuli. The evidence that led Thorndike to formulate the "law of effect" is as convincing as ever. On the other hand, the fact that organisms show spontaneous molar activity also implies that organisms placed under conditions of low or unchanging stimulation find increases in stimulation reinforcing. This was shown most dramatically in studies of human behavior under conditions of minimal stimulation (see the McGill studies; also Lilly, 1956). In fact, Hebb's notion of an optimal level of activation is an integrative concept of fair magnitude. However, the drive-reduction principle of reinforcement may be seen to be but half of this more general curvilinear principle.

However, this is probably not the whole story: It looks as if there were natively both positive and negative forms of exciting stimulation. There is evidence, for example, of the motivational effect of sexual excitement even when not permitted to continue to complete sexual satisfaction —suggesting that stimulation may be excitement-producing rather than excitement-reducing. Direct electrical stimulation of different areas of the brain suggests the existence of two forms of excitation, one positive and one negative, inbuilt into the organism. Evidence of innate (positive and negative) exteroceptive stimulation also comes from the work of Harlow (1958) refuting the development of love in infant monkeys through secondary reinforcement connected with the hunger drive. It looks as though certain types of stimulation may be positively reinforcing even though intense and exciting.

Conditioned Fear and Anxiety

There is also need to examine the notion that fear and anxiety are *always* inculcated as a consequence of traumatic experience of helplessness in the face of homeostatic or painful external stimulation. In the 1920's, Jones and Jones explained fear of a snake simply on the basis of maturation—an alternative hypothesis to that of conditioned fear. Holmes (1935) challenged both interpretations: Her results showed that fear responses in lower-class children were about half of those of upper-class children and lower for boys than for girls, even though lower-class children and boys are more likely to experience unmet homeostatic needs or painful external stimuli. Even more damaging to the notion of conditioned fear is the findings by Levine et al. (1956) that rats shocked in infancy showed no traumatic effect: Both the shocked and the petted animals showed less emotionality than their control and learned avoidance responses more rapidly.

An alternate explanation of fear is based on *incongruity* or *dissonance,* as postulated by Hebb, who found that young chimpanzees display innate fear of a familiar object presented in an unfamiliar guise. The feared object is one which excites receptors in a fashion which is incongruous with the central, sequential pattern of neural firings accrued as a residue of past experiences. The fear response is apparently unlearned beyond the fact that the familiar or expected aspects of the object need to have been previously established. The incongruence or dissonance hypothesis can explain Holmes' findings, although the possibility of a different explanation still exists. Acceptance of the incongruity–dissonance conception of the genesis of fear leads to interesting reinterpretations of a great many of the motivational phenomena, including fear of the dark and separation anxiety.

Motivation in Terms
of the Incongruity–Dissonance Principle

Hebb's incongruity–dissonance principle is a pervasive concept; it has a theoretical foundation in Hebb's own neurological theory, which postulates that the residue of past inputs is stored in semi-autonomous reverberating cerebral circuits which he calls *cell assemblies* (the neural analog of concepts), which, in turn, are sequentially integrated into what he calls *phase sequences.* It is this sequential organization which in time provides for the subjective phenomenon of expectation. When markedly incongruous receptor inputs disrupt this sequential organization, the process itself is felt as an unpleasant emotion. Slight degrees of incongruity which can be readily assimilated lend interest; greater incongruity is repelling and perhaps even devastating.

Piaget uses a similar notion to account for the development of intelligence and concepts in children. Helson speaks of the residues of immediate past experience in the typical psychophysical experiment as an *adaptation level.* Both Helson and McClelland see affective arousal as a matter of the size of the discrepancy between receptor input and the residue of immediate past experiences. Festinger's *theory of cognitive dissonance* likewise postulates that the discrepancy between belief about a situation and the perception of that situation acts as a drive, with the subject attempting to reduce dissonance by either withdrawing from the situation or changing his beliefs. Both Rogers and Kelly present relatively analogous positions.

It is worth noting that this incongruity–dissonance principle makes both motivation and reinforcement intrinsic to the organism's relations with its environment, i. e., intrinsic to the organism's information-processing. It is as if the organism operated like an error-actuated feedback system, with the error derived from the discrepancy between receptor-inputs of the present and the residues of past experience serving as the basis for anticipating the future.

In contrast, the dominant view of the past has held both motivation and reinforcement as extrinsic to information-processing, and has therefore placed a tremendous burden of responsibility for the management of affective motivation on parents, teachers, and others in positions of control. Visions of man completely controlled, as exemplified by George Orwell's *1984,* are conceivable only if we assume that the extrinsic motivation forces of homeostatic need and painful stimulation are completely dominant. Perhaps the task of developing the proper motivation is best seen, at least in nutshell form, as limiting the manipulation of external factors to that minimum of keeping homeostatic need and exteroceptive drive low, in favor of facilitating basic information-processing to maximize accurate anticipation of reality.

Comments

1. This most scholarly analysis of the newer concepts of motivation represents an alternative (or supplement) to the more traditional drive-reduction theory. Hunt's reinterpretation of the literature on motivation around the incongruity-dissonance principle also represents an alternative to that postulated by White (1959), whose motivational model revolves around the competency drive.

2. The incongruity–dissonance principle does not totally supersede the drive-reduction theory but rather points to its inadequacy as *the* (exclusive) explanation of motivation. The latter is now seen, not as incorrect, but rather as simply incomplete to explain all motivational phenomena. It is likely that parents and teachers will continue to rely primarily on drive reduction (via secondary reinforcement) as a system whose implementation and operational implications are somewhat more clear.

References

Festinger L. *A Theory of Cognitive Dissonance.* New York: Harper & Row, Publishers, 1957.

Harlow, Harry F. "The nature of love," *Amer. Psychol.,* 13: 673–685, 1958.

Helson, H. "Adaptation-level as a basis for a quantitative theory of frames of reference," *Psychol. Rev.,* 55: 297–313, 1948.

Helson, H. "Adaptation-level as a frame of reference for prediction of psychophysical data," *Amer. J. Psychol.,* 60: 1–129, 1947.

Holmes, Frances B. "An experimental study of the fears of young children," in A. T. Jersild & Frances B. Holmes. *Children's Fears.* Child Devel. Monogr., 20: 167–296, 1935.

Jones, H. E., and M. C. Jones. "A study of fear," *Childh. Educ.,* 5: 136–143, 1928.

Levine, S., et al. "The effects of shock and handling in infancy on later avoidance learning," *J. Pers.,* 24: 475–493, 1956.

Lilly, J. C. "Mental effects of reduction of ordinary levels of physical stimuli on intact, healthy persons," *Psychiatric Res. Rept.,* 5: 1–9, 1956.

McClelland, D. C., et al. *The Achievement Motive.* New York: Appleton-Century-Crofts, 1953.

U. Bronfenbrenner

The Changing American Child—
A Speculative Analysis *

Child-rearing patterns in the United States have changed appreciably over the past 25 years. Middle-class parents, especially, have moved away from the more rigid styles of discipline toward greater tolerance of the child's impulses, freer expression of affection, and increased reliance on "psychological" methods of discipline. At the same time, the gap between the social classes in their goals and methods of child-rearing appears to be narrowing, with the working-class parent adopting the values and the techniques of the middle class as both lower- and middle-class parents align their behaviors and values into greater correspondence with the attitudes and practices advocated by the experts. The question is what changes in the personality development of their children have occurred as a consequence.

A Strategy of Inference

Unfortunately, although it is possible to find appropriate data on the changing parental pattern, the relative unavailability of corresponding data on children precludes a direct and unequivocal approach to the study of the resulting changes in the latter's personality development. We can, nevertheless, arrive at some estimate of what the answer might be through a series of inferences. We do know that certain variations in the behavior of parents tend to be accompanied by systematic differences in the personality characteristics of their children. If we assume that these same relationships hold across different points of time, we can infer the possible effects on children of these changes in child-rearing patterns over the years.

Psychological Techniques of Discipline
and Their Effects

Research (Sears et al., 1957; Miller and Swanson, 1958, 1960) points to the greater efficacy of love-oriented techniques in bringing about the de-

* Adapted and abridged from *J. soc. Issues,* 17: 6–18, 1961. By permission of author and publisher.

sired behavior in the child. Such methods are especially favored by middle-class parents. Such parents are, in the first place, more likely to overlook offenses, and, when they do punish they reason with the youngster, isolate him, appeal to guilt, show disappointment—in short, convey in a variety of ways, on the one hand, the kind of behavior that is expected; on the other, the realization that transgression means the interruption of a mutually valued relationship (Bronfenbrenner, 1958). It appears that middle-class parents, though in one sense more lenient, are actually using disciplinary methods that are more compelling. Furthermore, the compelling power of these practices is probably enhanced by the more permissive treatment accorded to middle-class children in the early years of life; the more love present in the early years, the greater the threat implied in its withdrawal.

Children from middle-class families tend to excel those from lower classes in such desirable characteristics as self-control, achievement, responsibility, leadership, popularity, and general adjustment. If these differences in child behavior can be attributed to class-linked variations in parental treatment and if further an increasing number of parents have been adopting the more effective socialization techniques typically employed by the middle class, we might reach the optimistic conclusion that successive generations of children should show gain in the development of constructive behavior and desirable personality characteristics. Unfortunately, this welcome conclusion is premature.

Sex, Socialization, and Social Class

To begin with, the parental behaviors previously mentioned are differentially distributed not only by socio-economic status but also by sex. Girls are exposed to more affection and less punishment than boys and are more likely to be subjected to love-oriented discipline of the type that encourages the development of internalized control. Consistent with this line of reasoning, girls tend to be more obedient, cooperative, and in general better socialized than boys of comparable age—but also more anxious, timid, dependent, and sensitive to rejection. It seems that these more efficient methods of child-rearing employed with girls involve some risk of what might be called oversocialization (Bronfenbrenner, 1961).

It is possible, of course, that the contrasting behaviors of boys and girls stem from genetically-based maturational influences rather than from differential parental treatment. Contradicting this possibility is the fact that socialization techniques do contribute to individual differences *within the same sex* precisely in the type of personality characteristics noted above. Like girls, first-born children receive more attention, are more likely to be exposed to psychological discipline, and end up more anxious and more dependent whereas later children, like boys, are more aggressive and self-confident. Girls are rated by their teachers as more responsible, whereas boys obtain higher scores on leadership—a difference which can be anticipated from the tendency for girls to receive more affection, praise, and companionship, and for boys to be subjected to more physical punishment and achievement demands.

Quite unanticipated, however, was the finding that both parental affection and discipline appeared to facilitate effective psychological functioning in boys, but to impede the development of such constructive behavior in girls. Closer examination of our data indicated that both extremes of either affection or discipline are deleterious for all children, but that the process of socialization entailed somewhat different risks for the two sexes. Girls were especially susceptible to the detrimental influence of overprotection; boys to the ill-effects of insufficient parental discipline and support.

The qualities of independence, initiative, and self-sufficiency, which are especially valued for boys in our culture, apparently require for their development a somewhat different balance of authority and affection than is found in the love-oriented strategy characteristically applied to girls. Evidently, an affectionate context, while important for the socialization of boys, must be accompanied by and be compatible with a strong component of parental discipline. Otherwise, the boy finds himself in the same situation as the girl, who, having received greater affection, is more sensitive to its withdrawal—with the result that a little discipline goes a long way and strong authority is constricting rather than constructive (Bronfenbrenner, 1960).

This process may already be operating for boys from upper middle-class homes. To begin with, it is primarily at lower middle-class levels that boys get more punishment and girls receive greater warmth and attention; with an increase in the family's social position, direct discipline drops off, especially for boys, and indulgence and protectiveness decrease for girls. As a result, patterns of parental treatment for the two sexes converge as we move up the socio-economic scale. Correspondingly, the risk experienced by each sex in the process of socialization tends to be somewhat different at different social-class levels. The danger of overprotection for girls is greater in lower-class families and less in upper middle-class families; boys, on the other hand, are in greater danger of suffering from inadequate discipline and support in lower middle-class homes while the upper middle-class boy presumably runs the risk of being oversocialized and of losing some of his capacity for independent, aggressive accomplishment.

Accordingly, if our line of reasoning is correct, we should expect a changing pattern of sex differences at successive socio-economic levels. Specifically, aspects of effective psychological functioning favoring girls should be most pronounced in the upper middle class; those favoring boys in the lower middle. A recent analysis of some of our data bears out this expectation. Girls excel boys on such variables as *responsibility* and *social acceptance* primarily at the higher socio-economic levels. In contrast, boys surpass girls in such traits as *leadership, level of aspiration,* and *competitiveness* almost exclusively in lower middle class. Indeed, with a rise in a family's social position, the differences tend to reverse themselves with the girls now excelling boys.

Trends in Personality Development:
A First Approximation

The implications are clear: The love-oriented socialization techniques which have been increasingly employed by middle-class families over the past 25 years may have negative as well as constructive aspects. While fostering the internalization of adult standards, they may also have the effect of undermining capacities for initiative and independence, particularly in boys. Males exposed to this "modern" pattern of child-rearing might be expected to differ from their counterparts of a quarter-century ago in being somewhat more conforming and anxious, less enterprising and self-sufficient, and, in general, possessing more of the virtues and the liabilities commonly associated with feminine character structure.

Family Structure and Personality Development

Another factor to consider is the changing pattern of parental role differentiation. If our extrapolation is correct, the balance of power within the family continues to shift with fathers yielding parental authority to mothers and taking on some of the nurturant and affectional function traditionally associated with the maternal role. Again we can only infer the effect of such secular changes on successive generations of children by analyzing analogous data on contemporary relationships.

First, data suggest that it is primarily mothers who tend to employ love-oriented techniques of discipline and fathers who rely on more direct methods like physical punishment. However, this statement needs to be qualified for it is only in relation to boys that fathers use direct punishment more than mothers. In fact, each parent tends to be more active, firm, and demanding with a child of the same sex while he is more lenient and indulgent with a child of the opposite sex. Fathers especially tend to be stricter with boys and especially warm and solicitous with girls. In fact, generally speaking, it is the father who is more likely to treat children of the two sexes differently (Bronfenbrenner, 1960). However, these trends are pronounced only in the lower middle class. More specifically, it is almost exclusively in the lower middle class that fathers are more strict with boys and mothers with girls; to the extent that direct discipline is employed in upper middle-class families, it tends to be exercised by both parents equally.

What kind of children can we expect to develop in families in which the father plays a predominantly affectionate role and a relatively low level of discipline is exercised equally by both parents? A tentative answer is supplied by a preliminary analysis of our data, the results of which can be summarized as follows:

Both responsibility and leadership are fostered by the relatively greater salience of the parent of the same sex. Boys tend to be more responsible when the father rather than the mother is the principal disciplinarian; girls are more dependable when the mother is the major authority figure. In short, boys thrive in a patriarchal context, girls in a matriarchal. The most dependent and least dependable adolescents describe family arrangements that are neither patriarchal nor matriarchal, but equalitarian. To state the issue in more provocative form, our data suggest that the democratic family, which for so many years has been held up and aspired to as a model by professional and enlightened laymen, tends to produce young people who "do not take initiative," "look to others for direction and decision," and "cannot be counted on to fulfill obligations" (Bronfenbrenner, 1960).

In the wake of so sweeping a conclusion, it is important to call attention to the tentative character of our findings, which are based on a single study employing crude questionnaire methods and rating scales. Besides our interpretation is limited by the somewhat "attenuated" character of most of the families classified as "patriarchal" or "matriarchal" in our sample; had it been possible to obtain more extreme concentrations of power in one or the other of the parents, the data might have shown that such extreme asymmetrical patterns of authority might be even more detrimental to effective psychological development perhaps than equalitarian forms. On the other hand, our data find some peripheral support in the work of other investigators. Father absence, for example, apparently not only affects the child directly but also influences the mother in the direction of greater overprotectiveness, with especially critical effects on male children; boys from father-absent homes tend to be markedly more submissive and dependent. Research has also shown that schizophrenic patients more frequently than normal persons report that their mothers played a very strong, and the father a very weak, authority role. Complementary evidence also comes from the work of Miller and Swanson, who find that entrepreneurial families put considerably more emphasis on the development of independence and mastery and the use of psychological techniques of discipline. Bureaucratic homes, on the other hand, are more likely to be equalitarian.

Looking Forward

If Miller and Swanson are correct in their prediction that America is moving toward a bureaucratic society that emphasizes "getting along" rather than "getting ahead," then presumably we can look forward to an ever-increasing number of equalitarian families who, in turn, will produce successive generations of ever more adaptable but unaggressive "organization men." But recent signs do not all point in this direction. Data from recent studies suggest a slowing down in the trend toward greater permissiveness and reliance on indirect methods of discipline. We can anticipate something of a return to the more explicit discipline techniques of an earlier era, as forces emanating primarily from behind the Iron Curtain cause a shift in both the aims and the methods of child-rearing in America toward emphases on achievement, "education for excellence," and the maximal utilization of intellectual resources. But if a new trend in parental behavior is to develop, it must do so in the context of changes already under way. Consequently, since the focus of parental authority is shifting from husband to wife, perhaps we should anticipate that pressures for achievement will be enforced primarily by mothers rather than fathers and recent studies point to the matriarchal context as optimal for the development of *need for achievement.*

The prospect of a society in which socialization techniques are directed toward maximizing achievement has certain negative overtones. High achievement motivation, it seems, flourishes in a family atmosphere of "cold democracy," in which initial high levels of material involvement are followed by pressures for independence and accomplishment. It also seems that children from achievement-oriented homes excel in planfulness and performance but also are more aggressive, tense, domineering, and cruel. It would appear that education for excellence if pursued singlemindedly may entail some sobering social costs.

Comments

1.   As the author points out, there is a considerable element of speculation here: "But by now we are in danger of having stretched our chain of inference beyond the strength of our weakest link. Our speculative analysis has become far more speculative than analytic and to pursue it further would bring us past the bounds of science into the realms of science fiction." Nevertheless, the trends of which the author writes are indeed noticeable and the implications are relatively convincing. To the extent that the basic personality is set in the early years of life, we are, in a sense, predetermining the kind of people Americans of the generations to come will be.

2.   In view of the foregoing, the qualifications of the parents, who presumably are to be the architects in the matter, leave something to be desired. It is also true that other social agencies which share the responsibility are not themselves particularly clear as to their role or the im-

plications of their particular procedures, which are frequently accidental and haphazard rather than planned and systematic.

    3.   The socialization process does—and must—not only vary from culture to culture but also change with the changing nature of the social order and its objectives. Unfortunately, the pursuit of desirable goals does sometimes entail not-so-desirable side-effects. The fact that different child-rearing patterns prevail in other cultures is undoubtedly a factor of prime importance in matters of international relationships.

    4.   To the extent that the school is also involved in this process, it might behoove teachers to be aware of the implications of their procedures. Certainly, the school in recent years has emphasized the socialization–conformity syndrome, for example. It is now moving in the direction of excellence, with perhaps the same degree of uncertainty and ignorance as to the likely outcomes.

References

Bronfenbrenner, U. "Socialization and social class through time and space," in E. Maccoby et al. (eds.), *Readings in Social Psychology.* New York: Holt, Rinehart and Winston, Inc., 1958. Pp. 400–425.

Bronfenbrenner, U. "Freudian theories of identification and their derivatives," *Child Devel.,* 31: 15–44, 1960.

Bronfenbrenner, U. "Some familial antecedents of responsibility and leadership in adolescents," in L. Petrullo and B. M. Bass (eds.), *Leadership and Interpersonal Behavior.* New York: Holt, Rinehart and Winston, Inc., 1961.

Miller, D. R., and G. E. Swanson. *The Changing American Parent.* New York: John Wiley & Sons, Inc., 1958.

Miller, D. R., and G. E. Swanson. *Inner Conflict.* New York: Holt, Rinehart and Winston, Inc., 1960.

Sears, Robert R., et al. *Patterns of Child Rearing.* New York: Harper & Row, Publishers, 1957.

Jane Loevinger

Patterns of Parenthood
as Theories of Learning *

Gerhart Piers (in a talk which I quote from memory) has divided methods of learning into three types: learning by reinforcement, by insight, and by identification. All three types of learning unquestionably occur, and theories of learning espoused by professional psychologists must account for those facts, whatever they take as the prototype of all learning.

Any consistent method of child-rearing contains by implication a theory of how children function, particularly how they learn. One can easily set up a correspondence between well-known patterns of parenthood and the three types of learning. Corresponding to any pattern of child-rearing there is, then, a "theory of learning," emphasizing one type of learning at the expense of others. Theories of learning held by parents are, of course, far more naive and uncomplicated than similar theories held by psychologists. To avoid confusion, the term "parental theory" may be used to distinguish the implicit learning theory.

The disciplinarian parent apparently believes that any wrong thing a child does will be continued indefinitely if the parent does not see that it is punished. While psychological research has tended to emphasize rewards as more effective than punishments as reinforcing agents, disciplinarian parents emphasize punishments as reinforcers.

Apparently insight learning is assumed to predominate by those parents, once reputed to be numerous, who believe that every demand made on a child must be rationalized and explained.

Finally, the typical permissive parent must surely believe that the socialization of his child takes place by means of the child identifying himself with the well-socialized parent.

Consider the following situation. Five-year-old Johnny is beating on his two-year-old sister Sue. Mother comes in. Let us assume that every mother will want to prevent repetition of such behavior. What will she do?

Mother One believes that if Johnny does not feel pain, he will repeat the behavior at every coincidence of impulse and opportunity. She there-

* From *J. abn. soc. Psychol.*, 59: 148–150, 1959. By permission of author and publisher.

fore punishes him sharply, thus demonstrating her adherence to a parental reinforcement theory of learning.

Mother Two believes that Johnny can be shown how wrong his conduct is and sets about to persuade him. She believes in a parental insight theory of learning.

Mother Three believes that Johnny wants to grow up to be like his parents. If she punishes him harshly, he will learn that it is all right for the bigger one to be mean to the littler one if he or she feels like it; so his behavior is less likely to be repeated if reprimanded gently than if dealt with harshly. She believes in a parental identification theory of learning.

There is one fallacy common to all parental learning theories. Kelly (1955) points out that we are not victims of our history but only of our construction of that history. Kelly finds in that fact hope for the psychotherapist. But just as it gives hope for the therapist, it generates despair for the parent. A parent can decide to beat his child, but he cannot decide how the child will construe the beating. Nor, if he abstains from punishing, can he decide how the child will construe the abstention.

Rules for rearing children are beyond the scope of this note, indeed, beyond the competence of the writer. But one superordinate rule can safely be stated: Whatever the parent's theory of learning, the child will in fact be learning by an alternative method. Thus the son of Mother One is probably identifying with a punitive, disciplinarian adult; for the son of Mother Two it is being stamped in that beating on sister has no painful consequences; while the son of Mother Three has probably discerned, "Aha! I can get away with it." The explanation of why a child shifts his mode of learning to escape his parent's vigilant efforts at socialization is not difficult. He is attempting to defend the gratification of his impulses, and in this respect he is not altogether different from his parents.

The foregoing formulation helps to solve two riddles. Why is the battle between the generations fought, generation after generation, with such vigor? And why is it that experts on child-rearing are not conspicuously more successful at the art than those less expert?

The failure of expertise in child-rearing was foreshadowed in 1909 with Freud's (1925) publication of *Analysis of a Phobia in a Five-Year-Old Boy,* for little Hans was the child of two of Freud's followers. One should not make too much of the fact. He was not necessarily the most neurotic child in Vienna, merely the one that Freud had opportunity to observe and indirectly to treat. Nonetheless, the occurrence of so severe a phobia in the child was a striking omen.

Reasons have been advanced for the failure of children of experts to be vastly superior to others in their adjustment. Without disputing or discounting those reasons, one can focus on a slightly different one. The experts know what other parents did wrong, and they avoid those errors. But while they avoid the errors of parents in other houses, their children contrive to defend their instinctual gratification against the parents in their own house. In current terms, a shift in parentmanship is countered by a shift in childmanship.

The battle between the generations is commonly accounted for by the fact that parents have need to socialize their children, and the children forever battle against the socializing process. This view is the one being elaborated here. But it is not quite the whole story. A useful way to test a theory is to see what happens in the most extreme cases. Redl and Wineman (1957) have depicted extreme cases of "children who hate." Many of the sentiments of those children, such as "Grownups don't want kids to have any fun," are echoed occasionally in almost all homes. But the ferocity and implacability of the war with adults is entirely disproportionate to what takes place in an ordinary household. Were their parents, then, so rigorous in their attempts at socialization? On the contrary, the parents of those children presented a picture of impulsivity no less striking than that of the children. The abuses to which the children were subjected could hardly be called punishments; they did not appear to result from any theory of how children learn but rather were crude lashing out on impulse. The picture of parent–child relations in *The Aggressive Child* is a conspicuously undesirable one, both prima facie and in terms of outcome. It serves to demonstrate that not all parents are informed by a parental theory. The battle between the generations is never more vicious than when all pretense of representing the interests of society is dropped and it becomes the parent's impulsivity versus the child's.

A general theory of the battle between generations must account for all of the cases. It must therefore read that the child's impulse gratification conflicts with the needs of society, represented by parents, to socialize him, as well as with the parent's own impulse gratification. The normal parent, to be sure, satisfies many of his desires in and through his children. But moment by moment and day by day the needs which the children gratify are not always uppermost. The presence of an infant or child in the household necessarily imposes delay or surrender on many of the parents' wishes.

The conclusions of this discussion can be stated simply, though they do not exactly simplify life. Every consistent pattern of child-rearing embodies a theory of learning, and all those parental theories are substantially wrong. However, any parental theory is better than none.

Is it possible to base one's pattern of child-rearing on a more nearly realistic theory of learning? That is an intriguing question. In view of the adaptability of the normal child in shifting his tactics to match those of his parents, such a method would require constant reconsideration and change. Yet inconsistency, so the child-rearing experts tell us, is one of the worst faces a parent can turn to his child. Possibly, however, inconsistency got its bad name not from conscientious parents trying to outwit their children but from the label being applied to such parents as Redl and Wineman have sketched.

If, as the present discussion suggests, parental theories are more wrong than right, how does it happen that it is better to have one than not? The chief value of a parental learning theory may well be in providing a model for the child of curbing one's own impulses out of regard for the future welfare of another. The very oversimplification of parental theories may serve to make accessible to the child that his parent is acting on principle rather than on impulse. To say this is to lay emphasis on learning by identification. But probably most psychologists, whatever their professional theories, act in relation to their own children as if they expect them to learn chiefly by identification.

"All I say is by way of discourse, and nothing by way of advice. . . . I should not speak so boldly, if it were my due to be believed" (de Montaigne, 1913, p. 283).

Comments

1. The article raises interesting possibilities for all types of child-rearing practices as well as disciplinary measures in the classroom. It complicates the task of character development and discipline. It is a wonder parents succeed at all.

2. Flexibility of approach, or rather subscribing to a number of theories, may be bothersome to the theoretical purist. It also complicates the task of the parent who has to be familiar with a variety of approaches and makes child-rearing an art rather than a science.

References

de Montaigne, M. *The Essays of Michel de Montaigne.* Vol. III. C. Cotton (Trans.); W. C. Hazlitt (ed.). London: G. Bell, 1913.

Freud, S. "Analysis of a phobia in a five-year-old boy." In *Collected Papers.* Vol. III. London: Hogarth Press, Ltd., 1925. Pp. 149–289.

Kelly, G. A. *The Psychology of Personal Constructs. Vol. II. Clinical Diagnosis and Psychotherapy.* New York: W. W. Norton & Company, 1955.

Redl, F., and D. Wineman. *The Aggressive Child.* New York: Free Press, 1957.

That's What They Said

"People do not work because of their love for me. They work for pay, in the form of money, affection, and belongingness, and the status that permits self-approval. When this pay gets too low they will leave their jobs and seek something else."

> A. D. Woodruff. *The Psychology of Teaching.* New York: Longmans, Green & Co., 1951. [529]

"When children are confronted with a situation where the old techniques for satisfying their need for self-respect or security are not appropriate they will, if ready, learn new techniques for mastering the situation or, if unready, will use or discover methods for escaping from it."

> A. W. Combs and Donald Snygg. *Individual Behavior: A Perceptual Approach to Behavior.* New York: Harper & Row, Publishers, 1959. [381]

"The interdependence of pupils and of pupils and teachers for a mutual satisfaction of needs would seem to demand that each group receive training in understanding each other's social needs."

> Glenn M. Blair, et al. *Educational Psychology.* New York: The Macmillan Company, 1962. [289]

"This combination of emotional support and freedom is the foundation of emotional security."

> Louis Kaplan. *Foundations of Human Behavior.* New York: Harper & Row, Publishers, 1965. [165]

"In our own theory of behavior organization, we do not, of course, deny the existence of physiological needs but we do deny their primary status as activating agents. The normal condition of the behaving individual is activity, and we need postulate no poorly defined drives or motives to account for it."

> Karl U. Smith and Margaret F. Smith. *Cybernetic Principles of Learning and Educational Design.* New York: Holt, Rinehart and Winston, Inc., 1966. [471]

"If biological drives were the primary motivating mechanisms of the human being, 95 percent or more of our lives would be spent in non-constructive activities, or more realistically the human race would not have survived and been permitted the luxury of drive-less living most of the time."

Harry F. Harlow. "Motivation in monkeys and men." In Floyd Ruch (ed.), *Psychology*. Glenview: Scott, Foresman and Company, 1963. Pp. 589–594. [589]

". . . one can only wince at the current tendency to talk about such things as 'curiosity drives,' 'exploratory drives,' 'sensory drives,' 'perceptual drives,' etc. as if the 'activities' which are held to 'satisfy' each of the 'drives' (if indeed they are distinct) were just so much undifferentiated neutral pap that came by the yard."

S. Koch. "Psychological science versus the science-humanism antinomy," *Amer. Psychol.*, 16: 629–639, 1961. [633]

"The early glitter associated with study of the effect of parent on child has been tarnished by realization of the methodological obstacles that block quick and easy solutions to the critical problems. Questionnaires and retrospective reports are under heavy attack and the realization that parent behavior is subject to the reciprocal effect of the child's actions has led to greater caution in generalizing from cross-sectional data than was true a decade ago."

Jerome Kagan and Barbara A. Hencker. "Developmental psychology," *Ann. Rev. Psychol.*, 17: 1–50, 1966. [34]

"The general conclusion seems inescapable that a child's character is the direct product, almost a direct repetition of the way his parents treat him."

Robert F. Peck and Robert J. Havighurst. *The Psychology of Character Development*. New York: John Wiley & Sons, Inc., 1960. [178]

"Conscience develops or fails to develop as a function of the type of control techniques that are used with children in infancy. . . . Why should I label myself as a socialized person if the only reward from that is permission to punish myself. . . . He has no reason to develop a conscience or internalize parental standards, so that he remains low in anxiety, high in fear and shame, and high in direct self-gratification."

Boyd R. McCandless. *Children and Adolescents: Behavior and Development*. New York: Holt, Rinehart and Winston, Inc., 1961. [421]

"The American infant born in a hospital is a victim of mass efficiency. Removed to a nursery and fed on a bottle, he shares his mother's company only spasmodically. The neonate is being protected from infection and being exposed, at the same time, to a heartless regime. The psychological damage produced by his 'modern' pediatric routine may be more serious than the harm a few bugs are likely to do."

> Wayland F. Vaughn. *Personal and Social Adjustment.* New York: The Odyssey Press, Inc., 1952. [112]

"In disciplining children, parents on most occasions administer aversive stimuli some time after a deviation has occurred and fail to make its termination contingent on the child's expressing self-punitive responses. Consequently, punitive disciplinary techniques are not generally conducive either to the development of adequate response inhibition or the acquisition of 'guilt.' In contrast, when parents withhold or withdraw positive reinforcers, the reinstatement of these rewarding objects or experiences is usually made contingent on the child's complying with parental demands or on his making some kind of restitutive response. Consequently, it is not surprising that some investigators have reported that this method of discipline, especially when used by warm and affectionate parents, is associated with the development in children of self-controlling responses and guilt-reactions to transgression, whereas the use of aversive stimuli as a disciplinary measure is more likely to be associated with avoidance of the disciplinary agent."

> Albert Bandura and Richard H. Walters. *Social Learning and Personality Development.* New York: Holt, Rinehart and Winston, Inc., 1963. [221]

References

Abrahamson, S. "Needs theory applied to secondary schools," *Clearing House,* 30: 328–368, 1966.

Archambault, R. D. "The concept of needs and its relation to certain aspects of educational theory," *Harv. educ. Rev.,* 27: 38–62, 1957.

Rethlingshafer, Dorothy. *Motivation as Related to Personality.* New York: McGraw-Hill, Inc., 1963.

CHAPTER 3

Test Items

1. Which of the following is the least basic as an explanation of behavior?
   a. habit
   b. incentive
   c. inner tension
   d. motives
   e. purposiveness

2. The strongest and the weakest position given to purposiveness of behavior by learning theorists is that of _____ and _____ , respectively.
   a. Freud and Rogers
   b. Lewin and Watson
   c. Rogers and Lewin
   d. Thorndike and Guthrie
   e. Tolman and Skinner

3. Drive reduction occupies a central position in
   a. Freudian psychoanalysis
   b. Hull's classical conditioning
   c. Lewin's topological psychology
   d. phenomenological psychology
   e. Skinnerian (operant) conditioning

4. Drives are to energizing as motives are to
   a. directing
   b. energizing and reinforcing
   c. directing and reinforcing
   d. energizing, directing, and reinforcing
   e. reinforcing

5. Drives are to needs as
   a. extrinsic is to intrinsic
   b. incentives are to goals
   c. internal stimuli are to external stimuli
   d. physiological is to psychological
   e. none of the above; the two terms are essentially synonymous

6. Motives always imply
   a. a goal
   b. an external stimulus
   c. an internal stimulus
   d. need reduction
   e. a purpose

7. An incentive is best defined as
   a. an object or state having positive valence
   b. an object or state having negative valence
   c. a potential goal
   d. a previous reinforcing agent
   e. a reward

8. Opposite points of view as to the cruciality of motivation to learning
   are taken by _____ and _____, respectively.
   a. Freud and Combs
   b. Guthrie and Skinner
   c. Hull and Guthrie
   d. Thorndike and Hull
   e. Tolman and Skinner

9. Psychologists would agree that motivation is crucial to
   a. habit formation
   b. learning
   c. performance
   d. reinforcement
   e. the shaping of operant behavior

10. Which is the *incorrect* association? Hunger is to self-approach as
    a. drive is to need
    b. internal is to external
    c. physiological is to psychological
    d. primary is to secondary
    e. satiable is to insatiable

11. Psychological needs differ from physiological needs primarily in that
    they are
    a. insatiable
    b. less susceptible to modification (learning)
    c. more pervasive and longer lasting
    d. more specific and more intense
    e. of lower priority

12. The school child most likely to be frustrated in his need for achievement is the ——— child.
    a. aggressive
    b. average
    c. creative
    d. dull
    e. task-oriented

13. The major obstacle to satisfaction of one's needs lies in the area of
    a. conflict between concurrent needs
    b. limitations in the availability of satisfiers
    c. personal incompatibility with the environment
    d. personal limitations
    e. social and societal restrictions

14. The school's major responsibility with respect to the satisfaction of pupil needs lies in the area of
    a. allowing maximal freedom from direction so as to permit maximum leeway in pupil satisfaction
    b. providing a diversified program of activities within which all pupils can find some satisfaction
    c. providing for maximal pupil success in connection with the school's academic program
    d. providing within the framework of the school's program adequate outlets for the satisfaction of needs
    e. safeguarding the pupil from all frustration

15. The major objection to the drive-reduction theory as the exclusive theory of motivation is that
    a. it is based on essentially negative premises
    b. it is based on false homeostatic premises
    c. it conflicts with the concept of purposiveness
    d. it is unable to explain all motivational phenomena
    e. its validity is restricted to *primary* drives

16. Research suggests that ——— reinforcement produces responses most resistant to extinction.
    a. delayed
    b. direct
    c. immediate
    d. intermittent
    e. secondary

17. Research on the effectiveness of delayed reinforcement suggests that
    a. reinforcement is most effective when applied concurrently with the response and when given approximately five seconds after the response
    b. reinforcement has no effect whatsoever if not applied within 10 seconds of the response
    c. reinforcement retains its effectiveness over long periods of delay provided the connection can be reactivated at the time of reward
    d. the delay period can be longer for lower organisms with narrower focus than with human subjects
    e. the effectiveness of reinforcement is determined by its nature, not by the delay interval

18. Functional autonomy is best explained on the basis of
    a. the inapplicability of the principle of extinction to lower-order habits
    b. the insistence of an S–R, once established, to be used
    c. the self-reinforcement of habits
    d. the self-rewarding nature of needs
    e. the substitution of drives

19. The fundamental issue underlying objections to the drive-reduction theory is that
    a. behavior is too complex to be explained on the basis of a single theory
    b. the drive-reduction theory necessitates postulating a whole slough of secondary reinforcement
    c. homeostasis represents a nonattainable ideal
    d. need is not a sufficient condition for behavior, nor is need-satisfaction essential for its termination
    e. the organism is not an inert mass to which motion must be imparted by external forces, but rather an energy system in its own right

20. Probably the most comprehensive of the "stimulation" theories of motivation is
    a. Berlyne's curiosity drive
    b. Harlow's manipulatory drive
    c. Hill's activity drive
    d. Montgomery's exploratory drive
    e. White's competency drive

21. The special feature of the various drives postulated by the stimulation theories of motivation is

    a.   their dependence on primary drives
    b.   their externally determined basis
    c.   their functional autonomy
    d.   their orientation toward mastery
    e.   their susceptibility to extinction

22.   Need for achievement (N Ach) tends to be highest in homes in which
    a.   the atmosphere is permissive and supportive but nondemanding
    b.   the child is pushed into independent behavior from early life
    c.   the children are given maximum emotional security and freedom to grow
    d.   the father is friendly, self-confident, and highly successful
    e.   the home is dominated by a strong, supportive, strict, and achievement-oriented mother

23.   The present consensus concerning the need for stimulation is that
    a.   for every individual there is a certain level of stimulation that is optimal for his present well-being and continued development
    b.   a high level of stimulation is essential for early development
    c.   the ideal state, if it were attainable, is homeostasis
    d.   a maximum of stimulation is optimal for maximal development
    e.   the organism generates its own stimulation in amounts optimal for personal well being

24.   As a scientific concept, motivation
    a.   finds ample support in the empirical and theoretical evidence
    b.   has both practical value and theoretical validity
    c.   is sound; even though the drive-reduction principle is of questionable validity
    d.   tends to be circular; to simply describe what it alleges to explain
    e.   is theoretically sound but of limited practical (classroom) value

25.   The present consensus among psychologists as to the need for emotional security is that
    a.   the child should be given ample love but within the framework of reasonable expectations
    b.   the child should be given unconditional love and acceptance
    c.   consistency in expectation is a more fundamental determinant of emotional security than is love and affection per se
    d.   parental love and acceptance should be made conditional upon acceptable behavior
    e.   undue parental affection in early infancy tends to set a "spoiled" demanding pattern difficult to satisfy in later years

26. Which is the incorrect association of home climate and the children it tends to produce?

a. home: warm and democratic;   children: socially outgoing, original, and intellectually curious

b. home: permissive;   children: greater initiative, better socialization, better cooperation, less inner hostility

c. home: maternal coldness;   children: retarded in conscience development

d. home: high in mother warmth and affection and democratic permissiveness;   children: dependent, spoiled

e. home: high control, low democracy;   children: well behaved, lacking in aggression and originality

27. What is the most likely effect of maternal deprivation (e.g., extended institutionalization) on the development of young children?

a. Such children are likely to be apathetic and unresponsive to stimuli and to be retarded intellectually.

b. Such children tend to be less capable of adjusting to the demands of the school.

c. Such children tend to be socially insensitive, cold, isolated, and hard to reach.

d. Such children tend to be demanding, insistent on immediate gratification, unmanageable.

e. None of the above necessarily: the harm from early institutionalization apparently stems from *sensory* rather than maternal deprivation.

CHAPTER 4

The Self-Concept
and Self-Actualization

Because of its overriding effect on all that the individual will ever be or do, the self-concept deserves top priority in the school's concern for the child's welfare. Everything he does, every experience he undergoes, affects —in some way or another, for better or for worse—how he feels about himself. The newer emphasis on openness to experience, self-actualization, and more recently, *becoming* is especially exciting in the light of our present affluent society with its unlimited opportunities for the promotion of human welfare and human dignity. The teacher simply has no greater responsibility than to assist each child in the enhancement of the self. In the articles that follow, Lowe clarifies the nature of the self-concept, while Dildine presents a particularly interesting view of the individual as an open-energy system operating toward self-actualization and Will makes a strong plea for greater emphasis in teacher-education on the growth of the prospective teacher as a person.

C. Marshall Lowe

The Self-Concept:
Fact or Artifact? * [1]

"Notions concerning the self . . . like other human ideas . . . are inventions and not discoveries. The task is not that of discovering the 'true self' but instead of constructing those notions which increase understanding of human behavior. Just as the number of inventions is potentially unlimited, so there need be no limit on the number of constructions put upon the self. In this discussion, we will . . . consider the uses to which the different selves have been put" [p. 333].

(a) "The first self is the knowing self of structural psychology. Its function is to apprehend reality. The rational nature of man has always been in dispute and the New Look in perception has further undermined this conception. The article has cited studies which throw doubt on the ability of the self to perceive itself correctly in those areas which are of great value to it. It is the change in the self as perceiver of itself that is the aim of client-centered therapy. . . . Studies of client-centered therapy do not reveal whether therapy brings the client any closer to reality, but they do provide some evidence that the perceptions of self are brought closer to social expectancies" [p. 333].

(b) "The second construction of the self is that of motivator. This is the self of those who believe that the individual is motivated by a need for . . . self realization. . . . Attempts to validate this construct of the self have been carried on through work on *need achievement*" [p. 333].

* Adapted and abridged from C. Marshall Lowe, "The self-concept: Fact or artifact?" *Psychol. Bull.*, 58: 325–335, 1961. Copyright © 1961 by the American Psychological Association, and reproduced by permission.

[1] The article presents a concise review of the history of the self-concept as a heuristic construct in research and as a basis for the development of phenomenology in psychology. It includes a survey of the self-concept measures and their validation, an examination of the criterion of consistency, and a review of six possible interpretations of the self-concept. The present abstract is concerned only with the latter. The main theme is whether the self-concept is an objective entity suitable for scientific research or whether, on the contrary, it is simply a metaphysical construct created by psychologists to explain certain behaviors. The issue is basic not only with respect to the self-concept itself, but also with respect to the self theories of learning, for example.

(c) "The third construct . . . is the humanistic, semireligious conception of the self as that which experiences itself. It is the 'unique personal experience' of Moustakas (1957) and the experience of feeling in Rogers (1951). The difficulty . . . is that such a conception is more religious than scientific; it becomes a value-orientation . . . a highly controversial statement of what is the highest good (Lowe, 1959)" [p. 333].

(d) "The fourth approach views the self as organizer. This self is the psychoanalytic ego, the internal frame of reference of Snygg and Combs (1949), and the source of construct making in G. A. Kelly (1955). Any operational measure of self consistency would seem to imply the existence of such a self" [p. 333].

(e) "A fifth approach constructs the self as a pacifier. Such a self seems implied by Lewin (1936), who constructed his system of personality in terms of valences or tensions which the organism seeks to keep to a minimum. It seems present also in Angyal (1941) who views life as an oscillation about a position of equilibrium. The self in other words is seen as an adjustment mechanism which seeks to maintain congruence between the self and the nonself. It is the verification of this type of self that seems implied by . . . studies that show increased congruence of real and ideal self as a result of therapy" [pp. 333–334].

(f) "In the sixth view, the self is the subjective voice of the culture, being purely a social agent. . . . The self as an entity is denied, and behavioral consistency is seen as residing not in the individual, but in similar environmental events" [p. 334].

We can choose the particular conception of the self which best fits our theoretical frame of reference, but the choice seems to depend "more upon faith than upon logic, and the choice of one conception must of necessity deny other constructs. It seems impossible that the self can function as a motivator which constantly tries to change the status quo, and as a pacifier which minimizes the disparity between the real and the ideal self. There is a contradiction also between the self as motivator and the self as feeling, for in the latter case the self is accepted as it is, but in the former it is not. Differences are apparent also between the self as feeling and as pacifier. And finally, the self as agent of society is opposed to all other conceptions" [p. 334].

Conclusions

"Is the self-concept a fact which, having an objective existence in nature, is observed and measured; or is it an epiphenomenon of deeper reality, invented by man that he might better study his behavior" [p. 334]?

"The position of this paper must be that the self is an artifact invented to explain experience. If the self-concept is a tool, it must be well designed and constructed. We will conclude therefore with that construct of the self which best serves the 1960s. Such a construction combines the self of ego-involvement with the self of feeling. It is a self which is existential not to experience itself, but to mediate encounter between the organism and what is beyond. . . . It is as an artifact that the self-concept finds meaning" [p. 334].

Comments

1.   As Lowe points out, one of the difficult tasks for psychologists is that of relating observation of behavior to the study of mental processes. One approach has been to limit psychology to the study of behavior and leave to philosophy the task of speculating as to the existence and the nature of mind and soul. However, psychologists have attempted to make sense out of human action by postulating a self or ego as the basis for understanding the coherence and unity which they see in human behavior. As such, the self, the self-concept, or the self-image is simply a hypothetical construct having a usefulness rather than a reality or even validity.

2.   The author also discusses the difficulty of validating self-concept measures. This is especially evident in the thorough treatment given the subject by Ruth Wylie (1961). Perhaps it is more useful as a way of explaining and of thinking about human behavior than it is as an objective concept amenable to scientific research.

References

Angyal, A. *Foundations for a Science of Personality.* New York: Commonwealth Fund, 1941.

Kelly, G. A. *Psychology of Personal Constructs.* New York: W. W. Norton & Company, Inc., 1955.

Lewin, K. *Principles of Topological Psychology.* New York: McGraw-Hill, Inc., 1936.

Lowe, C. M. "Value orientation: An ethical dilemma," *Amer. Psychol.,* 14: 687–693, 1959.

Moustakas, C. *The Self.* New York: Harper & Row, Publishers, 1957.

Rogers, C. R. *Client-Centered Therapy.* Boston: Houghton-Mifflin Company, 1951.

Wylie, Ruth. *The Self-Concept: A Review of the Literature.* Lincoln: University of Nebraska Press, 1961.

Glenn C. Dildine

Energy—Basis of
Living and Learning *

Living is *action*. Anything alive moves, acts, and responds. What whirring, changing dynamos living creatures are!

Living is reaching for perfection. The unfolding panorama of life through the ages reveals living things in increasing variety climbing toward greater complexity and directing their energy toward more effective adaptation.

Living is capturing, controlling, and using energy. Each human is designed to capture and transform energy stored in food to the complex process of living, growing, and behaving. Every organ in the body is planned to play some essential part in a regular, intricate sequence of internal energy flow and change.

Living is also feeling. Our deepest satisfactions come as energy surges through us and we succeed in the jobs we have set for ourselves. If living is fundamentally energy flowing in intricately controlled patterns through a highly organized system, then emotion or feeling is our personal measure of the quality of our living.

Living is urge to learn. Being alive is really worthwhile when we feel we are growing more competent, better able to do things we want to do, learning to be the kind of person others expect. We are coming to see that *our most basic human quality is an inborn urge and drive to push our own development and self-realization to their limits*. We long to learn to use our energy in more and more effective ways of feeling, thinking, deciding and acting.

People of all ages, unless they have been too severely wounded, will face up to severe physical, emotional, and mental threat for the joy of working on through challenge toward greater competence and self-assurance. But this can happen only if the restrictions and demands from outside have not been too severe. A child's own memory must consistently tell him, "I have succeeded more often than I have failed." The fun of growing up and learning has far outweighed the necessary pain and defeat and restriction along the way. How exciting and enjoyable it is to use my energy to grow and learn!

* Adapted and abridged from *NEA J.* 39: 252–253, April 1950. By permission of author and publisher.

What must adults have done to cause so many growing children to deny this birthright? They have forced children to withdraw, already half licked by life, into a tentative, hesitant shell for protection against any more wounding. They have forced children to become so aggressive, in tense defiance of too much blocking, that they lose much needed affection, group acceptance, and opportunities for learning.

Living requires balancing and directing the energy budget. The energy we have must be spent on several vital jobs: keeping good machinery in good working order; growing up into a maturing person; using and expending our ability to feel; and learning to think, decide, and act more effectively. But each person has only one pool of energy to supply all these jobs—the energy he gets from the food he eats.

Since all essential activities draw their energy from the common pool, they must be intimately and inseparably interrelated. We should expect that efficiency in one means more energy for the others, and that defects in one will detract from the others. We can also anticipate that there must be some overall control to ensure that all energy available will be organized and used for the benefit and enjoyment of the whole person.

Anything that affects the child's physical health also affects the way he behaves as an individual. However, not only does physical health affect behavior, but the efficiency with which we organize our energy in order to control behavior plays an important part in physical health and growth. All phases of energy flow are inseparably interwoven. What each of us will do with his total energy pool depends partly on the mechanical efficiency of body physiology, and partly on the more complex patterns of individual psychological organization, especially on *what life has come to mean to each person.*

Comments

1.   The concept of the human organism as a dynamic energy system continuously converting energy into power for growth and activity is especially interesting. Dildine's premise regarding "our most basic human quality," namely, that of pushing one's development and self-realization to the limit, is simply another version of the position taken by Combs and Snygg and other phenomenologists that the basic human drive is the need for the preservation and enhancement of the self.

2.   In a sequel article, Dildine (1950) postulates that the individual's overt behavior, being the final or outgoing phase of energy use, depends on such factors as the efficiency of his body as an energy-transforming machine, the way he feels, thinks, and hopes about himself as a person, the things he likes to do, and how much of his energy he wants to expend. Adults, for example, may find the child restless and nervous, when in reality his high exuberance is nothing more than a reflection of high en-

ergy efficiency operating through a healthy body. Illness, on the other hand, causes a redirection of the body's energy output so that little may be left to deal with the other aspects of growth and environmental demands. The way the school child uses his energies depends on the extent to which schoolwork and adult demands appear significant and worthwhile to him as *he* sees it from his own personal world. The further away his background of experience is from the behavior the school expects, the less the chance that he will see much sense to the school program.

3. A teacher who considers a child "lazy" ought to be made to answer the question, "Is he really lacking in energy, or is he using his energy in the vigorous pursuit of nonacademic goals?" And, if the latter, "Why?"

Reference

Dildine, Glenn C. "Motivated to learn," *NEA J.,* 39: 356–357, 1950.

Richard Y. Will

The Education of the
Teacher as a Person *

Our present emphasis on the cognitive aspects of teacher education has led to a consequent neglect of the affective goals. To the extent that discussions of teacher effectiveness have placed a premium on the personal qualities, we need to concern ourselves with specifically what is being done to design a teacher-education curriculum conducive to the personal development of the prospective teacher. To the extent that desirable personal characteristics can be developed, experiences conducive to personal growth must be made a vital part of the teacher-education curriculum.

Most teacher-education programs are divided into two distinct parts, general education and professional education, with much controversy surrounding the relative degree of emphasis to be placed on each. Experiences involving direct involvement or practical experience, e. g., observation, participation and student teaching are generally considered from the standpoint of their potential contribution to cognitive learning. The contribution that they might make to the personal growth of the prospective teacher is usually ignored. Likewise, other face-to-face experiences such as student–advisor relationships and individual and group counseling experiences are generally thought of as student personnel services rather than crucial teacher-education experiences involving personal relationships and individual growth.

If teacher-education institutions see the provision of opportunities for students to accept responsibility for personal growth as one of their primary functions, face-to-face encounters must be emphasized and geared to the task. Qualities such as responsibility, sensitivity, openness to experience, and acceptance of self and others are not developed in isolation from their functional context, namely, the self and others in honest relationship. Like personal values, personal qualities are developed when the individual witnesses or is involved in emotionally charged situations with meaningful others.

Unfortunately, prospective teachers lacking in self-actualizing qualities are not provided the appropriate experiences and guidance to help

* Adapted and abridged from *J. teach. Educ.*, 18: 471–475, 1967. By permission of author and publisher.

them confront themselves as persons who need to grow in the direction of greater commitment, responsibility, and involvement. Most of their educational experiences deal with patterns of extreme importance to teaching in a fashion that is devoid of direct involvement, personal feelings, and personal meaning. The student spends most of his four years as a passive receptacle or as an impartial non-involved observer. There *is* a place for the prospective teacher to review teaching and life in general as an objective observer, but this should not be done at the expense of his growth as a person.

Student teaching is the one point in teacher education where student teachers become involved with self, others, and personal growth. Some learn to accept responsibility for their personal growth and become a little more like the healthy person described by Maslow, Rogers, and others. Some blot out the self and others to a large extent, simulate the desired behavior and, by playing the game, see themselves through student teaching with a minimum of real encounter. Some find the transition from the passivity of being a student to the active involvement of being a teacher too demanding; they feel that it is unrealistic to be asked to take responsibility for their action, to exhibit genuine feelings, and to become actors in, rather than reactors to, life. Maybe they are right. Why should prospective teachers who have become acclimated to passive and sterile roles in our classrooms be asked to become responsible during student teaching, a period when they are burdened with the other demands of teaching?

The purpose of both general and professional education is to develop the student's ability to interact with specific others in a way that enhances the possibility of effecting desirable changes in behavior. Regardless of the differences in educational philosophy, the development of the prospective teacher as a person is an essential responsibility of any teacher-education program. And because of the nature of the student-teaching experience, many students do encounter self and others and do accept responsibility during this period of training. However, many factors argue against delaying this focus on growth until the student-teaching period. The student teacher himself, for example, is often so concerned with the external demands of the situation that his desire for security overshadows his desire for growth. Anyway, the nature of personal growth is such that it cannot be developed in a short period of time under the press of many other demands and the guidance of a supervisor whose responsibility tends to hamper his acceptance of the student teacher's inadequacies, the starting point for honest relationship and growth. What is called for is a shift in emphasis from a curriculum characterized by prescription to one characterized by self discovery, from a curriculum characterized by reliance on external responsibility for growth to one characterized by personal responsibility for growth, and from a curriculum characterized by talking about ideas, values, and qualities to one characterized by the discovery and development of ideas, values, and qualities through personal involvement in a real and open relationship and experience. The teacher-education program must become a genuine dialogue between the prospective teacher and the significant experiences and significant others he may encounter throughout the program.

Comments

1. This article deals with a recurring theme, namely, that education is so often superficial, academic, aseptic, and devoid of personal meaning—the opposite of *Education for What is Real*. The need for personal confrontation is particularly important in prospective teachers whose hands will hold the destiny of the generations to come. Developing a teacher-education program capable of promoting this type of personal awareness within the framework of the typical college program with its large classes and its impersonal atmosphere is apparently difficult; we need to decide whether this goal is sufficiently important to warrant making the necessary changes in our operation.

2. Wilhelm (1967) presents a similar theme and outlines a program designed to meet this need which he has in actual operation.

3. The extent to which a program effective in this direction can be implemented under conditions of large classes held in relative isolation from the classroom where the action is may be a problem. Conant's concept of apprenticeship to a master teacher (Conant, 1963) might have considerable merit in this connection.

References

Conant, James B. *The Education of American Teachers*. New York: McGraw-Hill, Inc., 1963.

Wilhelm, Fred T. "Actualizing the effective professional worker in education," in Eli M. Bower and William G. Hollister (eds.), *Behavioral Science Frontiers in Education*. New York: John Wiley & Sons, Inc., 1967. Pp. 555–578.

That's What They Said

"Any value entering the system which is inconsistent with the individual's valuation of himself cannot be assimilated; it meets with resistance and is likely, unless a general reorganization occurs, to be rejected. This resistance is a natural phenomenon; it is essential for the maintenance of individuality."

> Prescott Lecky. *Self-Consistency: A Theory of Personality*. New York: Island Press, 1951. [153]

"To summarize, much behavior, both in and outside the classroom, is determined by the child's image and by his attempts to 'be himself'—the self that he perceives."

> Don C. Charles. *Psychology in the Classroom*. New York: The Macmillan Company, 1964. [73]

"Our concepts of ourselves and our environment constitute 'reality' for us, and this 'reality' forms the basis for our actions, feelings, thoughts, and decisions."

> Henry C. Lindgren. *Educational Psychology in the Classroom*. New York: John Wiley & Sons, Inc., 1962. [47]

"Each child strives to be himself, to realize his resources, to come into his own. In other words, he strives for selfhood. But while the self shows a powerful impetus to grow, it also, as part of its essential character, has a strong resistance to change."

> Arthur T. Jersild. *Child Psychology*. Englewood Cliffs: Prentice-Hall, Inc., 1954. [32]

"This above all: to thine own self be true and it must follow, as the night the day, thou canst not then be false to any man."

> "Polonius" in Shakespeare's *Hamlet*.

"Teachers should bear in mind that children generally behave in about the only way it is possible for them to behave considering the hereditary characteristics they possess, the kinds of experiences they have had, and the social pressures which are operating upon them at the moment."

> Glenn M. Blair et al. *Educational Psychology*. New York: The Macmillan Co., 1954. [366]

"Whatever we do in teaching depends upon what we think people are like. The goals we seek, the things we do, the judgments we make, even the experiments we are willing to try, are determined by our beliefs about the nature of man and his capacities."

> Arthur W. Combs. *Perceiving, Behaving, Becoming.* 1962 Yearbook. Washington, D.C.: Association for Supervision and Curriculum Development, 1962. [108]

"Briefly it may be put that the observed phenomena of change seem most adequately explained by the hypothesis that *given certain psychological conditions, the individual has the capacity to reorganize his field of perception, including the way he perceives himself, and that a concomitant or a resultant of this perceptual reorganization is an appropriate alteration of behavior.*"

> Carl R. Rogers. "Some observations on the organization of personality," in Alfred E. Kuenzli (ed.), *The Phenomenological Problem.* New York: Harper & Row, Publishers, 1959. Pp. 49–75. [57]

"The capacity for psychological self-repair appears to be very great."

> Arthur T. Jersild. *Child Psychology.* Englewood Cliffs: Prentice-Hall, Inc., 1960. [26]

"Given a healthy physical organism to provide the vehicle for perception, enough time, a stimulating environment, challenging and fruitful problems and a non-restrictive self-concept, there seems no end to the perceptions possible to the individual."

> Arthur W. Combs and Donald Snygg. *Individual Behavior.* New York: Harper & Row, Publishers, 1959. [216]

"The normal adjustment of the average, commonsense, well-adjusted man implies a continued successful rejection of much of the depths of human nature, both conative and cognitive. To adjust well to the world of reality means a splitting of the person. It means that the person turns his back on much in himself because it is too dangerous. But it is now clear that by so doing he loses a great deal, too, for those depths are also the sources of all his joys, his ability to play, to love, to laugh, and most important, to be creative. By protecting himself against the hell within himself, he also cuts himself off from the heaven within. In the extreme instance, we have the obsessional person, flat, tight, rigid, frozen, controlled, cautious, who can not laugh, or play, or love, or be silly or trusting or childish. His imagination, his intuitions, his softness, his emotionality tend to be strangulated or distorted."

> A. H. Maslow. "Creativity in self-actualizing people," in H. H. Anderson (ed.), *Creativity and Its Cultivation*. New York: Harper & Row, Publishers, 1959. Pp. 83–95. [91]

"A major purpose of education is to help every child reach his fullest potential for a creative and useful life, lived in dignity and freedom. We believe that each child has a potentially important contribution to make."

> Jane Franseth. "Does grouping make a difference in pupil learning?" in Margaret Rasmussen (ed.), *Toward Effective Grouping*. Washington: Association for Childhood Education International, 1962. Pp. 25–33. [25]

"To be competent in the world of tomorrow one needs to be able to do three things—to love, to work, and to play. To define these competencies operationally requires the courage of a lion tamer and the linguistic ability of a modern Shakespeare."

> Eli M. Bower. "The achievement of competency," in Walter B. Waetjen and Robert R. Leeper (eds.), *Learning and Mental Health in the School*. 1966 Yearbook. Washington,D.C.: Association for Supervision and Curriculum Development, 1966. [23]

"Two essential aspects of living organisms are the need to change, to grow, and differentiate toward greater complexity, and the need to integrate and to maintain equilibrium and wholeness, to consolidate our gains."

> Caroline Tryon and W. E. Henry. "How children learn personal and social adjustment," in N. B. Henry (ed.), *Learning and Instruction*. 49th Yearbook, National Society for the Study of Education, Part I. Chicago: University of Chicago Press, 1950. Pp. 156–182. [156]

"We can be very certain . . . that providing schools which facilitate the development of persons with adequate, fully functioning personalities is the best way to contribute some degree of stability to an uncertain future."

> Arthur W. Combs, 1962, op. cit. [253]

"We are, in my view, a science and a profession uniquely concerned with human effectiveness—with the establishment and maintenance of the effective performance of the members of society in all their required tasks, their social roles, and their human relationships. This is our challenge— and our opportunity."

> Arthur H. Brayfield. "Human effectiveness," *Amer. Psychol.*, 20: 645–651, 1965. [651]

CHAPTER 4

Test Items

1. The self-concept is best conceived as
   a. the counterpart of Freud's alter-ego
   b. the individual's phenomenological interpretation of reality
   c. the sum total of one's experiences acting as a guide to future interaction with the environment
   d. the system of attitudes revolving around one's evaluation of himself
   e. a system of values on which the individual bases moral decisions

2. According to Combs and Snygg, the basic human drive is
   a. to achieve personal success
   b. to actualize, maintain, and enhance the self
   c. to avoid and to resolve conflict
   d. to effect increased differentiation of the life space
   e. to promote psychomotion within one's life space

3. The development of the self-concept is best explained on the basis of
   a. deliberate cultivation as part of early dependency training
   b. habit formation
   c. incidental development, involving the simple accumulation of any and all experiences
   d. innate predispositions
   e. learning (in the same way that all attitudes are learned)

4. Conflict with the current self-concept is probably most clearly involved in
   a. the academic difficulties of the underachiever
   b. the antisocial behavior of the juvenile delinquent
   c. the defiance of children from the lower classes
   d. the nonconformity of boys in school
   e. the performance of teen-age girls in athletics

5. Probably the best way for the school to help the child build a positive self-concept is
   a. to coordinate community efforts toward a common set of values
   b. to help him generate a self-concept consistent with outside reality
   c. to provide each and every child with a meaningful curriculum in which he can experience challenge and general success
   d. to provide him with unconditional emotional security
   e. to shield him from all frustration and failure experiences

6. The primary mechanism by which the individual maintains consistency in his self-concept is
   a. avoidance and/or rejection of incompatible evidence
   b. judicious selection of experiences
   c. projection of one's shortcomings onto others
   d. reinterpretation of experiences to fit the existing self
   e. selective perception

7. Accentuation is primarily a form of
   a. cognitive confusion
   b. differential retention
   c. selective perception
   d. selective sensitivity
   e. stimulus distortion

8. A healthy self-concept is likely to be shown by the individual who maintains _____ discrepancy between his self-ideal and his self-concept.
   a. a high positive
   b. a slight positive
   c. a slight negative
   d. a strong negative
   e. none of the above; there is no relationship here

9. Psychologically speaking, *success* and *failure* are primarily a function of
   a. achievement on an absolute scale
   b. the adequacy of the reinforcement
   c. one's achievement relative to that of significant others
   d. one's level of aspiration
   e. the size of the reward in relation to the effort

10. Which of the following is the *least likely* resultant of continued failure?
   a. an erratic level of aspiration
   b. a lackadaisical effort toward an ill-defined goal
   c. reluctance to set a definite goal for attainment
   d. a sizable negative discrepancy between aspiration and ability to achieve
   e. a strong positive discrepancy between aspiration and ability to achieve

11.   Which of the following conditions is most conducive to a change in self-concept?
    a.   the highly unsatisfactory nature of present status
    b.   an intensive program of hard-sell pressures
    c.   a permissive environment
    d.   a state of high anxiety over present conditions
    e.   a systematic program of subtle pressures

12.   What is the consensus of psychologists concerning the effects of anxiety?
    a.   Anxiety is all bad; it should be avoided at all costs.
    b.   Anxiety is beneficial only in building inhibitions (e. g., conscience).
    c.   Anxiety is conducive to compulsive overachievement.
    d.   Anxiety has detrimental effects on personality development.
    e.   Some degree of anxiety is necessary for maximum self-realization.

13.   Anxiety differs from fear primarily from the standpoint of
    a.   clarity of the direction of response
    b.   the degree of differentiation of stimulus
    c.   duration
    d.   intensity
    e.   normality/abnormality

14.   The clearest effect of severe anxiety on behavior is
    a.   a greater sensitivity to appropriate cues
    b.   increased systematic efforts to achieve a solution
    c.   regression to a more primitive mode of behavior
    d.   renewed attempts to analyze the problem
    e.   rigidity and stereotypy of behavior

15.   The basic premise of the phenomenological school of psychology is that
    a.   all behavior is an attempt at the clarification of the individual's psychological space
    b.   behavior is a consequence of the interaction between internal and external forces
    c.   greater adequacy of behavior goes hand in hand with greater differentiation of the psychological space
    d.   the individual's behavior is a reaction to the demands of his psychological space
    e.   phenomena are meaningful only in a figure-and-group perspective

16. Anxiety is best conceived as a condition of
    a. abnormal fear
    b. guilt-laden fear
    c. intense fear
    d. undefined fear
    e. a combination of all of the above

17. High-anxiety subjects are most likely to outperform mild- or low-anxiety subjects in areas calling for
    a. a high quality of work
    b. the need to improvise
    c. persistence in routine tasks
    d. refined muscular skills
    e. reduction in errors

18. The best policy for the school concerning anxiety is
    a. to build up the child's security and competence
    b. to help the child develop a well-defined self-concept
    c. to grade the tasks the child has to perform so as to ensure his continuous success
    d. to provide the child with a well-defined environment in which he always knows precisely where he stands
    e. to safeguard the child from all instances of anxiety

19. The most highly differentiated element of the total life space is
    a. the phenomenal field
    b. the phenomenal self
    c. the physical environment (external of self)
    d. the self-image
    e. any of the above, depending on one's personality orientation

20. The key to the promotion of self-actualization among school children is
    a. a broad program of meaningful social interaction designed to promote self-discovery
    b. an effective curriculum designed to promote maximum competency
    c. a permissive, wholesome, and stimulating classroom designed to promote openness to experience
    d. a personalized program designed to capitalize on unique assets to promote individuality and originality
    e. a well-adjusted and competent teacher dedicated to promoting pupil growth

21. The primary element in effective communication between individuals is
    a. adequate motivation
    b. adequate socialization to the same culture
    c. commonness in experiential background
    d. commonness in phenomenological field
    e. commonness of interest

22. The Hartshorne and May studies of deceit demonstrated that
    a. the hierarchy of value on the basis of which the individual operates is internally (not necessarily socially) consistent
    b. honesty in the average person tends to be insufficiently generalized to guarantee consistency in a variety of situations
    c. honesty is situational
    d. most situations involving honesty are generally too complex to permit consistent behavior
    e. the self-concept is only one of many determinants of behavior

23. The success element of the self-actualizing person is
    a. an enlightened self-interest
    b. his favorable view of himself and others and his willingness to accept himself and others as is
    c. his high level of personal integration
    d. his openness to experience
    e. his social sensitivity

24. The inadequate person is characterized primarily by
    a. his inability to meet environmental demands
    b. his orientation toward progressively greater inadequacy
    c. his compulsive need to protect his self
    d. his reliance on ineffective means of coping with his world
    e. his unwillingness to clarify the threatening situations as the basis for effective action

PART II

The Child as a Developing Organism

CHAPTER 5

Growth and Development

Psychology has had a long history of wavering from one end to the other of the heredity–environment controversy. Early psychologists assumed a strong hereditarian position and, although Watson took an equally extreme environmental stand, this was soon counteracted by studies showing that maturation alone seemed sufficient to account for certain basic aspects of growth. Much time and effort was needlessly wasted in trying to apportion the relative contribution of heredity and environment—with the general consensus usually leaning strongly toward heredity as the more important of the two sets of factors determining the status of a given organism at a given time. The pendulum has swung once more; we still believe that heredity sets certain predispositions—and also certain limits—but the consensus today is that these limits are far less restrictive than was originally believed and, further, that the real limits are those resulting from accumulated failure in previous learnings. Not only has research into the biochemistry of the brain pointed to the critical role of environmental stimulation in cognitive development but there is considerable evidence to suggest that early environmental deprivation may result in irretrievable losses in all aspects of growth potential. The current emphasis is on development as the outcome of the complex and dynamic interaction of hereditary and environmental factors rather than a matter of the summation of their separate contribution.

Of particular pedagogical importance is the concept of readiness; we especially need to recognize that readiness interacts with method, that readiness is a matter of readiness for what, and, further, that children are typically ready for all kinds of activities much earlier than we are inclined to believe—provided we adapt our methods to the readiness they already have. Actually, our views on readiness have changed drastically over the past decade from a strong belief in its relative immutability (based on the assumption of maturation as its critical component) to a realization that readiness is primarily the result of previous learnings. Psychologists are recognizing more and more the importance of background experience in determining the kind of person the individual is to be. This more positive outlook as to the amenability of growth and development to environmental influences has had a strong impact on the education of the culturally disadvantaged. This has been reflected in the Head Start concept as an attempt to prevent and to counteract the deficiencies of lower-class children whose inadequate preschool background has traditionally been the stumbling block to their effective classroom functioning from the first grade to the time they drop out of school.

As long as we saw maturation as the crucial factor in development, our only recourse was to wait for the necessary maturation to emerge with time. The preschool child was simply left to grow; pressure to accelerate his growth was considered futile and potentially damaging. Now that we recognize the crucial role of early environmental stimulation—as discussed in the accompanying articles by Ausubel, Caldwell, and Hess and Shipman —the emphasis has shifted from hands-off to a substantial emphasis on cognitive and intellectual stimulation as a prerequisite to the realization of one's potentialities. The child from the lower socio-economic classes, for example, is especially handicapped by a relative lack of meaningful language experiences in early childhood—with resulting difficulties not only in communication but even more important also in the area of thinking, learning, etc., that is, in the development of intellectual and cognitive, as well as academic, competence. Just like primitive man, the lower-class child is handicapped by a lack of adequate tools. The article by Dawe, written some 30 years ago, presents rather dramatic evidence of the effect of systematic training in the language development of the young child. Evaluation of the results of current Head Start programs has, unfortunately, been less encouraging.

David P. Ausubel

Viewpoints from Related Disciplines: Human Growth and Development *

With respect to the field of human growth and development, unfortunately, we can offer at present only a limited number of very crude generalizations and highly tentative suggestions bearing on the issue. In a very general sense, of course, it is undeniable that concern with child development has had a salutary effect on the educational enterprise. On the other hand, premature and wholesale extension of developmental principles to educational theory and practice has caused incalculable harm. It will take at least a generation for teachers to unlearn some of the more fallacious and dangerous of these overgeneralized and unwarranted applications.

Much of the difficulty proceeds from failure to appreciate that human growth and development is a pure rather than an applied science. As a pure science it is concerned with the discovery of general laws about the nature and regulation of human development *as an end in itself.* Ultimately, of course, these laws have self-evident implications for the realization of practical goals in such fields as education, child rearing, and guidance. In a very general sense, they indicate the effects of different interpersonal and social climates on personality development and the kinds of methods and subject-matter content that are most compatible with developmental capacity and mode of functioning at a given stage of growth. Thus, because it offers important insights about the changing intellectual and emotional capacities of children as developing human beings, child development may legitimately be considered one of the basic sciences underlying education.

Actual application to practical problems of teaching and curriculum, however, is quite another matter. Before the educational implications of developmental findings can become explicitly useful in everyday school situations, much *additional* research at the engineering level of operations is necessary. Many of the better-known generalizations in child development —the principle of readiness, the cephalocaudal trend, the abstract-to-concrete trend in conceptualizing the environment, and others—are interesting and potentially useful ideas to curriculum specialists but will have little

* Adapted and abridged from *T. C. Rec.,* 60: 245–254, 1959. By permission of author and publisher.

practical utility in designing a social studies or physical education curriculum unless they are rendered more specific in terms of the actual operations involved in teaching these subjects.

Readiness and Grade Placement

It is fully agreed that readiness influences in a crucial way the effectiveness of the learning process; it often determines whether a given skill is learnable at all. Educators have also assumed that there is an optimal age for learning a particular task; postponing a given learning experience beyond this point not only wastes educational opportunity and valuable time but may actually increase the difficulty of its learning. Exposing a child to a given learning experience prematurely, on the other hand, will result in nonlearning of the subject matter and teach him negative attitudes of fear, dislike, and discouragement besides.

Up to this point, the principle of readiness is empirically demonstrable and conceptually unambiguous. Difficulty first arises when it is confused with the concept of *maturation* and when the latter concept, in turn, is equated with a process of "internal ripening." The concept of readiness simply refers to the adequacy of existing capacity in relation to the demands of a given learning task. No specification is made as to *how* this capacity is achieved. Maturation, on the other hand, has a different and much more restricted meaning. It encompasses those increments in capacity that take place in the demonstrable absence of specific practice experience. Maturation, therefore, is merely one of the two principal factors (the other being learning) that contribute to or determine the organism's readiness to cope with new experience. Whether or not readiness exists, in other words, does not necessarily depend on maturation alone but in many instances is solely a function of prior learning experience and most typically depends on varying proportions of maturation and learning.

To equate the principles of readiness and maturation not only muddies the conceptual waters but also makes it difficult for the school to appreciate that insufficient readiness may reflect inadequate prior learning on the part of pupils because of inappropriate or inefficient instructional methods. Lack of maturation can thus become a convenient scapegoat whenever children manifest insufficient readiness to learn, and the school, which is thereby automatically absolved of all responsibility in the matter, consequently fails to subject its instructional practices to the degree of self-critical scrutiny necessary for continued educational progress. In short, while it is important to appreciate that the current readiness of pupils determines the school's current choice of instructional methods and materials, it is equally important to bear in mind that this readiness itself is partly determined by the appropriateness and efficiency of the previous instructional practices to which they have been subjected.

The conceptual confusion is further compounded when maturation is interpreted as a process of "internal ripening" essentially independent of *all* environmental influences, that is, of both specific practice and incidental experience. Readiness then becomes a matter of simple genic regulation unfolding in accordance with a predetermined and immutable time-table; and the school, by definition, becomes powerless to influence readiness either through its particular way of arranging specific learning experiences or through a more general program of providing incidental or nonspecific background experience preparatory to the introduction of more formal academic activities.

Actually, the embryological model of development implicit in the "internal ripening" thesis fits quite well when applied to human sensorimotor and neuromuscular sequences taking place during the prenatal period and early infancy. The only truly objectionable aspect of this point of view is its unwarranted extrapolation to those more complex and variable components of later cognitive and behavioral development where unique factors of individual experience and cultural environment make important contributions to the direction, patterning, and sequential order of all developmental changes.

It is hardly surprising, therefore, in view of the tremendous influence on professional and lay opinion wielded by Gesell and his colleagues, that many people conceive of readiness in absolute and immutable terms, and thus fail to appreciate that, except for such traits as walking and grasping, the mean ages of readiness can never be specified apart from relevant environmental conditions. Although the modal child in contemporary America may first be ready to read at the age of six and one-half, the age of reading readiness is always influenced by cultural, subcultural, and individual differences in background experience, and in any case varies with the method of instruction employed and the child's IQ. Middle-class children, for example, are ready to read at an earlier age than lower-class children.

The need for particularizing developmental generalizations before they can become useful in educational practice is nowhere more glaringly evident than in the field of readiness. At present we can only speculate what curricular sequences might conceivably be if they took into account precise and detailed (but currently unavailable) research findings on the emergence of readiness for different subject-matter areas, for different sub-areas and levels of difficulty within an area, and for different techniques of teaching the same material. Because of the unpredictable specificity of readiness, valid answers to such questions cannot be derived from logical extrapolation but require meticulous empirical research in a school setting. The next step would involve the development of appropriate teaching methods and materials to take optimal advantage of existing degrees of readiness and to increase readiness wherever necessary and desirable. But since we generally do not have this type of research data available, except perhaps in the field of reading, we can only pay lip service to the principle of readiness in curriculum planning.

Breadth of Curriculum

A common criticism is that the broadening of elementary school curriculum to include social studies, art, science, etc., has been at the expense of competence in the fundamentals. Fortunately, the expansion of the curriculum has not resulted in a decline in the standards of the three R's. Evidently, the decreased amount of time spent on the latter subjects has been more than compensated for by the development of more efficient methods of teaching and by the incidental learning of the fundamentals in the course of studying these other subjects. There is still, however, a point beyond which further increase in the scope of the curriculum would have to be obtained through sacrificing mastery of the fundamentals. It is here that criteria of development can offer profitable guidelines.

Generally speaking, maximal breadth of the curriculum consistent with adequate mastery of its constituent parts is developmentally desirable at all ages because of the tremendously wide scope of human abilities. The wider the range of intellectual stimulation to which pupils are exposed, the greater are the chances that all of the diverse potentialities both within a group of children and within a single child will be brought to fruition. By the same token, a broad curriculum makes it possible for more pupils to experience success in the performance of school activities and thus to develop the necessary self-confidence and motivation for continued academic striving and achievement. The very fact that elementary school children are able to make significant progress in science and social studies also indicates that myopic concentration of the three R's would waste much available readiness for these types of learnings and thus compel junior and senior high schools to devote much of their instructional time to materials that are easily learnable in the lower grades.

The relationship between breadth and depth must also take into account the progressive differentiation of intelligence, interests, and personality structure with increasing age. The elementary school child is a "generalist" because both his intellect and his personality are still relatively unstable and uncrystallized and lack impressive internal consistency. Thus, many different varieties of subject matter are equally compatible with his interest and ability patterns. Furthermore, unless he has experience with many different fields of knowledge and gives each a provisional try, he is in no position to judge which kinds of intellectual pursuits are most congruent with his major ability and value systems. Hence, quite apart from the future life adjustment values of a broad educational background, it is appropriate on developmental grounds for elementary and early high school curricula to stress breadth rather than depth.

Toward the latter portion of the high school period, however, precisely the opposite kind of situation begins to emerge. Interests have crystallized and abilities have undergone differentiation to the point where greater depth and specialization are possible and desirable. Many students at this stage of intellectual development are ready to sink their teeth into more serious and solid academic fare, but unfortunately suitable instructional programs geared at an advanced level of critical and independent thinking are rarely available.

The Child's Voice in Curriculum Planning

One extreme point of view associated with the child-centered approach to education is the notion that children are innately equipped in some mysterious fashion for knowing precisely what is best for them. This idea is obviously an outgrowth of predeterministic theories (e. g., those of Rousseau and Gesell), which conceive of development as a series of internally regulated sequential steps that unfold in accordance with a prearranged design. According to these theorists, the environment facilitates development best by providing a maximally permissive field that does not interfere with the predetermined process of spontaneous maturation. From these assumptions it is but a short step to the claim that the child himself must be in the most strategic position to *know* and *select* those components of the environment that correspond most closely with his current developmental needs and hence are most conducive to optimal growth.

Proponents of this point of view argue that the child apparently knows what is best for him in all areas of growth and should be allowed to make his own selections even in matters of curriculum. A number of arguments can be presented questioning the validity of this position: One can never assume that the child's *spontaneously* expressed interests and activities are completely reflective of *all* of his important needs and capacities. Just because capacities can potentially provide their own motivation does not mean that they always or necessarily do so. It is not the possession of capacities that is motivating, but the anticipation of future satisfactions once they have been successfully exercised. But because of such factors as inertia, lack of opportunity, lack of appreciation, and preoccupation with other activities, many capacities may never be exercised in the first place. Thus, children typically develop *some* of their potential capacities, and their expressed interests cannot be considered co-extensive with the potential range of interests they are capable of developing with appropriate stimulation.

The current interests and spontaneous desires of immature pupils are simply not dependable guidelines for curriculum development. In fact, one of the primary functions of education should be to stimulate the development of motivations that are currently nonexistent. It is true that academic acheivement is greatest when pupils manifest felt needs to acquire knowledge as an end in itself. Such needs, however, are not endogenous but acquired—and largely through exposure to provocative, meaningful, developmentally appropriate instruction. While children might participate in designing the curriculum, it makes little developmental or administrative sense to entrust them with responsibility for significant policy or operational decisions.

Organization and Cognitive Development

What counts is not what a child knows at the end of a given grade but rather what he will know and be able to use in adult life. What is important then is not so much the subject-matter content of the curriculum but rather the organization, sequence, and manner of presenting learning experiences, their degree of meaningfulness, and the relative balance between conceptual and factual materials.

But obviously, before we could ever hope to structure effectively such instructional variables for the optimal realization of these designated objectives, we would have to know a great deal more about the organizational and developmental principles whereby human beings acquire and retain stable bodies of knowledge and develop the power of critical and productive thinking. This type of knowledge, however, will forever elude us unless we abandon the untenable assumption that there is no real distinction either between the logic of a proposition and how the mind apprehends it or between the logical structure of subject-matter organization and the actual series of cognitive processes through which an immature and developing individual incorporates facts and concepts into a stable body of knowledge. It is perfectly logical from the standpoint of a mature scholar, for example, to write a textbook in which topically homogenous materials are segregated into discrete chapters and treated throughout at a uniform level of conceptualization. But how closely does this approach correspond with highly suggestive findings that one of the major cognitive processes involved in the learning of any new subject is progressive differentiation of an originally undifferentiated field. Once we learn more about cognitive development than the crude generalizations that developmental psychology can currently offer, it will be possible to employ organizational and sequential principles in the presentation of subject matter that actually parallel developmental changes in the growth and organization of the intellect.

Many features of the activity program are based on the premise that the elementary school child perceives the world in relatively specific and concrete terms and requires considerable firsthand experience with diverse concrete instances of a given set of relationships before he can abstract genuinely meaningful concepts. Thus, an attempt is made to teach factual information and intellectual skills in the real-life functional contexts in which they are customarily encountered rather than through the medium of verbal exposition supplemented by artificially contrived drills and exercises. This approach has real merit, if a fetish is not made of naturalism and incidental learning, if drills and exercises are provided in instances where opportunities for acquiring skills do not occur frequently and repetitively enough in more natural settings, and if deliberate or guided effort is not regarded as incompatible with incidental learning. Even more important, however, is the realization that in older children, once a sufficient number of basic concepts are consolidated, new concepts are primarily abstracted from verbal rather than from concrete experience. Hence in secondary school it may be desirable to reverse both the sequence and the relative balance between abstract concepts and supportive data. There is good reason for believing, therefore, that much of the time presently spent in cook-book laboratory exercises in the sciences could be much more advantageously employed in formulating precise definitions, making explicit verbal distinctions between concepts, generalizing from hypothetical situations, and in other ways.

Another underlying assumption of activity and project methods is that concepts and factual data are retained much longer when they are meaningful, genuinely understood, and taught as larger units of interrelated materials than when they are presented as fragmented bits of isolated information and committed to rote memory. This, of course, does not preclude the advisability of rote learning for certain kinds of learning (for example, multiplication tables) *after* a functional understanding of the underlying concepts has been acquired. Unfortunately, however, these principles have made relatively few inroads on the high school instructional program, where they are still applicable. The teaching of mathematics and science, for example, still relies heavily on rote learning of formulas and procedural steps, on recognition of traditional "type problems," and on mechanical manipulation of symbols. In the absence of clear and stable concepts which serve as anchoring points and organizing foci for the assimilation of new material, secondary school students are trapped in a morass of confusion and seldom retain rotely memorized materials much beyond final exam time.

This brings us finally to a consideration of the mechanisms of accretion and long-term retention of ideational material. Why do high school and university students tend to forget so readily previous day-to-day learnings as they are exposed to new lessons? The traditional answer of educational psychology, based upon studies of short-term rote learning in animal and human subjects, has been that subsequent learning experiences which are similar to but not identical with previously learned materials exert a retroactively inhibitory effect on the retention of the latter. But wouldn't it be reasonable to suppose that all of the existing, cumulatively established ideational systems which an individual brings with him to any learning situation have more of an interfering effect on the retention of new learning material (proactive inhibition) than brief exposure to subsequently introduced materials of a similar nature (retroactive inhibition)? Because it is cognitively most economical and least burdensome for an individual to subsume as much new experience as possible under existing concepts that are inclusive and stable, the import of many specific illustrative items in later experience is assimilated by the generalized meaning of these more firmly established and highly conceptualized subsuming foci. When this happens the latter items lose their identity and are said to be "forgotten." Hence, if proactive rather than retroactive inhibition turned out to be the principal mechanism affecting the longevity with which school materials were retained, it would behoove us to identify those factors that counteract it and to employ such measures in our instructional procedures.

Comments

1. In this classic article, Ausubel points to some of the implications of human growth and development as a pure science for pedagogical practice; as teachers, we need to remember, for example, that children's lack of readiness often reflects nothing more than gaps and inadequacies in their prior learnings—possibly resulting from inadequacies in our teaching. We must also remember that maturation alone will not provide the child with the interests and motivations necessary to ensure his maximal development.

2. The distinction between logical and psychological organizations of subject-matter content has immediate bearing on curriculum development as well as on classroom teaching.

Bettye M. Caldwell

What Is the Optimal Learning Environment for the Young Child? *

A number of studies have investigated developmental sequences in children associated with various types of environment. These studies have, in the main, been simply descriptive. More recent studies contrasting middle and lower class family environment have implied that things could be better for the young child from the deprived segment of our culture. Even so, there has remained a justifiable reluctance about recommending or arranging any environment for the very young child other than the type regarded as his own natural habitat, namely within his own family.

Actually, we are constantly arranging to optimize the environment. Disturbed children, for example, are typically provided psychotherapy or even totally removed from their offending environment and placed on a temporary or prolonged basis in a milieu presumably more conducive to normal development. There is a massive milieu arrangement formalized and legalized as "education" which profoundly affects the life of all children once they reach the age of 5 or 6. This type of arrangement is not only tolerated but actually endorsed even to the point of strict enforcement.

However, there has been a great deal of timidity about conscious and planned arrangements of the developmental milieu for the very young child, as though we are operating on the implicit assumption that any environment which sustains life is adequate for this period. Considering the vast number of behavioral skills developing during this period and the increased evidence pointing to the relative permanence of any deficit that may be acquired during this period, it becomes mandatory that we give careful attention to the developmental environment during the first three years of life.

Conclusions from Inadequate Environments

A number of studies have concerned themselves with the development of contrasting patterns of intellectual functioning shown by a group

* Adapted and abridged from *Amer. J. Orthopsychiatry,* 37: 8–21, 1967. By permission of author and publisher.

of adopted adolescents who had been reared in institutions up to the age of 3 and then transferred to foster homes. It would seem that the former institution infants were less socially alert, less outgoing, less curious, less responsive, less interested in objects, and generally less advanced. Evidence of this type can be generalized into an explicit principle guiding our recommendations for optimal environments—learning or otherwise—for young children whenever any type of milieu arrangement is necessary. The optimal environment for the young child is one in which he is cared for in his own home in the context of a warm, continuous, emotional relationship with his own mother under conditions of varied sensory input. Implicit in this principle is (a) the conviction that the child's mother is the person best qualified to provide a stable and warm interpersonal relationship as well as the necessary pattern of sensory stimulation; and (b) the assumption that socio-emotional development has priority during the first three years and that, if this occurs normally, cognitive development, which is of minor importance during this period anyway, will take care of itself. At a still deeper level lurks the assumption that attempts to foster cognitive development will interfere with socio-emotional development. Advocacy of the principle also implies endorsement of the idea that most homes are adequate during this early period and that presumably no formal training for mothering is necessary.

However, there is always a large number of children for whom substitute milieu arrangements must be made. This is typically resolved by creating substitute families. The same holds when the parents themselves seek to work out an alternative child-care arrangement, say, because of maternal employment. The typical maneuver is to obtain a motherly person who will "substitute" for her (not supplement her). The behavioral and social sciences are becoming progressively more involved in planning for social action; in this context, it would be meaningful to question some of the hidden assumptions underlying our operating principle about the optimal environment for the young child.

Examining the Hidden Assumptions

(a)   Sensitized by knowledge of the deleterious effects of continued institutionalization of young children, a number of studies have investigated the consequence of short-term, intermittent mother–child separation. The evidence does not support the assumption that maternal deprivation such as exists in the institutional environment and maternal short-term intermittent separation are the same thing.

(b)   Is group upbringing invariably damaging? A sufficient number of exceptions have been reported to the social and cognitive deficits associated with continuous group care during infancy to warrant an intensification of the search for the true ingredients in group situations associated with the observed deficit. It would seem that the deficiencies of institutionalized children would disappear if it were possible to equate the comparison groups on the variable of environmental adequacy. As Gula (1965) suggests, merely because most institutions studied have been inadequate in terms of adult–child ratio, staff turnover, personal characteristics of some of the caretakers, etc., one is not justified in concluding *ipso facto* that group care is invariably inferior or damaging.

(c) Is healthy socio-emotional development the most important task of the first three years? Do attempts to foster cognitive growth interfere with social and emotional development? These two assumptions represent a closed system model of human development. They seem to conceptualize development as compartmentalized and with a finite limit so that, if a child progresses too much in one direction, he automatically restricts the amount of development that can occur in another area. Actually life is an open system in which development feeds upon development so that cognitive and emotional development tend to be positively rather than negatively correlated. If we accept the premise that intelligent behavior is adaptive behavior, it is difficult to see how cognitive advances imply discouraging healthy socio-emotional development. Ample data are available to suggest that quite the reverse is true. The emotional reinforcement accompanying the old "I can do it myself" declaration should not be undervalued. Fowler (1962), for example, questions whether there is any justification for the modern anxiety that cognitive stimulation may damage personality development. It would seem that, where damage occurred, the culprit was severe and harmful methods of stimulation rather than the process of stimulation per se.

(d) Do cognitive experiences of the first few months and years leave no significant residual? The assumption that the learnings of infancy are evanescent appears to be a fairly modern idea: Rousseau, for example, insisted that education should begin with the child still in the cradle. Interestingly enough, the view that early learnings disappear came from longitudinal studies suggesting that early intellectual status was largely irrelevant as a predictor of later intellectual performance. It does not follow, however, that the early months and years are unimportant for cognitive development; or the contrary, Bloom (1964), for example, suggests that marked changes in the environment in the early years can produce greater changes in intelligence than will equally marked changes in the environment at later periods of development.

(e) Can one expect that, without formal planning, all the necessary learning experiences will occur? Although it is possible for children surrounded by the necessary material to learn all there is to be learned about these materials, that this should necessarily occur with any frequency is quite another matter. Experience in operating nursery school programs for children with early experiential deficiencies leads to the increased conviction that such children are often totally unable to avail themselves of educational opportunities and must be guided into meaningful learning encounters. When one reflects on the number of carefully arranged reinforcement contingencies necessary to help a young child learn to decode the simple message, "No," it is difficult to support the position that, in early learning, nature should take its course.

(f)   Is formal training for child care during the first three years unnecessary? This assumption, obviously ridiculous, is nevertheless a logical deduction from the premise that the only adequate place for a young child is with his mother or a mother substitute. Since there is no adequacy test for motherhood, proclaiming that mothering is essential for the healthy development of the child implies that any mothering will do. Yet we have rigid certification statutes regulating the training of teachers. Perhaps it will now be possible to extend our efforts at social intervention to encompass a broader range of health, education, and welfare activities.

(g)   Are most homes and most parents adequate for at least the first three years? The clinical literature as well as the literature on social class differences make it abundantly clear that not all parents are qualified to provide even the basic essentials of physical and psychological care to their children. The low-income mother, for example, may be so overwhelmed by reactions of depression and inadequacy that behavior toward her child is largely determined by the needs of the moment rather than by any clear plan about how to bring up children and how to train them to engage in the kind of behavior that the parents regard as acceptable or desirable. Parents are blamed for many things but parental inadequacy during the first three years has not so far been considered a major menace. Perhaps when the various alternatives are weighed, it appears by comparison to be the least of multiple evils; but parental behavior of the first three years should not be regarded as any more sacrosanct or beyond the domain of social concern than that of the later years.

Planning Alternatives

At this point the exposition of this paper must come to an abrupt halt, for insufficient data about possible alternative models are available to warrant recommendation of any major pattern of change. One apparent limitation on ideas for alternatives appears to be thinking in terms of binary choices or dichotomies; we speak of individual care or group care; foster home or institution; etc., when actually environments for the very young child need not be any more mutually exclusive than they are for the older child. After all, our public education system is a combination of the efforts of the home plus an institution; we would tend to agree that the optimal environment for the older child is a combination of both rather than either singly.

A number of programs suggesting alternatives worth considering are currently in the early field trial stage. One of these, described by Caldwell and Richmond (1964), offers educationally-oriented day-care for culturally deprived children between six months and three years. The children spend the better part of five days a week in a group-care setting but return home each evening and maintain primary emotional relationships with their own families. Unfortunately, no evidence of their effectiveness at this stage is available, but effective social action can seldom await definitive data. Actually, in the area of child care the greatest demand for innovative action appears to be coming from a rather unlikely source—not from any professional group or from social planners—but from the mothers, or more specifically from working mothers who are looking for professional leadership to design and provide child-care facilities that help prepare their children for today's achievement-oriented culture. As a result, we are currently witnessing the early stages of the professionalization of the mother-substitute role—or as I would prefer to say, the mother-*supplement* role.

Another basis for planning alternatives is becoming available from the increasing knowledge concerning the process of development. The accumulation of data suggesting that the first few years of life are crucial for the priming of cognitive development calls for vigorous and imaginative action for these early years. Already a great deal is known which enables us to specify some of the essential ingredients in a growth-fostering milieu. Such an environment must contain warm and responsive people who, by their own interest, invest objects with value. It must be supportive and as free of disease and pathogenic agents as can possibly be arranged. It also must trace a clear path from where the child is to where he is to go developmentally; objects and events must be similar and yet novel enough to stimulate and attract. Such an environment must be exquisitely responsive, as a more consistent pattern of response is required to foster the acquisition of new forms of behavior than is required to maintain such behavior once it appears in the child's repertoire. The timing of experiences also must be carefully programmed. For children whose early experiences have been deficient and depriving, programming of the environment seems mandatory if subsequent learning difficulties are to be avoided.

Comments

1.   Caldwell's suggestion that we need to examine our present reluctance to institute a carefully designed program of social action for the very young child is probably scientifically and pedagogically correct. The sociological repercussions of such an attempt at this time may (or may not) be something else again. All of our efforts in this direction so far have been for the disadvantaged; it has apparently been assumed that middle-

class parents can provide all the necessary cognitive stimulation. This may bear investigation.

  2. Before we can decide what constitutes an optimal environment sufficiently superior to that of a given home to warrant taking over the educational function at that age, we need to clarify what we are trying to accomplish. Certainly, our answers would be different if we were to think of "day-care" custodial centers for children of working mothers or, in accordance with our more recent viewpoint, a preschool designed to promote maximal cognitive (as well as socio-emotional) development and overcome earlier developmental deficiencies.

  3. The crucial point here is the critical periods hypothesis, which postulates certain brief periods in the development of the individual during which he is optimally ready to profit from certain experiences. Failure to provide appropriate experiences during this period can result in irretrievable losses. Along these lines, it is felt that the lower-class child suffers irreparable losses as a result of stimulus deficiencies in his early environment.

References

Bloom, Benjamin S. *Stability and Change in Human Characteristics*. New York: John Wiley & Sons, Inc., 1964.

Caldwell, Bettye M., and J. B. Richmond. "Programmed day care for the very young—A preliminary report," *J. Marr. Family,* 26: 481–488, 1964.

Fowler, W. "Cognitive learning in infancy and early childhood," *Psychol. Bull.,* 59: 116–152, 1962.

Gula, H. Paper given at the Conference on Group Care for Children. Children's Bureau, January 1965.

Robert D. Hess and Virginia C. Shipman

Early Experience and the Socialization of Cognitive Modes in Children *

That children from deprived backgrounds score well below their middle-class peers on standardized measures of intelligence is well known. They come to school lacking in the skills necessary for coping with the first-grade curriculum. Their language, as well as their auditory and visual discrimination skills are relatively poor. In scholastic achievement, they are retarded by an average of 2 years by Grade 6; they are more likely to drop out of high school and less likely to go on to college. Years ago, the problem was discussed in terms of the relative contribution of hereditary and environmental factors; current interest centers on the mechanisms by which cultural experience is translated into cognitive behavior and academic achievement. It is no longer a question of whether social and cultural disadvantages depress academic ability; the focus is now more on conceptualizing social class as a discrete array or pattern of experience to be examined from the standpoint of their effect on the child's emerging cognitive equipment.

The present paper is concerned with the nature of cultural deprivation and its effect on the resources of the human mind; it presents the following arguments: (a) The behavior which leads to social, educational and economic poverty is learned in early childhood; (b) the central quality involved in the effects of cultural deprivation is lack of cognitive meaning in the mother–child communication system, and (c) the growth of cognitive processes is fostered in family control systems which offer and permit a wide range of alternatives of action and thought; conversely such growth is constricted by systems of control which offer predetermined solutions and few alternatives for consideration and choice. It postulates that the structure of the social system and of the family shape communication and language which, in turn, shape thought and cognitive (problem-solving) styles. More specifically, the nature of the parent–child control system within the

* Adapted and abridged from Robert D. Hess and Virginia C. Shipman, "Early experience and the socialization of cognitive modes in children," *Child Devel.,* 36: 869–886, 1965. Copyright © 1965 by the Society for Research in Child Development, and reproduced by permission.

disadvantaged family context restricts the number and kind of alternative actions and thought open to the child. This constriction discourages the tendency of the child to reflect, to consider, and to choose among alternatives; it develops modes for dealing with problems which are impulsive rather than reflective, which focus on the immediate rather than the future, and which are disconnected rather than sequential.

This position is based on the work of Bernstein (1961) who identifies two kinds of verbal communication styles, *restricted* and *elaborated*. Restricted styles are stereotyped, limited, and condensed; they lack the specificity and exactness required for precise conceptualization and differentiation. Sentences are short, simple, and often unfinished; there is little use of subordinate clauses. In elaborated codes, on the other hand, communication is individualized and made specific to a particular situation. Language here is more particular, more differentiated, and more precise; it permits the expression of wider and more complex arrangement of thought, leading to discrimination among cognitive and affective content.

Early experience with these styles not only affects communication and cognitive structure but it also establishes potential patterns of relations with the external world. According to Bernstein, language is used by participants of a social network to elaborate and express social and other personal relations and, in turn, is shaped by these relations. This reciprocal role of social interaction and language is illustrated by the distinction between two types of family control: One is oriented toward status appeal or ascribed role norms; the other toward persons. Actually, in the family, as in other social structures, control is exercised in part through status appeal; there is, however, a difference among families in the extent to which status-based control maneuvers are modified by orientation toward persons. In status-oriented families, behavior tends to be regulated in terms of role expectations; no consideration is given to the unique characteristics of the child as a factor in the decision-making process. In the person-oriented appeal system, on the contrary, the unique characteristics of the child modify the status demands. Behavior is justified in terms of feeling, preference, personal and unique reactions, and subjective states. This not so much permits as it actually demands an elaborated linguistic code and a wide range of linguistic and behavioral alternatives as part of interpersonal interaction.

These distinctions may be clarified by an example: Assume that the child is playing noisily when the telephone rings. In one home, the mother says: "Be quiet" or "Shut up." In the other, the mother says, "Would you keep quiet a minute, I want to talk on the phone." The point here is a difference in the inner response elicited in the child and its effect on his developing cognitive network of concepts and meanings. In the first instance, the child is simply called upon to comply: he is not called upon to reflect or to make mental discriminations. In the second instance, the child is required to consider two or three ideas: he must relate his behavior to a time dimension; he must consider his behavior in relation to its effects on another person; he must perform a more complicated task to follow the communication of his mother in that his relationship to her is mediated in part through concepts and shared ideas. His mind is stimulated by a more elaborate complex verbal communication initiated by the mother. As a consequence of these two divergent communication styles repeated in numerous ways in numerous circumstances during the preschool years, these two children might be expected to develop substantially different verbal styles and cognitive equipment by the time they enter school.

A person-oriented family encourages the child to achieve appropriate behavior by presenting role requirements in a specific context and by emphasizing the consequences of alternative behavior. Status-oriented families, by contrast, tend to present a rule in an assigned manner with compliance as the only possibility. The role of power is more obvious, with coercion and defiance likely interactional possibilities. Such families rely on a more rigid teaching-and-learning model in which compliance, rather than rationale, is stressed.

A central issue here is the nature of the responses elicited and permitted by the maternal style of communication. There are two axes in the child's behavior in which we have a particular interest: One is represented by an assertive initiatory approach to learning (in contrast to a passive compliant mode of engagement); the other deals with the tendency to reach solutions hastily or impulsively (as distinguished from the tendency to reason, to reflect, to choose among available options). These styles of cognitive behavior are related to the previously mentioned types of family control systems. A status-oriented statement tends to present rules of conduct based on arbitrary decisions rather than on logical consequences resulting from the selection among alternatives. Elaborated or personally-oriented statements, on the other hand, lend themselves more easily to a cognitive approach involving reflective comparisons. While status-oriented statements tend to be restrictive of thought, a request of "Will you keep quiet a minute, I want to speak on the phone" gives the child a rationale for relating his behavior to a wider set of considerations. He has been given a *why* for his mother's request and may possibly become more likely to ask *why* in other situations. It may be through this type of interaction that the child learns to look for action sequences in his own behavior and that of others.

The study concerns a group of 163 Negro mothers and their four-year-old children selected from four social-status levels: (a) upper-middle; (b) upper-lower; (c) lower-lower; and (d) an "Aid to Dependent Children" group. The procedure consisted of teaching each mother three simple tasks which she, in turn, was to teach to her child. The data lent support to the general lines of argument just presented.

(a)   Social-status differences: A major difference in the environments provided by the mothers was in their pattern of language use.

The most obvious social class difference was in the total verbal output of the mothers: An average of 82 lines of typescript for middle-class mothers as against an average of only 49 lines for the mothers of the other three groups. There were also differences in the *quality* of the language used: The middle-class mothers achieved an "abstraction" score (a tendency to use abstract words) of 5.6 as against 4.9, 3.7, and 1.8 for the second, third, and fourth group respectively.

(b) Control system: The mother's responses to questions as to what they would do in several hypothetical situations in school in which the child had broken a rule, failed to achieve, etc. revealed a strong relationship between higher social status level and the tendency to utilize person-oriented statements.

(c) Status differences in concept utilization: Another part of the study (data omitted here) revealed a significant decrease from cognitive to nonverbal response with decrease in social status: children of the two lower-class groups made very little use of relational and descriptive responses. The results seem to reflect the relatively undeveloped verbal and conceptual ability of children of homes with restricted ranges of verbal and conceptual content.

The study also found large differences among the social status groups in the ability of the mother to teach and of the child to learn. One mother, for example, would give explicit information about the task and what was expected; she offered support and help of various kinds, etc. Another mother, on the other hand, relied on nonverbal communication; she did not define the task for the child. The child was not provided with ideas and information he could grasp; he was neither told what was expected nor what the task was about, even in general terms. On the other hand, while gross differences appeared in the verbal and cognitive environment they provided, the mothers differed relatively little in the affective components of the interaction with their children.

Comments

1. This is a significant paper on the nature of cultural deprivation and its effect on the child. The view that educationally significant differences in readiness for school among children of different social classes are due to differences in the socialization process has interesting sociological implications.

2. If we start with the theoretical position that ability is something that develops as a result of productive interaction with the environment, we may be saying that the less able children are simply the outcome of ineffective maternal communication patterns of the status-oriented vari-

ety discussed in the present article. The dimension of impulsivity bears on the article by Jerome Kagan (Chapter 6).

Reference

Bernstein, B. "Social class and linguistic development: A theory of social learning," in A. H. Halsey et al. (eds.), *Education, Economy, and Society.* New York: Free Press, 1961.

Helen C. Dawe

A Study of the Effect of an Educational Program upon the Language Development and Related Mental Functions in Young Children *

The present study was concerned with the effects of training in the understanding and use of language symbols on language development and the relationship between language development and mental functions. More specifically, four types of training were involved: "(1) training in the understanding of words and concepts; (2) looking at and discussing pictures; (3) listening to poems and stories; (4) going on short excursions" [p. 200].

The training period consisted of some 50 hours of individual and group work, the former devoted to teaching the child the meaning of words, the latter devoted to stories, discussion of pictures, and excursions in groups of two to four children. The emphasis was on introducing new words and phrases into the child's functional vocabulary through the liberal use of explanatory comments. The children were encouraged to think critically, to notice relationships, and to avoid the careless use of language symbols. The subjects were 11 pairs of children attending the Iowa Soldiers' Orphans' Home. They were carefully matched on sex, chronological age, mental age, etc. The training period was distributed over some 8½ months; all training took place on the week-end.

The experimental group showed decidedly greater gains than their controls in all relevant variables; increases in the length and complexity of their sentences and in the intellectual caliber of their questions and comments reflected a corresponding increase in linguistic and analytical ability. Although probably associated in part with increase in age, some of the changes were so large as to indicate the operation of more fundamental factors.

* Adapted and abridged from Helen C. Dawe, "A study of the effect of an educational program upon the language development and related mental functions in young children," *J. exper. Ed.*, 11:200–209, 1942. Copyright 1942 by the American Psychological Association and reproduced by permission.

Comment

Dawe's well-known study is of particular interest in that it antedates the present emphasis on Head Start and other preschool programs. Her results, obtained at a time when the experts leaned heavily toward the "fixed maturation" concept, take on special significance with respect to the present recognition of the need for semiformal early childhood education, particularly for the culturally disadvantaged.

That's What They Said

"There is the possibility that a suitable and planned period of learning during the first few years of life might prepare a child to read at a much earlier age than children learn to read at present. This is a possibility, not an established fact, but one which opens new horizons for the planning of early education."

> Robert M. W. Travers. *Essentials of Learning.* New York: The Macmillan Company, 1963. [233]

"We are quite right in insisting that the demands of the school should not go beyond the child's capacity to perform. We are quite wrong if we do not add that the demands of the school should not be *below* the child's capacity. Since we cannot be perfect, which way shall we err?"

> Don Robinson. "Scraps from a teacher's notebook," *Phi Delta Kappan,* 43: 344, 1962.

"It appears that an appropriate level of stimulation is necessary not only to provide opportunities for learning but also to maintain normal maturational development."

> Karl U. Smith and Margaret F. Smith. *Cybernetic Principles of Learning and Educational Design.* New York: Holt, Rinehart and Winston, Inc., 1965. [456]

"The most provocative idea that has emerged from developmental research in the last dozen or so years is that there are critical periods in development for the establishment of environmentally organized behavior patterns."

> Karl U. Smith and Margaret F. Smith. 1965. ibid. [456]

"At each stage of our lives, we impose limits on the next stage, by the choices we make and the ways in which we organize what we have experienced. There is an important something that each individual must do for himself."

> Leona Tyler. "Toward a workable psychology of individuality," *Amer. Psychol.,* 14: 75–81, 1959. [81]

"The 'curriculum revolution' has made it plain even after only a decade that the idea of 'readiness' is a mischievous half-truth. It is a half-truth because it turns out that one *teaches* readiness or provides opportunities for its nurture, one does not simply wait for it. Readiness, in these terms, consists of mastery of those simpler skills that permit one to reach higher skills."

> Jerome S. Bruner. *Toward a Theory of Instruction.* Cambridge, Mass.: Belknap Press, 1966. [29]

"At birth, the infant, virtually lacking any knowledge at all, must spend an 'apprentice' phase acquiring the most elementary foundation discriminations and generalizations on the nature of the physical and social world. These concepts are perhaps the most difficult and slowest to come by. This is because the infant possesses no general frames of reference to serve as guides and conceptual leverages for learning. Stated in another way, the neonate or child for some time is, essentially, learning the process of how to learn; he is 'learning to learn' or is acquiring directional learning sets."

> William L. Fowler. "Cognitive learning in infancy and early childhood," *Psychol. Bull.,* 59: 116–152, 1962. [144]

"We are . . . inclined to push children along through their various stages of development, often faster than it is wise for them to proceed. It is therefore not surprising that many children resist and resent such pressure and react by refusing to behave as expected. Much of the problem behavior that plagues teachers and parents is the result of their attempt to enforce standards of behavior that are unrealistic in the light of the child's level of maturity."

> Henry C. Lindgren. *Educational Psychology in the Classroom.* New York: John Wiley & Sons, Inc., 1962. [297]

References

Deutsch, Martin. "The role of social class in language development and cognition," *Amer. J. Orthopsychiatry,* 35: 78–88, 1965.

Editor. "Giant in the nursery—Jean Piaget," *New York Times Mag.,* May 26, 1968. Pp. 25–27, 50–54, 59, 62, 77–80.

Pines, Maya. *Revolution in Learning: The Years from Birth to Six.* New York: Harper & Row, Publishers, 1967.

Rosenblith, Judy F., et al. "Contributions of Piaget to developmental psychology," *Merrill-Palmer Quart.,* 9: 243–286, 1963.

CHAPTER 5

Test Items

1. Maturation is to learning as
   a. growth is to development
   b. heredity is to environment
   c. heredity is to (growth and development)
   d. heredity is to nurture
   e. nurture is to nature

2. At the extremes of the heredity–environment continuum are
   a. Coghill–Watson
   b. Gesell–Ausubel
   c. Gesell–Carmichael
   d. McDougall–Watson
   e. Watson–Lorenz

3. Probably the best statement concerning the role of heredity in human development is that
   a. it sets definite developmental predispositions but these can be changed through environmental influences
   b. it probably sets certain maxima—which are never approximated
   c. it sets definite ceilings on every step of the developmental sequence
   d. it sets the general pattern of development but not its limits
   e. it sets both the limits and the pattern of human development

4. The major complicating factor in determining the relative influence of heredity and environment on human growth and development is
   a. the interactive nature of the influence of heredity and environment
   b. regression toward the mean
   c. the relative constancy of the environment
   d. the relatively infinite number of possible combinations of hereditary patterns
   e. the unavailability of suitable psychometric instruments

5. Probably the most educationally significant aspect of human growth and development is
   a. the change over age in the organization of developmental components

    b.   the range of individual differences in the rate of growth
    c.   the interdependence of the various components
    d.   the rate of maturation
    e.   uniformity in sequence of development

6.   The genes are best conceived as
    a.   complex DNA molecules
    b.   complex RNA molecules
    c.   cytoplasm
    d.   enzymes having self-generating properties
    e.   the nucleus of the chromosomes

7.   The genes passed by parents to their offspring are _____.
    a.   altered in abnormal cases only
    b.   frequently altered with respect to selected physiological functions
    c.   manufactured by them
    d.   modified by them
    e.   simply transmitted

8.   The best statement of the contribution of education to development is that
    a.   it accelerates the rate of intellectual (cognitive) maturation
    b.   it coordinates the various aspects of the child's growth and development
    c.   it increases one's knowledge, nothing more
    d.   it sets the direction of growth
    e.   it stimulates the rate as well as determines the direction of growth

9.   Environment has its greatest influence on development in the area of
    a.   the direction of behavioral growth
    b.   emotional balance
    c.   glandular balance
    d.   mental retardation
    e.   physical abnormality

10.   The most educationally significant feature underlying human growth and development is
    a.   the developing organism's inbuilt sense of direction of growth
    b.   the individual's tendency to revert to earlier modes of behavior
    c.   the individual's natural desire to grow
    d.   the strength of certain abilities even in the relatively inferior
    e.   the sufficiency of maturation to ensure adequate development of basic abilities

11. Generally speaking, the intellectually gifted child is
     a.   equally superior in any other trait selected at random
     b.   equally superior in all other desirable traits
     c.   above average in all other desirable traits
     d.   above average in any other trait
     e.   typically inferior in most other traits

12. The current consensus on early training is that such training
     a.   can be of some help but it can also be dangerous
     b.   can be of some help but is most uneconomical in time and effort
     c.   is essential to the child's optimal development
     d.   is generally productive in the development of skills but harmful
          in the area of personal adjustment
     e.   generally leads to the development of bad habits which can be
          detrimental to later proficiency

13. The aspect of readiness currently receiving greatest emphasis is
     a.   the emotional factors
     b.   the experiential factors
     c.   the maturational factors
     d.   the physiological factors
     e.   the psychological factors

14. Which of the following is not an accepted premise of the current em-
     phasis on preschool education?
     a.   Educational limits are typically set by experiential rather than
          by maturational factors.
     b.   Enriched preschool experiences are necessary to overcome short-
          comings in early upbringing.
     c.   Excess readiness in one aspect of growth can compensate to a
          slight extent for selective unreadiness in other areas.
     d.   Readiness must always be defined in relation to method as well
          as task or content.
     e.   Various aspects of growth are so closely interrelated that "unread-
          iness" in a certain aspect simply means "unreadiness" for that
          particular activity.

15. Readiness is to developmental task as
     a.   cognitive–intellectual is to social
     b.   heredity is to environment
     c.   introducing material too soon is to introducing it too late
     d.   maturation is to teachable moment
     e.   physiological factors are to psychological factors

16. Probably the most drastic about-face occurring during the past decade in the psychological premises underlying education has been with respect to
    a. the advisability of postponing training
    b. the effectiveness of readiness training
    c. the immutability of readiness to learn
    d. readiness as a prerequisite to learning
    e. the role of motivation in learning

17. One of the foremost critics of the fixed-maturation concept is
    a. Ausubel
    b. Gates
    c. Gesell
    d. Morphett
    e. Skinner

18. The strongest argument in support of early training comes from
    a. evidence concerning functional blindness in persons who gain their sight late in life
    b. evidence of irretrievable retardation resulting from sensory deprivation
    c. Harlow's concept of learning sets
    d. Hebb's concept of cell assemblies
    e. the relative success of readiness programs in the primary grades

19. Probably the most effective method of dealing with the readiness program in school is
    a. to adapt teaching methods to tap the readiness the child has
    b. to allow the child freedom to choose the activities for which he is ready
    c. to concentrate on formal readiness exercises
    d. to delay the introduction of certain materials till readiness is achieved
    e. to provide the child with a rich background of experience

20. Research evidence suggests that drastic inadequacies in early stimulation typically
    a. has detrimental effects on the cognitive domain only
    b. has detrimental effects on all aspects, including physical development
    c. has no effect whatsoever on final status
    d. results in irretrievable losses
    e. results in relatively minor *temporary* losses

21. Probably the most pedagogically sound method of dealing with individual differences in readiness is
    a. to accelerate maturation through readiness exercises
    b. to instigate an individualized remedial program for those who lag
    c. to provide a uniform sequence of readiness experiences going back to basic fundamentals
    d. to provide a massive program of compensatory education
    e. to wait for the most teachable moment

CHAPTER 6

Physical and Motor Development

The school must necessarily be concerned with the child's physical development, not only because of the interaction and interdependency of the various aspects of development but especially because of the extent to which one's psychological functioning revolves around one's body. One's physical status exerts a strong influence both on others and, more important, on oneself; late maturation, for example, has been shown to have a number of detrimental effects on the self-concept of adolescents. In a slightly different context, Kagan reports an "unexpected" relationship between body-build and impulsivity-reflectivity, a relationship which he attempts to explain in terms of reinforcement theory. In the area of psychomotor development, Fleishman distinguishes between the aptitudes relevant to the early stages in the development of a skill and those involved in the attainment of higher levels of proficiency.

Jerome Kagan

Body-build and Conceptual Impulsivity in Children *

Since Hippocrates, man has displayed sporadic interest in the relationship between physique and certain personality traits. Although there is considerable disagreement as to the significance of such a relationship, the evidence does point to a slight association between body-build and certain personality characteristics. We did not initially intend to study body-build as part of our inquiry of conceptual reflection versus impulsivity, but we were led to it by informal observations that boys with short–wide body-builds tended to be more impulsive on tests with high response uncertainty than tall–thin boys. The present paper summarized three independent attempts to assess this relationship.

The reflection–impulsivity dimension describes the degree to which a child reflects on the differential validity of alternative solution hypotheses in situations where many response possibilities are available simultaneously. In such problem situations, the children with fast tempos impulsively report the first hypothesis that occurs to them—and are typically wrong. The reflective child, on the other hand, delays a long time before reporting a solution hypothesis and is usually correct. The most sensitive test for this variable is the Matching Familiar Figure test (MFF) is which the child is shown a picture of a familiar object and six stimuli, only one of which is identical to the standard.

Study I

A large group of third-grade children from two schools were administered the MFF and measured as to height and chest girth. Splitting the distribution of height and girth at the median for each sex and for each of the two school populations provided four distributions with each subject falling into one of four cells: tall and broad, tall and narrow, short and broad, and short and narrow. Each child was also classified as reflective or impulsive depending on his performance on the MFF. Finally, each child was shown an array of nine silhouettes representing nine basic body-builds

* Adapted and abridged from *J. Pers.*, 34: 118–128, 1966. By permission of author and publisher.

of subjects between 9 and 10 years of age and asked to select the one that was most like his own body.

Table 1 presents the distribution of the four types of body-builds vs. reflectivity–impulsivity for boys and girls separately. While there was no significant difference between reflective and impulsive children for the two most populous cells—tall–broad and short–narrow—there was a sharp difference between the reflective and impulsive boys in the two less frequently occurring body types: Nine of the 14 tall–narrow boys were reflective whereas not one of the 17 short–broad boys was reflective. Boys who were shorter than their agemates but of slightly greater chest breadth were more likely to be impulsive, while boys with a tall–narrow body-build were more likely to be reflective. The results for the girls were different: There was a slight tendency for the shorter girls to be reflective and the taller girls to be impulsive.

In general, the subjects were relatively accurate in selecting the silhouette that matched their own height and girth. In terms of the discrepancy between their actual height and girth and that of the silhouette they chose to represent them, the impulsive boys were prone to perceive themselves as shorter than reflective boys of similar stature; when only the top 10 percent of the distribution of discrepancy scores is considered, a relatively greater proportion of the reflectives selected silhouettes taller than themselves and a correspondingly greater proportion of the impulsives selected shorter silhouettes. Thus, when the analysis is limited to extreme distortions, the impulsives perceived themselves as shorter and the reflective boys as taller than their actual statures. Again, in contrast, tall reflective girls picked silhouettes shorter than themselves while the short reflective girls picked silhouettes taller than they were.

The favored interpretation of this data rests on the assumption that the 10-year-old child is aware of the desirability of specific body types appropriate to his sex. Boys should be tall, girls should be small. The boy who is shorter than his peers is apt to develop feelings of impotence and inadequacy as a result of two related sets of experiences. First, the daily comparison between his height and that of his peers will lead to a negative

TABLE 1
Distribution of Body-Builds for Third-Grade Ss

	Tall–Narrow	Short–Broad	Tall–Broad	Short–Narrow
Reflective Boys	9	0	22	22
Impulsive Boys	5	17	21	20
Reflective Girls	6	10	13	17
Impulsive Girls	6	2	18	13

self-evaluation. The short boys will not be able to reach as high or throw as far as their peers—skills which are critical for the preadolescent boy. Second, it is likely that the shorter boys will be defeated in fights with age-mates and suffer the humiliation and anxiety over potency that are the sequellae of such defeats.

In explanation of the seeming contradiction of the above interpretation presented by the fact that impulsivity is more characteristic of the shorter boy with the broad chest than the short boy with a narrow girth, it is suggested that there are two fundamental reactions to anxiety: retreat and retaliation. An impulsive orientation is basically retaliative; the impulsive child does not withdraw from the risk of failure but attempts to minimize the potential danger associated with risky responses. It is possible that the extra muscle possessed by the short–broad boy permits him to react to risk of failure with retaliative responses with some degree of success that would be denied the short boy of more fragile build. In other words, to the extent that the short–narrow boy with minimal muscle is least likely to be successful at peer-valued tasks, he is likely to resort to withdrawal behavior. The fact that the short–broad, on the other hand, is likely to experience the occasional success would encourage the development of a pattern of attempted competitive involvement in an attempt at denying or attenuating anxiety over his potency. An impulsive orientation in problems of high response uncertainty is a reasonable reaction to expect from such a boy; he is not able to tolerate the delay necessary for him to select the best possible answer. This notion that impulsivity springs in part from anxiety over adequacy is supported by the girls' data. To the extent that there is a growing awareness among the girls of this age that girls are supposed to be small, one would expect impulsive girls to be taller and larger than reflective girls. The data support this prediction.

Study II: Replication on Actual Body-Build

A second study at the fourth- and fifth-grade level once again showed short–broad boys to be impulsive and tall–thin boys to be reflective. In

TABLE 2

Distribution of Body-Builds for
Fourth- and Fifth-Grade Ss

	Tall–Narrow	Short–Broad	Tall–Broad	Short–Narrow
Reflective Boys	4	1	5	2
Impulsive Boys	2	5	3	6
Reflective Girls	2	4	5	5
Impulsive Girls	4	1	2	2

terms of height (only), 70 percent of the impulsives were short whereas only 25 percent of the reflectives were short. The data for the girls also supported the earlier findings.

Study III: Replication on First-Grade Subjects

The interpretation of the relationship between body size and impulsivity—reflectivity is predicated on the assumption that preadolescent boys have learned anxieties over potency as a result of direct encounters with peers and knowledge of the ideal male physique in our culture. It would follow that this relationship would not obtain for younger children. The third study involved 155 first-grade children. As expected there was no significant association between height or height—girth and reflectivity—impulsivity for boys. The data for girls, on the other hand, were unusual in that the reflective girls were tall and broad while the impulsives were short and narrow.

Comments

1.   Kagan presents another instance of a relationship between body-build and behavioral variables, a relationship which he attempts to explain in terms of learned anxiety. As he emphasizes, it is not possible to rule out completely the possible influence of complex physiological factors antecedent to both body-build and behavioral variables, e. g., certain biochemical factors underlying a tendency toward hyperactivity.

2.   The concept of impulsivity-reflectivity has not received the attention it deserves from the teachers (and psychologists). It is one which undoubtedly has major educational and psychological significance; it might well be a factor in academic success, for example. See Kagan (1965, 1966) for a thorough treatment of the question.

3.   To the extent that Kagan is correct in his thesis that impulsivity is a reaction to anxiety, it might be expected that other anxious subgroups, e. g., the slightly below average child, would also be impulsive.

4.   It is interesting how psychologists are attempting to provide a learning interpretation to personality characteristics (e. g., Hill's discussion of the acquisition of values and character, Ch. 17.)

References

Kagan, Jerome. "Impulsive and reflective children: The significance of conceptual tempo," in John D. Krumboltz (ed.), *Learning and the Educational Process*. Skokie, Ill.: Rand McNally & Company, 1965. Pp. 133—161.

Kagan, Jerome. "Reflection-impulsivity: The generality and dynamics of conceptual tempo," *J. abn. Psychol.*, 71: 17—22, 1966.

Edwin A. Fleishman

A Comparative Study of Aptitude Patterns in Unskilled and Skilled Psychomotor Performances *

This study postulates that "the pattern of aptitude contributing to individual differences in performance early in training may be quite different from the aptitudes contributing to final performance levels" [p. 262]. More specifically, it involves a cross-sectional and a longitudinal comparison of the various abilities featured in the early and the late stages of proficiency on a variety of complex psychomotor tasks. The methodology consisted of a systematic appraisal of proficiency associated with practice on seven different tasks.

From a research point of view, psychomotor tasks present several advantages over nonmotor tasks: Not only do they have a good deal of "face" validity, even when studied in the laboratory, but rapid improvement in performance occurs with even brief amounts of practice. Besides, the criteria of proficiency can be made unequivocal and a high degree of control over the training schedule can be exercised.

The data were obtained from 200 basic trainee airmen in extended practice on complex criterion laboratory tasks. Two independent factor analyses were carried out on the intercorrelations among scores on the eight reference tests and those obtained from separate segments of practice on the criterion tasks, the first based on scores from the early stages of practice on each of the psychomotor tests, the second based on scores from later practice trials.

The results yielded a single factor common to the stages of practice on the criterion task and not to any of the reference tests. It appears that, at advanced proficiency levels, a large portion of the variance on such tasks is specific to habits and skills acquired on the task itself and not defined by other test variables. It was also found that a combination of measures provided a better prediction of advanced proficiency than a measure taken from early practice on the criterion task itself. The results confirm and extend previous findings suggesting that increases in proficiency on

* Adapted and abridged from Edwin A. Fleishman, "A comparative study of aptitude patterns in unskilled and skilled psychomotor performances," *J. appl. Psychol.*, 41, 263–272, 1957. Copyright 1957 by American Psychological Association and reproduced by permission.

complex tasks are accompanied by substantial systematic changes in the patterns of abilities contributing to said proficiency.

Comments

1. A subsequent study (Fleishman and Fruchter, 1960) confirms the present findings: Later proficiency appears to be less a function of general ability variables and more a function of specific habits acquired in training. This basic idea seems consistent with the modern position concerning the development of "ability." It finds a counterpart in the view that the knowledge (i. e., learning sets) which the learner brings to the situation is a better determinant of success in the learning of verbal material than is any index of general learning ability such as mental age (Gagné and Paradise, 1961; Tyler, 1964). This would be most obvious in a sequential activity: it would seem logical to expect general background in college mathematics (including Calculus I) to be a more pertinent determinant of success in Calculus II than scores on a numerical aptitude test.

2. "Aptitude" would probably play a more significant part— along with experiential factors—in the development of initial proficiency as a prerequisite to advanced proficiency. The argument becomes interestingly circular if we define "aptitude" as the sum total of relevant learnings the individual has accumulated to date (see Wesman, 1968, p. 223).

References

Fleishman, Edwin A., and B. Fruchter. "Factor structure and predictability of successive states of learning Morse Code," *J. appl. Psychol.,* 44: 97–101, 1960.

Gagné, Robert M., and N. E. Paradise. "Abilities and learning sets in knowledge acquisition," *Psychol. Monogr.,* 75, No. 14, 1961.

Tyler, F. T. "Issues related to readiness to learn," in E. R. Hilgard (ed.), *Theories of Learning and Instruction.* 63rd Yearbook, National Society for the Study of Education, Part I. Chicago: University of Chicago Press, 1964. Pp. 210–239.

That's What They Said

"A suit of armor worn by one of the fabled knights of the Middle Ages just will not fit a normal 13-year-old boy of today. It is too small."

Phi Delta Kappan, 42: 39, 1960.

"The typical high school teacher has neither achieved success nor made a contribution in the field he essays to teach. Usually he has accomplished nothing in the field and has had no experience with it except to pass some college courses. The most frequent exception to this is the physical education teacher who very often has athletic performance and successful competition on his record."

Don Robinson. "Scraps from a teacher's notebook," *Phi Delta Kappan,* 42: 401, 1961.

"I doubt whether it is good for society that the ordinary man should know much of the details of how his body works. The man who has learned to think of his heart as a pump, with valves that get out of order, is on the way toward having a weak one. Better let him think of it as the seat of love and generosity, and it will beat away happily till it stops."

Stephen Leacock. *Too Much College.* New York: Dodd, Mead & Company, Inc., 1939. [43]

Reference

Shaffer, Thomas E., et al. "What contributes to physical fitness," *Childh. Educ.,* 41: 62–81, 1964.

CHAPTER 6

Test Items

1. The most educationally significant aspect of physical growth is
   a. the differences in the generalized curve of various groups, e. g., boys versus girls
   b. the relative consistency of the individual's growth pattern
   c. its susceptibility to environmental inconsistencies
   d. its unpredictability
   e. the uniqueness of the individual's growth pattern

2. The factor typically having the greatest influence on the final status of physical growth is probably
   a. childhood illnesses
   b. dietary considerations
   c. glandular balance
   d. heredity
   e. maternal care during pregnancy

3. The usual physical growth curves most adequately represent
   a. group averages
   b. the interrelationships between physical and motor adequacy
   c. the irregularities occurring in the individual's growth pattern
   d. the irregularities occasioned by errors of measurement
   e. sex differences in growth pattern

4. The preadolescent growth spurt is of special significance from the standpoint of
   a. the effect it has on the adolescent's self-concept
   b. the detrimental effects it has on physical health and stamina
   c. the large individual differences in age of occurrence
   d. its relationship to the advent of sexual maturity
   e. sex differences in age of occurrence

5. Early or late attainment of pubescence has its detrimental effects on the individual largely as a consequence of
   a. the conflicting adult demands which it tends to sponsor
   b. the effects of sexual hormones on personality
   c. the reaction of the adolescent's peers and adults
   d. rejection by parents
   e. the social disruption it tends to promote

6. The outstanding feature of physical growth during childhood is
   a. the differences in the growth pattern of boys and girls
   b. the normality of the distribution of physical growth data
   c. the pattern of alternating rapid and slow growth
   d. its relative smoothness
   e. the wide range of individual differences among children of any one age or sex

7. The individual's physical status is of special importance from the standpoint of
   a. the attainment of various developmental tasks
   b. its effect on adult demands and expectations
   c. its effect on other aspects of growth
   d. its implications for physical health
   e. its relationship to personality types

8. Late maturing boys tend to be characterized by
   a. a high degree of rebelliousness, defiance, hostility, hyperactivity, restlessness, and mischievousness
   b. inferior physical status, especially in the area of health
   c. personal and social maladjustment
   d. a strong sense of dependency beyond the appropriate period
   e. strong group loyalty and conformity to group standards

9. The leadership qualities of the mesomorph are probably best explained on the basis of
   a. glandular balance underlying a high energy level
   b. innate aggressiveness backed by strength, energy, and skill
   c. the intercorrelation among desirable traits
   d. numerous factors essentially unknown
   e. social expectations based on stereotypes

10. The school's athletic program serves its major function by
    a. building school spirit
    b. contributing to the health of the youngster who has no other opportunity for exercise
    c. introducing diversity into an otherwise monotonous curriculum
    d. providing a different kind of outlet for the satisfaction of needs
    e. providing an orientation to leisure-time activities

11. Mesomorph body-build has been shown to be associated with
    a. delinquency
    b. emotional stability

    c.   leadership
    d.   physical health
    e.   tallness

12.   Endormorph is to ectomorph as
    a.   adjusted is to maladjusted
    b.   athletically oriented is to academically oriented
    c.   autocratic is to democratic
    d.   outgoing is to reserved
    e.   tall is to fat

13.   The best predictor of final proficiency in a complicated skill is
    a.   early proficiency in that skill
    b.   interest or motivation
    c.   muscular strength and coordination
    d.   the status of relevant aptitudes
    e.   the quality of the instruction provided

14.   Motor development is of special significance from the standpoint of
    a.   its effects on other aspects of growth
    b.   its encouragement of wholesome leisure-time pursuits
    c.   its health implications
    d.   the opportunity it provides children of lower class to excel
    e.   the opportunity it provides for different outlets for the satisfaction of needs

15.   The relative inferiority of elementary school girls to boys in most areas of motor proficiency is probably best explained on the basis of
    a.   differences in social expectations based on stereotypes
    b.   their inferior strength, size, and stamina
    c.   lack of opportunity for practice
    d.   the more sheltered life they lead
    e.   restrictions in stamina due to biochemical differences

16.   All-round proficiency in sports is best explained on the basis of
    a.   chance; somebody is bound to be good in everything
    b.   the common denominator in strength, coordination, and stamina
    c.   a high level of interest and motivation
    d.   the intercorrelation among desirable traits and aptitudes
    e.   opportunity for practice under supervision

CHAPTER 7

Emotional Development

An aspect of pupil growth whose importance is too easily and too often overlooked is that of emotional development. This is unfortunate, for in its broad sense, emotional development encompasses every aspect of the development of the individual as a person—the self-concept, freedom from anxiety, openness to experience, attitudes, personal and social adjustment, etc. It also underlies the whole of the educative process. Since most of these topics are covered in other sections, the present discussion is restricted to the more narrow meaning of "emotions." The following article by Fromm on the distinction between *self*-love and *selfish* love is as crucial today as it was in 1939; far from being reprehensible, enlightened self-interest is undoubtedly one of the most positive concepts from the standpoint of both personal and social welfare and enhancement.

Erich Fromm

Selfishness and Self-Love *

Modern culture is pervaded by a taboo on selfishness. It teaches that to be selfish is sinful and that to love others is virtuous. To be sure, this doctrine is not only in flagrant contradiction to the practices of modern society but it also is in opposition to another set of doctrines which assumes that the most powerful and legitimate drive in man is selfishness and that each individual by following this imperative drive also does the most for the common good. The existence of this latter type of ideology does not affect the weight of the doctrines which declare that selfishness is the arch evil and love for others the main virtue. Selfishness, as it is commonly used in these ideologies, is more or less synonymous with self-love. The alternatives are either to love others which is a virtue or to love oneself which is a sin.

This principle has found its classic expression in Calvin's theology. Man is essentially bad and powerless. He can do nothing—absolutely nothing—good on the basis of his own strength or merits. "We are not our own," says Calvin,[1] "therefore neither our reason nor our will should predominate in our deliberations and actions. We are not our own; therefore, let us not propose it as our end, to seek what may be expedient for us according to the flesh. We are not our own; therefore, let us, as far as possible, forget ourselves and all things that are ours. On the contrary, we are God's; to him, therefore, let us live and die. For, as it is the most devastating pestilence which ruins people if they obey themselves, it is the only haven of salvation not to know or to want anything by oneself but to be guided by God who walks before us." [2] Man should not only have the con-

* From *Psychiatry*, 2: 507–523, 1939. By permission of author and publisher.

[1] Calvin, Johannes. *Institutes of the Christian Religion* [translated by John Allen]. Philadelphia: Presbyterian Board of Christian Education, 1928 (1:688 pp.). —in particular Book III, Chapter 7, ¶ 1, p. 619.

[2] From "For as it is. . . ." the translation is mine from the Latin original (Johannes Calvini, *Institutio Christianae Religionis*. Editionem curavit A. Tholuk. Berolini 1835, par. I, p. 445). The reason for this shift is that Allen's translation slightly changes the original in the direction of softening the rigidity of Calvin's thought. Allen translates this sentence: "For as compliance with their own inclinations leads men most effectually to ruin, so to place no dependency on our own knowledge or will, but merely to follow the guidance of the Lord, is the only way of safety." However, the Latin *sibi ipsis obtemperant* is not equivalent to "follow one's own inclina-

viction of his absolute nothingness. He should do everything to humiliate himself. "For I do not call it humility," says Calvin, "if you suppose that we have anything left. . . . we cannot think of ourselves as we ought to think without utterly despising everything that may be supposed an excellence in us. This humility is unfeigned submission of a mind overwhelmed with a weighty sense of its own misery and poverty; for such is the uniform description of it in the word of God." [3]

This emphasis on the nothingness and wickedness of the individual implies that there is nothing he should like about himself. This doctrine is rooted in contempt and hatred for oneself. Calvin makes this point very clear; he speaks of "Self-love" as of a "pest." [4]

If the individual finds something in himself "on the strength of which he finds pleasure in himself," he betrays this sinful self-love. This fondness for himself will make him sit in judgment over others and despise them. Therefore, to be fond of oneself, to like anything about oneself is one of the greatest imaginable sins. It excludes love for others [5] and is identical with selfishness. [6]

There are fundamental differences between Calvin's theology and Kant's philosophy, yet, the basic attitude toward the problem of love for oneself has remained the same. According to Kant, it is a virtue to want the happiness of others, while to want one's own happiness is ethically "indifferent," since it is something which the nature of man is striving for and a natural striving cannot have positive ethical sense. [7] Kant admits that one

tions" but "to obey oneself." To forbid following one's inclinations has the mild quality of Kantian ethics that man should suppress his natural inclinations and by doing so follow the orders of his conscience. On the other hand, forbidding to obey oneself is a denial of the autonomy of man. The same subtle change of meaning is reached by translating *ita unicus est salutis portis nihil nec sapere, nec velle per se ipsum*, "to place no dependence on our knowledge nor will." While the formulation of the original straightforwardly contradicts the motto of enlightenment philosophy: *sapere aude*—dare to know, Allen's translation warns only of a dependence on one's own knowledge, a warning which is by far less contradictory to modern thought. I mention these deviations of the translation from the original which I came across accidentally, because they offer a good illustration of the fact that the spirit of an author is "modernized" and colored—certainly without any intention of doing so—just by translating him.

[3] Reference footnote 1; chapter 12, ¶6, p. 681.

[4] Compare reference footnote 1; chapter 7, ¶4, p. 622.

[5] It should be noted, however, that even love for one's neighbor, while it is one of the fundamental doctrines of the New Testament, has not been given a corresponding weight by Calvin. In blatant contradiction to the New Testament Calvin says: "For what the schoolmen advance concerning the priority of charity to faith and hope, is a mere reverie of a distempered imagination. . . ." Compare reference footnote 1; chapter 24, ¶1, p. 531.

[6] Despite Luther's emphasis on the spiritual freedom of the individual, his theology, different as it is in many ways from Calvin's, is pervaded by the same conviction of man's basic powerlessness and nothingness.

[7] Compare Kant, Immanuel. *Kant's Critique of Practical Reason and Other Works on the Theory of Ethics* [translated by Thomas Kingsmill Abbot]. London,

must not give up one's claims for happiness; under certain circumstances it can even be a duty to be concerned with one's happiness; partly because health, wealth, and the like, can be means which are necessary to fulfill one's duty, partly because the lack of happiness—poverty—can seduce a person from fulfilling his duty.[8] But love for oneself, striving for one's own happiness, can never be a virtue. As an ethical principle, the striving for one's own happiness "is the most objectionable one, not merely because it is false, ... but because the springs it provides for morality are such as rather undermine it and destroy its sublimity. . . . " [9] Kant differentiates in egotism, self-love, *philautia*—a benevolence for oneself; and arrogance —the pleasure in oneself. "Rational self-love" must be restricted by ethical principles, the pleasure in oneself must be battered down and the individual must come to feel humiliated in comparing himself with the sanctity of moral laws.[10] The individual should find supreme happiness in the fulfillment of his duty. The realization of the moral principle—and, therefore, of the individual's happiness—is only possible in the general whole, the nation, the state. Yet, "the welfare of the state—*salus rei publicae suprema lex est*—is not identical with the welfare of the citizens and their happiness." [11]

In spite of the fact that Kant shows a greater respect for the integrity of the individual than did Calvin or Luther, he states that even under the most tyrannical government the individual has no right to rebel and must be punished no less than with death if he threatens the sovereign.[12] Kant emphasizes the native propensity for evil in the nature of man,[13] for the suppression of which the moral law, the categorical imperative, is necessary unless man should become a beast and human society should end in wild anarchy.

In discussing Calvin's and Kant's systems, their emphasis on the nothingness of man has been stressed. Yet, as already suggested, they also emphasize the autonomy and dignity of the individual, and this contradiction runs through their writings. In the philosophy of the enlightenment

---

New York: Longmans Green & Co., 1909 (xiv and 369 pp.)—in particular Part I, Book I, Chapter I, ¶VIII, Remark II, p. 126.

[8] Compare reference footnote 7—in particular Part I, Book I, Chapter III, p. 186.

[9] Reference footnote 7—in particular *Fundamental Principles of the Metaphysics of Morals;* second section, p. 61.

[10] Compare reference footnote 7—in particular Part I, Book I, Chapter III, p. 165.

[11] Kant, Immanuel. *Immanuel Kants Werke.* Berlin: Cassierer, (8:xxix and 468 pp.)—in particular Der Rechtslehre Zweiter Teil I. Abschnitt, '49 p. 124. I translate from the German text, since this part is omitted in the English translation of the *Metaphysics of Ethics* by I. W. Semple [Edinburgh, 1871].

[12] Compare reference footnote 11—in particular p. 126.

[13] Compare Kant, Immanuel. *Religion Within the Limits of Reason Alone* [translated by Th. M. Greene and H. H. Hudson]. Chicago: Open Court, 1934 (xxxv and 200 pp.)—in particular Book I.

period the individual's claims and happiness have been emphasized much more strongly by others than by Kant, for instance by Helvetius. This trend in modern philosophy has found an extreme expression by Stirner and Nietzsche. In the way that they often phrase the problem—though not necessarily in their real meaning—they share one basic premise of Calvin and Kant: that love for others and love for oneself are alternatives. But in contradiction to those authors, they denounce love for others as weakness and self-sacrifice and postulate egotism, selfishness, and self-love—they too confuse the issue by not clearly differentiating between these phenomena—as virtue. Thus Stirner says: "Here, egoism, selfishness must decide, not the principle of love, not love motives like mercy, gentleness, good-nature, or even justice and equity—for *iustitia* too is a phenomenon of love, a product of love: love knows only sacrifice and demands self-sacrifice." [14]

The kind of love denounced by Stirner is the masochistic dependence which makes the individual a means for achieving the purposes of somebody or something outside himself. With this conception of love could he scarcely avoid a formulation which postulated ruthless egotism as a goal. The formulation is, therefore, highly polemical and overstates the point. The positive principle with which Stirner was concerned [15] was directed against an attitude which had run through Christian theology for many centuries—and which was vivid in the German idealism which was passing in his time; namely, to bend the individual to submit to and find his center in a power and a principle outside of himself. To be sure, Stirner was not a philosopher of the stature of Kant or Hegel, yet he had the courage to make a radical rebellion against that side of idealistic philosophy which negated the concrete individual and thus helped the absolute state to retain its oppressive power over the individual. Although there is no comparison between the depth and scope of the two philosophers, Nietzsche's attitude in many respects is similar to that of Stirner. Nietzsche also denounces love and altruism as the expressions of weakness and self-negation. For Nietzsche, the quest for love is typical of slaves who cannot fight for what they want and, therefore, try to get it through "love." Altruism

[14] Stirner, Max. *The Ego and His Own* [translated by Steven T. Byington]. London: A. C. Fifield, 1912 (xx and 506 pp.)—in particular p. 339.

[15] One of his positive formulations, for example, is: "But how does one use life? In using it up like the candle one burns. . . . Enjoyment of life is using life up." —Reference footnote 14; p. 426. Engels has clearly seen the onesidedness of Stirner's formulations and has attempted to overcome the false alternative between love for oneself and love for others. In a letter to Marx in which he discusses Stirner's book, Engels writes: "If, however, the concrete and real individual is the true basis for our 'human' man, it is self-evident that egotism—of course not only Stirner's egotism of reason, but also the egotism of the heart—is the basis for our love of man." [*Marx-Engels Gesamtausgabe;* Berlin, Marx-Engels Verlag, 1929 (1:1 and 540 pp.)—in particular, p. 6.]

and love for mankind is thus a sign of degeneration.[16] For him, it is the essence of a good and healthy aristocracy that is ready to sacrifice countless people for its interests without having a guilty conscience. Society should be a "foundation and scaffolding by means of which a select class of beings may be able to elevate themselves to their higher duties, and in general to their higher existence." [17] Many quotations could be added to document this spirit of sadism, contempt and brutal egotism. This side of Nietzsche has often been understood as *the* philosophy of Nietzsche. Is this true; is this the "real" Nietzsche?

To answer this question would require a detailed analysis of his work which cannot be attempted here. There are various reasons which made Nietzsche express himself in the sense mentioned above. First of all, as in the case of Stirner, his philosophy is a reaction—a rebellion—against the philosophical tradition of subordinating the empirical individual to a power and a principle outside of himself. His tendency to overstatements shows this reactive quality. Second, there were traits in Nietzsche's personality, a tremendous insecurity and anxiety, which explain that, and why he had sadistic impulses which led him to those formulations. Yet, these trends in Nietzsche do not seem to me to be the "essence" of his personality nor the corresponding views the essence of his philosophy. Finally, Nietzsche shared some of the naturalistic ideas of his time as they were expressed in the materialistic-biologistic philosophy, for which the concepts of the physiological roots of psychic phenomena and the "survival of the fittest" were characteristic. This interpretation does not do away with the fact that Nietzsche shared the view that there is a contradiction between love for others and love for oneself. Yet, it is important to notice that Nietzsche's views contain the nucleus from development of which this wrong dichotomy can be overcome. The "love" which he attacks is one which is rooted not in one's own strength, but in one's own weakness. "Your neighbor love is your bad love for yourselves. You flee into your neighbor from yourselves and would fain make a virtue thereof. But I fathom your 'unselfishness.' " He states explicitly, "You cannot stand yourselves and you do not love yourselves sufficiently." [18] The individual has for Nietzsche "an enormously great significance." [19] The "strong" individual is the one who has "true kindness, nobility, greatness of soul, which does not give in order to take, which does not want to excell by being

---

[16] Nietzsche, Friedrich. *The Will to Power* [translated by Anthony M. Ludovici]. Edinburgh and London: T. N. Foulis, 1910 (1:xiv and 384 pp.) and (2:xix and 432 pp.)—in particular stanza 246, 362, 369, 373 and 728.

[17] Nietzsche, Friedrich. *Beyond Good and Evil* [translated by Helen Zimmer]. New York: The Macmillan Company, 1907 (xv and 268 pp.)—in particular stanza 258, p. 225.

[18] Nietzsche, Friedrich. *Thus Spake Zarathustra* [translated by Thomas Common]. New York: Modern Library, Inc. (325 pp.)—in particular p. 75.

[19] Reference footnote 16; stanza 785.

kind;—'waste' as type of true kindness, wealth of the person as a premise." [20]

He expresses the same thought also in *Thus Spake Zarathustra:* "The one goeth to his neighbor because he seeketh himself, the other one because would he fain lose himself." [21]

The essence of these views is: love is a phenomenon of abundance, its premise is the strength of the individual who can give. Love is affirmation, "it seeketh to create what is loved!" [22] To love another person is only a virtue if it springs from this inner strength, but it is detestable if it is the expression of the basic inability to be oneself.[23]

However, the fact remains that Nietzsche left the problem of the relationship between self-love and love for others as unsolved antinomy, even if by interpreting him one may surmise in what direction his solution would have been found.[24]

The doctrine that selfishness is the arch-evil that one has to avoid and that to love oneself excludes loving others is by no means restricted to theology and philosophy. It is one of the stock patterns used currently in home, school, church, movies, literature, and all the other instruments of social suggestion. "Don't be selfish" is a sentence which has been impressed upon millions of children, generation after generation. It is hard to define what exactly it means. Consciously, most parents connect with it the meaning not to be egotistical, inconsiderate, without concern for others. Factually, they generally mean more than that. "Not to be selfish" implies not to do what one wishes, to give up one's own wishes for the sake of those in authority; *i.e.,* the parents, and later the authorities of society. "Don't be selfish," in the last analysis, has the same ambiguity that we have seen in Calvinism. Aside from its obvious implication, it means, "don't love yourself," "don't be yourself," but submit your life to something more important than yourself, be it an outside power or the internalization of that power as "duty." "Don't be selfish" becomes one of the most powerful ideological weapons in suppressing spontaneity and the free development of personality. Under the pressure of this slogan one is asked for every sacrifice and for complete submission: Only those aims are "un-

---

[20] Reference footnote 16; stanza 935.

[21] Reference footnote 18; p. 76.

[22] Reference footnote 18; p. 102.

[23] See reference footnote 16; stanza 820, and Nietzsche, Friedrich. *The Twilight of Idols* [translated by A. M. Ludovici]. Edinburgh: T. N. Foulis, 1911 (xviii and 281 pp.): stanza 35. Nietzsche, Friedrich. *Ecce Homo* [translated by A. M. Ludovici]. New York: The Macmillan Company, 1911 (xiv and 207 pp.); stanza 2. Nietzsche, Friedrich. *Nachlass.* Nietzsches Werke; Leipzig: A. Kroener (14: x and 442 pp.); pp. 63–64.

[24] Compare the important paper by Horkheimer, Max, Egoismus und Freiheitzbewegung. *Zeitschr. f. Socialforsh,* 5:167, 1936, which deals with the problem of egotism in modern history.

selfish" which do not serve the individual for his own sake but for the sake of somebody or something outside of him.

This picture, we must repeat, is in a certain sense one-sided. Beside the doctrine that one should not be selfish, the opposite doctrine is propagandized in modern society: have your own advantage in mind, act according to what is best for you—and by doing so, you will also bring about the greatest advantage for all others. As a matter of fact, the idea that the pursuit of individual egotism is the basis for the development of general welfare is the principle on which competitive capitalism has been built. It may seem strange that two such seemingly contradictory principles could be taught side by side in one culture. Of the fact, there can be no doubt. One result of this contradiction of ideological patterns certainly is confusion in the individual. To be torn between the one and the other doctrine is a serious blockage in the process of integration of personality and has often led to neurotic character formation.[25]

One must observe that this contradictory pair of doctrines has had an important social function. The doctrine that everybody should pursue his individual advantage obviously was a necessary stimulus for private initiative on which the modern economic structure is built. The social function of the doctrine "don't be selfish" was an ambiguous one. For the broad masses of those who had to live on the level of mere subsistence, it was an important aid to resignation to having wishes which were unattainable under the given socio-economic system. It was important that this resignation should be one which was not thought of as being brought about by external pressure, since the inevitable result of such a feeling has to be a more or less conscious grudge and a defiance against society. By making this resignation a moral virtue, such a reaction could to a considerable extent be avoided. While this aspect of the social function of the taboo on selfishness is obvious, another, its effect upon the privileged minority, is somewhat more complicated. It only becomes clear if we consider further the meaning of "selfishness." If it means to be concerned with one's economic advantage, certainly the taboo on selfishness would have been a severe handicap to the economic initiative of business men. But what it really meant, especially in the earlier phases of English and American culture, was, as has been pointed out before: Don't do what you want, don't enjoy yourself, don't spend money or energy for pleasure, but feel it as your duty to work, to be successful, to be prosperous.

It is the great merit of Max Weber [26] to have shown that this princi-

[25] This point has been emphasized by Horney, Karen. *The Neurotic Personality of Our Time*. New York: W. W. Norton & Company, Inc., 1937 (xii and 290 pp.), and by Lynd, Robert S. *Knowledge for What*. Princeton: Princeton University Press, 1939 (x and 268 pp.).

[26] Weber, Max. *The Protestant Ethic and the Spirit of Capitalism* [translated by Talcott Parsons]. London: Edward G. Allen & Son, Ltd., 1930 (xi and 292 pp.).

ple of what he calls *innerweltliche Askese* [inner worldly asceticism] was
an important condition for creating an attitude in which all energy could
be directed toward work and the fulfillment of duty. The tremendous economic achievements of modern society would not have been possible if
this kind of asceticism had not absorbed all energy to the purpose of thrift
and relentless work. It would transcend the scope of this paper to enter
into an analysis of the character structure of modern man as he emerged in
the 16th century. Suffice it to say here, that the economic and social
changes in the 15th and 16th centuries destroyed the feeling of security
and "belonging" which was typical of the members of medieval society.[27]
The socio-economic position of the urban middle class, the peasantry and
the nobility were shaken in their foundations; [28] impoverishment, threats
to traditional economic positions as well as new chances for economic success arose. Religious and spiritual ties which had established a rounded
and secure world for the individual had been broken. The individual found
himself completely alone in the world, paradise was lost for good, his success and failure were decided by the laws of the market; the basic relationship to everyone else had become one of merciless competition. The result
of all this was a new feeling of freedom attended, however, by an increased anxiety. This anxiety, in its turn, created a readiness for new submission to religious and secular authorities even more strict than the previous ones had been. The new individualism on the one hand, anxiety and
submission to authority on the other, found their ideological expression in
Protestantism and Calvinism. At the same time, these religious doctrines
did much to stimulate and increase these new attitudes. But even more important than the submission to external authorities was the fact that the authorities were internalized, that man became the slave of a master inside
himself instead of one outside. This internal master drove the individual to
relentless work and striving for success and never allowed him to be himself and enjoy himself. There was a spirit of distrust and hostility directed
not only against the outside world, but also toward one's own self.

This modern type of man was selfish in a twofold sense: He had little
concern for others and he was anxiously concerned with his own advantage. But was this selfishness really a concern for himself as an individual,
with all his intellectual and sensual potentialities? Had "he" not become
the appendix of his socio-economic rôle, a cog in the economic machine,
even if sometimes an important cog? Was he not the slave of this machine

---

[27] Harry Stack Sullivan has given particular emphasis to the need for security
as one of the basic motivating forces in man, while orthodox psychoanalytical literature has not paid sufficient attention to this factor.

[28] Compare Pascal, R. *The Social Basis of the German Reformation.* London:
C. A. Watts & Co., Ltd., 1933 (viii and 243 pp.). Kraus, Johann Babtist. *Scholastik,
Puritanismus und Kapitalismus.* Munchen: Dunker, 1930 (329 pp.). Tawney, R. H.
Religion and the Rise of Capitalism. London: John Murray, 1926 (xiii and 339 pp.).

even if he subjectively felt as if he were following his own orders? Was his selfishness identical with self-love or was it instead rooted in the very lack of it?

We must postpone answering these questions, since we have still to finish a brief survey of the doctrine of selfishness in modern society. The taboo on selfishness has been reinforced in the authoritarian systems. One of the ideological cornerstones of National-Socialism is the principle: "Public good takes precedence over private good." [29] According to the original propaganda technique of National-Socialism, the thought was phrased in a form purposed to permit the workers to believe in the "socialist" part of the Nazi program. However, if we consider its meaning in the context of the whole Nazi philosophy, the implication is this: the individual should not want anything for himself; he should find his satisfaction in the elimination of his individuality and in participating as a small particle in the greater whole of the race, the state or its symbol, the leader. While Protestantism and Calvinism emphasized individual liberty and responsibility even as it emphasized the nothingness of the individual, Nazism is focused essentially on the latter. Only the "born" leaders are an exception, and even they should feel themselves as instruments of someone higher up in the hierarchy—the supreme leader as an instrument of destiny.

The doctrine that love for oneself is identical with "selfishness," and that it is an alternative to love for others has pervaded theology, philosophy and the pattern of daily life; it would be surprising if one would not find the same doctrine also in scientific psychology, but here as an allegedly objective statement of facts. A case in point is Freud's theory on narcissism. He says, in short, that man has a certain quantity of libido. Originally, in the infant, all this libido has as its objective the child's own person, *primary narcissism*. Later on, the libido is directed from one's own person toward other objects. If a person is blocked in his "object-relationships," the libido is withdrawn from the objects and returned to one's own person, *secondary narcissism*. According to Freud, there is an almost mechanical alternative between ego-love and object-love. The more love I turn toward the outside world the less love I have for myself, and vice versa. Freud is thus moved to describe the phenomenon of falling in love as an impoverishment of one's self-love because all love is turned to an object outside of oneself. Freud's theory of narcissism expresses basically the same idea which runs through protestant religion, idealistic philosophy, and the everyday patterns of modern culture. This by itself does not indicate that he is right or wrong. Yet, this translation of the general principle into the categories of empirical psychology gives us a good basis for examining the principle.

[29] "Gemeinnutz geht vor Eigennutz."

These questions arise: Does psychological observation support the thesis that there is a basic contradiction and the state of alternation between love for oneself and love for others? Is love for oneself the same phenomenon as selfishness, is there a difference or are they in fact opposites?

Before we turn to the discussion of the empirical side of the problem, it may be noted that from a philosophical viewpoint, the notion that love for others and love for oneself are contradictory is untenable. If it is a virtue to love my neighbor as a human being, why must not I love myself too? A principle which proclaims love for man but which taboos love for myself, exempts me from all other human beings. The deepest experience of human existence, however, is to have this experience with regard to oneself. There is no solidarity of man in which I myself am not included. A doctrine which proclaims such an exclusion proves its objective insincerity by this very fact.[30]

We have come here to the psychological premises on which the conclusions of this paper are built. Generally, these premises are: Not only others, but also we ourselves are the "object" of our feelings and attitudes; the attitude toward others and toward ourselves, far from being contradictory, runs basically parallel.[31] With regard to the problem under discussion this means: Love for others and love for ourselves are not alternatives. Neither are hate for others and hate for ourselves alternatives. On the contrary, an attitude of love for themselves will be found in those who are at least capable of loving others. Hatred against oneself is inseparable from hatred against others, even if on the surface the opposite seems to be the case. In other words, love and hatred, in principle, are indivisible as far as the difference between "objects" and one's own self is concerned.

To clarify this thesis, it is necessary to discuss the problem of hatred and love. With regard to hatred one can differentiate between "reactive hatred" and "character-conditioned hatred." By reactive hatred I mean a hatred which is essentially a reaction to an attack on one's life, security, or ideals or on some other person that one loves and identifies oneself with. Its premise is one's positive attitude toward one's life, toward other persons and toward ideals. If there is a strong affirmation of life, a strong hatred necessarily is aroused if life is attacked. If there is love, hatred must be aroused if the loved one is attacked. There is no passionate striv-

[30] This thought is expressed in the biblical: "Love thy neighbor as thyself!" The implication is that respect of one's own integrity and uniqueness, love for and understanding of one's own self, cannot be separated from respect, love and understanding with regard to another individual. The discovery of my own self is inseparably connected with the discovery of any other self.

[31] This viewpoint has been emphasized by Horney, Karen, *New Ways in Psychoanalysis*. New York: W. W. Norton & Co., Inc., 1939 (313 pp.); in particular Chapters 5 and 7.

ing for anything which does not necessitate hatred if the object of this striving is attacked. Such hatred is the counterpoint of life. It is aroused by a specific situation, its aim is the destruction of the attacker and, in principle, it ends when the attacker is defeated.[32]

Character-conditioned hatred is different. To be sure, the hatred rooted in the character structure once arose as reaction to certain experiences undergone by the individual in his childhood. It then became a character trait of the person; he *is* hostile. His basic hostility is observable even when it is not giving rise to manifest hatred. There is something in the facial expression, gestures, tone of voice, kind of jokes, little unintentional reactions which impress the observer as indications of the fundamental hostility, which also could be described as a continuous *readiness* to hate. It is the basis from which active hatred springs if and when it is aroused by a specific stimulus. This hate reaction can be perfectly rational; as much so, as a matter of fact, as is the case in the situations which were described as arousing reactive hatred. There is, however, a fundamental difference. In the case of reactive hatred it is the situation which *creates* the hatred. In the case of character-conditioned hatred an "idling" hostility is *actualized* by the situation. In the case where the basic hatred is aroused, the person involved appears to have something like a feeling of relief, as though he were happy to have found the rational opportunity to express his lingering hostility. He shows a particular kind of satisfaction and pleasure in his hatred which is missing in the case of an essentially reactive hatred.

In the case of a proportionality between hate reaction and external situation, we speak of a "normal" reaction, even if it is the actualization of character-conditioned hatred. From this normal reaction to an "irrational" reaction found in the neurotic or psychotic person, there are innumerable transitions and no sharp demarcation line can be drawn. In the irrational hate-reaction, the emotion seems disproportionate to the actual situation. Let me illustrate by referring to a reaction which psychoanalysts have ample opportunity to observe; an analysand has to wait ten minutes because the analyst is delayed. The analysand enters the room, wild with rage at the offense done to him by the analyst. Extreme cases can be observed more clearly in psychotic persons; in those the disproportionality is still more striking. Psychotic hatred will be aroused by something which from the standpoint of reality is not at all offensive. Yet, from the standpoint of his own feeling it is offensive, and thus the irrational reaction is irrational only from the standpoint of external objective reality, not from the subjective premises of the person involved.

The lingering hostility can also be purposely aroused and turned into

---

[32] Nietzsche has emphasized the creative function of destruction. Reference footnote 23; *Ecce Homo*, Stanza 2.

manifest hatred by social suggestion; that is, propaganda. If such propaganda which wants to instill people with hatred toward certain objects is to
be effectual, it must build upon the character-conditioned hostility in the
personality structure of the members of the groups to which it appeals. A
case in point is the appeal of Nazism to the group which formed its nucleus, the lower middle class. Latent hostility was peculiarly the lot of the
members of this group long before it was actualized by Nazi propaganda
and that is why they were such fertile soil for this propaganda.

Psychoanalysis offers ample opportunity to observe the conditions responsible for the existence of hatred in the character structure.

The decisive factors for arousing character-conditioned hatred may be
stated to be all the different ways by which spontaneity, freedom, emotional and physical expansiveness, the development of the "self" of the
child are blocked or destroyed.[33] The means of doing this are manifold;
they vary from open, intimidating hostility and terror, to a subtle and
"sweet" kind of "anonymous authority," which does not overtly forbid anything but says: "I know you will or will not like this or that." Simple frustration of instinctual impulses does not create deep seated hostility; it only
creates a reactive hate reaction. Yet, this was Freud's assumption and his
concept of the Œdipus Complex is based on it; it implies that the frustration of sexual wishes directed toward the father or the mother creates hatred
which in its turn leads to anxiety and submission. To be sure, frustration
often appears as a symptom of something which does create hostility: not
taking the child seriously, blocking his expansiveness, not allowing him to
be free. But the real issue is not isolated frustration but the fight of the
child against those forces which tend to suppress his freedom and spontaneity. There are many forms in which the fight for freedom is fought and

---

[33] In recent years, a number of psychologists were interested in the problem of
uncovering the hostility, consciously or unconsciously, present in children. Some of
them were very successful in demonstrating the presence of strong hostility in very
young children. A method which proved to be particularly fruitful was to arrange
play situations in which the children expressed their hostility very clearly. According
to Bender, Lauretta, and Schilder, Paul, "Aggressiveness in children," *Genetic Psychology Monographs,* 18:410–425, 1936, the younger the children were the more directly they expressed hostility, while with the older ones the hate-reaction was already repressed but could be clearly observed in a play situation. Compare also
Levy, David M. *Studies in Sibling Rivalry* V. New York: American Orthopsychiatric
Association, 1937 (96 pp.). L. Murphey and G. Lerner have found normal children
who seem quite conventionally adjusted to the nursery-school play group, revealing
intense aggression in a free play situation, alone with one adult. J. Louise Despert
has come to similar conclusions: See her "A method for the study of personality
reactions in preschool age children by means of analysis of their play," *J. Psychol.,* 9:17–29, 1940. Hartoch, A., and Schachtel, E., have found expression of strong
aggressiveness in Rorschach tests in two to four year old children who did not show
proportionate amount of manifest aggressiveness in their behavior.

many ways in which the defeat is disguised. The child may be ready to internalize the external authority and be "good," it may overtly rebel and yet remain dependent. It may feel that it "belongs" by completely conforming to the given cultural patterns at the expense of the loss of its individual self—the result is always a lesser or greater degree of inner emptiness, the feeling of nothingness, anxiety and resulting from all that a chronic hatred, and *ressentiment,* which Nietzsche characterized very well as *Lebensneid,* envy of life.

There is a slight difference, however, between hatred and this envy of life. The aim of hatred is in the last analysis the destruction of the object outside of my self. By destroying it I attain strength in relative, although not in absolute terms. In envy of life, the begrudging attitude aims at the destruction of others too; not, however, in order to gain relative strength, but to have the satisfaction that others are being denied the enjoyment of things which—for external or inner reasons—I cannot enjoy myself. It aims at removing the pain, rooted in my own inability for happiness, by having nobody else who by his very existence demonstrates what I am lacking.[34]

In principle, the same factors condition the development of chronic hatred in a group. The difference here as in general between individual psychology and social psychology is only to be found in this: While in individual psychology, we are looking for the individual and accidental conditions which are responsible for those character traits by which one individual varies from other members of his group, in social psychology we are interested in the character structure as far as it is common to and, therefore, typical of the majority of the members of that group. As to the conditions, we are not looking for accidental individual conditions like an overstrict father or the sudden death of a beloved sister, but for those conditions of life which are a common experience for the group as such. This does not mean the one or the other isolated trait in the whole mode of life, but the total structure of basic life experiences as they are essentially conditioned by the socio-economic situation of a particular group.[35]

The child is imbued with the "spirit" of a society long before it makes the direct acquaintance with it in school. The parents represent in

[34] It should be noted that sadism has to be differentiated from hatred. As I see it, the aim of sadism is not destruction of the subject, but a seeking to have absolute power over it, to make it an instrument of oneself. Sadism can be blended with hatred; in this case it will have the cruelty usually implied in the notion of sadism. It can also be blended with sympathy in which case the impulse is to have the object as an instrument and, at the same time, to further him in any way excepting in one: letting him be free.

[35] See, on the method of analytic social psychology: Fromm, Erich, "Zur Aufgabe und Methode einer analytischen Sozialpsychologie," *Zeitschr. f. Sozialforschung* [Leipzig], 1:28–54, 1932.

their own character structure the spirit prevalent in their society and class and transmit this atmosphere to the child from the day of his birth onward. The family thus is the "psychic agency" of society.

The bearing on our problem of the differentiation in hatred will have become clear by now. While in the case of reactive hatred the stimulus which is at the same time the object, constitutes the "cause" for the hatred; in the case of character-conditioned hatred, the basic attitude, the readiness for hatred, exists regardless of an object and before a stimulus makes the chronic hostility turn into manifest hatred. As has been indicated, originally, in childhood, this basic hatred was brought into existence by certain people, but later it has become part of the personality structure and objects play but a secondary rôle. Therefore, in its case, there is, in principle, no difference between objects outside of myself and my own self. The idling hostility is always there; its outside objects change according to circumstances and it but depends on certain factors whether I myself become one of the objects of my hostility. If one wants to understand why a certain person is hated in one case, why I myself am hated in another case, one has to know the specific factors in the situation which make others or myself the object of manifest hatred. What interests us in this context, however, is the general principle that character-conditioned hatred is something radiating from an individual and like a searchlight focussing sometimes on this and sometimes on that object, among them myself.

The strength of basic hatred is one of the major problems of our culture. In the beginning of this paper, it has been shown how Calvinism and Protestantism pictured man as essentially evil and contemptible. Luther's hatred against the revolting peasants is of extraordinary intensity.

Max Weber has emphasized the distrust for and hostility toward others which runs through the Puritan literature replete with warnings against having any confidence in the help and friendliness of our fellow men. Deep distrust even toward one's closest friend is recommended by Baxter. Th. Adams says: "He—the 'knowing' man—is blind in no man's cause but best sighted in his own. He confines himself to the circle of his own affairs and thrusts not his fingers in needless fires. . . . He sees the falseness of it [the world] and, therefore, learns to trust himself ever, others so far as not to be damaged by their disappointments." [36]

Hobbes assumed that man's nature was that of a predatory animal, filled with hostility, set to kill and rob. Only by the consensus of all, submitting to the authority of the state, could peace and order be created. Kant's opinion of man's nature is not too distant from Hobbes'; he too thought that man's nature had a fundamental propensity for evil. Among psychologists, chronic hatred as an inherent part of human nature has been a frequent assumption. William James considered it as being so strong that

[36] *Work of the Puritan Divines* [quoted by Weber]. Reference footnote 26—in particular begin p. 222.

he took for granted that we all feel a natural repulsion against physical contact with other persons.[37] Freud, in his theory of the death instinct, assumed that for biological reasons, we all are driven by an irresistible force to destroy either others or ourselves.

Although some of the philosophers of the enlightenment period believed that the nature of man was good and that his hostility was the product of the circumstances under which he lives, the assumption of hostility as an inherent part of man's nature runs through the ideas of representative thinkers of the modern era from Luther up to our days. We need not discuss whether this assumption is tenable. At any rate, the philosophers and psychologists who held this belief were good observers of man within their own culture, even though they made the mistake of believing that modern man in his essence is not a historical product but is as nature made him to be.

While important thinkers clearly saw the strength of hostility in modern man, popular ideologies and the convictions of the average man tend to ignore the phenomenon. Only a relatively small number of people have an awareness of their fundamental dislike for others. Many have only a feeling of just having little interest or feeling for others. The majority are completely unaware of the intensity of the chronic hatred in themselves as well as in others. They have adopted the feelings that they know they are supposed to have: to like people, to find them nice, unless or until they have actually committed an act of aggression. The very indiscriminateness of this "liking people" shows its thinness or rather its compensatory quality a basic lack of fondness.

While the frequency of underlying distrust and dislike for others is known to many observers of our social scene, the dislike for oneself is a less clearly recognized phenomenon. Yet, this self-hatred may be considered rare only so long as we think of cases in which people quite overtly hate or dislike themselves. Mostly, this self-dislike is concealed in various ways. One of the most frequent indirect expressions of self-dislike are the inferiority feelings so widespread in our culture. Consciously, these persons do not feel that they dislike themselves: What they do feel is only that they are inferior to others, that they are stupid, unattractive or whatever the particular content of the inferiority feelings is.[38]

To be sure, the dynamics of inferiority feelings are complex and there are factors other than the one with which we are dealing. Yet, this factor is never missing and dislike for oneself or at least a lack of fondness for one's own person is always present and is dynamically an important factor.

---

[37] James, William. *Principles of Psychology.* New York: Holt, Rinehart and Winston, Inc., 1893 (1:xii and 689 pp.) and (2:vi and 704 pp.) in particular, 2:348.

[38] Industry, for instance, capitalizes the unconscious self-dislike by terrorizing people with the threat of "body odor." The unconscious dislike the average person has for himself makes him an easy prey for this suggestion.

A still more subtle form of self-dislike is the tendency toward constant self-criticism. These people do not feel inferior but if they make one mistake, discover something in themselves which should not be so, their self-criticism is entirely out of proportion to the significance of the mistake or the shortcoming. They must either be perfect according to their own standards, or at least perfect enough according to the standards of the people around them so that they get affection and approval. If they feel that what they did was perfect or if they succeed in winning other people's approval, they feel at ease. But whenever this is missing they feel overwhelmed by an otherwise repressed inferiority feeling. Here again, the basic lack of fondness for themselves is one source from which the attitude springs. This becomes more evident if we compare this attitude toward oneself with the corresponding one toward others. If, for example, a man who believes that he loves a woman should feel if she makes any mistake that she is no good, or if his feeling about her is entirely dependent on whether others criticize or praise her, we cannot doubt that there is a fundamental lack of love for her. It is the person who hates who seizes every opportunity to criticize another person and who does not miss any blunder.

The most widespread expression of the lack of fondness for oneself, however, is the way in which people treat themselves. People are their own slave drivers; instead of being the slaves of a master outside of themselves, they have put the master within. This master is harsh and cruel. He does not give them a moment's rest, he forbids them the enjoyment of any pleasure, does not allow them to do what they want. If they do so, they do it furtively and at the expense of a guilty conscience. Even the pursuit of pleasure is as compulsory as is work. It does not lead them away from the continual restlessness which pervades their lives. For the most part, they are not even aware of this. There are some exceptions. Thus, the banker, James Stillmann, who, when in the prime of life, had attained wealth, prestige and power reached only by but few people said: I never in my life have done what I wanted and never shall do so.[39]

The rôle of "conscience" as the internalization of external authorities and as the bearer of deep seated hostility against oneself has been seen clearly by Freud in the formulation of his concept of the Super-Ego. He assumed that the super-ego contains a great deal of the basic destructiveness inherent in man and turns it against him in terms of duty and moral obligation. In spite of objections to Freud's Super-Ego theory, which cannot be presented here,[40] Freud undoubtedly has sensed keenly the hostility and cruelty contained in the "conscience" as it was conceived in the modern era.

[39] Compare Robeson [Brown], Anna. *The Portrait of a Banker: James Stillmann.* New York: Duffield, 1927 (x and 370 pp.).

[40] See my discussion of the Super-Ego in the psychological part of *Studien über Autoritat und Familie* [Max Horkheimer, ed.]. Paris: Alcan, 1936 (xv and 947 pp.).

What holds true of hostility and hatred holds also true of love. Yet, love for others and self-love is by far a more difficult problem to discuss; and this for two reasons. One is the fact that while hatred is a phenomenon to be found everywhere in our society and, therefore, an easy object for empirical observation and analysis, love is a comparatively rare phenomenon, which lends itself to empirical observation only under difficulties; any discussion of love, therefore, implies the danger of being unempirical and merely speculative. The other difficulty is perhaps even greater. There is no word in our language which has been so much misused and prostituted as the word "love." It has been preached by those who were ready to condone every cruelty if it served their purpose; it has been used as a disguise under which to force people into sacrificing their own happiness, into submitting their whole self to those who profited from this surrender. It has been used as the moral basis for unjustified demands. It has been made so empty that for many people *love* may mean no more than that two people have lived together for 20 years just without fighting more often than once a week. It is dangerous and somewhat embarrassing to use such a word. Yet a psychologist may not properly succumb to this embarrassment. To preach love is at best bad taste. But to make a cool and critical analysis of the phenomenon of love and to unmask pseudo-love—tasks which cannot be separated from each other—is an obligation that the psychologist has no right to avoid.

It goes without saying that this paper will not attempt to give an analysis of love. Even to describe the psychological phenomena which are conventionally covered by the term "love" would require a good part of a book. One must attempt, however, the presentation necessary to the main trend of thought of this paper.

Two phenomena closely connected with each other are frequently presented as love—the masochistic and sadistic *love*. In the case of masochistic *love,* one gives up one's self, one's initiative and integrity in order to become submerged entirely in another person who is felt to be stronger. Because of deep anxieties which give rise to the feeling that one cannot stand on one's own feet, one wants to be rid of one's own individual self and to become part of another being, thus becoming secure and finding a center which one misses in oneself. This surrender of one's own self has often been praised as the example of "the great love." It is actually a form of idolatry, and also an annihilation of the self. The fact that it has been conceived as love has made it the more seductive and dangerous.

The sadistic *love* on the other hand springs from the desire to swallow its object to make him a will-less instrument in one's own hands. This drive is also rooted in a deep anxiety and an inability to stand alone, but instead of finding increased strength by being swallowed, strength and security are found in having a limited power over the other person. The masochistic as well as the sadistic kind of love are expressions of one basic need which springs from a basic inability to be independent. Using a biological term, this basic need may be called a "need for symbiosis." The sadistic *love* is frequently the kind of love that parents have for their children. Whether the domination is overtly authoritarian or subtly "modern" makes no essential difference. In either case, it tends to undermine the strength of the self of the child and leads in later years to the development in him of the very same symbiotic tendencies. The sadistic love is not infrequent among adults. Often in relationships of long duration, the respectives rôles are permanent, one partner representing the sadistic, the other one the masochistic pole of the symbiotic relationship. Often the rôles change constantly—a continuous struggle for dominance and submission being conceived as *love*.

It appears from what has been said that love cannot be separated from freedom and independence. In contradiction to the symbiotic pseudo-love, the basic premise of love is freedom and equality. Its premise is the strength, independence, integrity of the self, which can stand alone and bear solitude. This premise holds true for the loving as well as for the loved person. Love is a spontaneous act, and spontaneity means—also literally—the ability to act of one's own free volition. If anxiety and weakness of the self makes it impossible for the individual to be rooted in himself, he cannot love.

This fact can be fully understood only if we consider what love is directed toward. It is the opposite of hatred. Hatred is a passionate wish for destruction; love is a passionate affirmation of its "object" [41] That means that love is not an "affect" but an active striving, the aim of which is the happiness, development, and freedom of its "object." This passionate affirmation is not possible if one's own self is crippled, since genuine affirmation is always rooted in strength. The person whose self is thwarted, can only love in an ambivalent way; that is, with the strong part of his self he can love, with the crippled part he must hate. [42]

The term *passionate affirmation* easily leads to misunderstanding; it does not mean intellectual affirmation in the sense of purely rational judgment. It implies a much deeper affirmation, in which one's personality takes part as a whole: one's intellect, emotion and senses. One's eyes, ears and nose are often as good or better organs of affirmation than one's brain. If it is a deep and passionate one, the affirmation is related to the essence of the "object," not merely toward partial qualities. There is no stronger expression of God's love for man in the Old Testament than the saying at the end of each day of creation: "And God saw that it was good."

[41] Object is put into quotation marks because in a love relationship the "object" ceases to be an object; that is, something opposite to and separated from the subject. Not accidentally do "object" and "objection" have the same root.

[42] Sullivan has approached this formulation in his lectures. He states that the era of preadolescence is characterized by the appearance of impulses in interpersonal relations which make for a new type of satisfaction in the pleasure of the other person (the chum). Love, according to him, is a situation in which the satisfaction of the loved one is exactly as significant and desirable as that of the lover.

There is another possible misunderstanding which should particularly be avoided. From what has been said, one might come to the conclusion that every affirmation is love, regardless of the worthiness of the object to be loved. This would mean that love is a purely subjective feeling of affirmation and that the problem of objective values does not enter into it. The question arises: Can one love the evil? We come here to one of the most difficult problems of psychology and philosophy, a discussion of which can scarcely be attempted here. I must repeat, however, that affirmation in the sense here used is not something entirely subjective. Love is affirmation of life, growth, joy, freedom and by definition, therefore, the evil which is negation, death, compulsion cannot be loved. Certainly, the subjective feeling can be a pleasurable excitement, consciously conceived in the conventional term of love. The person is apt to believe that he loves, but analysis of his mental content reveals a state very different from what I have discussed as love. Much the same question arises with regard to certain other problems in psychology, for instance, the problem as to whether happiness is an entirely subjective phenomenon or whether it includes an objective factor. Is a person who feels "happy" in dependence and self-surrender happy because he feels to be so, or is happiness always dependent on certain values like freedom and integrity? One has always used the argument that the people concerned are "happy" to justify their suppression. This is a poor defense. Happiness cannot be separated from certain values, and is not simply a subjective feeling of satisfaction. A case in point is masochism. A person can be satisfied with submission, with torture, or even with death, but there is no happiness in submission, torture or death. Such considerations seem to leave the ground of psychology and to belong to the field of philosophy or religion. I do not believe that this is so. A sufficiently refined psychological analysis, which is aware of the difference in the qualities of feelings according to the underlying personality structure, can show the difference between *satisfaction* and *happiness*. Yet, psychology can be aware of these problems only if it does not try to separate itself from the problem of values. And, in the end does not shrink from the question of the goal and purpose of human existence.

Love, like character-conditioned hatred, is rooted in a basic attitude which is constantly present; a readiness to love, a *basic sympathy* as one might call it. It is started, but not caused, by a particular *object*. The ability and readiness to love is a character trait just as is the readiness to hate.[43] It is difficult to say what the conditions favoring the development of this *basic sympathy* are. It seems that there are two main conditions, a positive and a negative one. The positive one is simply to have experienced love from others as a child. While conventionally, parents are supposed to *love* their children as a matter of course, this is rather the excep-

[43] It would be most unfortunate to assume that these respective readinesses are characteristics of different personalities. Many people present concomitant readinesses of both varieties.

tion than the rule. This positive condition is, therefore, frequently absent. The negative condition is the absence of all those factors, discussed above, which make for the existence of a chronic hatred. The observer of childhood experiences may well doubt that the absence of these conditions is frequent.

From the premise that actual love is rooted in a *basic sympathy* there follows an important conclusion with regard to the *objects* of love. The conclusion is, in principle, the same as was stated with regard to the objects of chronic hatred: The objects of love do not have the quality of exclusiveness. To be sure, it is not accidental that a certain person becomes the *object* of manifest love. The factors conditioning such a specific choice are too numerous and too complex to be discussed here. The important point, however, is that love for a particular *object* is only the actualization and concentration of lingering love with regard to one person; it is not, as the idea of *romantic love* would have it, that there is only *the* one person in the world whom one could love, that it is the great chance of one's life to find that person, and that love for him or her results in a withdrawal from all others. The kind of love which can only be experienced with regard to one person demonstrates by this very fact that it is not love, but a symbiotic attachment. The basic affirmation contained in love is directed toward the beloved person as an incarnation of essentially human qualities. Love for one person implies love for man as such. The kind of "division of labor" as William James calls it; namely, to love one's family, but to be without feeling for the "stranger," is a sign of a basic inability to love. Love for man as such is not, as it is frequently supposed to be, an abstraction coming "after" the love for a specific person, or an enlargement of the experience with a specific *object;* it is its premise, although, genetically, it is acquired in the contact with concrete individuals.

From this, it follows that my own self, in principle, is as much an object of my love as another person. The affirmation of my own life, happiness, growth, freedom is rooted in the presence of the basic readiness of and ability for such an affirmation. If an individual has this readiness, he has it also toward himself; if he can only *love* others, he cannot love at all. In one word, love is as indivisible as hatred with regard to its *objects*.

The principle which has been pointed out here, that hatred and love are actualizations of a constant readiness, holds true for other psychic phenomena. Sensuality, for instance, is not simply a reaction to a stimulus. The sensual or as one may say, the erotic person, has a basically erotic *attitude* toward the world. This does not mean that he is constantly excited sexually. It means that there is an erotic *atmosphere* which is actualized by a certain object, but which is there underneath before the *stimulus* appears. What is meant here is not the physiologically given ability to be sexually excited, but an atmosphere of erotic readiness, which under a magnifying glass could be observed also when the person is not in a state of actual sexual excitement. On the other hand, there are persons in whom this erotic readiness is lacking. In them, sexual excitement is essentially caused by a stimulus operating on the sexual instinct. Their threshold of stimulation can vary between wide limits, but there is a common quality in this type of sexual excitement; namely, its separateness from the whole personality in its intellectual and emotional qualities. Another illustration of the same principle is the sense of beauty. There is a type of personality who has a readiness to see beauty. Again, that does not mean that he is constantly looking at beautiful pictures, or people, or scenery; yet, when he sees them a continuously present readiness is actualized, and his sense of beauty is not simply *aroused* by the object. Here too, a very refined observation shows that this type of person has a different way of looking at the world, even when he looks at objects which do not stimulate an acute perception of beauty. We could give many more examples for the same principle, if space permitted. The principle should already be clear: While many psychological schools [44] have thought of human reactions in terms of stimulus-response, the principle presented here is that character is a structure of numerous *readinesses* of the kind mentioned, which are constantly present and are actualized but not caused by an outside stimulus. This view is essential for such a dynamic psychology as psychoanalysis is.

Freud assumed that all these readinesses are rooted in biologically given instincts. It is here assumed that although this holds true for some of them, many others have arisen as a reaction to the individual and social experiences of the individual.

One last question remains to be discussed. Granted that love for oneself and for others in principle runs parallel, how do we explain the kind of *selfishness* which obviously is in contradiction to any genuine concern for others? The *selfish* person is only interested in himself, wants everything for himself, is unable to give with any pleasure but is only anxious to take; the world outside himself is conceived only from the standpoint of what he can get out of it; he lacks interest in the needs of others, or respect for their dignity and integrity. He sees only himself, judges everyone and everything from the standpoint of its usefulness to him, is basically unable to love. This selfishness can be manifest or disguised by all sorts of unselfish gestures; dynamically it is exactly the same. It seems obvious that with this type of personality there is a contradiction between the enormous concern for oneself and the lack of concern for others. Do we not have the proof here that there exists an alternative between concern for others and con-

---

[44] Although the reflexological viewpoint seems to be similar to the one taken here, this similarity is only a superficial one. The reflexological viewpoint means a pre-formed readiness of neurones to react in a certain way to a certain stimulus. Our viewpoint is not concerned with these physical conditions and, what is more important, by *readiness* we mean an actually present but only lingering, or willing attitude, which makes for a basic atmosphere or *Grundstimmung*.

cern for oneself? This would certainly be the case if selfishness and self-love were identical. But this assumption is the very fallacy which has led to so many mistaken conclusions with regard to our problem. Selfishness and self-love far from being identical, actually are opposites.

Selfishness is one kind of greediness.[45] Like all greediness, it contains an insatiability, as a consequence of which there is never any real satisfaction. Greed is a bottomless pit which exhausts the person in an endless effort to satisfy the need without ever reaching satisfaction. This leads to the crucial point: Close observation shows that while the selfish person is always anxiously concerned with himself, he is never satisfied, is always restless, always driven by the fear of not getting enough, of missing something, of being deprived of something. He is filled with burning envy of anyone who might have more. If we observe still closer, especially the unconscious dynamics, we find that this type of person is basically not fond of himself but deeply dislikes himself. The puzzle in this seeming contradiction is easy to solve. The selfishness is rooted in this very lack of fondness for oneself. The person who is not fond of himself, who does not approve of himself, is in a constant anxiety concerning his own self. He has not the inner security which can exist only on the basis of genuine fondness and affirmation. He must be concerned about himself, greedy to get everything for himself, since basically his own self lacks security and satisfaction. The same holds true with the so-called narcissistic person, who is not so much overconcerned with getting things for himself as with admiring himself. While on the surface it seems that these persons are very much in love with themselves, they actually are not fond of themselves, and their narcissism—like selfishness—is an overcompensation for the basic lack of self-love. Freud has pointed out that the narcissistic person has withdrawn his love from others and turned it toward his own person. While the first part of this statement is true, the second one is a fallacy. He neither loves others nor himself.[46]

It is easier to understand this mechanism when we compare it with overconcern and overprotectiveness for others. Whether it is an oversolicitous mother or an overconcerned husband, sufficiently deep observation shows always one fact: While these persons consciously believe that they are particularly fond of the child or husband, there actually is a deep repressed hostility toward the very objects of their concern. They are overconcerned because they have to compensate not only for a lack of fondness but for an actual hostility.

The problem of selfishness has still another aspect. Is not the sacrifice of one's own person the extreme expression of unselfishness, and, on the

---

[45] The German word *Selbstsucht* (addiction to self) very adequately expresses this quality common to all *Sucht*.

[46] Since Freud thinks only in the framework of his instinctual concepts, and since a phenomenon like love in the sense used here does not exist in his system, the conclusions to which he comes are all but inevitable.

other hand, could a person who loves himself make that supreme sacrifice? The answer depends entirely on the kind of sacrifice that is meant. There is one *sacrifice,* as it has been particularly emphasized in recent years by Fascist philosophy. The individual should give himself up for something outside of himself which is greater and more valuable; the Leader, the race. The individual by himself is nothing and by the very act of self-annihilation for the sake of the higher power finds his destiny. In this concept, sacrificing oneself for something or someone greater than oneself is in itself the greatest attainable virtue. If love for oneself as well as for another person means basic affirmation and respect, this concept is in sharp contrast to self-love. But there is another kind of sacrifice: If it should be necessary to give one's life for the preservation of an idea which has become part of oneself or for a person whom one loves, the sacrifice may be the extreme expression of self-affirmation. Not, of course, an affirmation of one's physical self, but of the self in the sense of the kernel of one's total personality. In this case the sacrifice in itself is not the goal; it is the price to be paid for the realization and affirmation of one's own self. While in this latter case, the sacrifice is rooted in self-affirmation, in the case of what one might call the masochistic sacrifice, it is rooted in the lack of self-love and self-respect; it is essentially nihilistic.

The problem of selfishness has a particular bearing on psychotherapy. The neurotic individual often is *selfish* in the sense that he is blocked in his relationship to others or overanxious about himself. This is to be expected since to be *neurotic* means that the integration of a strong self has not been achieved successfully. To be *normal* certainly does not mean that it has. It means, for the majority of *well-adapted* individuals that they have lost their own self at an early age and replaced it completely by a *social self* offered to them by society. They have no neurotic conflicts because they themselves, and therefore the discrepancy between their selves and the outside world, have disappeared. Often the neurotic person is particularly *unselfish,* lacking in self-assertion and blocked in following his own aims. The reason for this *unselfishness* is essentially the same as for the *selfishness.* What he is practically always lacking is self-love. This is what he needs to become *well.* If the *neurotic* becomes well, he does not become *normal* in the sense of the conforming *social self.* He succeeds in realizing his self, which never had been completely lost and for the preservation of which he was struggling by his neurotic symptoms. A theory, therefore, as Freud's on narcissism which rationalizes the cultural pattern of denouncing self-love by identifying it with *selfishness,* can have but devastating effects therapeutically. It increases the taboo on self-love. Its effects can only be called *positive* if the aim of psychotherapy is not to help the individual to be himself; that is, free, spontaneous and creative—qualities conventionally reserved for *artists*—but to give up the fight for his self and conform to the cultural pattern peacefully and without the noise of a neurosis.

In the present era, the tendency to make of the individual a powerless atom is increasing. The authoritarian systems tend to reduce the individual to a will-less and feelingless instrument in the hands of those who hold the reins; they batter him down by terror, cynicism, the power of the state, large demonstrations, fierce orators and all other means of suggestion. When finally he feels too weak to stand alone, they offer him satisfaction by letting him participate in the strength and glory of the greater whole, whose powerless part he is. The authoritarian propaganda uses the argument that the individual of the democratic state is *selfish* and that he should become unselfish and socially minded. This is a lie. Nazism substituted the most brutal selfishness of the leading bureaucracy and of the state for the selfishness of the average man. The appeal for unselfishness is the weapon to make the average individual still more ready to submit or to renounce. The criticism of democratic society should not be that people are too selfish; this is true but it is only a consequence of something else. What democracy has not succeeded in is to make the individual love himself; that is, to have a deep sense of affirmation for his individual self, with all his intellectual, emotional, and sensual potentialities. A puritan-protestant inheritance of self-denial, the necessity of subordinating the individual to the demands of production and profit, have made for conditions from which Fascism could spring. The readiness for submission, the pervert *courage* which is attracted by the image of war and self-annihilation, is only possible on the basis of a—largely unconscious—desperation, stifled by martial songs and shouts for the Führer. The individual who has ceased to love himself is ready to die as well as to kill. The problem of our culture, if it is not to become a fascist one, is not that there is too much self-ishness but that there is no self-love. The aim must be to create those conditions which make it possible for the individual to realize his freedom, not only in a formal sense, but by asserting his total personality in his intellectual, emotional, sensual qualities. This freedom is not the rule of one part of the personality over another part—conscience over nature, Super-Ego over Id—but the integration of the whole personality and the factual expression of all the potentialities of this integrated personality.

Comments

1. The distinction between self-love and selfish love is as crucial today from a philosophical, psychological, and sociological point of view as it was in 1939 when the article was written; it is basic, for example, to the all-important concept of enlightened self-interest which underlies social and emotional maturity.

2. The article obviously reflects concern over the upsurge of totalitarian philosophy which characterized the Nazi, fascist, and communist movements of the pre-World-War period.

That's What They Said

"Yet the pupil is an emotional being who responds to stress and decision-making on the basis of how he feels as well as what he knows. He may be threatened and bullied into achieving a high test score, yet come to loathe the subject, the school, and all things academic."

> F. G. Watson. "Research in teaching science," in N. L. Gage (ed.), *Handbook of Research on Teaching.* Skokie, Ill.: Rand McNally & Company, 1963. Pp. 1031–59. [1054]

"Our findings indicate that the normal person comes to terms with himself and views himself more on an emotional basis than on an intellectual basis. The self feeds, as it were, more on feeling than on thought."

> Arthur T. Jersild. *In Search of Self.* New York: Teachers College, Columbia University, 1952. [54–55]

"When emotional factors in learning are seen to be important not only in problem cases but also in a large proportion—if not all—of the student body, guidance becomes a preoccupation of every day, rather than the subject of a semi-annual visit to the dean."

> L. B. Murphy and H. Y. Ladd. *Emotional Factors in Learning.* New York: Columbia University Press, 1946. [9]

". . . much of what goes under the name of self-control is a denial, a repudiation, an evasion of life, of genuineness, and of integrity. Control, which means not real control nor realization nor even self-denial but a form of self-eradication, is not a good rule of health."

> Arthur T. Jersild, *op. cit.* [44]

"There is a very delicate balance between the facilitating and the frustrating effects of emotion. In their early stages and after the phase of momentary disorganization, emotions are facilitating. But if blocking continues for some time, the organism becomes frustrated and what may have been behavior well on the road toward the solution of the problem presented by the situation, now becomes disorganizing and even may hamper effective reaction."

> John E. Anderson. "The relation of emotional behavior to learning," in N. B. Henry (ed.), *The Psychology of Learning.* 41st Yearbook, National Society for the Study of Education, Part II. Chicago: University of Chicago Press, 1942. Pp. 333–352. [343]

"Knowing that a child is intellectually capable of tough work is relatively useless if he is emotionally incapable. As we cannot by sheer will power raise his intellect neither can we by mere insistence improve his emotional capacity."

> Don Robinson. "Scraps from a teacher's notebook," *Phi Delta Kappan,* 44: 191, 1963.

"Many other children find the educational scene so filled with failure, so full of reminders of their limitations, and so harsh in giving these reminders that they hate school. School is such a threat to their self picture that it is almost intolerable, but they drag themselves back to school day after day because the alternative of not going would be even more painful and threatening."

> Arthur T. Jersild, *op. cit.* [100]

"We take advantage of one another in order to satisfy our emotional needs and to work out our personal tensions and anxieties. Most of the time most people use one another as targets for their own psychological needs. The amount and degree of psychological exploitation in human association is so pervasive that it is taken for granted. It is shocking to discover . . . the degree to which all individuals seek to impose their particular ways of thinking, feeling, and acting, upon others."

> Nathaniel Cantor. *The Teaching Learning Process.* New York: Holt, Rinehart and Winston, Inc., 1953. [265–266]

"The fact that three-year-old children are quite often negative is considered evidence that negativism is inherent in the nature of three-year-olds, and the concept of the negativistic age or stage is then regarded as an explanation (though perhaps not a complete one) for the appearance of negativism in a given particular case!"

> Kurt Lewin. "Conflict between Aristotelian and Galilean modes of thought," *J. gen. Psychol.,* 5: 141–171, 1931. [153]

CHAPTER 7

Test Items

1. Emotions are most closely related to
   a. attitudes
   b. conscience
   c. motivation
   d. personality adjustment
   e. personality development

2. Probably the most fundamental component of emotions is
   a. a certain feeling tone
   b. the directional drive
   c. the impulse to action
   d. the neurophysiological basis
   e. the visceral changes

3. Emotions are under the control of
   a. the autonomous nervous system
   b. the central nervous system
   c. the lower brain centers (e. g., the hypothalamus)
   d. the parasympathetic nervous system
   e. the sympathetic nervous system

4. The one gland that is not under the dual (antagonistic) control of both components of the autonomic nervous system is
   a. the adrenal gland
   b. the endocrine gland
   c. the hypothalamus
   d. the liver
   e. the pancreas

5. Which of the following is not a feature of emotional development?
   a. a change from all-or-none to a graduation of emotional expression
   b. a change in emotional susceptibility
   c. a change in emotional susceptibility from the concrete to abstract stimuli
   d. a gradual decline in emotional sensitivity
   e. a gradual increase in the relative ratio of positive-to-negative emotions

6. Failure of adults to identify the specific emotion displayed by the newborn infant is primarily due to
   a. failure of adults to recognize the specific symptoms
   b. failure of the infant to know the particular stereotypes through which emotion is displayed
   c. the inability of his physiological equipment to display the emotions he has
   d. his lack of emotional differentiation
   e. the overlap in the behavioral patterns used to express different emotions

7. Emotions have their maximal facilitating effects in situations which call for
   a. ability to improvise
   b. clear thinking
   c. gross muscular strength, speed, and stamina
   d. persistence
   e. routine behavior

8. The damaging effect of persistent emotions to physical health stems primarily from
   a. the body's inability to consume the resulting blood sugar
   b. the danger of physical violence
   c. inability to think clearly
   d. the overstimulation of the lower brain centers
   e. their relationship to mental illness

9. In the differentiation of various emotions,
   a. affection appears before fear
   b. anger and affection appear relatively simultaneously
   c. distress and delight appear relatively simultaneously
   d. fear and jealousy appear relatively simultaneously
   e. the "negative" emotions tend to differentiate before the "positive" emotions

10. The differentiation of emotions according to Bridges is
    a. apparently a process involving both learning and maturation in equal degree
    b. a maturational process as to direction but not sequence nor timing
    c. a maturational process as to sequence but not timing
    d. primarily a maturational process as to both timing and sequence
    e. strictly a learning process

11. The best approach to helping the child toward wholesome emotional development is
    a. to expose him to a systematic program of both positive and negative emotions under conditions of moral support
    b. to increase his security and his competence
    c. to keep him under conditions of relative freedom from emotional tensions
    d. to minimize the number of negative emotions to which he is exposed
    e. to protect him from emotion-producing situations

12. What constitutes an emotion-producing situation is a function of
    a. the individual's perceived ability to meet the demands of the situation
    b. the individual's phenomenological interpretation of the nature of the stimulus
    c. the individual's status as to health, accumulated frustration, etc.
    d. the nature of the situation
    e. the relative discrepancy between the individual's competency and the demands of the situation

13. Patriotism is to prejudice as
    a. enlightened self-interest is to exploitation
    b. in-group is to out-group
    c. large-group loyalty is to small-group loyalty
    d. loyalty is to clannishness
    e. loyalty is to disloyalty

14. Patriotism is most harmful when
    a. it leads to categorization of people on the basis of group membership
    b. it leads to intergroup rivalry
    c. it means acceptance of the in-group in preference to the out-group
    d. it means rejection of the members of the out-group
    e. it restricts meaningful social interaction with members of the out-group

15. Anger is to fear as
    a. attack is to flight
    b. cumulative is to current
    c. hostility is to insecurity
    d. localized focus is to vague focus
    e. relative competence is to relative incompetence

16. Unusual hostility is often a case of
    a. accumulated frustration dating back to early infancy
    b. conditioning to a previous traumatic experience
    c. defense against feelings of insecurity
    d. prejudice
    e. projection of resentment of one's own shortcomings

17. The decline in temper tantrums after the age of three is generally due to
    a. the discovery of more subtle and safe ways of registering anger
    b. an increase in frustration tolerance as an aspect of maturation
    c. an increase in inhibition as the socialization process becomes effective
    d. an increase in security accompanying an increase in competence
    e. a trend toward cooperation as the positive emotions mature

18. Control of anger through punitive measures leads to
    a. the development of an irrational-conscientious morality
    b. an increase in inner hostility
    c. an increase in overt cooperation
    d. an increase in rebelliousness and overt aggression
    e. reliance on displaced aggression

19. Concerning the display of anger, psychologists would agree that
    a. anger is bad only when it results in harm to others
    b. anger is typically bad because it generates counteranger
    c. anger is typically a bad adjustment that should be avoided
    d. anger may be all right on occasions but it carries the danger of progressive abuse
    e. anger tends to contribute to personal adjustment and social mal-adjustment

20. The primary reason for the widespread use of anger as an adjustment mechanism is that
    a. it has a relatively stable base in personal insecurity
    b. it induces a reciprocal anger which reinforce one another
    c. it is probably an inherited predisposition nurtured by the constant frustration encountered from the environment
    d. it is the resultant of an inborn need to safeguard one's interests
    e. it tends to be reinforced on an intermittent basis

21. Excessive fear of examinations and of robbers have in common
    a. conditioning to early trauma
    b. generalized guilt

c. personal incompetence
d. personal incompetence and insecurity
e. a traumatic experience

22. Which of the following is *not* a typical feature of the fear response?
a. extension to phobic reactions
b. extinction
c. spontaneous recovery
d. stimulus discrimination
e. stimulus generalization

23. The primary determinant of fear is
a. the nature of the stimulus
b. the perceived gap between personal competence and situational demands
c. personal incompetence
d. personal insecurity
e. previous experience with fear-producing situations

24. The most clearly detrimental aspect of fear is that
a. it destroys the individual's self-confidence
b. it detracts from the individual's ability to cope with difficult situations
c. it discourages the individual from developing the necessary competencies
d. it promotes guilt feelings
e. it quickly extends itself to phobia

25. The most clearly beneficial effect of fear is that
a. it acts as a basis for socialization and conscience development
b. it increases alertness to danger and to potential solutions
c. it prevents the individual from tackling potentially dangerous situations
d. it promotes a certain degree of prudence and preparedness
e. it promotes regulation-abiding behavior

26. The most effective method of eliminating fear is
a. conditioning to a positive stimulus
b. development of the necessary competencies
c. imitation of group behavior
d. reassurance
e. simply maturation

27. A form of pleasure insufficiently emphasized as a school incentive is
    a. a game approach to learning
    b. peer recognition
    c. praise
    d. pride in personal accomplishment for accomplishment's sake
    e. problem solving and discovery

28. The inborn component of affection appears to be
    a. its amenability to conditioning to primary drives
    b. the capacity for love
    c. its direct amenability to positive reinforcement
    d. its glandular basis
    e. the human predisposition toward affiliations

29. The most personally satisfying and socially beneficial form of affection is
    a. altruistic love
    b. enlightened self-interest
    c. maternal love
    d. self-centered love
    e. selfish love

30. The most plausible explanation of homosexuality is
    a. glandular (excess of opposite-sex hormones)
    b. learning (conditioning of fear reaction to members of the opposite sex)
    c. medical (individual is biologically of the wrong sex)
    d. psychological (failure to develop heterosexuality as a developmental task)
    e. sociological–situational (unavailability of members of the opposite sex)

31. Probably the most significant feature of emotional security is
    a. ability to channel emotional tensions into constructive activities
    b. emphasis on emotional expression rather than repression
    c. freedom from tensions arising from negative emotions
    d. skill in fitting into the social setting
    e. willingness to forego one's needs for the social welfare

32. The school's responsibility in the area of emotional development is that of
    a. channeling emotional tensions, thereby minimizing classroom disruptions

b. providing a positive program geared to the promotion of emotional maturity

c. providing a program of cognitive-academic development; emotional development follows as a by-product

d. safeguarding the child from undue school-generated frustrations

e. suppressing objectionable emotional outbursts

CHAPTER 8

Social Development

Another aspect of pupil growth that is too frequently neglected by the school in its concern over academic goals is that of social development. Whereas the crucial factors in the child's social growth are probably the early socialization occurring in the home in infancy and the later interaction with the peer group, the school cannot afford to make its contribution in this important connection a matter of chance. Actually, the school has a particular opportunity here in that it provides the child with his first systematic opportunity to interact in a miniature social context under conditions of guidance and support. Indeed, the fact that everything that the child undergoes in school takes place in a social setting is often the crucial factor in the over-all situation. Unfortunately, too often teachers view their classes as an aggregate of separate individuals and, in an ill-advised effort to prevent pupil interaction within the classroom from interfering with school learning, discourage interpupil contacts. To the extent that a major function of the school as an agent of democratic society is to promote effective citizenship, managing the classroom as a social vacuum is the last thing an intelligent teacher should want to do.

Of particular interest in view of the well-recognized difficulties boys experience in our schools are the articles by McNeil, who finds a possible connection between the academic disadvantages under which boys operate and the female-dominated atmosphere of the typical classroom, and by Meyer and Thompson, who find that women teachers do indeed have more negative contacts with boys than with girls. Another aspect of the problem, namely, the relationship between social status and social striving is the topic of the Douvan article. To the extent that the education of the child occurs in a social context, both questions are of concern to the operation of the school. Lynn traces the differences in sex role to fundamental differences between boys and girls in the process of parental identification. The final selection is taken from the excellent booklet by Sheviakov and Redl on the ever-present problem of classroom discipline.

John D. McNeil

Programmed Instruction versus Usual Classroom in Teaching Boys To Read *

That boys experience greater difficulty than girls in learning to read is a common observation; boys outnumber girls roughly 3 to 1 among enrollees in reading clinics, for example. This fact has been variously explained on the basis of (a) the slower rate of maturation of boys, (b) the lesser appeal to boys of present instructional materials, and (c) the negative treatment of male learners by female teachers. The present study tested the hypothesis that the inferiority of young males in learning to read might be the result of the failure of teachers to adapt their procedures to certain behavioral tendencies of boys as well as they do to the behavioral tendencies of girls. The subjects were 72 boys and 60 girls in kindergarten of an average IQ of 107 and an average age of 5–6. In Phase One of the study, the children were presented with programmed instruction consisting of daily lessons over a period of 17 days. Each child sat in an individual laboratory-type cubicle equipped with headphones through which he heard a taped commentary. The cubicle also contained a response and confirmation panel, consisting of three buttons with which to signal his answers and a green and red light for feedback as to the correctness of his answers. He saw the daily sequence presented by film on a 6 x 8 screen at the front of the room, while simultaneously hearing the accompanying tape commentary.

Relevant features of the auto-instructional procedures included: (a) Boys and girls made individual confirmations; (b) because the pupils were in individual cubicles, interaction among them was not encouraged; (c) boys and girls were presented with identical frames at a common pace and received the same taped comments of encouragement, and (d) boys and girls were given equal opportunity to respond; the same number of responses was demanded daily from all learners.

A post-test consisting of 51 multiple-choice items similar in format to the programmed instruction was then administered with oral instructions. None of the items of the post-test was identical with any of the frames of

* Adapted and abridged from John D. McNeil, "Programmed instruction versus usual classroom in teaching boys to read," Amer. educ. Res. J., 1: 113–119, 1964. Copyright by American Educational Research Association.

the program. Contrary to expectation based on results from previous studies of beginning reading, the boys earned significantly higher scores than the girls.

In Phase Two of the study, these children were assigned to regular classrooms staffed by women teachers, who were not aware of the nature of the investigation. During a period of four months, each reading group was given approximately 20 minutes of direct teacher instruction daily and 20 minutes of seat work. Following this period of classroom instruction, these same boys who had been significantly superior to the girls at the end of the period of auto-instruction were now found to be inferior to the girls ($p. < .01$) on a similar test covering teacher-taught words.

Interview data revealed that boys received significantly more negative comments than girls ($p. < .01$), they were seen as given less opportunity to read ($p < .05$) and more frequently than girls assessed by the teachers as having little or no motivation or readiness for reading ($p < .01$). There was a correlation of .313 ($p < .01$) between the number of times an individual pupil was perceived as receiving negative comments from the teacher and his drop in rank from the first to the second criterion. Drop in rank also correlated .238 with perceived deprivation of opportunity to read. The results support the hypothesis that teachers treat boys and girls differently and suggest an association between teachers' behavior and performance in beginning reading. The results also suggest that a study of the features of auto-instruction may be useful in developing teaching procedures more appropriate for boys than those in current use.

Comments

1. As McNeil suggests, there are apparently factors in the regular classroom that mitigate against maximum academic performance by young males. A possible cause of this difficulty is the conflict of the self-concept of the male child to the school situation with its overall female orientation (see Lecky, 1945). As early as 1909, Ayres (*Laggards in Our Schools*) pointed to the difficulties which the overfeminization of the school presented for boys. McNeil refers to the effects of peer group interaction in causing boys to display aggression or for other reasons failing to attend to the lesson at hand. The elimination through autoinstructional devices of this factor as an obstacle to beginning reading cannot be considered apart from the effect of such elimination on the other aspects of pupil growth.

2. McNeil attempted to control the factor of the differential appeal which the mechanical gadgetry might have for boys and girls; boys and girls did not differ in their preference for autoinstruction.

3. The findings of this study are in line with the modern psy-

chological position that readiness is a function of the adaptation of teaching methods to the present development of the child.

4.   The apparent incompatibility of women teachers and first-grade boys raises a question concerning the preponderance of women in the primary grades. (There is, of course, no evidence that different results would have been obtained with male teachers.) The negative orientation of primary teachers to the behavioral tendencies of boys is interesting from the standpoint of the school adjustment of boys. The latter point has been questioned by Davis and Slobodian (1967), who did not find (convincing) evidence of discrimination against boys by women teachers in a regular classroom situation. But then they did not find the usual inferiority of boys in reading either—thereby supporting, rather than refuting, the McNeil thesis of a relationship between negative treatment and reading retardation. (See also Meyer and Thompson, 1956.) Ingle and Kephart (1966) also raise a number of questions regarding the McNeil study.

References

Ayres, Leonard P. *Laggards in Our Schools*. New York: Russell Sage Foundation, 1909.

Davis, O. L., and June J. Slobodian. "Teacher behavior toward boys and girls during first-grade reading instruction," *Amer. educ. Res. J.*, 4: 261–270, 1967.

Ingle, Robert B., and William J. Gephart. "A critique of a research report: Programmed instruction versus usual classroom procedures in teaching boys to read," *Amer. educ. Res. J.*, 3: 49–53, 1966.

Lecky, P. *Self-Consistency: A Theory of Personality*. New York: Island Press, 1945.

William J. Meyer and George G. Thompson

Sex Differences in the Distribution of Teacher Approval and Disapproval among Sixth-Grade Children *

The study was designed to test the following hypotheses: (a) To-the extent that boys are more aggressive and "unmanageable" than girls, they are more likely than girls to receive disapproval contacts from their teacher, "who is usually a woman from the middle socio-economic stratum of our society" [p. 386]. (b) Conversely, girls being more conforming and generally quiescent than boys, are more likely to receive approval contacts than boys, and (c) both boys and girls are aware of the sex differences in teacher approval and disapproval. The data for Hypotheses 1 and 2 were obtained from a total of thirty hours of observation for each of the three sixth-grade classrooms, during the course of which all teacher-initiated contacts of an approval or disapproval nature were recorded; and from a modified "Guess Who" technique, asking each child to nominate four classmates for each of a number of situations describing teacher approval or disapproval of pupils. The subjects were three women teachers and their 39 boys and 39 girls.

As anticipated, boys received a significantly larger number of blame or disapproval contacts than girls. "These differences may be interpreted according to our hypotheses as supporting the notion that teachers are responding with counter-aggression to the greater expression of aggression by boys" [p. 387]. However, contrary to hypothesis, the boys also received more approval contacts. Perhaps teachers are trying to reinforce any positive behavior that boys display—or, on the other hand, perhaps their behavior reflects a compensatory reaction arising from feelings of guilt generated by their excessive aggressiveness toward boys. Both boys and girls—but especially boys—listed boys as receiving more teacher disapproval than girls; on the other hand, the "Guess Who" technique gave conflicting results as to whether boys or girls received more approval contacts.

* Adapted and abridged from William J. Meyer and George G. Thompson, "Sex differences in the distribution of teacher approval among sixth-grade children," *J. educ. Psychol.*, 47:385–396, 1956. Copyright 1956 by American Psychological Association, and reproduced by permission.

Comments

1. The authors note that apparently teachers react to the aggressive behavior of boys with counteraggression, a vicious circle for both pupils and teacher. While the behavioral tendencies of girls are generally in closer agreement with those of the teacher, the aggressive behavior of boys tends to be resented. Wickman's study, for example, showed that teachers considered aggressiveness one of the more serious symptoms of maladjustment. According to the authors, the consistent trends in their findings imply a lack of appreciation on the part of teachers of the fact that in our culture outgoing behavior is as normal in the male as quiescent nonassertive behavior is in the female. The teacher who attempts to inhibit this behavior, i.e., to socialize boys through dominative counteraggression, can only meet with resistance. A more reasonable plan to follow would seem to be one in which the boys' excessive energy is discharged in some constructive activity. "Perhaps most important of all, however, is the knowledge that some degree of aggressive behavior is a normal part of the development of both boys and girls and should be treated not as a personal threat to the teacher but as a sign of 'normal' social and personality development" [p. 393].

2. Wide discrepancies in teacher approval–disapproval also exist within each sex group. The bright child, for example, is less likely to receive disapproval than is the dull child; the creative child is less appreciated than his more "convergent" counterpart of equal ability. A factorial (research) design based on such dimensions as sex, personality orientation, intellectual status, etc. together with male and female teachers, might provide interesting results.

Elizabeth Douvan

Social Status and Success Strivings *

To the extent that middle-class parents stress accomplishments and impose on their children earlier and more persistent demands for personal achievement than do their lower-class counterparts, it can be hypothesized that the need for achievement would be more generalized in middle-class children than in children of the lower class. The reaction of lower-class children to success–failure cues, on the other hand, should generally be more responsive to changes in the reward potential of the situation.

The present study contrasted the degree of achievement motivation manifested by members of the middle- and the lower-class in two success–failure situations differing in reward potential. "In one situation, success was defined in terms of personal satisfaction derived from having attained an abstract norm; in the other, successful performance offered, in addition, a material reward. The specific hypothesis to be tested was that working-class youth would manifest a significantly greater difference in achievement strivings under two (different) reward conditions than would youngsters from the middle class" [p. 219].

The subjects were 336 high school seniors randomly assigned to one or the other of the two motivational conditions. Under the material reward conditions, the examiner announced before the test series that a $10 reward would be given to any student whose overall score reached the average score of the other high school seniors who had taken the test. However, in order to create a failure experience, he announced a falsely high average, after which a projective measure of achievement motivation was given.

No class differences were noted in the monetary reward situation. But, as predicted, the middle-class youngsters manifested more generalized striving; their performance under the two conditions remained essentially alike. While the achievement motivation of the working-class subjects dropped significantly when the material reward was removed, the motivation of the middle-class subjects remained high. Even under conditions of comparative failure, the latter manifested significantly higher need to

* Adapted and abridged from Elizabeth Douvan, "Social status and success strivings," *J. abnorm. soc. Psychol.*, 52: 219–223, 1956. Copyright 1956 by the American Psychological Association and reproduced by permission.

achieve than their working-class counterparts, even though group recognition was not involved since only the student knew his own score.

Comments

1. In contrast to middle-class children who have a greater momentum and who can work at school work even though it is dull, children of the lower classes need more consistent and constant arousal by one means or another if they are to participate wholeheartedly. The problem is aggravated by the fact that the middle-class oriented curriculum is often unrelated to their needs. Experience with these school activities may well have conditioned lower-class children to work for an external reward as the only meaningful aspect of schooling. If this is true, it may pose problems for the school which is essentially attempting to work for long-range goals, the benefits of which are sometimes difficult to see in the immediate present.

2. Undoubtedly, certain lower-class homes have adopted middle-class values and vice versa. In Douvan's study, these children were excluded from the comparison.

3. A large number of studies have investigated the social differential in child-rearing practices. The middle-class home tends to make earlier and more consistent demands for personal attainment.

4. Of interest in this connection is the finding (French, 1956) that persons with a high affiliation motivation tend to choose as work partners someone they like. The achievement-oriented person, on the other hand, tends to select as a work partner someone who is good at performing the task in question.

Reference

French, Elizabeth G. "Motivation as a variable in work-partner selection," *J. abn. soc. Psychol.*, 53: 96–99, 1956.

David B. Lynn

Sex-Role and Parental Identification *

The article presents a theoretical formulation postulating basic sex differences in the *nature* of sex roles and parental identification as a relevant basic difference in the *process* of achieving such identification. According to typical developmental patterns in our culture, both male and female infants learn to identify with the mother. However, the girl has with her the same-sex parental model with which to identify more than the boy has the same-sex model with him; much incidental learning which she can apply directly in her life simply takes place from constant contact with her mother. For boys, on the other hand, their initial learned identification with their mother naturally weakens as a consequence of the process of reinforcement of the culture's highly developed system of rewards for indications of masculinity and punishment for signs of femininity. Thus, whereas girls tend to identify with specific aspects of their own mother's role, boys, on the contrary, tend to identify with a culturally-defined stereotype of the masculine role. In other words, we must distinguish between masculine *role* identification in males and mother identification in females.

It is postulated that the task of achieving these separate kinds of identification for each sex requires separate methods of learning. The girl typically has her mother with her a relatively large portion of the time so that she learns her mother-identification lesson in the context of an intimate personal relationship with the mother—partly by imitation and partly through the mother's selective reinforcement of mother-similar tendencies. What she needs to learn is not to abstract underlying principles defining the feminine role, but rather simply to identify with her specific mother. The boy, on the other hand, as he gets aware that he does not belong in the same sex category as the mother must find a proper sex-identification role. Furthermore, since the desired behavior is rarely defined positively but rather negatively as something he should not do or be (e. g., sissy), from very early in life the boy must either stumble on the right course or bear repeated punishment without warning when he accidentally enters the wrong path. This he must do at the urging of negative admonishings, often

* Adapted and abridged from David B. Lynn, "Sex-role and parental identification," *Child Devel.,* 33: 555–564, 1962. Copyright 1962 by the Society for Research in Child Development, Inc., and reproduced by permission.

made by women and often without benefit of a male model. In other words, he must abstract the principles defining the masculine role.

One of the basic steps in this formulation can now be taken. It is assumed that, in learning the appropriate identification, each sex is thereby acquiring separate methods of learning which are subsequently applied to learning tasks generally. The little girl applies a learning method which primarily involves: (a) a personal relationship and (b) imitation rather than restructuring the field and abstracting principles. On the other hand, the little boy acquires a different learning method which primarily involves: (a) defining the goal; (b) restructuring the field, and (c) abstracting principles.

The following hypotheses can be considered to follow from the above formulation:

(a)   The girl in the context of a close personal relationship with the mother is reinforced by appropriate rewards for signs that she is learning the mother-identification lesson. As a consequence, maintaining this rewarding relationship should acquire strong secondary drive characteristics. By generalization, the need for affiliation in other situations should also have strong secondary drive characteristics. Since the boy, on the other hand, receives his rewards for learning the appropriate principles of masculine role identification as they are abstracted from many contexts, the need for affiliation should not acquire much strength as a secondary drive. Consequently, females will tend to demonstrate greater need for affiliation than males.

(b)   The mother identification lesson does not require that the girl deviate from the *given,* but rather that she learn the lesson as presented. For boys, the problem of masculine role-identification must be solved through admonishings derived from many contexts serving as guides in defining the masculine role; he must restructure the field. *Consequently, females tend to be more dependent than males on the external context of a perceptual situation and hesitate to deviate from the given.*

(c)   In the process of solving the masculine role-identification problem, the male acquires a method of learning which should be applicable in solving other problems. The female learning method, on the other hand, is not well geared to problem solving. Consequently, it might be expected that males will surpass females at problem-solving skills.

(d)   The need for abstracting principles characteristic of the masculine learning method should generalize to other problems including the acquisition of moral standards. If one is very responsive to the moral standards of others, it is relatively unnecessary to internalize standards. If one, on the other hand, tends to learn moral standards by abstracting moral principles rather than being highly responsive to the standards of others, then one *does* need to internalize one's standards. Consequently, males will tend to be more concerned with internalized moral standards than females.

(e)   Conversely, since the girl learns the identification lesson through imitation without restructuring it, such a learning method should generalize to the acquisition of standards. Consequently, we might expect females to be more receptive to the standards of others than males.[1]

In general, the hypotheses that were generated by this theoretical formulation seem consistent with the data. Thus, by postulating a separate learning method for the two sexes as derived in the process of acquiring appropriate identification, one can formulate hypotheses which are consistent with very diverse findings ranging from the males' superior problem-solving skills to the females' greater need for affiliation.

Comments

1.   Lynn's formulations are based on the Woodworth–Schlosberg distinction between a learning *lesson* and a learning *problem:* With a problem to master, the learner must explore the situation and identify the goals, whereas in the case of the learning lesson the problem-solving phase is omitted, or at least minimized. The distinction in the present context has broad sociological and educational implications.

2.   The problem is somewhat complicated in the case of the young girl who attends nursery school and kindergarten (perhaps as a result of the mother's employment) and is then unable to rely so totally on imitation of a single person. The fact that parental identification is gradually replaced in part by identification with peers, teachers, etc. would also complicate the picture. This does not deny that early experiences may be more crucial than those occurring later.

3.   A more comprehensive and up-to-date version of Lynn's theoretical position is to be found in "The process of learning parental and sex-role identification," *J. Marr. Fam.,* 28: 466–70, 1966.

[1] The article marshals research evidence in support of these basic postulations.

George V. Sheviakov and Fritz Redl

Discipline for Today's Children and Youth *

Before You Go Back to Your Classroom—Remember This

We do not believe the tremendous issue of "discipline" can be taught in a few sententious words. However, an occasional guidepost is often a help to the hurried practitioner on the job. We would, therefore, like to end this rather detailed discussion in a somewhat untraditional way, by suggesting the following thoughts for the teacher who is stepping into a classroom after reading all this:

1. *Routine tricks aren't the whole show. You can't sew discipline together out of rags.* Often, especially when we get jittery or when nonunderstanding superiors or colleagues put the thumb-screws upon us for the wrong things, we develop undue admiration for the organizational "gadget." We develop the illusion that the gadget could do the trick for us, would save us thinking, planning, loving, and understanding. Well, it won't. If you overload your group atmosphere with the rattle of organizational machinery—try to have a "rule" for everything under the sun and another principle of revenge, if that rule is broken, for everything under the moon—you are just going to thwart your best efforts in the long run. Don't think you have to run around with your belt stuck full of guns and lollipops all the time, either. Rely a little more on yourself, your "person," and your sense of humor. It saves you lots of headaches and leads to disciplinary poise.

2. *The "mystery of personality" is good, when it works. But it is a poor excuse for failure.* This second statement is to keep you from falling into the opposite extreme after reading the first. While our personality—and the way we get it across to children—establishes most of what we call "respect" and "leadership," there is also the "everyday trifle"

* Adapted and abridged from Fritz Redl, "Part II. Before you go back to your classroom—remember this." George V. Sheviakov and Fritz Redl, *Discipline for Today's Children and Youth*. New revision by Sybil K. Richardson. Washington, D.C.: Association for Supervision and Curriculum Development, 1944 and 1956, pp. 62–64. Reprinted with permission of the Association for Supervision and Curriculum Development and the authors. Copyright © 1944 and 1956 by the Association for Supervision and Curriculum Development.

that is more easily settled through a rule or common agreement than by your magic gaze. Children have, although sometimes they are unconscious of it, considerable need for regularity and predictability in what is expected. If their *whole* life is dependent on the whims of your genius, little frictions begin to increase. So, don't extend your contempt for using routine tricks instead of personality into mistaken contempt for *any* planning and organization.

3. *Don't try to wash all your laundry with the same cake of soap.* Sometimes we discover two or three nice little tricks that work. Then we develop the delusion that, if we just keep on sticking to these tricks, the rest of the problems of life will dissolve. Well, it won't wash. Don't expect tricks to work under all circumstances and don't blame yourself or the children. Blame those tricks or, better, blame the way you translated them without enough planning.

Watch out when you begin to tell "anecdotes" of how this or that "always works," for these are the moments when mental petrification begins.

4. *Children are at least as complicated as a piece of wood.* So you had better find out about their texture, elasticity, and grain fiber before you apply your various tools and machinery upon them. Sometimes we want to get places fast and then we spoil the whole show by using too coarse an instrument. If you do that, don't blame it on the instrument but upon your incomplete analysis of your material.

5. *If you make a fool of yourself, why not be the first one to find out and have a good laugh about it?* The worst superstition about discipline is that "respect" and "leadership" melt as easily as a chocolate bar. It is not true. If they do, they never were "real" respect and leadership to begin with.

So don't be jittery for fear that you will "jeopardize" your dignity in the eyes of your youngsters if they find out you aren't the Archangel Michael after all. The fear of exposure to ridicule has caused more intangible discipline problems than anything else. There is a difference between the laughter you start and ridicule. Real, especially self-directed humor is the most disarming thing in the world with children that you could find.

6. *Don't develop suicidal fantasies, just because you aren't almighty after all.* There are limits to the power of the biggest magician among us as well as to the omnipotence of the most conscientious scientist. Every once in awhile we run up against those discoveries. If you do so, don't blame your youngsters because they can't be cured by you, nor blame yourself. The biggest hurdle in our work is time. It takes at least as many months of planful work to undo a wrong trait in a child as it took years of planful mishandling to build the wrong trait. But don't forget, many things can be started on the right track through long-range planning, though those same things can't be followed through to their final development. Don't be afraid of making mistakes. It isn't one particular mistake that produces

distorted children—it is the wrong way of reacting to the mistakes after we make them. And that is entirely in your power.

7. *What do you want to be, anyway, an educator, or an "angel with the flaming sword"?* It is upon your answer to this question that your decisions about discipline techniques will finally depend. For it requires one type of person to be the proud avenger of infantile wrongs and sins against defied "rules and regulations," and another to be the guide of human beings through the turmoil of growth. You have to make up your mind.

8. *Remember you're human, too.* Many of the understandings required of you as a teacher today come into conflict with values learned before you can remember. In our earliest years, we accept certain behaviors of adults toward children and of children toward adults as "right" and natural. These convictions were learned in close emotional relationship with our own parents and teachers and are painful to change. It is hard to be objective about the child who still exists within each of us. Perhaps you have already realized that not all parents are like yours and that each child must be helped to grow wholesomely in his world as it is. Then you are well on your way to the emotional maturity, the sense of perspective and the freedom from threat needed by leaders of today's children and youth.

That's What They Said

"A necessary condition for socialization in both the sense of social response and social control is learning that other people are necessary and that one should therefore modify his behavior in accordance with their needs and wishes as well as his own."

> Boyd R. McCandless. *Children and Adolescents: Behavior and Development.* New York: Holt, Rinehart and Winston, Inc., 1961. [315]

"The process of growing up is unlearning psychological subservience to authority and replacing it with rational acceptance of authority."

> Don Robinson. "Scraps from a teacher's notebook," *Phi Delta Kappan,* 44: 235, 1963.

". . . when the middle-class child begins to emerge into middle-class society, he discovers that his attempts to escape from guilt within the family involve him in guilt outside it. He is now expected to be purposeful, independent, and competitive. He is expected to 'do things,' to accomplish, perhaps to lead in some endeavor, like other children. . . . At first he felt guilty only if he failed to love and obey, . . . now, however, the god-monsters will be appeased only by a combination of submission in his role of child-in-family and assertiveness in his play group, school–pupil, and other roles enacted outside the home. An integration of these conflicting roles is impossible. . . . He is damned if he does and damned if he doesn't. He is embraced by a psychological Iron Maiden; any lunge forward or backward only impales him more securely on the spikes."

> Eric Larrabee. "Childhood in twentieth-century America," in Eli Ginzberg (ed.), *The Nation's Children.* 1960 White House Conference on Children and Youth. New York: Columbia University Press, 1960. [v. 3: 211]

"Democracy . . . cannot condone development of the individual at the expense of the group. Nor can democracy condone development of the group at the expense of the individual."

> Ruth Cunningham et al. *Understanding Group Behavior of Boys and Girls.* New York: Teacher's College, Columbia University, 1951. [211]

"The leader must be at the same time sufficiently like his constituents to relate to them and be accepted as one of them and different enough to be recognized as unique, and therefore qualified for leadership."

> Don Robinson. "Scraps from a teacher's notebook," *Phi Delta Kappan,* 45: 474, 1964.

"Education has long neglected the problem of what inhibitions should be developed and how they should be developed. The neglect is to a great extent a residual of the philosophy of education which emphasized the need for removal of the inhibiting factors in the environment of the child and the necessity for providing conditions in which the child could grow without the existence of resistive forces. We know today that this is a poor way to develop the characteristics that this philosophy stressed."

> Robert M. W. Travers. *Essentials of Learning.* New York: The Macmillan Company, 1963. [137]

"The authoritarian–democratic construct provides an inadequate conceptualization of leadership behavior."

> Richard C. Anderson. "Learning in discussions: A résumé of the authoritarian–democratic studies," *Harv. educ. Rev.,* 29: 201–215, 1959. [212]

"Yet in the normal course of events in this country it is safe to say that we have the choice of educating the people or exercising authority over them. Obviously the choice is not as simple as that, but we have shifted the emphasis, and are continuing to shift the emphasis, from exercising authority over people to educating all the people for self-discipline. We are assuming that man controls life surely as much as he must submit to it. And though we have not yet perfected the methods of educating all persons for responsible self-governing, we are not on that account going to give up the effort and return to the authoritarian philosophies."

> Don Robinson. "Scraps from a teacher's notebook," *Phi Delta Kappan,* 44: 389, 1963.

"The true measure of the value of 'discipline' is in the rapidity with which it renders itself unnecessary."

> Morris B. English. *Dynamics of Child Development.* New York: Holt, Rinehart and Winston, Inc., 1961. [92]

"One of the fundamental tenets of modern education is that an adequately motivated child disciplines himself, and that need for extraneous forms of discipline is evidence of failure to provide the kind of motivation needed for adequate performance."

> Henry Beaumont and F. G. Macomber. *Psychological Factors in Education.* New York: McGraw-Hill, Inc., 1949. [225]

"Troublemakers are trying in the only way they know to say that conditions are very unpleasant for them. . . . 'Getting after' such students merely increases the unpleasantness of the situation for them without removing any of its undesirable or frustrating elements."

> A. D. Woodruff. *The Psychology of Teaching.* London: Longmans, Green & Co., Ltd., 1951. [141]

"Many teachers are afraid that anarchy will erupt if they do not 'enforce' compliance. But countless difficulties result from such ill-advised efforts to press children into submission. Children become only more defiant, for their cooperation cannot be gained through humiliation and suppression. Without realizing it, the teacher then becomes more interested in her power and authority than in the welfare of the children. As soon as she becomes resentful, frustrated, annoyed, she stops being a leader and an educator and becomes just a fighting human being, fighting for her rights, her position, prestige, and superiority. No understanding of the situation and of herself is then possible; the teacher is in no condition to recognize the nature of her actions which may be responsible for the child's behavior."

> Rudolf Dreikurs. *Psychology in the Classroom.* New York: Harper & Row, Publishers, 1968. [8–9]

"Far from seeking a single model type of teacher, we recognize the advantages for school children of experiencing relationships with a diversity of teacher personalities as an important part of their psycho-social learning."

> Viola W. Bernard. "Teacher education in mental health," in Morris Krugman (ed.), *Orthopsychiatry in the School.* New York: American Orthopsychiatric Association, 1958. Pp. 184–203. [189]

CHAPTER 8

Test Items

1. The ultimate goal of social development is the promotion of
   a. enlightened self-interest
   b. social adequacy
   c. social conformity
   d. social responsibility
   e. social sensitivity

2. The key concept in socialization is
   a. compliance
   b. conformity
   c. coordination
   d. social responsibility
   e. social welfare

3. The primary determinant of individual differences in social development is probably
   a. glandular structure
   b. maturation of inherited predispositions
   c. motivational structure
   d. the self-concept
   e. social reinforcement

4. The agency most directly involved in the socialization of the child is
   a. the church (and other character-formation agencies)
   b. the home
   c. the larger community (including the news media, etc.)
   d. the peer culture
   e. the school

5. The role of the kindergarten is gradually shifting to an emphasis on
   a. acclimation to classroom routine
   b. cognitive and language development
   c. the correction of physical and nutritional deficiencies
   d. the promotion of emotional security
   e. social adjustment

6. The most significant benefit from nursery school is
   a. familiarity with academic routine

b. greater independence
c. improved self-expression, adaptability, and initiative
d. improved sociability
e. increased emotional security

7. The nursery school serves its primary function by providing
    a. emotional security to children from inadequate homes
    b. experience in social give-and-take
    c. readiness for later school success
    d. relief to the mother
    e. remediation for the ills of bad upbringing

8. The most acceptable statement of the research evidence as to the effects of kindergarten experience is that
    a. its effects are inconclusive because of failure in experimental control
    b. it facilitates entry into first grade
    c. it has distinct across-the-board beneficial effects
    d. it has limited effect on social adjustment
    e. it promotes the linguistic development of the culturally disadvantaged

9. The current emphasis on Head Start programs of preschool education is predicated upon
    a. empirical evidence of effectiveness in promoting school adjustment
    b. deductions from accepted theories of learning
    c. evidence of success in promoting basic security and socialization among lower-class children
    d. inference from related animal studies of the effects of early sensory deprivation
    e. substantial empirical evidence of its effectiveness regarding later academic success

10. The major contribution of the peer group to the socialization of the child is that
    a. it defines acceptable social behavior
    b. it encourages the development of strong loyalties
    c. it encourages social sensitivity
    d. it promotes the ability to conform
    e. it provides security necessary for effective exploration of the world

11. What effect does insecurity tend to have on peer-group interrelation-ships?
    a. It interferes with the attainment of group goals.
    b. It leads to the break-up of the group.
    c. It leads to hostility and rebellion.
    d. It makes for strong intermember ties.
    e. It promotes undue loss of individuality and initiative.

12. The relative stability of social orientation is primarily a function of
    a. one's in-built glandular structure
    b. the consistency of the social reinforcement structure
    c. the corresponding stability of the environment
    d. the general momentum generated by any on-going process
    e. the reciprocal effects between individual and his environment

13. The advent of puberty is of special importance because of
    a. its attending physiological changes
    b. its pervasive effects on the self-concept
    c. its relationship to the attainment of sexual maturity
    d. the sex differential in age of occurrence
    e. society's recognition of puberty as the beginning of adulthood

14. The choice of friends rests primarily on
    a. convenience (availability of a car, etc.)
    b. geographic proximity
    c. mutual need satisfaction
    d. similarity in age, socio-economic status, etc.
    e. similarity in interest

15. The basic element of the group for maximum effectiveness and benefit to its members is
    a. cohesiveness
    b. compatibility
    c. effective communication
    d. a sense of purpose
    e. strong leadership

16. The popularity of an idol tends to be based on
    a. his social sensitivity
    b. his social status
    c. his superiority in certain valued assets, e. g., good looks
    d. his symbolic value for need satisfaction
    e. his understanding of group psychology

17. Probably the best guarantee of adequate development of sympathy
    in children is
    a. emotional security
    b. experience with tragedy
    c. freedom from repressed hostility
    d. reinforcement of sympathetic behavior
    e. systematic emphasis on the need to be considerate

18. Psychologists look on negativism as
    a. evidence of failure in socialization
    b. a form of emotional immaturity
    c. a manifestation of repressed hostility
    d. a manifestation of social ineptness
    e. a natural phase of development

19. Quarreling among siblings is best seen as
    a. a natural aspect of social interaction
    b. evidence of incompatibility
    c. part of the process of learning to meet the outside world
    d. the result of faulty early child-rearing practices
    e. a symptom of maladjustment

20. The effectiveness of democratic group processes as a method of
    classroom operations is primarily a function of
    a. the competence of the teacher in group techniques
    b. the congruence of the overall classroom atmosphere with demo-
        cratic principles
    c. the diversity and adequacy of the talents to be found in the group
    d. the way the school defines its role and its function
    e. our views on the competition/cooperation issue

21. Leadership is determined primarily by
    a. flexibility, chameleon-like ability to espouse popular causes
    b. followership and follower needs
    c. skill in manipulating people
    d. social sensitivity
    e. superiority in relevant assets

22. The leader's primary task is that of
    a. acting as a sounding board for the ideas of the group
    b. acting as a spokesman for the group
    c. clarifying the goals toward which the group is to strive
    d. directing the efforts of the group toward worthwhile goals
    e. facilitating the process by which each member can make his
        maximum contribution

23. The Lewin et al. study of group climate has shown that
    a. an authoritarian classroom climate tends to provide the greatest security
    b. a democratic classroom organization tends to maintain group tension at an optimal level
    c. a democratic classroom organization tends to produce the highest level of productivity
    d. a laissez-faire classroom atmosphere tends to promote creativity and initiative
    e. none of the above is necessarily true: The results are only suggestive as far as the classroom operation is concerned

24. The major difficulty in applying the results of research on group dynamics to the classroom is that
    a. the average teacher has had only limited leadership training
    b. the classroom group has limited freedom in selecting its goals
    c. the classroom is not a "group" in the true sense of the word
    d. much of the curriculum does not lend itself to group procedures
    e. research findings were not based on group size of 30

25. The best way to "rehabilitate" the isolate is for the teacher
    a. to allocate him/her to a compatible group
    b. to encourage one of the stars to adopt him/her
    c. to help him/her increase his/her acceptability by eliminating obnoxious traits
    d. to increase his/her ability to contribute by helping him/her develop skills
    e. to provide acceptance and security while the isolate finds his/her way

26. The result of the Anderson et al. study suggests that
    a. authoritarian leadership destroys initiative
    b. children profit more from firm teacher direction
    c. domination incites resistance
    d. a permissive atmosphere is conducive to "horseplay"
    e. ultrademocratic classroom procedures are generally anxiety-producing

27. Group work leads to increased per-capita productivity
    a. when members have strong competitive tendencies
    b. whenever group talents supplement one another
    c. whenever meaningful goals are involved
    d. when there is a strong emphasis on consensus
    e. rarely, if ever

28. The effect the group has on the personality development of its members depends on
    a. the adequacy of the leader as a leader
    b. the effectiveness of the group's program of self-improvement
    c. the group climate
    d. the security the group provides for each member
    e. its success in achieving individual and group goals

29. Teachers are most likely to underrate the sociometric status of pupils who are
    a. academically disinterested and unwilling to abide by classroom regulations
    b. highly responsive to adult direction
    c. members of a small well-knit clique
    d. of lower socio-economic status
    e. prominent in school activities

30. Discipline is best approached from the standpoint of
    a. behavior control
    b. character formation
    c. effective social interaction
    d. social conformity
    e. social sensitivity

31. The key to the development of effective discipline is
    a. consistency in reinforcement
    b. conversion of appropriate behavior to the habit level
    c. freedom to experiment with misbehavior
    d. permissiveness within the context of emotional security
    e. a system of well-defined but gradually expanding freedom

32. The goal of effective discipline is
    a. conformity to social expectations
    b. effective self-direction
    c. a sense of personal and social responsibility
    d. inhibition of misbehavior
    e. sensitivity to the consequences of one's behavior

33. The best way to present discipline to children is as a set of
    a. arbitrary conventions based on tradition
    b. group-imposed standards of conduct
    c. mutual agreements essential for social interaction
    d. regulations existing in their own right
    e. well-recognized taboos

34. Misbehavior is best seen as
    a. an attempt at establishing what is and what is not acceptable
    b. an attempt to satisfy one's needs
    c. a manifestation of an inborn tendency toward evil
    d. a reaction against society's attempt at socialization
    e. a symptom of deeper personality difficulty

35. The school's primary task in the area of discipline is
    a. to deter misbehavior
    b. to prevent misbehavior from becoming habitual
    c. to prevent misbehavior from interfering with the attainment of
        the schools' objectives
    d. to promote positive behavior
    e. to provide suitable outlets for the release of tension

36. In dealing with misbehavior, the teacher's approach should be
    a. consistent and systematic
    b. diagnostic
    c. firm but not punitive
    d. indulgent
    e. retributive

37. The most effective weapon against wholesale misbehavior in the
    classroom is
    a. a considerate and respected teacher
    b. an effective and challenging curriculum
    c. an effective student government assuming responsibility for
        discipline
    d. firm discipline-oriented teachers
    e. a permissive and supportive classroom climate

38. The present consensus concerning the effectiveness of punishment
    as a disciplinary measure is that
    a. punishment can be effective but it tends to destroy interpersonal
        relationships
    b. punishment deters misbehavior by forcing a change in basic
        motivation
    c. punishment has strong deterring effects but can be harmful
        to personality development
    d. punishment is always harmful in that it interferes with iden-
        tification and conscience development
    e. punishment tends to inhibit misbehavior so that acceptable be-
        havior occurring as a substitute can be reinforced

39. Probably the greatest single contributor to pupil misbehavior in the classroom is
    a. failure to understand the true purposes of discipline
    b. the lack of a constructive and meaningful program
    c. poor personality on the part of the teacher
    d. teacher incompetence
    e. teacher's lack of understanding of children and their needs

40. Social maturity is best defined in terms of
    a. contribution to group goals
    b. enlightened self-interest
    c. relative freedom from subservience to the group
    d. a sense of social responsibility and service
    e. social sophistication

41. The school's greatest asset in the task of promoting social maturity is
    a. its dedication to the survival and promotion of social values
    b. its organization as a miniature social group
    c. its orientation toward the solution of social problems
    d. the life lessons incorporated in its curriculum
    e. its very existence as a major agency of the social order

CHAPTER 9

Intellectual Development

Intelligence, as the component of growth and development with which the school is most directly concerned, is best seen as an aspect of readiness which, like its other components, develops through experience and is subject to the same influences and restrictions, no more, no less. This constitutes a drastic shift in our views on the subject from a strong belief in intelligence as an innate, relatively immutable capacity which, barring drastic environmental deprivation, more or less came up to preset levels to one of intelligence as a form of overall readiness developed through experience. This modern view, as expounded by Combs, Hunt, and Wesman in the articles that follow, simply places intelligence in the context of accumulated learnings providing the basis for effective, i. e., "intelligent," behavior in broad areas of environmental demands. The emphasis is on the basic concepts of *learning* (readiness, experience, perception, learning sets, problem solving, etc.) with nonintellectual factors such as motivation, intellectual curiosity, openness to experience, etc. playing their usual role. In a sense, this constitutes one of the greatest operational principles in recent years—that intelligence is fundamentally a function of learning. There is not complete agreement on this point, of course. British psychologists (e.g., Burt, Vernon, and others), perhaps reflecting the more class-conscious British social structure, maintain a much stronger orientation toward its biologically innate nature. More recently, Jensen of Berkeley, in a much-discussed article, has also questioned the current environmental emphasis.

Actually, the issue is of more than simple academic interest: it makes a difference whether we believe intelligence is inherited, never to be changed, or if, on the other hand, we believe it is primarily the product of experience. In a sense, the British system of providing different educational opportunities to its pupils on the basis of ability and America's current emphasis on Head Start experience highlight the contrast.

Hereditary limitations undoubtedly still exist, and certainly learning theorists have always been concerned with the nature of the organism doing the learning. But it now seems clear that educators and psychologists have been far too prone to blame inherited deficiencies for learning difficulties and poor test performance that are more correctly a reflection of a lack of *readiness* in the usual sense—perhaps due to inadequacies in previous learning. Even today, many teachers still see the IQ as an indicator of innate potential and, to make matters worse, use this false conception of ability as the basis for irreversible decisions about youngsters, and to excuse themselves from having to teach children who, despite arguments to the contrary, can learn.

The articles selected for this chapter are classics in the field. They include (a) Guilford's well-known article on the structure of the human intellect; (b) thoughtful papers on the development of intelligence as the product of experience by Combs, Hunt, and Wesman; (c) a forceful defense of the traditional IQ by McNemar; and (d) a speculative interpretation of the relationship between IQ changes and certain nonintellective personality variables by Kagan et al. These papers present a broad picture of the current psychological thinking on this important subject; they should be evaluated in conjunction with the articles in the previous section on growth and development.

Reference

Jensen, Arthur R. "How much can we boost IQ and scholastic achievement?" *Harv. educ. Rev.*, 39: 1–123, 1969.

J. P. Guilford

Three Faces of Intellect *

Our understanding of the components of the human intellect has evolved in the past 25 years largely as the outcome of the earlier work of Thurstone, the wartime research of the Air Force, and more recently, the Aptitude Project at the University of Southern California. Whereas the latter's findings pertaining to creativity have received the greatest attention, to me its most significant contribution has been the development of a unified theory of the human intellect capable of ordering intellectual abilities into unitary structure.

Factor analysis suggests that the various human abilities can be conceptualized according to a three-way classification involving (a) processes or operations performed (e.g., memory, divergent thinking, etc.); (b) materials or contents involved (e.g., figural, symbolic, semantic, or behavioral); and (c) products generated through the application of certain operations upon certain contents. This arrangement can be represented by a 5 x 6 x 4 three-dimensional solid model, comprising 120 cells (see Figure 1), each identifying a special ability defined in terms of a specific operation, content, and product. These can be discussed one layer at a time.

The Cognitive Abilities

The cognitive abilities interacting with contents and the six products provide 18 cells or unique abilities, 15 of which have already been identified.

(a)   The figural-units cell represents the ability to recognize familiar objects in silhouette form, some of the parts of which may be masked out to make the test more difficult. The cell also covers auditory figures (as in the recognition of melodies) and kinesthetic forms.

(b)   The symbolic-units cell represents the ability to identify the vowels missing from P–W–R or to rearrange the letters to make a word out of R A C I H.

(c)   Cognition at the units level is best represented by the well-known verbal comprehension as generally measured through a vocabulary test.

* Adapted and abridged from J. P. Guilford, "Three faces of intellect," *Amer. Psychol.*, 14, 469–479, 1959. Copyright 1959 by American Psychological Association and reprinted by permission.

FIGURE 1
A Cubical Model Representing the Structure of Intellect

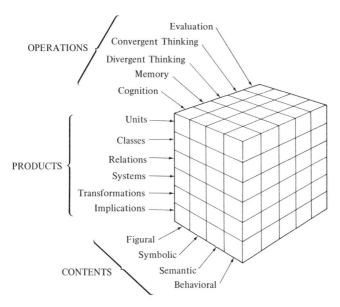

The Memory Abilities

This area has been somewhat less explored so that only seven of the possible 18 cells are now occupied. The memory factors represented by the symbolic-units cell can be measured through memory span for numbers or letters; memory for ideas in a paragraph would fall in the memory-semantic units category.

The Divergent-thinking Abilities

These call for a variety of responses in which the product is not completely controlled by the information given. The ability to list words beginning with the letter "s" or words ending in "tion" would represent divergent production at the symbolic-units level. Ideational fluency would fall in the divergent thinking–semantic-units category.

(a)   Divergent production of class ideas would reflect spontaneous flexibility, a typical test of which might ask the examinee to list all the uses he can think of for a common brick. If he simply lists building a house, a barn, a garage, etc., he would display ideational fluency but little spontaneous flexibility since all of his uses are in the same class. Making a door stop or a paper weight, drowning a cat, driving a nail, etc. would, on the other hand, suggest greater ideational flexibility.

(b)   Divergent thinking at the level of transformations provides a number of interesting factors. In the figural column lies adaptive flexibil-

ity as might be tested through the Match-Problem test in which the examinee is told to take away a given number of matches to leave a certain number of squares with nothing left over. At the semantic level is the factor of
originality as might be involved in asking the examinee to come up with
novel, unusual, clever, or far-fetched ideas. In the Plot-Titles test, a short
story is presented and the examinee is asked to list as many appropriate ti-
tles as he can to head the story. Another test of originality might call for
writing punch lines for cartoons.

Convergent Production Abilities

Twelve of the eighteen convergent-production abilities presented by
the model have already been identified. Convergent productions having
to do with relationships would include the deduction of correlates as might
be required in items calling for completion rather than a choice among
alternatives, e.g., pots, stop; bard, drab; rats, __?__. Convergent production
of implications is represented by the ability to draw conclusions from given
information, e.g., Form Reasoning in the figural column, or logical deductions in the semantic column, e.g., Charles is younger than Robert; Charles
is older than Frank; who is older: Robert or Frank?

Evaluative Abilities

Evaluation calls for reaching a decision as to the accuracy, suitability,
or adequacy of information. In the figural column of the evaluation-units
category is the factor of perceptual speed. Sensitivity to problems would
represent evaluative ability having to do with implications.

Some Implications of the Structure of Intellect

For Psychological Theory

Clarification of the nature and structure of the human intellect facilitates the understanding of individuals as functioning organisms; the five
kinds of intellectual abilities in terms of operations represent five different
ways of functioning. Intellectual abilities classified according to varieties of
intellectual contents and of products represent a classification of the basic
kinds of knowledge. This way of looking at the human intellect presents a
view of the organism as an agency for dealing with information of various
kinds in various ways, a view which is likely to be productive in future investigations of learning, memory, problem solving, invention, and decision
making.

For Vocational Testing

"With about 50 intellectual factors already known, we may say that
there are 50 ways of being 'intelligent.' It has been facetiously suggested
that there seem to be a great many more ways of being stupid, unfortu-

nately. The structure of intellect is a theoretical model that predicts as many as 120 distinct abilities, if every cell of the model contains a factor. Already we know that two cells contain two or more factors each, and there probably are actually other cells of this type. Since the model was first conceived, 12 factors predicted by it have found places in it. There is consequently hope of filling many of the other vacancies, and we may eventually end up with more than 120 abilities" [p. 477]. This implies that the appraisal of the individual's intellectual resources calls for a large number of scores although, inasmuch as some factors are intercorrelated, we may be able to cover the important abilities with a more limited number of tests. At any rate, a multiscore approach to the assessment of intelligence is clearly indicated for the purpose of vocational guidance.

Classification of the different kinds of ability according to content suggests four kinds of intelligence. Ability to deal with figural content may be considered a form of "concrete" intelligence as might be basic for mechanics, engineers, artists, and musicians. Abilities in the area of symbolic and semantic content represent two kinds of "abstract" intelligence; language and mathematics would depend upon symbolic ability while the understanding of verbal concepts might rely on semantic intelligence. The behavioral column suggests 30 abilities in the area of "social" intelligence, some having to do with understanding, some with productive thinking about behavior, and others with the evaluation of behavior. These abilities are of primary importance for people who have to deal with others, e. g., teachers, social workers, politicians, etc.

For Education

Such a model has major implications for education. It leads us to see the learner as the agent for dealing with information, along the lines of a computer in which we feed information to be stored for later use in generating new information; it also presents a concept of learning as discovery of information rather than simply the formation of S–R connections.

Although we do not know the relative influence of heredity and environment in the development of the various components of the human intellect, the best position for educators to take is that possibly every factor can be developed to some extent through experience and that the development of each factor provides a goal for which to strive. Our task lies in the choice of curricula and teaching methods that will best promote this development as defined by the content, operation, and product involved. The perspective provided by the model puts us in a good position to see what abilities, if any, are being neglected in education; it is being recognized, for example, that we have not been too successful in producing creative individuals. Apparently we need a better balance in emphasis between divergent and convergent (critical) thinking.

This particular structure of the intellect may or may not stand the test of time; even if the general form persists, there will probably be need for some modifications. Meanwhile, the multiplicity of intellectual abilities seems well established. "There are many individuals who long for the good old days of simplicity when we got along with one unanalyzed intelligence. Simplicity certainly has its appeal. But human nature is exceedingly complex, and we may as well face that fact. . . . Humanity's peaceful pursuit of happiness depends upon our control of nature and of our own behavior; and this, in turn, depends upon understanding ourselves, including our intellectual resources" [p. 479].

Comments

1. This is undoubtedly one of the major contributions to the understanding of human intelligence since Thurstone's postulation of primary mental abilities, of which it can be considered a refinement and an extension. In a sense, it constitutes a model along the lines of the periodic table for ordering and identifying the elements; not only does it permit the classification of intellectual abilities already known, but it structures research into the discovery of other factors. The original should be consulted for further details; a more complete and up-to-date report is to be found in Guilford (1967).

2. The present model constitutes a different way of looking at intelligence which is bound to have major implications for psychological and educational practice. Its full implementation will, of course, have to await the development of more of the necessary measuring instruments, no easy task if we are to judge from recent criticism of creativity (divergent thinking) as a unitary trait (see Thorndike, 1963). More fundamentally, we must bear in mind that this model is simply a *way* of conceptualizing intelligence, that these abilities are not entities, but simply descriptive categories (see Wesman, 1968, pp. 223–227).

References

Guilford, J. P. *The Nature of Intelligence*. New York: McGraw-Hill, Inc., 1967.

Jensen, Arthur R. "How much can we boost I.Q. and scholastic achievement?" *Harv. educ. Rev.*, 39: 1–123, 1969.

Thorndike, Robert L. "Measurement of creativity," *T. C. Rec.*, 64: 422–424, 1963.

Arthur W. Combs

Intelligence from a Perceptual Point of View *

If, by intelligence, we refer to the effectiveness of one's behavior and if, further, we see behavior as dependent on perception, then intelligence is simply a function of the adequacy of one's perceptions of the events of his phenomenal field at the time of behavior. If one's perceptions are vague and ill-defined, his behavior will be correspondingly vague and ineffective. Intelligence, then, becomes a function of the factors that limit the scope and clarity of one's phenomenal field.

A distinction must be made between *potential* and *functional* perceptions, the former referring to perceptions which exist in the individual's field of awareness and which *could* but do not necessarily occur. While this potential intelligence may be of interest in judging human capacity, what we measure are the subject's functional perceptions, i. e., the differentiations he actually makes when confronted with the necessity to do so. To the extent that intelligence is a function of the richness and variety of perceptions possible to him at a given moment, there is need for us to be concerned with the factors that limit the individual's perceptions from what he could perceive to what he actually does perceive at the given moment of behaving.

Some Factors Limiting Perception

Physiological Limitations

The differentiations possible in the individual's phenomenological field are affected by prenatal anomalies, impairment of sense modalities, and even chronic fatigue and malnutrition, all of which impair his ability to make adequate perceptions—although here we must recognize that the perceptions of the "handicapped" may be simply different, rather than necessarily poorer than ours.

Environmental Opportunity as a Limitation

Differentiations of one's phenomenological field are also affected by opportunities for actual or symbolic perception. Certainly the Eskimo

* Adapted and abridged from Arthur W. Combs, "Intelligence from a perceptual point of view," *J. abnorm. soc. Psychol.,* 47:662–673, 1952. Copyright 1952 by American Psychological Association and reproduced by permission.

would be limited in his understanding of *banana* just as the African bush-man would have difficulty with *snow*. Problems of this kind exist in connection with appraising the intellectual status of culturally disadvantaged groups, for example. The individual in a particular culture perceives those aspects of his environment that, from his point of view, he needs to perceive in order to maintain and enhance his self in the world in which he lives.

Time as a Limitation

Exposure to a given event must be long enough to make differentiation possible. In fact, the richness of one's perceptions is partially a function of how long he has contact with a given experience. However, being confronted with a given experience is not the equivalent of having had *contact* with it. The child exposed to a curriculum day by day may actually have very little experience with it; to the extent that perceptions are a function of previous differentiations, he cannot grasp multiplication until he has perceived addition. All this takes time.

"In this sense, intelligence . . . is continually increasing as long as the individual remains alive and operating. That intelligence seems to level off at age sixteen or later is probably a mere artifact of our methods of observation. So long as the individual remains at school we have at least a modicum of comparable experience which can be tested in different persons. After the school years, when individuals are free to go their separate ways, this modicum of comparable experience rapidly disappears. The older one gets, the more diverse is his experience. Intelligence tests based on comparability of experience may thus fail to evaluate properly the effectiveness of adults" [pp. 665–666].

The Individual's Goals and Values as Limiting Factors

"From a phenomenological view, the individual is forever engaged in a ceaseless attempt to achieve satisfaction of his needs through the goals and values he has differentiated as leading to that end. These goals and values may by explicit or implicit, simple or complex, but they are always unique to the personality itself. . . . The individual's goals may be either positive or negative. That is, in the course of his experience, the person may differentiate some things as matters to be sought, while other things may be differentiated as matters to be avoided" [p. 666].

The individual's goals and values have an important effect on the perceptions he makes. The experiences of the child who values schooling are far different from those of the child who tries to avoid school at all cost. "If the fundamental thesis of this paper is accurate, that intelligence is a function of the variety and richness of the perceptive field, then the individual's goals must have a most important effect upon intelligence" [p. 666]. But, inasmuch as individual goals have an equal effect on the constructor of intelligence tests, we are faced with "the very confusing situation wherein the test constructor with one organization of goals perceives certain experiences to be marks of intelligence for another person who may or may not have similar goals" [p. 666]. Consequently, low scores may simply reflect a divergence in perceptual field between examinee and examiner.

Cultural Effects of Goals as Limitation

The goals that determine one's perceptual field are themselves the result of previous experience and are thus deeply affected by cultural factors. Cultures both restrict and encourage the formulation of goals. Indeed, the selective effects of the culture pretty well determine the goals the individual seeks and those he avoids. To the extent that these goals, in turn, exert important effects on perceptions that become part of his later perceptive field, it may be that the child of low apparent intelligence is not so much the product of an unfortunate heredity as an unfortunate constellation of goals and values.

The Self-Concept as a Limitation

The individual's self-concept plays a vital role in the selection of the perceptions which become part of his perceptual field, and thus, in the "intelligence" of one's behavior. Certainly the child who has a concept of himself as "unable to read" is going to be relatively stupid as far as reading is concerned. More important, the self-concept corroborates and perpetuates itself in the behavior it tends to promote.

"Every clinician has had experience with children of ability who conceive of themselves as unable, unliked, unwanted, or unacceptable and perceive and behave in accordance with their perceptions. And this effect is not limited to children alone. It seems to me one of the great tragedies of our society that millions of people in our society perceiving themselves able to produce only X amount, behave in these terms. Society, in turn, evaluates them in terms of this behavior and so lends proof to what they have already conceived. Compared to this waste of human potential in our society, our losses in automobile accidents seem like a mere drop in the bucket. It is even conceivable in these terms that we create losses in intelligence. If, in our schools, we teach a child that he is unable and if he believes us and behaves in these terms, we need not be surprised when we test his intelligence to discover that he produces at the level at which we taught him" [p. 668]!

Psychology has perhaps unwittingly contributed to the situation by emphasizing the static conception of intelligence and human capacity. To the extent that we believe that the child's capacities are comparatively fixed, we may be in large measure determining the child's intellectual level by the circular effect of our behavior on his self-concept.

Threat as a Limiting Factor

When he feels threatened, the individual tends to narrow his perceptive field to the threatening object in a condition generally known as "tunnel vision," particularly evident in moments of crisis. In fact, not only does threat reduce the possibility of a broader range of perception but it also causes him to cling to the perceptions he already has, i. e., he develops perceptual and behavioral rigidity—and often stupidity.

"If the conception of intelligence we have been discussing . . . should prove accurate, it seems to me to raise serious questions about some of our common assumptions with respect to intelligence and, at the same time, opens some exciting new possibilities for the treatment or education of persons we have often assumed to be beyond help. It implies that our conception of the limiting factors of intelligence may be too narrow" [p. 670]. This is not to deny the existence of physiologic limits in intelligence; we can demonstrate limitations in mongolism and other conditions of abnormality but we do not have similar evidence of limitations in the capacity of "normal" individuals. "Until it can be definitely established that limitations exist as biological functions, our task as psychologists is to assume that they may just as well be social or psychological in character and to work just as hard exploring the matter in our discipline as we expect the biologist to work in his" [p. 670].

Some Implications

Also in need of careful scrutiny is the area of intelligence testing. If intelligent behavior is a function of the variety and richness of one's perceptions, we need be sure that our tests of "intelligence" represent a proper sampling of the perceptual field. "Is the delinquent, with rich and varied perceptions on how to elude the police, less intelligent or has he simply not perceived things society wishes he had" [p. 671]? On what basis can we justify developing a test of intelligence geared to middle-class need structure? "Can we blame the machinist for his lack of perceptions about foreign affairs without asking the diplomat to be equally skilled in the machinist's field of perceptions" [p. 671]?

If intelligence does indeed depend on one's perceptions, we need to provide the individual with opportunities for the required perceptions to occur. Our task may be to free the individual from the restraints precluding his perceptions. Simply providing the child with the opportunity for certain experiences is not enough. "Has the child in school who is so worried about his relationships with his peers that he cannot perceive what his book is saying truly been provided an opportunity to perceive" [p. 672]? We also need to consider the extent to which satisfying the individual's most pressing needs might result in the systematic release of his perceptions. We attend to the satisfaction of the child's biological needs: Should his psychological needs be any less pressing or important? Satisfying the child's needs for love and affection, prestige, etc. might enable us to dispense with frantic efforts to motivate him or to blame him for not being motivated. We also need to create in the child needs, goals, and values from which rich perceptions can be expected to emerge. It is especially important that we provide children with a positive self-concept. "What differences in the richness and variety of perception might result from a generation of people with an 'I can' rather than 'I can't' conception of themselves" [p. 672]? We have not yet begun to scratch the surface in producing more adequate perceptions—and thus more adequate behavior —through a systematic effort at producing more adequate self-concepts. We particularly need to remove threat if we are to release the individual's ability to perceive more adequately.

Comments

1.   The phenomenological view of intelligence, as presented by Combs, relates directly to the degree of functionality of one's behavior. His discussion of the ways in which the individual's perceptual field and hence his intelligence can be improved is particularly challenging. Of interest in this connection is the Dollard and Miller (1950) thesis that the neurotic person is a stupid person, not so much that he lacks "intelligence" in the traditional sense, but rather that his neurosis so restricts his perceptual field that he cannot cope effectively with environmental demands.

2.   The view of behavior as a function of one's perceptions is important from the standpoint of both intelligence and adjustment. The central theme here is that nothing but short-sighted behavior can come from short-sighted perceptions and that the individual's behavior will improve only as his perceptions improve. Combs' discussion of the impediments to effective perception—and thus, to intelligent behavior—is interesting in the light of the more recent statements on the development of intelligence. (See Hunt, Wesman, and others, pp. 216–227, this text.) A comparative analysis of these different positions should prove a profitable exercise.

Reference

Dollard, John, and Neal F. Miller. *Personality and Psychotherapy*. New York: McGraw-Hill, Inc., 1950.

J. McV. Hunt

How Children Develop Intellectually *

The task of maximizing the intellectual potential of our children has acquired new urgency. Two of the top challenges of our day lie behind this urgency. First, the rapidly expanding role of technology decreases opportunity for persons of limited competence and skills, while it increases opportunity for those competent in written language, in mathematics, and problem solving. Second, the challenge of eliminating racial discrimination requires not only equality of employment opportunity and social recognition for persons of equal competence but also an equalization of the opportunity to develop the intellectual capacity and skill upon which competence is based.

Until recently, any idea of increasing intellectual capacity was considered unrealistic. Recent changes in the conception of the nature of man have now introduced the possibility that we might counteract some of the worst effects of cultural deprivation and raise substantially the average level of intellectual capacity. The present article discusses the nature, rationale, and implications of these changing concepts.

Changing Beliefs

Fixed Intelligence

The notion of fixed intelligence goes back to Darwin and his emphasis on heredity; his position, that the improvement of man lay not in education but in the selection of superior parents, became the theme of early American psychologists, including the leaders of the intelligence testing movement. This emphasis reflected a strong belief in the constancy of the IQ: when longitudinal studies showed only low correlation between IQ at the preschool level and age 18, the inconsistency was sloughed off by pointing to the limited validity of infant tests.

Predetermined Development

Underlying the concept of fixed intelligence was the principle of predeterminism, the view that development is predetermined by heredity; G. Stanley Hall, for example, held that each behavior pattern displayed by

* Reproduced from CHILDREN, May–June 1964 with permission from the U.S. Department of Health, Education, and Welfare, Children's Bureau.

the child is simply a natural stage with which no one should interfere. The work of Gesell was largely predicated on similar hereditary premises. The theory of predetermined development got support from research findings (e.g., Coghill, Carmichael, etc.) showing, for example, that maturation was alone sufficient for salamanders to swim. There was discordant evidence, of course; chicks kept in the dark for 20 days after hatching were no longer able to learn how to peck effectively. Furthermore, it appears that infantile experience becomes progressively more important as we move upward on the phylogenetic scale.

Static Brain Function

Early S–R psychologists (e.g., Thorndike) used the telephone as a mechanical model of the brain's operation: the brain operated like a static switchboard through which a given stimulus could be connected to a variety of responses. Research produced evidence suggesting a more active role in the brain and we now see the computer as a more adequate model of brain functioning. Furthermore, differences in the relative proportion of the brain connected with incoming and outgoing fibers in lower and higher animals indicate an anatomic basis for the role of early experiences in development; evidence suggests that the chemical factors incorporated in the genes may have more complete control in lower animals (e.g., salamanders, frogs, etc. which provided most of the evidence supporting the belief in predetermined development) than they have in species higher up on the phylogenic scale.

Motivation by Need, Pain, and Sex

Our concept of motivation is also undergoing change. Until recently, it was assumed that behavior was motivated by painful stimulation, homeostatic need, or by sexual appetite, or by acquired motives based thereon. The operation of these needs is still accepted. But the claim that *all* behavior is so motivated would imply that, in the absence of such needs, the organism would become quiescent. Observation denies this assumption: Children play in the absence of such motivation; animals explore, manipulate, etc. There is apparently some additional basis for motivation.

Reflex Versus Feedback

There has also been a change in our conception of the nervous system from the reflex arc as the functional unit to the feedback loop; the fact that the neural activity which results when cats are exposed to a given stimulus is markedly affected when they are simultaneously exposed to the sight of a mouse reflects the influence of feedback in sensory input.

Incongruity as Motivation

The feedback loop (as the new conceptual unit of neural function) supplies the basis for a new motivational mechanism. This feedback loop, which Miller et al. have called the Test-Operate-Test-Exist (TOTE) unit, operates like a room thermostat. Having been set at a given temperature, the thermostat is continually testing the room against this standard: if the temperature falls below the standard, the test registers incongruity which starts the furnace. If the test yields congruity with the standard, the furnace stops and the system exists. A similar pattern of operation can be ascribed to living organisms, although several classes of operating standards (rather than a single standard) are likely to exist. Not only does incongruity with these standards instigate action, but there also seems to be an optimum level of incongruity: too little produces boredom, too much causes stress. While this optimum of incongruity is still not well understood, it seems to involve the matching of incoming information with standards based on information already coded and stored within the cerebrum. This optimum is probably an individual matter but the search for this optimum apparently explains "growth motivation" postulated by Froebel and Dewey as the basic motivation underlying the quest for knowledge.

Emotional versus Cognitive Experience

Another fundamental change in our outlook is with respect to the importance attributed to early preverbal experience. Traditionally, in keeping with the prevailing concept of predetermined development, infantile experiences were considered largely irrelevant. Freud saw the importance of preverbal experience but from an emotional rather than a cognitive point of view. It now appears that the opposite may possibly be more nearly true. Rats subjected to early traumatic experiences actually tend to develop a sort of immunity to such experiences; children from the lower classes who have frequently experienced painful stimulation tend to be less fearful than middle-class children who have more rarely experienced pain. By contrast, experiments based on Hebb's theory have consistently demonstrated the importance of early perceptual and cognitive experience. In the early phases of development, the variety of circumstances encountered appears to be most important; later, the responsiveness of the environment to the infant's activities appears to be central; and still later, the opportunity to understand the causation of various mechanical and social relationships seems most significant.

Motor Output and Receptor Input

Another traditional belief about psychological development that may have to be changed concerns the relative importance of motor response and receptor input in the development of the autonomous central processes mediating intellectual capacity. Early psychologists emphasized perceptual input but, in keeping with the static brain concept of the post–WWI era, emphasis shifted to response output. This is now being questioned.

Counteracting Cultural Deprivation

The intellectual inferiority of children from homes of lower educational and socio-economic status is already evident by the time they begin kindergarten. These children are apt to have various linguistic liabilities: limited vocabularies, poor articulation, and syntactical deficiencies that are revealed in a tendency to reply in unusually short sentences with faulty grammar. They also display perceptual deficiencies and, perhaps more important, they tend to have fewer interests than their middle-class counterparts. These deficiencies make for a poor start in scholastic competition. As long as intelligence was assumed to be fixed and development predetermined, the intellectual inferiority of these children had simply to be accepted; now with the previously mentioned changes in our conception of intellectual development, there is hope.

Clues from Intrinsic Motivation

Piaget's work suggests three stages in the development of intrinsic motivation. In the first stage, the infant is simply responsive: any change in the on-going perceptual input attracts attention. During the second stage, the infant manifests interests in (and efforts to retain) something newly recognized as familiar. The third stage begins with this interest in the novel in the context of a familiar situation and typically becomes noticeable toward the end of the first year; it is the basis for "growth motivation." It would also appear that the more the child encounters different visual and auditory changes during the first stage, the more of these he will recognize with interest during the second, and the more these will provide novel features to attract him during the third stage.

Effects of Social Environment

Such developments prepare the child to go on growing. But continued development appears to require a relationship with adults who enable the infant to pursue his locomotor and manipulative intentions and who answer his endless questions. Without these supports during the second, third, and fourth years of life, the child cannot continue to profit no matter how favorable his circumstances during the first year. It seems unlikely that the infant from the low socio-economic family suffers great deprivation during the first year; it is even conceivable that, because of crowding, he actually encounters a wider variety of visual and auditory input than his middle-class counterpart. During the second year, however, as he begins to move about, he is likely to get in the way of adults who are already ill-tempered from their own discomforts and frustrations. In such an atmosphere, his opportunity to carry out activities required for his development must almost inevitably be sharply curbed. Too seldom do his questions bring suitable answers; too often they bring punishment. There is also a shortage of suitable playthings and models for imitation. These ill-effects become more serious during the fourth and fifth year; the longer they exist, the more likely are their effects to be lasting. Research with animals, for example, has shown that extended deprivation can result in irreparable damage.

Possible Counteracting Measures

Such observations suggest that if nursery or day-care centers were arranged for the culturally disadvantaged child from the age of 4—or preferably 3—some of the worst effects of his home rearing might be substantially reduced. He should be given the opportunity to encounter a wide variety of objects, pictures, and appropriate behavioral models, as well as to receive adequate social approval for appropriate behavior. The setting should encourage him to indulge his inclinations to scrutinize and manipulate the new objects as long as he is interested and should provide him with meaningful answers to his questions. Such varied experiences would foster the development of representative imagery which can serve as referents for spoken words and later for written language. He should hear people who provide syntactical models of standard grammar and be given other experiences that would enable him gradually to overcome the handicaps of his lower-class upbringing.

There is, of course, a danger in attempting to prescribe remedies for cultural deprivation at this stage of knowledge. Any prescription about specific objects, pictures, etc. may fail to provide the proper degree of incongruity with the impressions the young child has already coded and stored in the course of his lower-class experiences. What seem to be appropriate behavioral models may merely produce conflict. Because of differences in coded information stored in the lower-class child from that stored in his middle-class peer with whom middle-class teachers are more familiar, it is dangerous for the latter to prescribe intuitively or on the basis of their experience in teaching middle-class children. We need to provide the child with the opportunity to find particular circumstances which match his particular phase of development and introduce the proper degree of incongruity for intrinsic motivation.

Comments

1. As Hunt points out, no one can blueprint a program of preschool enrichment that can be guaranteed as an antidote for cultural deprivation. Yet with more functional assumptions replacing the traditional beliefs about the development of human capacity, we can hope that ulti-

mately an effective program of preschool education will be devised—not only for the culturally disadvantaged but for the maximal development of all the children of all the people.

2. This most scholarly article on recent developments should be read in connection with the author's more comprehensive treatment of the same theme (Hunt, 1961; 1964), and his treatment of the newer conception of motivation as presented in Chapter 3.

3. The various changes in psychological viewpoint which Hunt reviews are certainly among the most dramatic and productive developments of modern psychology. Evidence from a number of sources has provided a new perspective and a theoretical basis for effective programs of compensatory education. We have moved to an optimistic position of relatively unlimited potentiality for the future welfare of mankind. In this connection, we might recall the skepticism which met the Iowa findings of substantial IQ increases connected with attendance at nursery school when reported in the 1930s; apparently, we have come a long way—and are willing to put our money where our beliefs are. It is interesting to speculate how in a couple of generations we might be able to wipe out a good deal of the current cultural deprivation and thereby raise the intellectual standards of the nation, particularly among the lower classes. In a nation as enlightened as ours, this should pose no insurmountable problem.

4. In a related article, Schwebel (1965) presents the ghetto problem in historical perspective. He points out that today's "socially deprived" are the Negroes and the Puerto Ricans; a few years back, they were the central and eastern Europeans, the Italians, and the Orientals, and before that the Scandinavians, the Germans, and the Irish. These people occupied the lowest paid positions in their country of origin and filled a similar occupational role in this country. As the years passed, each group retained essentially the same characteristic: lowest positions, lowest income, highest unemployment rate, poorest housing; educationally, their position was one of lowest IQ, no educational tradition, little formal schooling, preoccupation with survival, etc. If today's situation is complicated by race, previously it was religion, foreign language, and alien culture. At least we are now helped by advances in knowledge. Many of today's practices, unfortunately, are still based on the faulty assumptions of earlier days, that the lower classes could not and need not (perhaps should not) be educated, that they were destined to labor, not to think. The advent of the IQ helped to document their intellectual inferiority. However, if we begin with different assumptions concerning their learning ability and provide suitable educational experiences, other answers can be had. Indeed, current thinking about the development of mental processes permits us to be optimistic about our ability to raise the educational level of the nation.

References

Hunt, J. McV. *Intelligence and Experience.* New York: The Ronald Press Co., 1961.

Hunt, J. McV. "The psychological basis for using preschool enrichment as an antidote for cultural deprivation," *Merill-Palmer Quart.,* 10: 209–243, 1964.

Schwebel, Milton. "Learning and the socially deprived," *Pers. Guid. J.,* 43: 646–653, 1965.

Alexander G. Wesman

Intelligent Testing *

Despite the fact that the nature of intelligence has been a favorite subject for contemplation for centuries, there appears to be no greater agreement as to its general nature or the most valid means for its measurement than there was 50 years ago. "It is my conviction that much of the confusion which plagued us in the past, and continues to plague us today, is attributable to our ignoring two propositions which should be obvious: (a) Intelligence is an attribute not an entity; (b) intelligence is the summation of the learning experiences of the individual" [p. 267].

Intelligence is best defined as the summation of one's learning experiences; each act in which intelligent behavior is displayed "represents a response the organism has learned; each learned response in turn predisposes the organism to learn additional responses which permit the organism to display new acts of intelligent behavior. . . . We start with an organism which is subject to modification by interaction with the environment; as a product of that interaction, the organism has been modified. Further interaction involves a changed organism—one which is ready to interact with its environment in a new way" [p. 267]. Organisms differ in their susceptibility to modification as a result of such interaction with experience; whether these differences arise from differences in neurological endowment or in the quality of the environment is not clear.

The "bits" or "modules" which constitute intelligence may be information or skills (i. e., content or process). Furthermore, they are multidimensional: The toy ball is first seen in terms of size, shape, and color. But these modules are consistently shifting and modifying, particularly in the direction of taking on increased complexity. We have to assume that further learning depends on previous learning, that the more complex modules cannot exist without the antecedent modules from which they grow.

This conception of intelligence, although oversimplified, does no essential violence to any of the current theories; on the other hand, it has merit with regard to a number of issues which currently confront us:

(a) *The classification of ability tests into aptitude, achievement, and intelligence measures.* If we agree that what we know and what

---

* Adapted and abridged from Alexander G. Wesman, "Intelligent testing," *American Psychology*, 23: 267–274, 1968. Copyright 1968 by American Psychological Association and reproduced by permission.

we can do intellectually is the result of learning, the distinction between intelligence, aptitude, and achievement tests becomes strictly academic. Historically, we have always argued that whatever intelligence tests measured was independent of learning phenomena. We have distinguished between aptitude (what the individual *can* learn) and achievement (what the individual *has* learned). "One gets a strong impression that the aptitude instrument is perceived as measuring the innate potential of the individual as distinguished from what is to be achieved (i. e., learned) . . ." [p. 268].

Actually, "all ability tests—intelligence, aptitude, and achievement —measure what the individual *has* learned and they often measure through similar content and similar process" [p. 269]. The justification for labeling them *intelligence* tests, *aptitude* tests, or *achievement* tests resides entirely in the *purpose* for which a particular instrument is used, not in the instrument itself. If we want to determine how much the examinee has learned in a particular course, we devise what we call an "achievement" test. If our intent is to predict the individual's likely success in learning a new skill, we identify previous learnings presumably related to future learning and label the test an "aptitude" test. If, on the other hand, we wish to predict future learning over a broad area of environmental exposure, we select those previous learnings, the possession of which is relevant to as many important future learning situations as we can anticipate. This we call an "intelligence" test. The items may or may not differ "but in each case what is being measured is what has been previously learned. We are not measuring different abilities; we are merely attending to different criteria. It is the *relevance* of the learnings we select for investigation that basically determines how we name our test, and whether we will succeed in our purpose" [p. 269].

(b) *The utility of culture-free and culture-fair tests.* By definition, a culture-free test—i. e., one which presumably probes learnings which are not affected by environment—is sheer nonsense. A culture-fair test, on the other hand, focusses on those learnings which are common to many cultures—and therefore violates our basic purpose. "The implicit intent in any attempt to create a culture-free or culture-fair test is somehow to measure intelligence without permitting the effect of differential exposure to learning to influence scores. This contains the tacit assumption that 'native intelligence' lies buried in pure form deep in the individual, and needs only to be uncovered by ingenious mining methods" [p. 269]. We can, of course, probe learning in the non-verbal, non-numerical domains but this raises the question of the relevance of these special domains to the kinds of learning we want to predict. "If we wish to predict whether an individual will profit appreciably from additional exposure to learning, our best predictor must be a measure which appraises what prerequisite learning he has acquired heretofore. Appropriate verbal abilities are more relevant to the largely verbal learning we usually wish to predict than other abilities are" [p. 270].

It has been advocated that tests be specially developed to incorporate content peculiar to a given subculture on the premise that such tests would be a fairer measure of the "intelligence" or "readiness to learn" of the members of that subculture. The question is "readiness to learn what?" If our purpose is to distinguish members of that subculture from each other with respect to how much of that special subculture they have assimilated, such a test might be useful. If, as is more likely the case, we wish to predict future learnings of the content of the more general culture . . . , tests designed for the subculture will be less relevant than those from the general culture. . . . As long as our educational system and our general culture are dependent on conventional verbal abilities, those who aspire to progress in that system and that culture will need to command those abilities. In a verbal society, verbal competence cannot sensibly be ignored" [p. 270].

(c) *Verbal ability and intelligence.* This does not mean that verbal ability is the only important component of "intelligence," or the exclusive component of all learning domains. "Many domains require the possession of other abilities as well [it may be more important to perform a mechanical skill than to describe it], but our appraisal methods tend to be inadequate to reveal that need. Because it is easier to employ verbal criteria, or more convenient—or because we have given insufficient thought to criterion validity—we predetermine the finding that verbal abilities will dominate the scene" [p. 270]. There is, of course, the need for education to become increasingly "realistic with respect to what its criteria *should* be" [p. 271].

(d) *The growth and decline of "intelligence."* Psychologists have been concerned about their inability to predict the IQ of a teenager from his IQ as an infant. This should come as no surprise: To the extent that we are measuring in different ability domains at these two age levels, we should not expect accurate prediction from one level to the other. The same applies at the other end of the age spectrum: The scores of older people on our conventional measures of intelligence decline with age. The trouble is that the relevance of what conventional intelligence tests measure to the kinds of learning individuals engage in from the age of 30 onward becomes increasingly remote with each passing year. To the extent that what people learn as they grow older occurs in a variety of relatively specialized endeavors, it is virtually impossible to find a common core on which adults can be compared. As a consequence, we can talk of decline performance on tests designed for younger adults but hardly of declining "intelligence."

(e) *The search for purity.* Factor analysis facilitates the organization of data as the basis for investigating interesting and often fruitful research hypotheses. It has had a strong influence on test construction and has stimulated the development of theories concerning the structure of the intellect, but the power of the tool does not necessarily assure the validity of the product. Yet, even though the factors are merely descriptive categories, "The temptation to discover a psychological structure analogous to the periodic table of the elements is too powerful to resist. We then hear of 'primary mental abilities,' and are shown the 'three faces of intellect' " [p. 273], with the distinction between the reality of the descriptive categories and the illusion of underlying functional entities not always clearly kept in mind. Mental behavior is multifaceted and complex; "to assume that we can abstract from a host of such activities a pure and simple entity is to ignore the psychological meaning of intelligent behavior" [p. 273].

"To what view of a structure of intellect am I led by the ideas I have enunciated here? Essentially, I believe intelligence is *un*structured. I believe that it is differently comprised in every individual—the sum total of all the learning experiences he has uniquely had up to any moment in time. Such structure as we perceive is structure which we have imposed. We can so select samples of previous learning to examine as to reveal a general factor, or group factors, or specifics. We can sample from domains that are relatively homogeneous and apply labels such as verbal, numerical, spatial; we can sample from wider variety of learnings, apply labels such as 'general mental ability' or simply 'intelligence' " [p. 273].

The most reasonable basis for selecting the kinds of learning to be sampled is that of predictive purpose; the previous learnings to be probed are those which are most relevant to the particular future learnings we wish to predict. "The critical issue, then, is not which approach measures intelligence—each of them does, in its own fashion. No approach save sampling from every domain in which learnings have occurred—an impossible task—fully measures intelligence. The question is rather which approach provides the most useful information for the various purposes we wish the test to serve" [p. 273].

Comments

1. This is, no doubt, one of the clearest expositions of the intellect as the result of the interaction of the individual with his environment. The concept of learning as the basis for intellectual functioning has broad sociological, philosophical, as well as educational implications, particularly with respect to the education of the "culturally deprived." It also has special bearing on a number of current issues concerning the nature of the intellect and its appraisal: "I wish at least a few of my psychometric colleagues would leave off searching for *the* structure of the intellect, and

devote their wisdom and energy to learning more about the learning process, and to teaching–learning theories about testing" [p. 268].

      2.   Also of interest in this connection are the comments by
Humphreys (1962): "I have been disturbed for several years at two related
tendencies in the work on human abilities. One is the proliferation of factors as more and more experimental test batteries have been intercorrelated and factored. . . . The other is the continued tendency to think of
factors as basic or primary, no matter how specific, or narrow, or artificial
the test behavior may be that determines the factor." Humphreys also
points out that factor analysis is a useful tool—in hypothesis *formation,*
but not in hypothesis *testing.* He prefers the hierarchical model presented
by British psychologists—e. g., Vernon (1950): At the top of the hierarchy is *g,* the general factor, then major group factors, then minor group
factors, and finally the specific factors.

References

Humphreys, Lloyd G. "The organization of human abilities," *Amer. Psychol.,*
    17: 475–483, 1962.
Vernon, Philip E. *The Structure of Human Abilities.* New York: John Wiley &
    Sons, Inc., 1950.

Quinn McNemar

Lost: Our Intelligence. Why? *

"Apparently one reason why concepts are discarded or modified beyond recognition is that too much has been claimed for them. Among the supposed strikes against general intelligence are the following: the earlier false claims about IQ constancy; prediction failures in individual cases; unfounded claims that something innate was being measured . . . ; equally unfounded assertions that nothing but cultural effects were involved; the bugaboo that IQ tests reflect middle-class values . . ." [p. 871].

Spearman championed the theory of general intelligence, although he did concede that factors other than *g* might also exist. But then, Thurstone in his first major application of the centroid factor method claimed that no general common intellectual factor had been located. Spearman, reanalyzing Thurstone's data, rediscovered *g,* plus some group factors. "He charged that Thurstone's rotational process had simply submerged the general factor" [p. 871].

Thurstone's seven primary mental abilities constituted an attractive package in that these "so-called primaries were more amenable to specific definition than the old hodgepodge called general intelligence" [p. 872]. A problem arose in that, in one study based on the Stanford-Binet, *g* refused to be rotated out. "But, rather than admit that this might be some kind of general intelligence, the author renamed it 'maturational level.' Incidentally, this illustrates the first cardinal Principle of Psychological Progress: *Give new names to old things"* [p. 872].

"The second disturber of the neat little set of primaries, sans a *g,* resulted when Thurstone took the next logical step, that of constructing tests to measure the primaries. It was found that the primaries were themselves intercorrelated. . . . The Thurstones readily admitted that a general factor was needed to explain this interrelatedness of the primaries. This eventually led to the idea of oblique axes, which axes were regarded as representing the primaries as first-order factors, whereas the general factor pervading the primaries was dubbed a second-order factor. It began to look as though Spearman was being revisited, except for the little matter of labeling: Anything called second-order could not be regarded as of much im-

* Adapted and abridged from Quinn McNemar, "Lost: our intelligence. why?" *Amer. Psychol.,* 19: 871–882, 1964. Copyright 1964 by the American Psychological Association and reproduced by permission.

portance. . . . Thus it became easy for most American factorists to drop the concept of general intelligence and to advocate that tests thereof, despite their proven usefulness over the years, should be replaced by tests of the primaries" [p. 872].

Meanwhile, our British cousins did not tag along with the factor methods preferred on this side of the Atlantic. After all, it is possible to use factor methods that permit a sizable general factor, if one exists, to emerge as the very first factor. Being first, it is, presto, the most important, as indeed it is as a factor explaining, for the starting battery as a whole, more variance for more tests than attributable to any American-style primary factor. The methods preferred by the British also yield group factors apt to bear the same name as the primaries, but of attenuated importance. Apparently, the British are skeptical of the multitude of ability factors being "discovered" in America. The structure of the intellect that requires 120 factors may very well lead the British, and some of the rest of us, to regard our fractionization of ability, into more and more factors of less and less importance, as indicative of scatterbrainedness" [p. 872].

"In practically all areas of psychological research the demonstration of trivially small minutia is typically doomed to failure because of random errors. Not so if your technique is factor analysis, despite its being based on the correlation coefficient—that slipperiest of all statistical measures. By some magic, hypotheses are tested without significance tests. This happy situation permits me to announce a Principle of Psychological Regress: *Use statistical techniques that lack inferential power.* This will not inhibit your power of subjective inference and consequently will progress you right back to the good old days when there was no strangling stat or sticky stix to make your insignificant data insignificant" [p. 872].

"It may be a long time before we have an ivory tower, strictly scientific resolution of the issue as to whether a scheme involving primary abilities plus a deemphasized *g* is preferable to one involving an emphasized *g* plus group factors. With bigger and better computers we will have bigger, though not necessarily better, factor-analytic studies, but it seems unlikely that such studies will, in and of themselves, settle the issue under discussion. Until such time as some genius resolves the broader question . . . of the place, if any, of correlational methods in a science that aspires to be experimental, we may have to turn to the criterion of social usefulness as a basis for judging whether it is wise to discard general intelligence" [p. 872].

The Bearing of Social Usefulness

"In practice, if you believe that the concept of general intelligence has outlived its usefulness, you may choose from among several differential, or multiple, aptitude batteries, which will provide measures of some of the so-called primary mental abilities. If you happen to believe that there is something to general ability, you can find tests to use. The novice . . . may have to alert himself to the first Principle of Psychological Progress—the test labels may have changed from 'general intelligence' to 'general classification' or 'scholastic aptitude.' If you enjoy riding the fence, you might become a devotee of the practice of the College Boards, and others, and measure just two abilities: Verbal and Quantitative" [p. 873].

"This is certainly not the place to review the voluminous literature that amply demonstrates the practical utility of tests of general intelligence. Nor is it the place to catalog the misuses of the Stanford-Binet for purposes which Terman never claimed for it, or the misuses of the Wechsler scales for purposes which Wechsler *has* claimed for his scales. . . . Of the many group tests that appeared between 1920 and 1945 it can be said that few, if any, proved unidimensional measures of general intelligence. The chief difficulty is that most lead to a total score based on a mixture of verbal and mathematical material. Thus, with two main sources of variance, marked qualitative differences can exist for quantitatively similar scores" [p. 873].

In considering the extent to which multiple aptitude batteries have contributed to the demise of general intelligence, one encounters a paradox: "Some test authors want to eat their cake and have it too—they attempt to measure factors and g with the same instrument" [p. 874]. Some publishers have apparently g-garnished a factor cake while others have factor-iced a g cake, presumably "to make them more palatable in the market place. . . . Some multitest batteries . . . have a Madison Avenue advantage: The advertising claims the measurement of not only factors but also g; not only g but also factors. This measurement absurdity is all too apt to go unrecognized by many test users, and hence a sales advantage for the aptitude battery that produces both factor scores and an IQ" [p. 874].

Just how successful have the multitest batteries been—particularly with respect to the school where most extensive use lies? For the Differential Aptitude Test (DAT), the only battery for which adequate validity data exist—and the battery which has fared best in the hands of the reviewers—"one could by gracious selection [from the 4096 validity coefficients reported] "show" that the DAT is the answer to the prayer of every counselor . . . or, by malicious selection one could "prove" that the DAT is far worse than any test ever published" [p. 874]. The DAT validities show the Verbal Reasoning and the Language Usage tests best, followed by Numerical Ability as the best predictor of achievement in school math (but not as good a predictor of science grades as Verbal Reasoning). Of the remaining six tests, only Spelling has predictive ability. Data from the other multiple aptitude test batteries tend to confirm the DAT findings. Aside from tests of numerical ability having differential value in predicting school grades in math, it seems safe to conclude that the worth of the multitest batteries as differential predictors of achievement in school has not been demonstrated.

"And now we come to a very disturbing aspect of the situation. Those who have constructed and marketed multiple test batteries, seem never to have bothered to demonstrate whether or not multitest batteries provide better predictions than the old-fashioned scale of general intelligence. . . . It is far from clear that tests of general intelligence have been outmoded by the multitest batteries as the more useful predictor of school achievement" [p. 875]. A combination of the Verbal Reasoning (Analogies) and Numerical Ability test of the DAT—essentially a measure of general intelligence—predicts as well as, and in most instances, better than any single test taken in the differential sense. While the manual of the DAT interprets this to mean that the DAT makes the use of an intelligence test unnecessary, one could "with better justification, say that an intelligence test can serve nearly all, if not all, the purposes for which a multiple aptitude battery is given in the schools because the former, in general, is a better predictor and because . . . the differential clues are too fragmentary to be of use to the counselor. And there is a bonus: one classroom period of testing, compared to six periods. A second bonus: much less costly. A third bonus: fewer scores to confuse the already confused minds of most school counselors" [p. 875].

"Thus, we come to the conclusion that general intelligence has not been lost in the trend to test more and more abilities; it was merely misplaced by a misplaced emphasis in the hope that . . . factors, when and if measured, would find great usefulness in the affairs of society. By the criterion of social usefulness, the multiple aptitude batteries have been found wanting" [p. 876].

Intelligence Elsewhere

Another area of the alleged inadequacies of general intelligence is that of creativity. "Anyone who peeks over the fence into this field is apt to be astonished at the visible chaos. The definition of creativity is confounded by the diversity of subareas within the field, the criterion problems are far from licked, and so little is known about the creative process that measuring instruments are, seemingly, chosen on a trial-and-error basis" [p. 876]. "One elaborate study came up with. . . . 150 *criteria* of scientific productivity and creativity. By combining some factors and eliminating others, the number . . . was reduced to 48. A thorough factor analysis of the intercorrelations of the 48 reduced the number to 14 'categories'. . . . The fact that the intercorrelations among the 14 criterion categories . . . range from $-.08$ to $+.55$, with a median of only .18, indicates either criterion complexity or else a whale of a lot of vagueness as to what is meant by productivity and creativity in science" [p. 877]. A total of 2210 "validity coefficients" produced an essentially random-sampling distribution centering on zero. Correlation coefficients of 16 predictors based on aptitude tests with 17 criterion measures (a total of 272 validities) also turned out to be not significantly different from zero: Apparently, aptitude ain't important in scientific productivity and creativity" [p. 877]. A number of other criterion-based studies have been interpreted to have shown that intelligence plays only a minor role in creative achievement, but "it must be remembered that drastic but unknown or unspecified curtailment of the range exists for both ability and criteria. Why do correlational studies under such adverse circumstances" [p. 878]?

"Next we turn to studies of creativity which cannot be criticized because of restriction of range on the criterion—these studies simply avoid this problem by never having actual criterion information. The approach is to claim that certain tests . . . *are* measures of creativity, with no evidence whatsoever that the tests have predictive validity for nontest, real-life creative performance. This bit of ignorance does not prove to be a handicap to those who think that creativity can be studied without the nuisance of obtaining criterion measures" [p. 878].

"We first note that general intelligence has not emerged as a correlate of so-called creativity tests in the factor-analytic studies of creativity. The explanation . . . is easily found—no measures of general intelligence are used in these studies." Presumably, we must look well beyond the boundaries of the IQ if we are to fathom the domain of creativity. "Does the failure to include an IQ test help one learn the extent to which we must go beyond the boundaries of the IQ to fathom creativity? In one sample ($n = 7648$) of Project Talent, IQ and creativity correlated .67. A substantial correlation between IQ and creativity seems to have been involved in the Getzels and Jackson study, despite a considerable attenuation because of such factors as the usual measurement errors, the restriction of range in IQ, and the fact that the IQ was a mixture of scores derived from three different scales.

"Much has been made of the finding that the creativity tests tended to correlate higher than did IQ with the verbal-content school achievement. Again the IQ comes in for an unfair drubbing because of the same mixture of IQ scores and, what is more pertinent, because of explicit selective curtailment of the IQ variable and only incidental selection of the creativity variable" [p. 879].

Of greater importance to the present paper is the comparison of the academic achievement of a highly creative and a high IQ group. The fact that the high creatives did as well on academic achievement as did their bright counterparts despite the latter's 23 IQ point advantage comes as no surprise to anyone familiar with a three-variable problem. Furthermore, the high IQ and the high creative groups did equally well in school achievement despite an unreported difference in mean creativity. "Utilizing the half-blind logic of the authors, one can say that creative ability is not as important as IQ for school achievement—just the opposite of their position" [p. 879]! "Now the fact that seven of nine replications of this study have confirmed the original findings merely indicates that repetition of the same faulty design and faulty logic will lead to the same false conclusions. . . . I cannot refrain from saying at this point that, although discouraged, I am still hopeful that people who do statistical studies will learn a modicum of elementary statistics" [p. 879].

"The . . . renewed interest in 'gifted' children, along with the flurry of creativity studies, has led to a reexamination of methods for identifying the gifted. . . . The argument against the IQ is now being reinforced by the claim that the selection of the top 20% on IQ would mean the exclusion of 70% of the top 20% on tested creativity. This startling statistic . . . is being used to advocate the use of creativity tests for identifying the gifted" [p. 880]. However, to say that creativity tests are better for this purpose than the IQ tests because of the lack of constancy of the IQ overlooks the fact that absolutely nothing is known about the constancy of creativity test scores.

The IQ is linked with *learning* as an outmoded educational objective to be replaced with emphasis on *thinking*. "Somehow . . . creativity, not general intelligence, is being associated with thinking. The horrible idea of underachievers and overachievers, in terms of expectancies based on IQ, will be abolished. But no thought has been given to the fact that the use of creativity tests will simply define a new crop of under- and overachievers" [p. 880].

"An additional difficulty is not being faced by those who would replace the IQ tests by creativity tests, or creative-thinking tests. The factor-analytic studies indicate either no, or a trivially small, general creativity factor in these tests, yet these . . . reformers do not hesitate to advocate a total score which is nearly devoid of meaning. Changing the curriculum to the teaching of . . . creative thinking will not overcome this measurement difficulty. Again, I express the hope that the IQ is replaced by something better rather than something worse" [p. 880].

"There are other areas such as reasoning, problem solving, and concept formation in which one might expect to find some consideration of intelligence as an aspect. One might also expect that investigators of thinking would have something to say about individual differences in thinking being dependent on intelligence, but for some unintelligent reason these people seem never to mention intelligence. Surely, it cannot be inferred that thinking about thinking does not involve intelligence" [p. 880].

Comments

1.   "It has been the thesis of this paper that the concept of general intelligence, despite being maligned by a few, regarded as a sec-

ond-order function by some, and discarded or ignored by others, still has a rightful place in the science of psychology and in the practical affairs of man" [p. 880]. In his defense of general intelligence, McNemar puts into perspective some of the claims of the advocates of tests of differential aptitude and of creativity. He is far from convinced that the case against general intelligence has been "proved" and that it is being discarded in favor of something better.

      2.   In his conclusions, McNemar refers to the work of Hayes who presents a motivational–experiential theory of intelligence in which he postulates "experience-producing drives" which, in conjunction with environmental differences, produce differences in experience. These, in turn, by way of learning lead to differences in ability, so that differences in ability, capacity, aptitude, intellectual skill, or whatever you call them are nothing more than acquired abilities. He laments the fact that this area has been "too long dominated by ever-increasing fractionization by factor analysis, with little thought as to how the fractured parts get put together into a functioning whole" [p. 881].

      3.   Also critical of the emphasis on creativity as allegedly distinct and independent of the type of abstract intelligence measured by established "intelligence" or scholastic aptitude tests is an article by Thorndike (1963), who questions whether there is a common component running through these tests to which a common term *creativity* might legitimately be applied. He urges a great deal of tentativeness in the use of a global and value-laden term such as *creativity* to represent a quantity as ill-defined as the area of creative thinking currently seems to be.

References

Hayes, Keith J. "Genes, drives, and intellect," *Psychol. Rep. (Monogr. Suppl.* 2), 10: 299–342, 1962.

Thorndike, Robert L. "The measurement of creativity," *T. C. Rec.,* 64: 422–424, 1963.

Jerome Kagan *et al.*

Personality and IQ Change *

Research on mental development during the last 20 years suggests that the IQ remains only relatively constant. The purpose of this study was to investigate the relationship between changes in IQ during childhood and certain personality predispositions: (a) need for achievement, (b) competitive striving, (c) curiosity about nature, and (d) passivity. It was assumed that "need for achievement, competitive strivings and curiosity about nature motivate the acquisition and improvement of cognitive abilities and by so doing facilitate increases in tested IQ" [p. 261]. More specifically, it was hypothesized that children showing marked IQ increases would produce more achievement imagery on the TAT, that they would report more aggressive content on the Rorschach, and that they would reveal greater curiosity through showing interest in nature and its phenomena. On the contrary, they would be less likely to characterize their TAT heroes as passive in attitude or behavior.

The subjects represented the top and bottom quarter in IQ gain ($n = 70$ and 70) of the population of the Fels Research Institute longitudinal study. These children had been tested twice yearly from the ages of 2½ through 6 and annually from the ages of 6 through 11. The two groups were relatively equivalent in IQ at age 6 but, by age 10, Group A (the ascenders) had gained an average of 17 points while Group D (the IQ descenders) had lost some 5 points.

The results supported all four hypotheses: (a) Group A reported more achievement imagery than Group D. (b) A larger number of boys in Group A (than in Group D) reported aggressive images on the Rorschach, the difference bordering on significance; no difference was found for girls. (c) Group A told significantly more themes of interest in the stars and heavens than Group D. (d) Group A gave significantly fewer passivity themes than Group D. The results suggest that "high motivation to achieve, competitive strivings, and curiosity about nature may motivate the acquisition of intellectual skills and knowledge which, in turn, facilitates increases in

* Adapted and abridged from Jerome Kagan et al., "Personality and IQ change," *J. abnor. soc. Psychol.*, 56: 261–266, 1958. Copyright 1958 by the American Psychological Association, and reproduced by permission.

tested IQ" [p. 264]. The fact that boys outnumbered girls in Group A two to one supports the present interpretation.

Comment

The article touches upon the important role of personality variables in the development of the intellect. To the extent that intelligence is something that one develops as a result of interaction with the environment, nonintellective factors are bound to play a differential role in the extent to which innate potential is actually developed. The article also bears on the motivational–experiential theory of intelligence postulated by Hayes (1962), as mentioned in the previous article by McNemar.

That's What They Said

"One thing seems clear: If all students are helped to the full utilization of their intellectual powers, we will have a better chance of surviving as a democracy in an age of enormous technological and social complexity."

> Jerome S. Bruner. *The Process of Education.* Cambridge: Harv. Univ. Press, 1960. [10]

"Intelligence appears to me . . . to be a dynamic succession of developing functions with the more advanced and complex functions in the hierarchy depending on the prior maturing of earlier simpler ones."

> Nancy Bayley. "On the growth of intelligence," *Amer. Psychol.,* 10: 805–818, 1955. [807]

"It is highly inconsistent to conceive of the mind as being represented by a single score or even by a handful of scores or dimensions that are present in our current intelligence tests. The brain which underlies the mind is far, far too complex to hope that all its intellectual activities can be represented by only a single score or by only a handful of dimensions. In fact, it might be considered an insult to the brain and human mind to continue to do so."

> Calvin W. Taylor. "A tentative description of the creative individual," in Walter B. Waetjen (ed.), *Human Variability and Learning.* Fifth Research Institute. Washington: Association for Supervision and Curriculum Development, 1961. Pp. 62–79. [64]

"Intelligence then from a perceptual point of view becomes a function of the factors that control the richness, extent, and availability of perception in the perceptual field."

> Arthur W. Combs and Donald Snygg. *Individual Behavior.* New York: Harper & Row, Publishers, 1959. [214]

"Valuable as our intelligence testing has been, it does have some limitations. The most commonly used tests measure capacities which are primarily related to what schools have taught in the past. These, of course, are the usual academic or verbal learnings. While these learnings are very important and significant, questions are being asked increasingly as to whether or not there are other kinds of important and significant learning products which schools should foster. The question might be phrased like this: Do our schools adequately measure capacity to develop rich, meaningful concepts; capacity to solve problems of personal and social living; or capacity to think creatively?

> Gordon N. Mackenzie. "Freeing capacity to learn: Implications for curriculum and instruction," in Alexander Frazier (ed.), *Freeing Capacity To Learn*. Fourth Research Institute. Washington: Association for Supervision and Curriculum Development, 1960. Pp. 1–9. [2]

"The problem for the management of child development is to find out how to govern the encounters that children have with their environment to foster both an optimally rapid rate of intellectual development and a satisfying life."

> J. McV. Hunt. *Intelligence and Experience*. New York: The Ronald Press Co., 1961. [362–363]

"Education in this country has unfortunately been too much dominated by the learning theories based upon the stimulus–response model of Thorndike, Hull, and Skinner. People, after all, are not rats (with a few exceptions), and they are not pigeons (with similar exceptions). Let us make full use of the human brains that have been granted to us. Let us apply a psychology that recognizes the full range of human intellectual qualities. We must make more complete use of our most precious natural resource—the intellectual abilities of our people, including their creative potentialities."

> J. P. Guilford. "Factors that aid and hinder creativity," *T. C. Rec.*, 63: 380–393, 1962. [392]

". . . we are shifting . . . from a notion that intelligence is fixed and immutable and unchangeable and a fact that one simply must accept, to a very powerful notion that we can do something about a youngster's intelligence by the nature of the experiences we provide for him."

> Ira J. Gordon. *Changing View of Childhood*. Address to Florida Association for Supervision and Curriculum Development, 1964. (See also 1966 Association for Supervision and Curriculum Development Yearbook. [56])

"There are two aspects to intelligence which must be considered: the innate potential of the individual and the functional expression of that potential as usable and used ability. The former is physiological, the latter behavioral. Since we cannot 'get to' innate intelligence, educational measurement has reflected the functional ability."

Allen J. Edwards and Dale T. Scannell. *Educational Psychology: The Teaching–Learning Process.* Scranton: International, 1969. [7]

Reference

Roger Reger. "Myths about intelligence," *Psychol. Sch.,* 3: 39–44, 1966.

CHAPTER 9

Test Items

1. Probably the most basic aspect of intellectual growth is the gradual increase in
   a. ability to cope with abstract symbols
   b. ability to deal with stimuli remote in time and space
   c. convergent reasoning ability
   d. divergent reasoning ability
   e. memory

2. Modern psychologists look on intelligence as
   a. a composite of verbal and numerical aptitude
   b. a multidimensional organization of primary (innate) mental abilities
   c. the product of previous learning
   d. a relatively innate ability to reason
   e. a single global capacity to cope with environmental demands

3. Guilford's model conceptualizes intelligence into the following dimensions:
   a. abstract, concrete, social
   b. aptitude, content, and process
   c. cognitive, memory, and reasoning
   d. concrete, symbolic, and behavioral
   e. process, content, and product

4. Spearman is to Thurstone as
   a. a general factor is to group factors
   b. a general factor is to a multitude of specific independent neural connections
   c. *g* is to specific factors
   d. *g* is to primary mental abilities
   e. group factors are to specific factors

5. The modern consensus is that intelligence
   a. develops primarily through a maturational process
   b. is a composite of relatively specific skills and knowledges
   c. is a composite of relatively independent aptitudes

    d.   is fundamentally an aspect of readiness
    e.   is primarily something one develops through experience

6.   Hayes has postulated that the hereditary mechanism underlying intelligence lies primarily in the relative adequacy of one's
    a.   biochemical balance
    b.   early experiences
    c.   experience-producing drives
    d.   lower brain centers
    e.   neurological assets

7.   Piaget views intellectual growth as
    a.   the acquisition of symbolic processes
    b.   the development of ability to deal with causal relationships
    c.   the development of an effective experience-retrieval system
    d.   growth in the effective use of language
    e.   a matter of sequential stages in the ability to deal with logical operations

8.   The stages in the child's thought processes, according to Piaget, are in sequence
    a.   preconceptual—intuitive—formal
    b.   preconceptual—intuitive—causal
    c.   sensimotor—concrete operations—formal operations
    d.   sensimotor—formal—inferential
    e.   preconceptual—syncretic—intuitive

9.   Which of the following is not a major criticism of Piaget's position?
    a.   The age sequence is not as rigid as Piaget suggests.
    b.   It covers only a small segment of "intelligence."
    c.   He has misplaced the age at which certain abilities appear.
    d.   He implies too strong an hereditary stand.
    e.   He postulates stages rather than continuous development.

10.   The fact that oldsters do more poorly on "intelligence" tests than they did when they were younger is best explained on the basis of
    a.   the gradual erosion of neurophysiological processes with age
    b.   the inappropriateness of test content for the types of activities oldsters engage in
    c.   the invalidity of the test norms
    d.   the lack of interest (motivation) of oldsters in the content typically incorporated in IQ tests
    e.   the resistance and rigidity with which oldsters approach the test situation

11. Other things being equal, the child with the *greatest intellectual ability* is
    a. Child A: CA = 8;   IQ = 150
    b. Child B: CA = 10;   IQ = 100
    c. Child C: CA = 10;   IQ = 125
    d. Child D: CA = 12;   IQ = 75
    e. Child E: CA = 12;   IQ = 110

12. The relative constancy of the IQ is best considered
    a. an artifact of the relative constancy of the environment
    b. an artifact of the tendency for any composite measure to average out
    c. a natural consequent of innate ability
    d. a reflection of the insensitivity of current IQ tests
    e. a relative myth, hardly supported by the evidence

13. The better performance of World War II inductees (than their World War I counterparts) is best explained on the basis of
    a. their better educational background
    b. their greater wisdom
    c. differences in the calibration of the instruments
    d. biological improvement of the species over one generation
    e. the gradual deterioration of test instruments over time

14. What is the best statement of the effect of schooling on intelligence?
    a. Only when it emphasizes problem solving does schooling increase intelligence.
    b. Schooling has no effect on intelligence.
    c. Schooling promotes intelligent behavior but not an increase in intelligence.
    d. Schooling promotes intelligent behavior—and that is intelligence.
    e. Schooling raises the IQ by invalidating the test norms.

15. The major difficulty in establishing the validity of intelligence tests is
    a. ambiguity as to the meaning of intelligence
    b. ambiguity as to the meaning of validity
    c. inability to isolate "intelligence" from "learning"
    d. unavailability of a suitable criterion
    e. the wide diversity of background of the various examinees

16. The best interpretation of the IQ obtained by a culturally disadvantaged child on current tests of intelligence is that
    a. it is a meaningful index of the degree of his retardation

b.   it is a meaningful index of his innate potential

c.   it is a meaningful index of likely future status but is relatively meaningless as an index of his present ability

d.   it is totally invalid and meaningless

e.   it is a valid indication of what the child can do now in certain areas

17.   John has an IQ of 132. This means that

a.   he is bright today; there is no telling as to his final intellectual status

b.   he is intellectually superior to some 98 percent of the general population

c.   he obtained a high score on the test, nothing more

d.   he is twice as bright as Tom who has an IQ of 66

e.   he will do well academically

18.   The fact that college seniors do better on IQ tests than they did as freshmen implies that

a.   college makes students more test-wise

b.   college motivates students toward higher achievement

c.   intelligence can apparently be raised

d.   the IQ can be raised, nothing more

e.   the test norms can be invalidated

19.   According to Sontag, the children most likely to display an accelerating mental growth curve are

a.   the bright

b.   children who are aggressive and highly competitive

c.   the emotionally dependent children

d.   the girls

e.   the well adjusted

20.   The best position to take as to the various criticisms of current IQ tests is that

a.   because of the diversity of experiential background, they are wrong as often as right

b.   they are meaningful only when used on middle-class whites, ages 6 through 25

c.   they are predictive only within the range of the school years

d.   they have definite predictive value within the context of our present educational system

e.   only culture-fair (and culture-free) tests provide meaningful IQs for all

21. The most damaging of the Davis and Eells criticisms of the cultural bias of current IQ tests is that
    a. they are based on content responsive to differences in cultural background
    b. they incorporate content relying heavily on academic competence
    c. they measure ability rather than capacity
    d. they measure what has been achieved rather than what can be achieved
    e. they perpetuate an educational system that is not particularly suited to the interests, background, and needs of the lower-class child

22. Strictly speaking, an intelligence test would be free from *cultural bias* if
    a. it counterbalanced items so as to equate the advantages/disadvantages of each socio-economic strata on the test as a whole
    b. it gave each of the different socio-economic strata of our society the same mean IQ
    c. it incorporated items which either everyone or no one had an opportunity to learn
    d. it measured ability directly, i.e., independently of experience
    e. it measured intelligence in exact relationship to the influence of the environment

23. Probably the major cause of the lower IQ of the culturally disadvantaged is
    a. constant dietary inadequacies
    b. their genetic inferiority
    c. lack of prenatal care
    d. the relative sensory deprivation in early years
    e. the typically inadequate vocabulary of people of the lower classes

24. The failure of infant IQ tests to predict IQ at, say age 18, is best explained on the basis of
    a. the different content of the tests at age 1 and age 18
    b. the differential effects of intervening environmental influences
    c. errors arising out of the difficulty of testing young children
    d. the evolving hierarchical changes in the composition of intelligence
    e. the inadequacy of tests, particularly infant tests

25. In which of the following alternatives are all writers on the same side of the heredity-environment IQ controversy?
    a. Burks—Skeels—Woodworth

    b.   Newman—Thorndike—Moore
    c.   Fowler—Hunt—Chauncey
    d.   McNemar—Kirk—Wellman
    e.   Galton—Dawe—Goddard

26. The most realistic stand for today's teachers to take in the issue of heredity versus environment regarding intelligence is that
    a.   the best the school can do is to have the child use to constructive purposes the intelligence with which heredity has provided him
    b.   environment plays a very crucial role in developing inherited and intellectual potential
    c.   heredity sets a very real ceiling on intellectual functioning
    d.   there are definite IQ levels required for mastery of most of the school's tasks
    e.   whatever possibilities existed for raising the child's intelligence are gone by the time he gets to school

27. What is the best statement of the relationship between IQ and vocational adjustment?
    a.   Intelligence tests can identify jobs for which a person is either too bright or too dull.
    b.   IQ is a strong determinant of the relative success of people both within and between occupational groups.
    c.   There is a definite hierarchy of IQ from one occupational level to another.
    d.   There is a gradual increase in IQ as we progress up the occupational scale but there is also much overlapping.
    e.   Vocational adjustment is determined more by interest than by IQ.

28. Probably the factor most directly involved in the greater moral adjustment of the bright is
    a.   the coincidence of the values of their homes with those of society
    b.   the discouragement of unacceptable behavior by the home
    c.   the greater availability of outlets for the satisfaction of needs
    d.   their greater ability to avoid detection
    e.   their greater ability to foresee consequences

CHAPTER 10

Individual Differences

That individual differences among its citizens constitute the major asset of democratic society is indisputable. It is equally obvious, however, that individual differences do indeed complicate the routine of the classroom. Actually, the school's approach to the problem of inter- and intra-individual differences in the past has not been particularly imaginative nor enlightened. Rather than capitalize on individual talents for the benefit of the group, the school has typically attempted to minimize these differences in the interest of uniformity of operation—with the result often a matter of frustration on the part of the less able, boredom on the part of the more capable, and homogeneous mediocrity all around. More fundamentally, the problem seems to revolve around the apparent inability of teachers to devise an effective approach to the dual problem of helping children realize their potentialities to the fullest while at the same time having the class achieve a basic set of educational objectives. The possibilities of encouraging security, openness to experience, and self-actualization, on the one hand, as a means of releasing potentialities, and allowing maximal flexibility in curriculum and methodology (through independent study, programed instruction, etc.), on the other hand, is worthy of serious consideration as a partial solution to the problem. The person in the process of *becoming* can be expected to make full use of his potentialities and of the opportunities that present themselves.

The articles in this chapter cover a variety of topics. In an older article, Coffield and Blommers suggest that nonpromotion, besides being academically unprofitable, is not particularly effective in reducing the range of individual differences in the classroom. Peltier discusses a number of issues related to sex differences in the operation of the school. Tyler, reacting to the increasing unwieldiness of our present approach to the appraisal of individual differences, suggests as an alternative the dual principles of choice and organization. The last paper, by Wolfle, expounds on the benefits of planned one-sidedness, i. e., the benefits of having at least a few outstanding individuals of exceptional ability concentrate on a limited number of specialties to the relative neglect of their other talents.

William H. Coffield, and Paul Blommers

Effects of Non-Promotion on Educational Achievement in the Elementary School *

The relative merits of liberal promotion standards versus promotion based on rigid minimum standards of achievement have been the subject of serious debate by educators over the past 50 years. There has been a definite trend in the direction of a decrease in the frequency of non-promotion from 50 percent of the pupils having experienced failure by the completion of their elementary school in 1900 to approximately 10 percent in 1954. This does not settle the issue, however. Arguments ranging from the extra cost of education associated with non-promotion to the fear that, unless minimal standards are maintained, children will lose respect for scholarship still abound.

The present study compared the performance of 93 out of 147 seventh-grade pupils who had experienced failure once from the third to the sixth grade with that of a carefully matched control group of equally inadequate but yet promoted classmates. Each of the remaining 54 students were similarly matched with a promoted control from another school. In effect, each failed pupil was compared with himself and with a promoted matchee in order to give both an internal and an external comparison. The criterion was the five subtests of the Iowa Tests of Basic Skills.

Analysis of the data showed that: (a) The failed pupils approximated six months in educational progress in their repeat year, still failing to achieve the norms for the grade involved. The progress of the failed pupils during the two years following failure is not significantly greater than that made by the matched non-failed group in a single year in the next grade. (b) The educational status of the seventh-graders who had been retained once is about equal to that of the matched seventh-graders who had spent one year less in school and about eight months less than that of the matched regularly-promoted eighth-graders who had spent the same number of years in school. (c) The rigidity or leniency of the school's promotional policy does not affect significantly the general level of achievement

* Adapted and abridged from William H. Coffield and Paul Blommers, "Effects of non-promotion on educational achievement in the elementary school," *J. educ. Psychol.*, 47: 235–250, 1956. Copyright 1956 by American Psychological Association and reproduced by permission.

in its seventh-grade class. Rigid promotional policies, however, tend to increase by about ten percent the number of overage seventh-grade students.

While the study does not encompass all the variables operating in the situation, the data suggest that non-promotion as a device for ensuring greater mastery of elementary school subject-matter does not appear justifiable. ". . . it would seem that slow-learning children who are required to repeat a grade and [equally] slow-learning children who are promoted, ultimately perform at the same level when this performance is measured in the same higher grade, in spite of the fact that the failed pupils have each spent an added year in attaining this higher grade" [p. 249].

Comments

1. Despite considerable research, no clear-cut solution of the problem has been achieved. As the investigators point out, the problem is many-faceted and no one solution is applicable to all students. Both promotion and non-promotion present problems; promotion seems to be the lesser of the two evils. Perhaps the question should be a matter of individual decision rather than of schoolwide policy. In the final analysis, it is not whether a child is promoted or retained that matters but rather what the school does for him after that. A year spent in dull repetition of the previous year's work is not likely to be overly profitable. Special attention also needs to be given to the emotional and social effects of non-promotion.

2. We especially need to look at the curriculum to see that it is not generating its own failures by its incompatibility with the true needs of a substantial minority of its clientele. This may be where the real problem lies; once cured, the question of non-promotion may well become insignificant. We need to keep in mind that overemphasis on academic excellence might work to the detriment of certain children.

3. A good review of the issues involved is presented by Goodlad (1954, 1962), who points out, for example, that neither promotion nor retention alone can change the child's basic learning rate. He argues that what is needed is an organization that facilitates continuous progress for all children in each of the many facets of their development; the long-term answer, as he sees it, is "the elimination of grade barriers that give rise to a host of fallacious notions about pupil progress of which the fantasy that children should arrive precisely at a given 'norm' each June is the most preposterous."

References

Goodlad, John I. "To promote or not to promote," *Childh. Educ.*, 30: 212–215, 1954.

Goodlad, John I. "To promote or not to promote? Several answers; short-term or long-term," in Margaret Rasmussen (ed.), *Toward Effective Grouping.* Washington: Association Childhood Education International, 1962. Pp. 34–38.

Gary L. Peltier

Sex Differences in the School: Problem and Proposed Solution *

Although, traditionally, leadership positions in our society have been held by males, it is the female who more often finds success in our educational system. In many ways, the young male starts life's struggle with gross handicaps. He matures less rapidly than girls, he is susceptible to situational stress and trauma, he displays a greater incidence of mental deficiency and mental illness and a greater preponderance of behavioral and school adjustment problems. Nearly two thirds of all grade repeaters are boys; more boys than girls by a huge margin are underachievers and poor readers; three times as many boys as girls stutter.

Although girls appear to be more successful in school, research has failed to provide consistent sex differences in scholastic performance. Some studies have found boys scholastically inferior to girls in the elementary grades, whereas others have shown that in most areas boys achieve as well and in some cases better than girls. Project Talent did not find any startling sex differences in standardized test performance, although the girls in grades nine through twelve did finish slightly more items than the boys. However, boys typically receive lower grades and thus a lower class standing, and there is a considerably higher failure rate among boys in first and second grade. Even though there is evidence to suggest that boys do somewhat better than girls in mathematics and science where they are expected to, all in all, there appear to be a number of social, psychological, and institutional factors within the framework of American education which apparently hinder boys.

Socialization

The socialization process in contemporary America is so organized that behavioral expectations tend to be more clearly defined and more consistent for girls than they are for boys. Girls are provided with more opportunity for sex-identification and for acceptance of the sex role. Boys, on the other hand, are expected to be more aggressive and rebellious; yet such

* Adapted and abridged from *Phi Delta Kappan*, 50: 182–185, 1968. By permission of author and publisher.

behavior is clearly unacceptable (and unaccepted) in many settings, including the school. Too much identification with mother or with the teacher is likely to bring disapproval, e.g., being called mamma's boy, sissy, or teacher's pet. In general, boys are discouraged from taking on a significant portion of what is generally defined as appropriate male behavior, e.g., aggressiveness, dominance, the exercise of authority, etc. The boy is expected to exhibit overt aggression but the opportunities for him to do so are few and the limitations of these opportunities are often ill defined.

Psychological Differences

A number of psychological differences are apparent. Boys are typically more aggressive, independent, and outspoken. They avoid displays of emotion. They are generally superior in analytical thinking, problem solving, and scientific pursuits. Girls, on the other hand, display greater conformity and passivity and greater sensitivity to human relations. Boys and girls tend to develop different thinking styles.

The School's Role

The problem is complicated by the fact that the school tends to be an essentially sex-neutral institution, treating unequals as equals. We expect first-grade boys to write as well as their female counterparts even though their small-muscle coordination is less well developed. We expect both to progress through school at the same pace, despite the slower rate of maturation of boys. Socially accepted roles of aggressiveness and dominance bring boys in direct conflict with the teacher's role as the authority figure in the classroom. Allowing boys to behave like boys upsets classroom decorum; this teachers consider intolerable.

The large number of female teachers in the elementary school also tends to work to the disadvantage of boys; boys often create difficulties for themselves by making too many decisions on their own rather than responding to teacher suggestions (perhaps reflecting a lack of social sensitivity). Research has shown that girls tend to receive more teacher approval. Women teachers tend to scold boys more often and more harshly than they do girls—which only leads to greater aggressiveness on the part of boys.

There also appears to be a difference in the way men and women think. If this is true, boys are handicapped by their different style of thinking, their inability to comprehend female language, and their unwillingness to conform to a feminine value system. For boys, the classroom may well be perceived as a place in which they must be quiet and neat and must think like girls—all of which appears to conflict with their embryonic ideas of what a boy should be.

Proposed Solutions

A number of suggestions have been made to deal with the problem, e.g., to admit boys to school six months or so later than girls. Although European schools have traditionally segregated boys and girls, American educators have generally rejected both separate classes and separate schools, apparently on the argument that social learning is also important. Another suggestion is to group children on the basis of maturational readiness for learning. It has also been suggested that additional instructional time may have to be given boys in certain subjects.

Direction

Obviously, further research is necessary before any mandate for a major educational change is in order. In the meantime, elementary schools would do well to experiment with special classes for boys in areas where boys appear to be at a disadvantage. Such classes should be more masculine in tone, more exploratory in nature, and more oriented toward areas of masculine interest. Coeducational classes could be retained in the social studies and certain other subjects in order to retain the social advantages of coeducational interaction. There is a definite need to attract more men teachers to the elementary school to provide appropriate sex models, particularly in view of the many fatherless families. This may involve upgrading the prestige of elementary teachers, in general. Allowing prospective men teachers to serve as aides in elementary schools during their college years could serve to awaken them to the challenge and the reward of elementary school teaching. At the junior and high school level, we need to overcome traditional taboos as to "socially appropriate" activities based on false sex-role stereotypes; planning science classes from a female point of view might attract more talented girls into the sciences, for example.

Comments

1. While the existence of sex differences cannot be challenged, the specific nature of these differences is subject to considerable disagreement. What is more important, however, are the antecedents of these differences. Boys in the first grade tend to have difficulty in learning to read under present arrangements; they do not seem to have difficulty under different reading conditions (see McNeil, pp. 180–182, this text). In 1937, Gates suggested that whether a child learns to read or does not at a given level of development may well be a function of the particular style of teaching to which he is subjected. Rather than continue our unprofitable tendency to catalog the difficulties experienced by boys as if it were their fault, not ours, we might do better to adapt the school's curriculum—

indeed, its overall program, its very orientation—to capitalize on their strengths.

    2.   Some people would take strong issue with the suggestion of having boys enter school later than girls, especially in view of the generally greater expectations placed on the male in our culture. It might be noted that with respect to the culturally disadvantaged we have taken the position that the less well developed the child is, the earlier he should be subjected to the influence of the school. If we are to believe Bruner, adapting our instructional procedures to their readiness level might be a more effective and acceptable alternative.

    3.   For more comprehensive treatment of sex differences, see Josef E. Garai and Amram Scheinfeld, "Sex differences in mental and behavior traits," *Genet. Psychol. Monogr.*, 77: 169–299, 1968; and Tyler, Leona E. *The Psychology of Individual Differences*. New York: Appleton-Century-Crofts, 1965.

Leona E. Tyler

Toward a Workable Psychology of Individuality *

Individuality has so many champions nowadays that "conformity" has almost become a nasty word. "Adjustment," for years a central concept in psychology, is becoming suspect. People are recoiling in horror from Whyte's "Organization Man," while novelists are highlighting the individual's search for personal identity. Our task as psychologists is to convert this idea of individuality into a workable concept capable of generating good research hypotheses, of producing a technology of assessment, and of being applied in the day-to-day activities of people who are not psychologists. "The problem as I see it is: 'How can we modify the system of psychological principles and skills that are now being applied in all these situations so that the uniqueness of the individual is really taken into account?' " [p. 75].

Over the past 60 years, differential psychology has worked out techniques for measuring hundreds of traits, each of which can be thought of as an axis along which any one person's position can be located. "In this system the *uniqueness* of the individual is defined by his *combination* of measurements along all possible dimensions. A person is represented by a point in n-dimensional space. No one else occupies exactly the same position" [p. 76].

"Useful as this approach has been, I have found myself questioning more and more whether it is really adequate at this stage in the development of our science. For one thing, it does not *feel* quite right. Most people find it hard to think of themselves as points in n-dimensional space. . . . For another thing, the system shows signs of becoming completely unworkable . . . because of the proliferation of dimensions. It looked for a time as though factor analysis would . . . simplify it, but there are now so many factors and their relationships with each other are so complex that factor theory does not really constitute a simplification. But the most important reason I see for questioning the adequacy of this way of looking at things is that we are no longer making the progress with it that we have a right to expect. Correlations with criteria significant for theory or for

* Adapted and abridged from Leona E. Tyler, "Toward a workable psychology of individuality," *Amer. Psychol.*, 14: 75–81, 1959. Copyright 1959 by American Psychological Association, and reproduced by permission.

practice are not going up very much. . . . The addition of new dimensions and the increasing refinement in the ways we measure the old ones are not really 'paying off' very well. The possibility is at least worth considering that we are approaching the limit of what can be done with this particular system" [p. 76].

A number of personality theorists—Freud, Adler, Gordon Allport, Murray, and others—have been concerned with the question of individual uniqueness and how it can be best conceptualized. Unfortunately, none of these concepts drawn from personality theory has been particularly workable from the standpoint of technology. "By and large, the vast majority of so-called personality *tests* are measures of either general maladjustment, the extent to which an individual deviates from hypothetical average or of general 'normality,' or they are measures of the particular *variety* of neurotic or psychotic trends he shows" [p. 76]. Even in cases where the concepts derived from personality theory have led to methods of personality assessment, it is still on the basis of assumption that differences among persons can be measured in terms of traits or dimensions. A score on a personality test identifies the testee's position on a given trait in relation to the members of some reference group.

"What I have come to believe is that individuality will continue to elude us as long as we restrict our thinking to models based on dimensions or trait continua. Little by little, evidence has been accumulating that some of the crucial defining features of psychological individuality are to be found in two aspects of experience and behavior that are not easily expressed in dimensions and that can be best thought of as discontinuous. I call these two aspects of individuality *choice* and *organization* . . ." [p. 77].

"Partly what led me to a reorganization in my ideas about individuality around these concepts was a sort of inherent reasonableness about them. With the swift passage of the years one becomes acutely aware that . . . only a small fraction of the potentialities with which his life begins can ever become realities. By the time his infancy is over, a considerable number of them have already been ruled out by the fact that he has spent his most formative years in one particular kind of home rather than in another. But the person is still confronted at each step of his life with an incredibly complex assortment of stimulating conditions and behavior possibilities. In order to function at all, each of us must choose from this plethora of possibilities and organize what he has chosen" [p. 77].

As the individual interacts with a complex environment, he develops certain patterns of choice that serve to let some things in and to keep others out. In addition, there is an organizational process acting on the experiences which the individual has chosen. It is in these two concepts of choice and organization that we come close to the meaning of individuality.

"A person's life is always bounded by limits of one kind or another;

he is not free to do anything he wants to do or to go in any direction. . . . Certainly at any one time a large number of behavior possibilities are ruled out by external circumstances, by personal inadequacies, and by previous commitments. But within these analyzable limits there is a larger and smaller space in which movement of different sorts is possible. It is this movement in one direction rather than another, within defining limits, that I am calling *choice*" [p. 77].

While a large part of the choice process is unconscious, the small part of this choice process of which we are aware is what we call *freedom*; it is this awareness in human choices which "changes the nature of the total situation and thus leads to choices that may be different from those that would have been made unconsciously. And in this small margin of difference that awareness makes lies our best hope for progress in living our own lives wisely and helping those it is our responsibility to help" [p. 77].

"A workable psychology of individuality would provide us with ways of recognizing significant patterns of choices that have been made at previous stages of life, consciously or unconsciously, and of widening the margin of awareness in any individual's present experience. To accomplish this we need a different approach, a different kind of assessment from the customary measurements of traits or dimensions" [p. 78].

Scaling the degree of a given trait or dimension simply misses the main distinction. The correlation of the numerical scores on the Strong Interest Inventory with various measures of success and satisfaction have invariably been rather low, but what is important is that such scores are predictive of a special kind of criteria, viz., the way the individual will make his choices at later junctures of his life. What these correlations show is simply that a measure of the nature of one's complex pattern of occupational choices predicts later complex choices in the same area.

"The main point I am trying to make here is that to work out technology of choice measurements we must use classifications with regard to choices rather than continua, validate our assessments using choice criteria rather than measures of degrees of happiness or success, and state the relationships as probabilities that one thing will lead to another rather than as correlation coefficients" [p. 79]. This shift from traits to discontinuous patterns of choice does not require that we abandon the concept of predictive validity; we simply need to identify criteria that represent choices rather than distances along some scale, e.g., staying in school (vs. dropping out) as opposed to GPA.

It is also important to consider *how* as well as *what* individuals choose. Involved is not only the matter of awareness of choice but also the stage at which these choices are made and whether these choices are made positively or negatively. One person chooses an occupation to avoid low prestige or low pay, while another is motivated through a strong desire to try different things. Another important point to consider is how much thoughtful consideration of possible alternatives has gone into these choices. Most important of all in certain ways, even though hardest to investigate, is the question of how central or deeply rooted any given pattern of choice is for a given individual, for "it is these basic unalterable choices that give the person a firm sense of self. Just making choices with regard to separate objects and actions is not enough. It is necessary that a person in some way *choose to be himself*" [p. 80].

To sum up, the present discussion is centered around *choice;* this is not to minimize the importance of *organization* but this is left to others to develop.[1] Other possibilities of investigation in this concept of choice and organization exist. "What interests me most right now, however, is the significance of concepts of choice and organization in an inclusive psychology of the development of the individual. We are coming to see development as a life-long process in which choice and organization play a crucial part. In a certain sense each individual is a 'self-made man.' At each stage of our lives, we impose limits on the next stage, by the choices we make and the ways in which we organize what we have experienced. There is an important something that each individual must do for himself" [p. 81].

Comments

1.   The article relates the psychology of individual differences to basic issues in the conceptualizations of personality and its assessment. It emphasizes the basic weaknesses in our current approach. On the other hand, it may be easier to recognize limitations in our present emphasis on psychological traits than it is to work out the details of an alternative approach.

2.   The extent to which one's freedom of choice is gradually restricted by the choices he has made previously (as well as by his role in life, also partially of his own choosing) is an interesting concept. As Tyler points out, the individual, in all reality, has true control of only a small segment of the behavioral "choices" he makes minute by minute. The fact that you are reading this now is really an inevitable consequence of the decision made a couple of months ago regarding taking the course. In fact, it is really a delayed consequent of the particular "choice" of parents you made before birth. If we agree that ability and personality are rather clearly set as a result of the experiences of the first few years, one's "choice" horizon is rather drastically reduced by the time he enters school. The self-concept is another aspect of this restriction of "choice."

[1] The author mentions briefly a number of sorting techniques designed to investigate the orientation of the individual's relationships to other significant people in his life.

Dael Wolfle

Diversity of Talents *

"A problem of continuing concern is the extent to which we are properly developing and utilizing the nation's intellectual resources. For both realistic and practical reasons, it is desirable that we make better provisions than we have in the past for the full development of human talent. The more fundamental reason is that one of the basic ideals of a free society is the provision of opportunity for each person to develop to his full capacity" [p. 535].

There is also an urgent practical reason: In contrast to our needs in our early history, the critical need in our nation today is "for men and women with ideas and highly developed talents . . . men and women who can roll back the boundaries of ignorance, who can manage complex organizations, who can perform the diverse and demanding tasks on which the further development of a free industrial society depends" [p. 535]. Prior to WW II, we lived in the worst depression of our history; our need then was for work for the people we had. Before that, most of the labor force was engaged in farming and other vocations that made relatively little demand on man's intellectual capacity. WW II created a need for brains and proved to us that invention could be planned.

Research has shown that many bright students do not go to college. Bridgman (1961) reports that out of the 30% at the top of the ability distribution, approximately 55% do not graduate from college; about 11% do not even finish high school. The picture is even worse for girls: Only 30% of the girls in the top 30% in ability graduate from college. We need to be more active in encouraging talented students. "There may be exceptions, but it is neither safe nor realistic to assume that high ability is always accompanied by high motivation, that human talent will override obstacles to find its own way to fruition. Nor is it safe to assume that the necessary inspiration or encouragement will always be provided by the family" [p. 537]. Swanson (1955) found that the clearest difference between bright students who had gone to college and those who had not was

* Adapted and abridged from Dael Wolfle, "Diversity of talents," *Amer. Psychol.*, 15: 535–545, 1960. Copyright 1960 by American Psychological Association and reproduced by permission.

that someone—a teacher, a minister, a relative, or a friend—had encouraged the former to go to college.

However, it is not sufficient simply to encourage the talent we find. A more interesting question is that of devising an underlying strategy of talent development. "I suggest that it is time for those of us who are professionally most concerned to consider the policy issues and to try to develop a strategy that will maximize the achievement and social value of the persons whose talents we seek to identify and develop" [p. 539]. This implies a need, first of all, for the full development of all forms of socially useful talents, and secondly, for a better understanding of the social and cultural factors that stimulate or retard the development of talent.

However, besides identifying talented youngsters and helping them secure an education commensurate with their ability, "we must also consider how the talents we are developing can be so distributed as to result in the greatest accomplishment. The recommendation that I will make on this point is likely to be controversial. . . . In the selection and education of persons of ability, it is advantageous to a society to seek the greatest achievable diversity of talent: Diversity within an individual, among the members of an occupational group, and among individuals who constitute a society" [p. 539].

"I am not talking about the well-rounded individual, or the broad scholar, or the man of many talents. These are qualities we ordinarily respect; but I wish to make a case for the opposite, for the man who has developed some of his talents so highly that he cannot be well-rounded, for the one who may be called uneven or one-sided but in whom at least one side has been developed to the level of real superiority" [p. 539].

We do not want to maximize diversity by having some people very bright and others very dull; "obviously we want each person to reach the highest level of which he is capable. But . . . a strong case can be made for the proposition that the value of a nation's intellectual resources—or the total achievement—would be maximized by maximizing the variety of abilities within and among individuals" [p. 539].

Actually, a number of forces constantly operate in the opposite direction, causing us to be more, rather than less, alike and tending to prevent the uneven development of the talented individual; parents don't want their children to be different; teachers tend to want their children alike. The point is well illustrated by Harold Benjamin's *The Cultivation of Idiosyncrasies* (1955), where all the animals had to take all the subjects.

Let us start with two assumptions on which there is general agreement: (a) Individuals vary in the total amount of talent they possess; and (b) ability is not a unitary trait but rather expresses itself in various forms of special abilities. Now suppose a given individual has 1000 units of ability: If he wishes to be completely well-rounded, he could assign 50 units to each of 20 abilities. Or he might elect to assign 100 units to each of 10 abilities he considers most important and neglect completely the other 10. Or, at the extreme, he might stake his whole 1000 units on one ability and neglect the other 19. Which of those strategies would be best for the individual and for society calls for consideration of values in real life. The price tag which society places on different levels of accomplishment is not directly proportional to the ability or achievement involved; rather it increases sharply with ability. Not only is the distribution of salaries badly skewed to the right, but it is generally agreed that the salaries paid to the most able fall far short of being commensurate with their worth.

This is not to say that every scholar should be a narrow specialist; we do need scholars of wide interest and knowledge to bridge the gaps between various areas of knowledge. "As to how far we should go in the direction of diversity, I have only two suggestions, and both must be stated in general terms. One is that we should go as far as we can. The other is that the greater the ability with which we are dealing, the greater the amount of idiosyncrasy we can tolerate" [p. 542]. An implication of the foregoing is that we ought to make wider use of tests of special abilities and aptitude as a means of minimizing the danger of overlooking students with unusual potential that is not well measured by tests of general ability. This would increase the size of the talent pool from which we can draw. In the study by Little (1958), about 20% of the students identified by their teachers as specially gifted in some field had not ranked in the upper quarter of their graduating class in either general ability or general scholastic achievement.

Comments

1. The article's major contribution is with respect to its third point—admittedly controversial—namely, the optimal deployment of talent by maximizing diversity on the part of individuals of high potential in a specialized area. While narrow eccentricity on a wholesale basis is undoubtedly objectionable, there is a considerable reaction against the "nothing good–nothing bad" assembly-line mediocrity that seems to characterize some of our operations.

2. The issue also bears on the "liberal education" concept: there is agreement that everyone must be able to use English effectively, that the effective operation of democratic society calls for some commonality of background on socio-political issues, etc. The issue is, of course, one of balance between general education and specialization, with the point of optimal individual and social benefit obviously indeterminate. It must also be recognized that "division of labor" and social interdependence imply some degree of specialization in certain areas and relative incompetence in others.

References

Benjamin, Harold. *The Cultivation of Idiosyncrasy.* Cambridge: Harvard University Press, 1955.

Bridgman, D. S. *Losses of Intellectual Talent from the Educational System prior to Graduation from College.* Washington: National Science Foundation, 1961.

Little, J. K. *A State-Wide Inquiry into Decisions of Youth about Education beyond High School.* Madison: University of Wisconsin, 1958.

Swanson, E. O. "Is college education worthwhile?" *J. counsel. Psychol.,* 2: 176–181, 1955.

That's What They Said

"Every major tenet of our culture and every major principle of our democracy tell us that the most valuable asset existing in a group is the uniqueness of individuals within the group, a principle that is denied daily."

H. G. Morgan. "Impact of cultural change on school grouping practices," in Margaret Rasmussen (ed.), *Toward Effective Grouping.* Washington: Association for Childhood Education International, 1962. Pp. 3–16.

"True education makes for inequality; the inequality of individuality, the inequality of success; the glorious inequality of talent, of genius; for inequality, not mediocrity, individual superiority, not standardization, is the measure of the progress of the world."

Felix E. Schelling

"It seems clear . . . that the most striking characteristics of students in the elementary and secondary schools are the very great individual differences in patterns of aptitude and ability and the lack of sound educational planning based on a full understanding of the significance of the unique potential of each student."

John C. Flanagan. "Student characteristics: Elementary and secondary," in Robert L. Ebel (ed.), *Encyclopedia of Educational Research.* New York: The Macmillan Company, 1969. Pp. 1330–1339. [1338]

"The closer we come to attaining equality of educational opportunity the greater become the inequalities of education, as the capable come closer to reaching their potential and widen the gap between themselves and the less competent."

Don Robinson. "Scraps from a teacher's notebook," *Phi Delta Kappan,* 47: 157, 1965.

". . . I believe the highest goal that measurement and evaluation psychologists can strive for is the development of those instruments and techniques required by a society which aspires to capitalize to the fullest upon the fact that most men are created unequal."

Paul Horst. "Most men are created unequal," *Sci. Monthly,* 72: 318–324, 1951. [324]

"We hold these truths to be self-evident . . . that all men are created equal."

The Declaration of Independence.

"The magnitude of these differences is difficult to determine because we have very few measurements which can be expressed in absolute units such as we use in the measurement of height and weight. But a quick glance at a set of norms for the different grades on almost any standardized test will convince the reader. Inspecting the norms for a well-known and carefully developed battery of aptitude tests, we note that an average of about 40 per cent of ninth-grade students exceed the scores made by the lowest third of twelfth-grade students. On several of the tests, 50 per cent of the ninth-grade students exceed the lowest third of the twelfth-grade students."

Benjamin S. Bloom. "Testing cognitive ability and achievement," in N. L. Gage (ed.), *Handbook of Research on Teaching.* Skokie, Ill.: Rand McNally & Company, 1963. Pp. 379–397. [382]

"There is a persistent conspiracy to make learning hard when there is every reason to make it easy. In some schools teachers are still considered 'good' if they give a high percentage of failing grades. It would seem that an effective teacher would have a low rate of failure, and the ideal teacher would have no failure at all."

Don Robinson. "Scraps from a teacher's notebook," *Phi Delta Kappan,* 48: 416, 1967.

"Schools have always tried to cope with the problem of individual differences, usually in ways which really have been designed in the hope of eliminating or minimizing differences."

G. Max Wingo. "Implications for improving instruction in the upper elementary grades," in N. B. Henry (ed.), *Learning and Instruction.* 49th Yearbook, National Society for the Study of Education, Part I. Chicago: University of Chicago Press, 1950. Pp. 280–303. [297]

"Once upon a time, the animals decided they must do something heroic to meet the problems of 'a new world.' So they organized a school.

"They adopted an activity curriculum consisting of running, climbing, swimming, and flying. To make it easier to administer the curriculum, *all* the animals took *all* the subjects.

"The duck was excellent in swimming, in fact better than his instructor; but he made only passing grades in flying and was very poor in running. Since he was slow in running, he had to stay after school and also drop swimming in order to practice running. This was kept up until his web feet were badly worn and he was only average in swimming. *But average was acceptable in school, so nobody worried about that except the duck.*

"The rabbit started at the top of his class in running, but had a nervous breakdown because of so much make-up work in swimming.

"The eagle was a problem child and was disciplined severely. In the climbing class he beat all the others to the top of the tree, but insisted on using his own way to get there.

"The prairie dogs stayed out of school and fought the tax levy because the administration would not add digging and burrowing to the curriculum. They apprenticed their child to a badger and later joined the groundhogs and gophers to start a successful private school."

C. H. Reavis. "The animal school," *Tech Training,* 11, May 1948. [7]

"Whether individual differences in ability are innate or are due to environmental differences, we must deal with them imaginatively and constructively."

John W. Gardner. *Excellence.* New York: Harper & Row, Publishers, 1961. [58]

"Although such facts should be basic data in educational thinking, traditional school organization and curriculum practices ignore them. The idea of homogeneous groups of people receiving uniform instruction by means of educational techniques from uniform textbooks dies hard. The assumptions persist: that grade levels signify rather definite stages of educational achievement, that the course of study for a grade is the prescribed academic requirement to be administered uniformly to all pupils, that all pupils in a grade should be capable of coping successfully with the work outlined for that grade, that a pupil should not be promoted to a grade until he is able to do the work outlined for that grade, that when individual differences are provided for all pupils can be brought up to standard, that maintaining a passing mark results in homogeneous instructional groups, and that when relative homogeneity of a class does not prevail it is the result of poor teaching or lax standards."

Walter W. Cook. "Individual differences and curriculum practice," *J. educ. Psychol.,* 39: 141–148, 1948. [141–142]

"Had Rip Van Winkle been a teacher, and had he dozed off in 1934 while deliberating the fate of thirty youngsters, be might have resumed his deliberations quite naturally on awakening in 1954. Not a soul would laugh; not a soul would consider his activities bizarre. Only the thankful thirty, spared through Rip's somnolent sojourn, might rejoice that the belated decisions would now have no bearing upon their lives."

> John I. Goodlad. "To promote or not to promote," *Childh. Educ.*, 30: 212–215, 1954. [212]

"The crux of the promotion issue is that there ought not to be any alternatives. *There ought not to be a decision to make. Promotion and non-promotion are both inconsistent with certain significant insights into children and their learning. . . .*"

> John I. Goodlad. "To promote or not to promote? Several answers: Short-term and long-term," *Membership Serv. Bull.*, 5-A, 1962. Washington: Childhood Education International, 1962.

"The theory that keeping a child back to repeat a grade or class will improve his academic standing has not been realized in practice."

> J. C. Parker and D. H. Russell. "Ways of providing for individual differences," *Educ. Lead.*, 11: 168–174, 1958. [169]

"Acceleration of a year or two or three, however desirable, is but a fraction of what is needed to keep a gifted child or youth working at his intellectual best."

> Lewis M. Terman. "The discovery and encouragement of exceptional talent," *Amer. Psychol.*, 9: 221–230, 1954. [227]

"In short, it appears that acceleration has caused much less social maladjustment than has ordinarily been supposed. A little care in selection and guidance of accelerated students should make difficulties even less common. Increase in the number of accelerated individuals should decrease difficulties even more."

> S. L. Pressey. *Educational Acceleration.* Columbus: Ohio State University, 1949. [138]

"A plan for continuous growth is widely recognized as more desirable than the experience of annual evaluation followed by promotion or non-promotion. Learning is continuous and must progress according to individual rate and ability. Schools cannot, therefore, justify continuance of annual promotion or retardation as sound practice."

> Helen Heffernan et al. "The organization of the elementary school and the development of a healthy personality," *Calif. J. elem. Educ.*, 20: 129–153, 1952. [135]

"Failure to develop the very bright to their highest capacity represents waste of the kind that we can least afford."

C. S. Berry. *Special Education.* New York: Appleton-Century-Crofts, 1931. [549]

"The best single reason for using computers for instruction is that computer technology provides the only serious hope for recognition of individual differences in subject-matter learning."

Allen B. Coderman. "Computer-based instructional systems," in Richard R. Goulet (ed.), *Educational Change: The Reality and the Promise.* New York: Citation Press, 1968. Pp. 231–244. [234]

CHAPTER 10

Test Items

1. Probably the widest differences in human beings are
   a. the differences among the different aptitudes within any one in-
      dividual
   b. the differences between men and women
   c. the differences connected with aging
   d. the differences that exist from one racial group to another
   e. the diversity of the members of any one group

2. In which of the following are sex differences likely to be *least?*
   a. academic achievement as measured by standardized achievement
      tests
   b. adjustment to the school's routine
   c. mechanical aptitude
   d. social sensitivity and docility
   e. verbal fluency and clerical perception

3. Which of the following differences is *least?*
   a. age differences in IQ
   b. socio-economic differences in attitudes and values
   c. socio-economic differences in health and physical size
   d. sex differences in IQ
   e. sex differences in verbal fluency

4. Of the following, the least difference in actual achievement would
   probably be that between
   a. the achievement of pupils in successive grades in elementary
      school
   b. the grades of boys and girls in the same English class
   c. the grades of elementary school children of high and of low socio-
      economic status
   d. grades of children in the top and bottom quarter of a given grade
   e. over-all knowledge of the average high school and college seniors

5. The school needs to look at individual differences as
   a. a challenge to routine
   b. a decided help to good operation
   c. the individual's most important asset

d. an obstacle to effective classroom operation
e. a priceless asset to social welfare

6. Probably the most justifiable means of dealing with individual differences in the classroom is
   a. acceleration / nonpromotion
   b. ability grouping
   c. modification of the curriculum
   d. modification of teaching procedures
   e. reduction of curricular requirements to minimal essentials

7. Nonpromotion is best justified as a means of
   a. helping the child catch up
   b. maintaining standards
   c. providing for optimal grade placement
   d. reducing individual differences within a given grade
   e. reducing unhealthy pressures on the child

8. Probably the least justified means of dealing with individual differences is
   a. to fail the laggards
   b. to let every child set his own pace, e. g., by using teaching machines
   c. to provide extra classes, e. g., summer school
   d. to set classroom objectives at the least common denominator
   e. to standardize the curriculum

9. The main objection to ability grouping is that
   a. it creates administrative difficulties beyond the benefits it provides
   b. it disregards other important components of child growth
   c. it negates the democratic values of our society
   d. it often involves de facto segregation of the races
   e. it promotes feelings of superiority / inferiority

10. Generally speaking, the best way of dealing with the gifted child in high school is
    a. to allow him to skip a grade
    b. to allow him to take an extra class through the school's early or late shift
    c. to give him encouragement and freedom to work out his own adjustment
    d. to place him in a special class with other gifted children
    e. to provide a program of independent study for extra credit

11. The most constructive way for the school to deal with its dull-child problem is
     a. to have teachers concentrate on the slower children of the class
     b. to provide evening sessions for all children who need help
     c. to provide a preschool Head Start program
     d. to provide special classes
     e. to redefine its objectives to eliminate all but the essentials

12. Probably the most crucial feature of any program of ability grouping in high school is that
     a. assignment to any given group be continuous throughout high school
     b. the instructional program be varied accordingly
     c. it be based on over-all GPA rather than IQ
     d. it be flexible and reversible
     e. it be specific to each subject area

13. The greatest danger to the mentally retarded child in the regular classroom is that
     a. constant pressures will result in personality distortion
     b. he will become a compulsive overachiever
     c. he will become progressively more inept as his foundation of previous learnings becomes progressively less adequate
     d. he will resort to delinquency in order to satisfy his needs
     e. inability to meet demands will result in his refusal to try

14. In dealing with individual differences, teachers should strive
     a. to capitalize on group activities in which everyone can make a contribution
     b. to encourage each child to cultivate a specialty with which he can identify
     c. to place the child on a self-actualizing schedule where he can make his own plans
     d. to plan a variety of activities from which children can choose what they like
     e. to substitute individual standards for currently uniform group standards

15. The key to the effective dealing with individual differences in the classroom is
     a. an alert, sensitive, and competent teacher
     b. a flexible system of ability grouping
     c. freedom from administrative restrictions and constraints
     d. a suitable curriculum
     e. a workable up-to-date pupil record system

16. Individual differences in physical size among people of the same age and sex are probably greatest in
    a. adult men of different socio-economic class
    b. adult women
    c. adolescent boys
    d. grade-school boys
    e. preschool girls

17. Sex differences related to the academic setting are most pronounced with respect to
    a. ability as measured by IQ tests
    b. motivation, docility, and social sensitivity
    c. performance as reflected in grades
    d. performance in basic skills (e. g., reading, arithmetic)
    e. performance on standardized tests

18. During the adolescent and preadolescent period, girls tend to be superior to boys in
    a. academic performance
    b. personal adjustment
    c. physical health and stamina
    d. social and emotional maturity
    e. verbal and quantitative aptitude

19. At what age does mental functioning begin to decline?
    a. anytime after birth
    b. around age 16
    c. in early adulthood
    d. shortly after age 50
    e. it varies from one mental function to another

20. The most pronounced differences connected with socio-economic status are in the area of
    a. antisocial predispositions
    b. attitudes and values
    c. intelligence
    d. personal and social adjustment
    e. physical size

21. The overlap between the distribution of 9th- and 12th-graders in general academic competence is of the order of _____ percent.
    a. 2   d. 40
    b. 10   e. 60
    c. 20

22. According to current thinking, the greatest contributor to the wide range of individual differences in academic competence in the primary grades is/are
    a. early sensory stimulation
    b. inadequate instruction
    c. inherited limitations
    d. failure to abide by sound promotional policies
    e. failure to provide remedial help where needed

23. The most convincing argument against reliance on ability grouping as the "solution" to the individual-differences problem is that
    a. it is in violation of the democratic framework within which the school exists
    b. it promotes social isolation along intellectual lines
    c. it promotes feelings of inferiority/superiority
    d. the teacher still has to reckon with individual differences within an ability-grouped class
    e. none of the above; there is no major objection to ability grouping

24. The key concept that should influence any retention/promotion decision is
    a. academic standards (the reputation of the diploma)
    b. character development (accepting the consequences of one's shortcomings)
    c. frustration tolerance (helping the child cope with disappointment)
    d. mental health (safeguarding the child from psychological harm)
    e. optimal grade placement (how can we best help the child)

25. Probably the least adequate way of dealing with the individual difference problem in the classroom is
    a. accelerating the bright
    b. failing the dull
    c. eliminating the yearly promotion system
    d. eliminating testing, grading, and pass–fail
    e. providing tutorial instruction (e. g., programed instruction)

26. The most appropriate way of grouping high-school students is on the basis of
    a. general IQ
    b. past grades in major academic subjects
    c. performance on standardized tests of academic achievement
    d. special ability in relevant areas
    e. teacher recommendation relative to motivation, citizenship, and general maturity

27. Grade retention and/or double promotion are particularly effective in
     a. facilitating the task of the teacher
     b. maintaining scholastic standards
     c. motivating students
     d. reducing the range of individual differences within a given class
     e. none of the above; they are not particularly effective

28. Which of the following has *not* voiced direct support for the accelera-
     tion of the gifted?
     a. The Fund for the Advancement of Education
     b. Gesell
     c. Learned and Wood
     d. Pressey
     e. Terman

29. Probably the most profitable thing the teacher can do with regard to
     individual differences in the classroom is
     a. to adapt the curriculum to individual needs
     b. to be alert to learning difficulties that impede growth
     c. to help each child achieve the security necessary for him to be-
         come maximally open to experience
     d. to organize the curriculum around broad projects toward which
         each child can contribute
     e. to provide each child with a thorough grasp of the fundamentals,
         e. g., the basic skills

PART III

The Process of Learning

CHAPTER 11

General Nature of Learning

The psychology of learning is the study of the process of behavior modification through experience. Many psychologists see learning, in its broad sense, as the central problem in the study of behavior. Although there is some question as to how effectively the findings accumulated to date can be generalized to the education of children, few people would disagree with the premise that the key to effective classroom operation lies in the effective application of the principles of learning. There is a general feeling, however, that educational psychology will make only a limited contribution to educational practice until such time as it reorients itself toward real problems as they occur in the setting of the classroom.

An understanding of how, and under what conditions, people learn can be considered to be the major contribution of psychology to pedagogical practice. If they are to be more than mere technicians, teachers need to understand the psychology of the learning process, to note its outstanding features and characteristics, to study variations in the learning process itself as well as in its elements, and to examine the implications of learning principles for the management and the measurement of learning experiences. Such an understanding, along with the skills necessary to convert it into effective teaching–learning strategies, is essential to the professional preparation of teachers. Actually, as we have seen in connection with learning theories, there are many explanations of the way learning takes place and how it can be facilitated. Although each theory claims to cover the learning phenomenon in all its manifestations, it is unrealistic to expect a single formulation to cover equally well all aspects of the educational enterprise—verbal materials, psychomotor skills, attitudes and values, etc. Gagné (1962), for example, did not find the general principles derived from traditional psychology of learning particularly applicable to the "teaching" of military skills.

In the two papers in this chapter, Bayles, in an article published in the early 1950s, presents the field (cognitive) view of learning as the development of insight. Kendler, on the other hand, presents a relatively current version of the S–R position as it applies to audiovisual education.

Reference

Gagné, Robert M. "Military training and principles of learning," *Amer. Psychol.*, 17: 83–91, 1962.

Ernest E. Bayles

The Idea of Learning
as Development of Insight *

Theory regarding the nature of learning lies close to the heart of teaching theory. Lack of clarity regarding the former leads to a corresponding lack of clarity regarding the latter. This is not to say that learning theory is the whole of teaching theory; far from it. With the confusion that still surrounds current professional thinking regarding the nature of learning, further discussion of the question seems in order.

Lack of clarity of connectionism was brought home to me early in the twenties when as a supervisor of practice teachers I was supposed to help beginners achieve competence in handling the learning process. But connectionist principles always pointed to wrong procedures. Repetitive drill was obviously wrong. Yet, both the logic of the theory and the nature of teaching materials available at the time pointed inevitably to repetitive drill. Then Gestalt theory appeared, threads of clarity began to penetrate the confusion, and order began to emerge. Later Thorndike acknowledged that repetition (per se) has little, if any, effect on learning and proposed the concept of "belongingness."

Looking at the matter through mid-twentieth century eyes, individuals appear to behave on the basis of the principle of least action; *to act in such a way as to achieve an adopted pattern of goals in the quickest and easiest way that they sense or comprehend as available under existing circumstances.* In other words, we seem to be inherently lazy, to seek always the easiest way to get done what appears necessary or desirable.

Insight and the Principle of Least Action

Reliance on the principle of least action means that we base the interpretation of behavior on three factors: *goal*—what a person wants or intends to do; *confronting situation*—what he will meet in proceeding to attain the goal; and *insight*—the way he sizes up the situation. You will note that in our basic premises we do not say the quickest and easiest way available; but rather the quickest and easiest way which is sensed *as* available. We do not take paths that we know nothing about.

* Adapted and abridged from Ernest E. Bayles, "The idea of learning as development of insight," *Educ. Theory*, 2: 65–71, 1952.

Learning frequently is defined as a change in behavior; but not every behavioral change means learning. A change in behavior will accompany a change in goal, or in the confronting situation, even though in neither case has learning necessarily occurred. Evidently, and this seems to be amply supported by experimental and experiential evidence though as yet not so recognized in the psychological literature, learning represents and is confined to a *change in insight*.

The Meaning of "Insight"

By insight, we do not mean any linguistic expression; rather we refer to what lies back of any word statement; to that which one catches even before he has words to express it, such as the swing of a ball bat or an idea for which one cannot quite find the right word. Developing insight means establishing a sense of, or "feel" for, pattern. It may require looking sharply but imaginatively into a confronting situation in order to make the pattern "jump out at you," as when we look for hidden faces in a cleverly designed drawing or for strange animals in fleecy clouds. Or it may require closing the eyes and trying intently to visualize a situation, possibly not yet fully observed. Then, catching the point, we act with precision and exactitude. It is less of learning by doing and more of learning by seeing, even though with "the mind's eye." Emphasis in the process of learning shifts from going through the motions to conceptualization.

This does not imply that we are to dispense with practice. But practice is to be something other than repetitive stamping-in. On the contrary, practice in the framework of learning as the development of insight implies doing things differently each time from the way they were done before. What counts is the grasp the learner gains rather than simply the number of times a given thing has been done.

And this "grasp" is very much of a mental phenomenon, whether the subject is basketball, woodwork, appreciation of an art object, or mastery of a proposition in mathematics or science. Once one "gets the hang of a thing," the feel for pattern, one does not have to repeat and repeat in order to make perfect. We need to get completely away from repetitive drill. The present writer feels thoroughly justified in insisting that *"Whenever repetitive drill is invoked, learning will suffer."*

Practice within the context of learning as development of insight is no longer a matter of repetition; in spelling, for example, practice is a search for hidden patterns and leads to the study of words that fit this pattern and those that do not. In a sense, this represents a return to spelling rules. But there is a difference between learning rules by rote, as they were learned years ago, and having rules evolve out of the words that are being studied—with such rules holding only as long as they perform in a fairly satisfactory manner. This is no longer a matter of "rules" but rather of insight.

Belongingness and Repetition

Thorndike recognized that belongingness had to accompany repetition, for repetition by itself had little, if any, effect. Although he did not define belongingness, it seems highly reasonable that it can, and should, mean insight as we are using the term. Furthermore, insight may be gained without repetition; in fact, to the extent that life is forever new, we continually have to act correctly the first time or be hopelessly incompetent.

The proof of the insight theory of learning is operational: To the extent that observable facts turn out as anticipated or deduced from the generalized theory, the theory can be assumed to have been demonstrated. Whenever sharp and precise deductions disclose the possibility of observable differences, the findings have consistently favored overwhelmingly the insight theory. It seems that the more painstaking or meticulous the analysis, the more convincing is the showing.

In summary, then, it seems that, if teaching is to be most effectual, the learning theory to be employed should be one that seeks consistently to develop insight. Procedural emphasis shifts from repetition to conceptualization, from learning by doing to learning by "seeing." Learning is not a function of the number of times an act is repeated. It is the "feel" for pattern that is caught during a performance—the insight gained—that counts. Learning as development of insight does not mean the elimination of practice, although an overall reduction of practice time may reasonably be expected.

Comments

1. Bayles' views on the importance of learning as development or modification insight have been presented in a number of publications—e.g., Bayles (1960). The article above, published in 1952, makes a strong case against repetition and drill based on Thorndikean premises. Bayles is also noted for his strong emphasis on democratic teaching procedures which, he presumably believes, are highly compatible with the idea of learning as development of insight.

2. Bayles' views are in line with the current emphasis on meaningfulness. Perhaps the problem is how to develop this meaningfulness; it does not follow, for example, that the problem-solving approach or teaching through discovery is necessarily the only way of having students develop meaningfulness, and Bayles himself has repeatedly taken pains to point this out.

Reference

Bayles, Ernest E. *Democratic Educational Theory*. New York: Harper & Row, Publishers, 1960.

Howard H. Kendler

Stimulus Response Psychology and Audio-Visual Education *

Before one can control behavior, it is necessary to describe it. Stimulus response psychology is one attempt to do so. To the extent that conditioning provides the clearest picture of how a response becomes associated with a stimulus, and how this connection is strengthened or weakened, observing it closely will permit us to uncover the secrets of the learning process.

It must be recognized, however, that there is no automatic connection between a theory, whether in physics or psychology, and its successful application to a practical problem. Before a theoretical principle can be applied, its essence must be converted to fit the needs of a practical problem. And there is no simple rule to describe how this conversion is done successfully. We must rely on those applied scientists who possess the gift for making things work. In short, the learning theorist cannot, no matter how adequate his theory, take the place of the audio-visual educator. He can offer advice and give direction, but, in the final analysis, the creation of effective audio-visual programs must emerge from the distillation of theoretical principles with practical "know-how." And only the audio-visual educator can perform that function.

According to S–R psychology, for learning to take place the organism must make the correct response when the appropriate stimulus occurs and the necessary conditions for associative learning are available. These conditions are easily arranged in a laboratory but are much more difficult to manipulate in a typical educational situation. Too often, the stimulus situations presented in the classroom are such that the learner never encounters them again. A more serious problem for the audio-visual educator is to develop techniques that will permit the reinforcement of appropriate responses to the stimuli presented. This means, for example, that if the audio-visual educator is to formulate an effective training program, he must know precisely what responses he desires students to learn and arrange for them to be reinforced for making these responses. To the author, the difficulty contained therein has been greatly exaggerated; if the se-

* Adapted and abridged from *AV Comm. Rev.,* 9: 33–41, 1961. By permission of author and publisher.

quence is successful in presenting the appropriate stimulus and instigating the correct response, learning will more than likely take place.

In dealing with complex behavior, particularly of humans, learning theorists generally assume certain mediating processes occurring between the presentation of an external stimulus and the organism's response to this stimulus. The all important feature of this mediational mechanism is that the behavior of the subject is controlled by a cue he himself emits. Therefore, the audio-visual educator interested in teaching a skill involving a mediational mechanism—for example, a verbal skill—must arrange a training sequence that elicits similar mediational responses among the various members of the audience. The educational process is easily controlled by giving the learner the opportunity to make, whenever the stimulus is presented, an overt response which can be rewarded when correct and left unrewarded when incorrect. Difficulties arise when the responses are unknown so that reinforcement cannot be administered.

Some efforts within the traditional audio-visual educational program can be made to overcome these difficulties. One is to require the audience to make an overt response where it is feasible. Another possibility lies in instructing the audience as to what they should do during the film to facilitate training. Still another is to recognize the limitations of the audio-visual medium and to supply the necessary training of the response in another setting. The final possibility may be best of all: And that is to combine audio-visual with autoinstructional techniques.

Comments

1. The need to specify the exact conditions under which learning is to take place in a given situation is a primary consideration in arranging for optimal learning proficiency. Too often educators seem simply to assume that if "they teach" students will obviously learn. The article bears on the whole issue of what constitutes effective teaching.

2. There is need for further clarification of the bearing of S–R psychology to learning in other nonaudio-visual settings. There is also need for similar clarification of the cognitive or field bases for the various aspects of educational practice.

3. The fact that a theory of learning does not automatically lead to a blueprint for educational practice should be kept in mind. Nevertheless, the practitioner needs to be clear as to what the ingredients of an effective learning situation are and whether they are present.

That's What They Said

"There is much less agreement among psychologists and educators today on the nature of the learning process, on the conditions under which it occurs, or on the means of maximizing learning according to the school's objectives."

> Ernest A. Haggard. "Learning: A process of change," *Educ. Lead.*, 13: 149–156, 1955. [150]

"Viewed in its broadest dimensions, learning is the search for meaning."

> Henry C. Lindgren. "The teacher helps the learner interpret his experiences," in D. H. Russell and S. K. Richardson (eds.), *Learning and the Teacher.* 1959 Yearbook. Washington: Association for Supervision and Curriculum Development, 1959. Pp. 81–104. [87]

". . . the Law of Effect is fundamentally inadequate as a guide to understanding in the domain of achievement-oriented activity. Success does not invariably produce a strengthening of the tendency to undertake the same activity on another occasion. Sometimes success weakens the subsequent tendency to engage in the same activity. The individual strongly motivated to achieve normally raises his level of aspiration following success: His behavior changes."

> John W. Atkinson. "The mainspring of achievement-oriented activity," in John D. Krumboltz (ed.), *Learning and the Educational Process,* Skokie, Ill.: Rand McNally & Company, 1965. Pp. 25–66. [59]

"To the situation 'a modifiable connection being made between an S and an R and being accompanied or followed by a satisfying state of affairs' man responds, other things being equal, by an increase in the strength of that connection. To a connection similar, save that an *annoying* state of affairs goes together or follows it, man responds, other things being equal, by a decrease in the strength of that connection."

> Edward L. Thorndike. *Educational Psychology.* Vol. 1: *The Original Nature of Man.* New York: Teachers College, Columbia University, 1913. [172]

"Probably the most insidious and subtle barrier to formal learning today is the exposure to what is called the sensory overload—the impact of too many different messages and exposure to too much 'noise' beyond an individual's capacity to deal with either adequately."

Lawrence K. Frank. "Four ways to look at potentialities," in Alexander Frazier (ed.), *New Insights and the Curriculum.* 1963 Yearbook. Washington: Association for Supervision and Curriculum Development, 1963. Pp. 11–37. [35]

"There is no decisive proof that any particular method of teaching (inductive, deductive, individual, group) or any particular philosophy of teaching (teacher-dominated lesson or socialized lesson) will guarantee better results than any other method or philosophy, so far as achievement is concerned."

I. A. Dodes. "The science of teaching mathematics," *Math. Teach.*, 46: 157–166, 1953. [163]

"Most of today's textbooks are pleasant to look upon and easy to read. What they lack, it seems to me, is the rough texture of honesty—the kind of gritty detail that slows up the reading but speeds up the thinking. The slick, effortless prose flows on and on without a ripple, while the student, half asleep, floats atop the glossy surface. The whole idea, it would seem, is not to rock the boat."

Richard J. Margolis. "The well-tempered textbook," *T. C. Rec.*, 66: 663–670, 1965. [663]

"A careful review of the research does not reveal evidence that there is any best pattern of instruction for every teacher in every situation."

Lindley J. Stiles. "Methods of teaching," in Walter S. Monroe (ed.), *Encyclopedia of Educational Research.* New York: The Macmillan Company, 1950. Pp. 745–753. [748]

"There is no unitary good teacher; instead there is a broad range of ways of doing good teaching."

Barbara Biber. "Teacher education in mental health," in Morris Krugman (ed.), *Orthopsychiatry in the School.* New York: American Orthopsychiatric Association, 1958. Pp. 169–183. [177]

"The status and role of the teacher has changed dramatically in the twentieth century. Trends are going toward making the teacher less an information-dispenser and more a catalyst and facilitator of independent study. The teacher's role and status are a reflection of the forces which influence the nature of education. The teacher is what the educational system demands; thus, study of attributes and roles of the teacher is an appropriate method of inquiry into the nature of education."

Ted W. Ward and John E. Ivey. "Improvement of educational practice," in Robert L. Ebel (ed.), *Encyclopedia of Educational Research.* New York: The Macmillan Company, 1969. Pp. 626–633. [631]

CHAPTER 11

Test Items

1. Learning is best defined as
   a. the accumulation of knowledge and skills
   b. the change in behavior resulting from experience
   c. the formation of S–R bonds, learning sets, and other functional operations
   d. the improvement in performance resulting from deliberate practice
   e. the modification of behavior over time

2. Controversy as to the definition of learning stems primarily from
   a. differences in terminology
   b. the differences in theoretical premises and perspective
   c. individual differences in learning styles
   d. the variety of contents to be learned
   e. the variety of processes involved in different learnings

3. The reason that learning is rarely sudden and immediate is that
   a. it takes time for it to consolidate
   b. learning can only occur within the context of a wide network of related data
   c. learning does not occur on an all-or-none basis
   d. learning involves a repeated back-and-forth movement between differentiation and integration
   e. learning is always part of an on-going process so that nothing is ever completely learned

4. Which of the following is *not* one of the steps of the learning process?
   a. application
   b. obstacle
   c. readiness
   d. reinforcement
   e. response

5. What purpose do the laws of learning serve?
   a. They express empirical relationships between learning and certain antecedent conditions.
   b. They identify causal factors underlying learning.
   c. They identify the physiological basis of learning.

    d.   They provide hypotheses for the study of learning process.

    e.   They provide the scientific explanation of how and why learning takes place.

6. The following, application, motivation, obstacle, readiness, reinforcement, and response, as parts of the learning process are based on ——— premises.

    a.   associationistic

    b.   conditioning

    c.   eclectic

    d.   gestalt

    e.   phenomenological

7. Thorndike's law of effect relates most closely to

    a.   the concept of operant conditioning

    b.   the law of exercise

    c.   the law of readiness

    d.   the principle of classical conditioning

    e.   the principle of reinforcement

8. What are the primary educational implications of Thorndike's law of exercise as currently viewed?

    a.   It discourages unsupervised practice.

    b.   It explains the effectiveness of periodic review.

    c.   It provides a justification for drill.

    d.   It serves no purpose at all; it is basically false.

    e.   It underscores the role of motivation in effective practice.

9. The extent to which a problem situation is a matter of trial and error or insight depends primarily on

    a.   the adequacy of the learner's relevant learning sets

    b.   the complexity of the situation

    c.   the degree of logical means–end relationships involved in the situation

    d.   the intelligence of the learner

    e.   the learner's mind set in relation to the solution

10. What Köhler called "insight" would now more properly be explained in terms of

    a.   clarification of the life space

    b.   cognitive restructure

    c.   learning sets

    d.   the "shaping" of behavior

    e.   trial-and-error behavior

11. Trial-and-error behavior is
    a. haphazard and random
    b. lacking in purpose
    c. more correctly called, trial-and-success
    d. oriented toward an ill-defined goal
    e. totally lacking in insight

12. Thorndike's law of belonging is best seen in the context of
    a. belonging as one of the psychological needs
    b. cohesiveness as a necessary condition for effective group work
    c. continuity in the sequence of learning
    d. meaningfulness of content
    e. self-contained "unity" of the material to be learned

13. Product is to process as
    a. curriculum is to objectives
    b. formal is to incidental
    c. instructional materials are to instructional methods
    d. learning is to teaching
    e. philosophy is to psychology

14. Learning to dislike mathematics because of a poor teacher would be classified as _____ learning.
    a. concomitant
    b. formal
    c. indirect
    d. informal
    e. instrumental

15. Dewey suggests that very often the most important aspect of a given lesson, say in the social studies, is
    a. its formal goals
    b. the concomitant learnings that accompany the lesson
    c. the interpersonal skills that come as a by-product
    d. secondary learnings, e. g., sidelights not specifically stressed
    e. the verbalisms and misconceptions that creep in as a substitute for learning

16. Probably the most efficient learning is _____ learning.
    a. concomitant
    b. incidental
    c. informal
    d. instrumental
    e. trial-and-error

17. Psychologists relate learning to
   a.   the acquisition of knowledge and skills
   b.   all changes in the behavior of organisms due to experience
   c.   all changes in human behavior
   d.   any and all changes occurring in and to living organisms
   e.   the learning of academic material only

18. What is the present status of the physiology of learning?
   a.   All theories of learning carefully avoid stipulating a neuro-phys-iological basis to learning.
   b.   Psychologists are interested only in the behavioral aspects of learning.
   c.   Psychologists are showing progressively greater interest in the neuro-chemistry of learning.
   d.   Thorndike showed convincingly that learning is not predicated on a physiological basis.
   e.   Regardless of its relation to learning, neuro-physiology has nothing to contribute to the *psychology* of learning.

19. Reinforcement, as a concept, is fundamental to
   a.   association theories only
   b.   classical conditioning only
   c.   cognitive theories only
   d.   the phenomenological version of field theories only
   e.   essentially all learning theories

20. Learning refers to
   a.   all changes occurring to the organism during its lifetime
   b.   all changes in behavior occurring as a consequence of interaction with the environment
   c.   changes in behavior resulting from deliberate intent (and practice)
   d.   changes in inherited predispositions as a consequence of systematic (selective) reinforcement
   e.   the improvement of behavior with systematic practice

21. Which of the following is the incorrect association as to how learning takes place?
   a.   Hull—classical conditioning
   b.   Köhler—perceptual reorganization
   c.   Lewin—cell assemblies
   d.   Skinner—instrumental conditioning
   e.   Thorndike—S–R bonds

22. Which of the following is not typically listed as one of the steps of the learning process?
    a. goal
    b. obstacle
    c. punishment
    d. reinforcement
    e. response

23. The preceding formulation of the steps of the learning process (Question 22) is devised from _____ specifications.
    a. associationistic
    b. cognitive
    c. neuro-physiological
    d. phenomenological
    e. topological

24. Thorndike's law of effect is best seen as
    a. an aspect of the broader principle of reinforcement
    b. an earlier (now discarded) explanation of trial-and-error learning
    c. an earlier version of the current concept of feedback
    d. a complement to the Law of Exercise
    e. a simplified version of Hull's drive-reduction theory

25. Which of the current theories of learning appears to have the greatest validity and relevance to classroom learning?
    a. cognitive theories in general
    b. Hull's (Estes') conditioning
    c. Skinnerian conditioning
    d. Tolman's purposivism
    e. none of the above; no theory has clear-cut superiority over the others

26. What is the present status of Thorndike's Law of Exercise?
    a. It has been totally discredited.
    b. It operates within the framework of the Law of Effect.
    c. It proves that practice is a necessary and sufficient condition for learning to take place.
    d. It still serves as the justification for practice as a precondition to learning.
    e. Its validity is restricted to the development of psychomotor skills.

27. _____ practice is essentially, if not totally, ineffective.
    a. Concentrated
    b. Distributed

    c. Unguided
    d. Unmotivated
    e. Unsystematic

28. A reappraisal of Thorndike's Law of Exercise has led to a shift in classroom emphasis from
    a. concentrated to distributed practice
    b. punishment to reward
    c. routine drill to meaningfulness
    d. teacher lecture to student discussion
    e. trial and error to insight

29. The reason Thorndike's experimental animals relied on trial and error —rather than insight—to solve their problems is related to
    a. their limited "intelligence"
    b. the nature of the problem (and its solution)
    c. their past experiences
    d. tunnel vision (resulting from anxiety)
    e. the unavailability of adequate reward

30. Process is to product as
    a. formal is to incidental
    b. learning is to teaching
    c. psychology is to philosophy
    d. skill is to knowledge
    e. teaching is to learning

31. Attitudes toward a given subject generally fall within the context of _____ learnings.
    a. collateral
    b. incidental
    c. formal
    d. instrumental
    e. conditioned

CHAPTER 12

Guiding
the Learning Process

The fact that the school exists for the purpose of promoting pupil learning carries with it a mandate for pedagogical efficiency. Unfortunately, after well over half-a-century of study and research, our knowledge of the psychology of learning is still largely an accumulation of findings based on animal experiments, rote memory, laboratory studies—all of which have little bearing on the learning of meaningful materials in the setting in which children are taught. Data on the "psychology" of teaching per se are relatively nonexistent. A few rather gross studies have been conducted regarding the effectiveness, for example, of two general methods of instruction, typically with little effort made to conceptualize the teaching–learning situation in psychological terms and to identify its psychologically significant components.

In the papers in this chapter, Worthen reports an actual study of the relative merit of discovery and exposition as teaching methods, and, in a parallel theme, Pulliam cautions against the overuse of the lecture as an expedient in meeting soaring enrollments and suggests certain safeguards. The third selection, Macdonald's "Myths about Instruction" is both timely and provocative; maybe we don't know as much as we thought we did, little as that was. We can't expect to resolve our various instructional problems while making the wrong assumptions and asking the wrong questions; Cook, for example, questions some of the assumptions underlying the earlier use of programed instruction. Also included in this chapter is

Riessman's well-known paper on learning style, a concept which has particular relevance to the education of the disadvantaged. It has bearing on Kagan's *cognitive* style presented in Chapter 6 and suggests once again that readiness for a given activity is not independent of the method through which the activity is presented. The possibility that learning styles vary across socio-economic lines and that teachers are typically middle class may well have a bearing on the academic difficulties experienced by lower-class children.

Blaine R. Worthen

A Study of Discovery and
Expository Presentation:
Implications for Teaching *

Adherents to the discovery method of teaching have been vociferous in their claims of its superiority over other methods of teaching. They have claimed that learning through discovery enhances retention, transfer, motivation, and learning how to discover. Discovery learning is not without critics, however; some have discounted it as pedagogically impractical and have argued that it offers little that cannot be achieved equally well by good expository teaching. They have pointed out that little, if any, research can be cited to support the claims of its proponents and that, despite its alleged advantages, the majority of teachers rely on expository methods. The research evidence is conflicting, partly because of semantic inconsistencies in labelling; teaching methods labelled the same in different studies are often so unlike in reality that any comparison of the results is meaningless.

The present study had two basic purposes: (a) to explore some of the teaching–learning variables operative in the discovery process; and (b) to compare discovery and expository methods of instruction in the naturalistic setting of the classroom. The study dealt with the learning, retention, and transfer of elementary mathematics concepts presented by teachers competent in the use of both instructional methods.

The instructional materials consisted of several mathematical concepts selected on the basis of their suitability to both discovery and expository teaching and their probable unfamiliarity to students at the inception of the study. Two complete sets of materials were developed, one for use with each of the two methods. The specific instructional procedures were devised to conform to the requirements of the method and followed the structural sequence of the materials to be presented. The various aspects of teacher behavior—interjection of teacher knowledge, introduction of generalizations, methods of answering questions, control of pupil interaction, method of eliminating false concepts—were carefully specified and integrated into the instructional procedures so as to maintain the integrity of

* Adapted and abridged from *J. teach. Educ.*, 19: 223–242, 1968. By permission of author and publisher.

the two methods; in discovery, for example, verbalization of each generalization was delayed until the end of the instructional sequence so as to maximize the possibility that the pupils would arrive at the generalization on their own as a result of the presentation of an ordered and structured series of examples. No explanation of the examples were given, nor was there any hint of the existence of an underlying principle to be discovered.

Many studies comparing two teaching methods have run into the difficulty that the teachers are unable to vary their teaching behavior sufficiently to effect a real test of the methods under study. To obviate such criticism, the present study relied on pupil and observer rating of teacher behavior, both of which confirmed that the two methods were indeed dissimilar and further that instruction in both treatments followed prescribed teaching models almost to perfection and equally well.

The experimental subjects consisted of 432 fifth- and sixth-grade pupils from 16 classes in eight elementary schools in Salt Lake City. In each school, two classes were taught the arithmetic concepts by the same teacher, one by Treatment D (Discovery), the other by Treatment E (Expository). The study controlled length of time on the learning tasks, amount of verbalization in the teacher's presentation, pre-experimental mathematical background, IQ, etc. The experimental period consisted of six weeks of instruction. Teachers and raters underwent training both before and during the experiment.

Results

The expository group outperformed ($p < .01$) the discovery group on the criterion test at the end of the experimental period. However, on retention tests given 5 weeks and 11 weeks after instruction, the discovery group outscored the expository group ($p < .05$ and $< .025$ respectively). The data also showed that pupils in Treatment D transferred the concepts learned during the instructional period somewhat more readily ($p < .08$) than those in Treatment E. No difference was found between the two treatments in negative transfer or in attitude but ability to transfer heuristics was greater for Treatment D.

In general, the results of the study support the major claims made by proponents of the discovery method. The most dramatic finding was the sharp reversal in the relative effectiveness of the method from superiority of the expository group at the end of the experimental period to inferiority in retention 5 and 11 weeks later. Pupils taught by the discovery method retained significantly more material over the postexperimental period despite the fact that they knew significantly less on the initial test. These findings strongly suggest that presenting mathematical concepts to upper elementary school pupils through discovery sequencing causes the learner to integrate the content conceptually in such a manner that he can retain it

TABLE 1

Summary of Analyses of Covariance
of Criterion Measure Posttest Scores
between Treatments D and E

Measure	F	p	Direction
Concept Knowledge Test	7.435	<.01	D<E
Concept Retention Test 1	3.918	<.05	D>E
Concept Retention Test 2	5.868	<.025	D>E
Concept Transfer Test	3.089	<.08	D>E
Neg. Concept Transfer Test	.098	n.s.	
Sem. Diff. Attitude Scale	.161	n.s.	
Statement Attitude Scale	1.173	n.s.	
Written Heuristic Trans.	5.004	<.05	D>E
Oral Heuristic Trans.	5.720	<.025	D>E

more readily than when the concepts are presented to him through exposition. The discovery approach also increases significantly the pupils' ability to use discovery problem-solving approaches in new situations, both those requiring pencil-and-paper applications and those involving verbal presentation by the teacher.

Comments

1.   Whether the results as to the relative superiority of the discovery method would hold equally well in subjects other than mathematics, where the principles to be discovered are less obvious or might not exist, would be worth considering. Science, for example, should be particularly amenable to a discovery approach. Perhaps the key is for the teacher to know when to use expository and when to use discovery teaching and to be skilled and knowledgeable in their use.

2.   A number of studies on discovery as a method of teaching were conducted in the 1950s—with conflicting results. The method is probably not used as much as its effectiveness in an appropriate setting would warrant. The fact that many teachers are more interested in a superficial coverage of content as required to pass examinations than in deep insights and long-term memory may have something to do with it. On the other hand, as Ausubel (1961) points out, rather exaggerated claims have been made as to its superiority. (See Kersh and Wittrock, 1962 for a review of recent research.)

3.   The article discusses a number of implications from the standpoint of future research, teaching, and teacher education. It must be noted, for example, that the teachers in this study were able to shift their teaching behavior from one model to the other while still maintaining a high degree of fidelity to each model. To the extent that it would be bene-

ficial for teachers to be able to supplement expository teaching with the inclusion of discovery teaching, where appropriate, teachers will need to develop skills and sensitivities that teacher education programs so far have typically failed to provide.

References

Ausubel, David P. "Learning by discovery: Rationale and mystique," *N.A.S.S.P. Bull.*, 45: 18–58, December 1961.
Kersh, Bert Y., and Merl C. Wittrock. "Learning by discovery: An interpretation of recent research," *J. teach. Educ.*, 13: 461–468, 1962.

Lloyd Pulliam

The Lecture—Are We Reviving
Discredited Teaching Methods? *

The need to reduce educational costs has led administrators to place increasing reliance on the lecture. While it has always been a major teaching method in college, it is now being extended, through team teaching and educational TV, into all levels of the educational system. If we are to prevent fiscal success from becoming educational failure, we need to evaluate carefully just what students learn from the lecture.

Historically, the lecture evolved largely because of the scarcity of hand-copied books in medieval universities; since only the doctors had a book, it became customary for them to read from the book while the students took notes. The lecture was later expanded to include the synthesis of various points of view and the presentation of a changing field of knowledge.

Two major studies are relevant to our evaluation of the lecture as a teaching–learning procedure. Nichols and Stevens found that, no matter how carefully he listens, the average person grasps only about half of what he hears; two months later he remembers half of that. It would seem that the lecture is not particularly effective as a learning method. The second group of studies are those of Lewin, showing that group decision is much more likely to result in changed behavior than is listening to a carefully prepared lecture.

The most obvious limitation of the lecture stems from the fact that it is teacher-centered rather than learner-centered. It is largely a *teaching* method in its focus, its orientation, and its lack of concern with what is happening to the learner. The lecturer is occupied with the question: "What shall I say?" rather than with "What kind of experiences can I lead students into that will increase their positive learnings?" In order to prepare his lecture notes, the teacher does much reading and studying, and, therefore, acquires most of the learning. The student, on the other hand, does not learn just from listening; he learns as he makes knowledge, skills, and attitudes his own in such a manner that he gains meaning from them for his own life and is able to use that knowledge in a variety of contexts.

* Adapted and abridged from *Phi Delta Kappan*, 44: 382–385, 1963. By permission of the publisher.

He learns through self-discovery and experience in a socio-cultural context where his discoveries and experiences are interpreted and evaluated, accepted or rejected, learned or not learned. This is an active process on the part of the learner, not something his teachers can do for him.

To the extent that the student learns as he interacts with others, the lack of such interaction in the lecture situation contributes to its ineffectiveness. The lecture places the student in an isolated socio-cultural situation where he has no chance to test his ideas through interaction with members of the group. Nor does the lecture permit the lecturer to become aware of misconceptions which he might try to correct. Furthermore, inasmuch as the lecture is typically confined to giving information *about* biology, literature, etc., rather than focussing on the understanding of its application, it often leads to verbalism instead of meaningful learning.

It is a common practice for the lecture system to be organized around a master teacher, who lectures to large groups. Then small discussion groups are organized under the direction of student assistants or, in the case of TV classes, under the guidance of classroom teachers. This means that there is no interaction between the lecturer and the students to clarify subject matter and attitudes and to give the lecturer the feedback he needs to evaluate the effectiveness of his lectures. Most of the student learning occurs in the small groups, under the guidance of teachers who are usually less competent than the lecturer.

Recent research indicates that the success or failure of the master teacher's lecturing to a large group is largely determined by the personal influence of the small group leaders, who may either reinforce or negate the lecturer's efforts. Unless the master teacher works closely with his group leaders, his influence may actually be diminished rather than extended. On the other hand, when properly used, the lecture may make a valuable contribution to student learning. Its effectiveness revolves primarily around what happens to the students after the lecture is over; if it does not stimulate students into activity, it will essentially fail as a learning method. This kind of activity does not usually follow unless it is structured into the lecture itself.

Lectures may be designed to inspire new thoughts and actions, to lead directly to new experiences, e.g., readings, laboratory experiments to test ideas, field work to lend concreteness to verbalized theory, a thought-provoking discussion, etc. The lecturer should demand that student activity follow his remarks; he should suggest specific references that will support, clarify, and make application of the ideas he presents. The lecture is most effective when used in conjunction with other methods and is confined to a group of not more than 30 students. A class of this size enables the lecturer to shift to other methods with relative ease, using discussion, audio-visual aids, demonstrations, and other methods to clarify subject matter and attitudes that may otherwise be distorted if the lecture is used alone. Supplementing the lecture with other methods also gives the flexibility needed to work effectively with the wide range of ability and interests found in most classes.

Where lack of funds dictates large classes, it should be remembered that learning in such situations will not come directly from the large-class lectures but rather from the activities of students, individually and in small groups. Special effort should be made to make these an extension of the work of the master-teacher. The major role of the master-teacher, then, would not be so much that of presenting lectures as that of coordinating associate teachers, demonstrating effective teaching practices, and suggesting appropriate learning activities and resources. This does not eliminate the master-teacher's lectures, but simply changes the emphasis of his role to that of stimulating, supporting, coordinating and providing leadership for the activities of the small groups.

Comments

1.   The author's words of caution are unquestionably worthy of careful consideration. The evidence does not warrant the wholesale condemnation of the lecture method but rather a reconsideration of where and how it can be used. While there is need to emphasize that the ultimate purpose of lecturing is to promote student learning and that this calls for student, rather than lecturer, activity, it does not follow that the lecture is completely devoid of merit.

2.   It must be recognized that, except for very large classes, colleges tend to rely on the lecture-discussion rather than on the lecture alone. To the extent that the average college professor brings in materials from sources too varied and diverse for the average student to locate on his own, the lecture, as part of his overall teaching strategy, is an indispensable approach to effective teaching. The problem is that it is frequently used exclusively to do things for which it is not particularly suited.

3.   Pulliam's emphasis on the need for effective coordination of the smaller discussion groups with the lecture, where large lecture sections are involved, is well taken.

Reference

Nichols, Ralph G., and Leonard A. Stevens. *Are You Listening?* New York: McGraw-Hill, Inc., 1957.

James B. Macdonald

Myths about Instruction *

The "Trouble with Education" may be that it is already dead as a meaningful enterprise, and the efforts of the "establishment" are not attempts to cure symptoms at all but really a series of episodes of digging up and reburying the corpse so that society won't find out. We have in effect accepted uncritically the view that we are sick and need new prescriptions to make us well, rather than acknowledge that education is dead or that perhaps it is the social perspective defining our symptoms that is sick rather than education itself.

We live in a world of metaphors and other symbolic pictures which help us make sense out of potential chaos. But we must remember that our metaphors and symbols do not exist in a one-to-one correspondence with reality. We must especially refrain from prescribing action on the basis of metaphors as if they were reality. Metaphors become myths when they are accepted uncritically, when they are used as the basis of prescriptions for action without subjecting them to some reasoned, phenomenological, or empirical process of validation. Our instructional metaphors are possibly valid; they are possible but are they probable? In effect, we prescribe instructional practice on the basis of metaphors of possible but unknown probability of validity.

We might consider six common instructional myths, each of which has been used as a basis for prescribing instructional practice; each is a possible way of looking at instruction; but each has an unknown probability of being a valid view of instruction, and each possesses powerful motivating forces for acceptance as a basis for prescriptions which emanate from sources outside the context of the instructional setting.

1. The Myth of Learning Theory

Learning theory is descriptive. It is after the fact. It tells what happened. As such it is not necessarily a basis for prescribing what to do. Just because learning is alleged to take place in small increments built up

* Adapted and abridged from James B. Macdonald, "Myths about instruction," *Educ. Leader.*, 22(8): 571–576, 609–618, May 1965. Reprinted with permission of the Association for Supervision and Curriculum Development and the author. Copyright © 1965 by the Association for Supervision and Curriculum Development.

through the process of reinforcement does not necessarily mean that this is the best way in which learning tasks should be presented. It certainly points out the *possibility* that this is so, but it says little about the validated probability of this being true. For example, if Skinner is correct in his premise that reinforcement in the classroom is far from being sufficiently systematic, the results of programed instruction should surpass those of the usual approaches by "extremely large actual as well as statistically significant differences." But, to date, there is no evidence of the overwhelming superiority, or even consistent statistical superiority. In other words, the wholesale adoption and instructional prescription in education on the basis of psychological metaphors such as learning theory is primarily an act of faith.

2. The Myth of Human Development

Although everyone admits the possibility that developmental knowledge has relevance for instructional practice, human growth and development can offer only a very limited number of very crude generalizations and highly tentative suggestions bearing on educational practice. Ausubel, for example, points to the concepts of readiness and self-selection as examples of unwarranted extrapolation of developmental knowledge to the more complex and variable components of educational practice. Developmental metaphors are interesting and reasonably valid within the context in which they were developed; when extrapolated and projected onto instructional settings, they become much less probable as valid bases for prescribing instructional strategies.

3. The Myth of the Structure of the Disciplines

Convinced that each discipline has a set of fundamental ideas or principles about which the fabric of its knowledge is woven, academic scholars have insisted that what is needed is a well-planned instructional program to communicate this structure to the student. The basic fallacy in this argument is that structure is an after-the-fact description of the way knowledge can be organized by the mature scholar; it is not the basis from which the knowledge itself is developed, nor is it the way to organize knowledge in the instructional setting. As a metaphor, the concept of structure suggests interesting possibilities for instruction; as a prescription, it has much less probability of validity for instruction than it has in the realm of philosophical discourse about the nature of knowledge. As a prescriptive base for instruction it is simply a metaphor of unknown validity.

4. The Myth of Modes of Inquiry

The same general argument applies here: Modes of inquiry are what mature scholars say they do as they reflect on what they have done. They are abstractions from behavior. There is, in other words, no necessary logic that says because man can be said to discover knowledge in a given way that ipso facto his instruction should be organized and presented for learning purposes in the same fashion. To the extent that each discipline tends to have its own unique mode of inquiry, the case for distinct modes of inquiry—beyond general reflective thinking—becomes tenuous. In any case, the probability of providing reasonably valid instructional prescription from the concept of modes of inquiry is not necessarily high, even if the possibility is an intriguing one.

5. The Myth of Interaction Analysis

One of our own scholarly myths is that of interaction analysis. Again it seems that the description of what *is* going on in the classroom has become confused with the prescription of what *ought* to be going on in the classroom. Flanders' direct and indirect categories of teacher behavior, for example, are being misused by many educators as rationale for prescribing indirect teacher behavior. This was not the intention of the originators of these analyses, nor is it necessarily embodied in the assumptions of the methodology. As long as we remember that any system of interaction is a matter of created reality, rather than necessarily a natural phenomenon, there is no problem; but any interaction system becomes a myth when used to prescribe practice.

6. The Myth of Rational Decision-making

Tyler, Herrick, and others have advocated a rational decision-making approach to the instructional process; the recommended instructional strategy is for the teacher to make a series of rational decisions about objectives, learning experiences, organization, and evaluation. This too is a myth: It is possible that teaching can be viewed as a rational decision-making process, but the action probability of validity is rather slim. A perhaps more defensible premise is that our objectives are known to us in a complete sense only after the completion of our act of instruction; objectives by this rationale are heuristic devices which provide initiating sequences which become altered in the course of instruction.

In summary, the six propositions just presented are simply myths created to describe the instructional process. Although they are possible ways of talking about instruction, we must recognize that they have unknown probability of being valid as a basis for prescribing instructional practice. We could just as easily create other metaphors which may have better probabilities of being valid. Heubner, for example, has suggested two other possibilities, the aesthetic and the moral, each of which, it seems to me, has as much reasonable possibility of providing prescriptions for in-

struction as any of the previous ones mentioned, and their probability of
being valid might even be greater.[1]

In conclusion, we have considered a number of metaphors about instruction which have been raised to the level of myths; they are being used
to prescribe instruction patterns, when, in reality, they are only possible
ways of viewing instruction, with uncertain probabilities of validity. They
are simply descriptive theories that have been used to prescribe practice.
They are not necessarily wrong, but we need to recognize the tentativeness
of our instructional language. In a broader sense, the need is for conceptual plurality and prescriptive variety in instructional programs, lest we
arouse rather startlingly in the not-too-distant future, tightly enmeshed in
the grip of some pathological possibilities which will effectively slam the
door on future progress.

Comment

The article calls for a reconsideration of the premises from which instruction strategies have been derived and a recognition of their tentative
nature; this should prove beneficial in the long run. The issues it raises
bear on the development of theories of teaching, in contrast to the theories
of learning and while Macdonald has not identified specific alternatives, he
does raise significant questions as to some of our present viewpoints.

[1] These are discussed in the actual article; they are omitted here for the sake of
brevity.

John O. Cook

Superstition in the Skinnerian *

"Teaching machines were the outgrowth of the Skinner box and they bear—particularly the early models—unmistakable marks of their origin. Thus, the design of teaching machines not only reflects certain theoretical principles about behavior; it also exhibits a number of irrelevant features of the Skinner box—features that had to be incorporated into it because of the very limited symbol-manipulating capacity of rats and pigeons. In short, I am saying that the teaching machine, even today, is just too faithful a copy of the Skinner box" [p. 516].

Early designers of airplanes made the mistake of having them flap their wings—simply because that was the way birds fly. "The principles of physics that underlie the flight of birds and the flight of rigid-wing airplanes are the same, but the manner in which these two things operate in the air is quite different; flapping wings is not a feature that is necessitated by the underlying physical principles. . . . I still think that they [the designers of teaching machines] are making the same mistake—the mistake of confusing features that are dictated by theoretical principles with features that are dictated by the specific characteristics of the learning task, by the nature of the learning organism, or by some other non-theoretical consideration" [p. 516]. In other words, it seems that devout Skinnerians have incorporated into the teaching machine a strong element of superstition transferred bodily from the training of a pigeon in the Skinner box.

Pigeons trained in the Skinner box make overt responses—so human beings trained by teaching machines are required to make overt responses. "Yet, it has been repeatedly demonstrated that for many tasks it makes no difference whether the subject makes overt responses or implicit ones" [p. 517]. In the same way, the pigeon is always reinforced *after* it has made the correct response, so the teaching machine provides for reinforcement after the correct response. Yet, research suggests some advantage in giving the correct answer before the response, rather than after.

"This story has three morals, but they are all very simple. The first is that not all the features of a gadget are dictated by theoretical principles. The second is that what works beautifully in one context may not work so

* Adapted and abridged from John O. Cook, "Superstition in the Skinnerian," *Amer. Psychol.,* 18: 516–518, 1963. Copyright 1963 by American Psychological Association and reproduced by permission.

beautifully in another. The third moral is that superstitious behavior is not restricted to pigeons" [p. 518].

Comment

As Cook points out, these criticisms are more appropriate to the weaknesses of the early Skinnerian position. The basic issue is not the adequacy of the teaching machine but rather the possibility that our operations are often unnecessarily complicated by useless, if not adverse, features derived from false or unwarrantedly extended premises. It would, no doubt, benefit all of us—and enhance the productivity of our efforts—if we were to stop periodically to question some of our practices and their underlying rationale.

Frank Riessman

Styles of Learning *

In any classroom, probably no two pupils learn the same thing in the same way at the same pace. Everyone has a distinct style of learning peculiar or unique as his personality, although some people may use more than one style. A common characteristic of the disadvantaged, for example, is his physical approach to learning. He has had very little exposure to reading, because his parents rarely have the time to read to him. As a consequence, it may be easier for him to learn by acting out the words rather than hearing them spoken by the teacher.

For years, teachers and guidance workers have tended to ignore individual differences in learning style as they typically blamed the student's failure to measure up to his learning potential on lack of instruction or some emotional block or personality conflict. Little attention has been given to how the pupil's learning could be improved simply by concentrating on the way he works and learns. Teachers have been trained to look on learning in a general way; their preparation predisposes them to neglect personal idiosyncrasies in learning. Many teachers, for example, assume that the best way to study a reading assignment is to first survey the chapter: this is the way most people learn best but some students become so anxious and disturbed at having to take such an overall view that they cannot function. In the same way, some students do their best studying in a noisy place. Styles are also very much involved in taking tests; some people become so anxious that they become disorganized.

An individual's basic style of learning is probably laid down early in life and is not subject to fundamental change. The pupil who likes to learn by listening and speaking is not likely to change into an outstanding reader. The first step is to help him discover his particular style so that, once he is aware of the way he learns, he can schedule his learning activities accordingly. In the case of the physical learner, for example, we might even try role playing. The challenge to every teacher is first how to identify the learning strengths in his pupils and then how to utilize them in overcoming weaknesses. This is the central problem in the strategy of style.

* Adapted and abridged from *NEA J.*, 55: 15–17, 1966. By permission of author and publisher.

Comments

1.　The idea of learning style is interesting; there is a question as to how far one ought to rely on a favorite approach to learning to the neglect of others presumably more effective in the general case and—further—the extent to which teachers ought to attempt to cater to each child's peculiar learning style. It might be argued that part of education entails learning how to adapt to a variety of situational demands and we may be doing the student no great service by encouraging him to cut himself off from normal avenues of experience. The same argument is presented by Kliebard in connection with tailoring the curriculum to fit the immediate needs of the disadvantaged, thereby cutting them off from avenues of upward mobility. To the extent that the school cannot tailor its approach to the idiosyncrasies of each and every pupil, beyond allowing flexibility for people to make their own adjustments, it may be more logical to expect the child to develop at least minimal ability to adapt to standard classroom patterns. This is not to deny the need for some degree of adaptation of teaching methods and contents to meet the need of special groups of children.

2.　Some people might want to take issue with the immutability implied in Riessman's statement that an individual's basic learning style is set early in life and not subject to fundamental change. Early learning patterns should probably not preclude the development of certain minimal skills in this connection.

That's What They Said

". . . I have been struck by the fact that when allowed to pace themselves, the slower learners simply take more time doing, apparently precisely the same things that a fast learner does. Where a fast learner will look at a frame and do what it tells him to do with dispatch, a slow learner will stare at the frame for a relatively long time and attempt a response only after much deliberation. Typically, the fastest and the slowest learning rates differ by a factor of four or five."

John D. Carroll. "School learning over the long haul," in John D. Krumboltz (ed.), *Learning and the Educational Process*. Skokie, Ill.: Rand McNally & Company, 1965. Pp. 249–269. [260]

"Feedback is a more descriptive term since school situations involve both informational contingencies and reinforcement contingencies."

Lawrence M. Stolurow. "Model the master teacher and master the teaching model," in John D. Krumboltz (ed.), *Learning and the Educational Process*. Skokie, Ill.: Rand McNally & Company, 1965. Pp. 223–247. [237]

". . . support is given to nondirective approaches, apparently because they keep alive the searching behavior important to divergent thinking. Teachers who are insistent on quiet, orderly behavior, who teach by informative statements, produce task-oriented behavior favorable to convergent thinking; teachers who show personal interest and who avoid critical individual evaluation tend to favor the more creative products of divergent thinking."

Pauline S. Sears and Ernest R. Hilgard. "The teacher's role in the motivation of the learner," in E. R. Hilgard (ed.), *Theories of Learning and Instruction*. 63rd Yearbook, National Society for the Study of Education, Part I. Chicago: University of Chicago Press, 1964. Pp. 182–209. [208–209]

"Learning by self-discovery is superior to learning with external direction only insofar as it increases student motivation to pursue the learning task."

Bert Y. Kersh. "The motivation effect of learning by directed discovery," *J. educ. Psychol.*, 53: 65–71, 1962. [70]

"Altogether it should be emphasized . . . that the belief in the superiority of discovery (Socratic method) over traditional teaching still rests
more on intuitive conviction than on well established experimental generalizations."

> Jan Smedslund. "Educational psychology," *Ann. Rev. Psychol.*, 15:
> 251–276, 1964. [273]

"A review of the arguments and evidence on teaching by discovery
leads one to suspect that much of the opposition stems from construing the
learning-by-discovery hypothesis in an extreme form; that learners should
be deprived of all cues and left completely unguided in their search for a
concept or principle, or that teaching by discovery should be used always
for all aspects of all subjects. A more reasonable position, supported by
considerable evidence, is that guided discovery—giving the learner only
some of the cues he needs—can be used in teaching some aspects of some
subjects with advantages for learning, retention, and transfer. Such a mod-
erate position, both on the nature of the discovery method and the extent
to which it should be used, seems to be supported by both research and
common sense."

> N. L. Gage. "Teaching methods," in Robert L. Ebel (ed.), *Encyclopedia
> of Educational Research*. New York: The Macmillan Company, 1969.
> Pp. 1446–1458. [1456]

"Frequently a class discussion consists of a campaign of self-defense
and self-vindication, with tenacious evasion of facing a truth or an implication that is threatening to the self."

> Arthur T. Jersild. *In Search of Self*. New York: Teachers College, Co-
> lumbia University, 1952. [19]

"If I were faced with the problem of improving training, I should not
look for much help from the well-known learning principles like reinforcement, distribution of practice, response familiarity, and so on. I should
look instead at the technique of task analysis and at the principles of component task achievement, intratask transfer, and the sequencing of subtask
learning to find those ideas of greatest usefulness in the design of effective
training."

> Robert M. Gagné. "Military training and the principles of learning,"
> *Amer. Psychol.*, 17: 83–91, 1962. [90]

"The evidence on massed versus spaced practice in *learning* verbal
tasks indicates that spaced practice facilitates learning only under a highly

specialized set of conditions and even then the magnitude of the effect is so small as to have no applied consequence."

Benton J. Underwood. "Laboratory studies of verbal learning," in E. R. Hilgard (ed.), *Theories of Learning and Instruction*. 63rd Yearbook, National Society for the Study of Education, Part I. Chicago: University of Chicago Press, 1964. Pp. 133–152. [150]

"In certain situations of high interference between tasks, spaced practice may actually impede learning. However, under such situations, spaced practice may facilitate retention."

Benton J. Underwood. 1964. Ibid. [151]

"Present thinking would strongly recommend the spaced practice if the interference is produced by associations which are 'unwanted'; that is, if they are *not* produced by interference from other school tasks, the retention of which is also at stake. The reason for this is that certain evidence indicates that the spacing procedures produce their effect by eliminating or extinguishing the conflicting associations, or at least the term involved in the associations."

Benton J. Underwood. 1964. Ibid. [151]

"Although Skinner places his major emphasis on the way in which his machines handle the subtle contingencies of reinforcement in the learning process, his major and revolutionary contribution may lie in two other features of his approach. First, he conceives of competence in any subject, including the symbolic skills, as approximations to total mastery, not as a point on a distribution curve for an age or grade in achievement. Thus, the significant dimension of assessment becomes how far a pupil has gone toward full competence, not how he stands generally in relation to his fellows. Second, to insure steady progress at the student's own pace toward whatever degree of competence he can attain, the material to be learned is 'programmed' in such a fashion that any given point is basic to the next point to be studied and thus it is thoroughly understood before the next point is tackled. The important thing here is that the material to be learned is so programmed that the pupil never moves on to a new topic until he has acquired a repertoire of responses that enable him to deal correctly with the topic fundamental to it. He never, therefore, carries with him any errors learned in earlier sequences into later ones."

Edward J. Shoben. "Viewpoints from related disciplines: Learning theory," *T. C. Rec.*, 60: 272–282, 1959. [277]

"A number of recent studies suggest the absence of any correlation between class size and academic achievement. This may be not because class size is irrelevant to learning but because teachers have failed to take advantage of smaller classes to use appropriate teaching techniques."

> Don Robinson. "Scraps from a teacher's notebook," *Phi Delta Kappan,* 49: 411, 1968.

"The common complaint that time does not permit such diagnostic work with an individual pupil is not sensible. Failure to do such work inevitably involves the teacher in many wasted minutes working with a 'stupid' pupil, when a little corrective work could often set the pupil on his own feet and enable him to go ahead with the group."

> A. D. Woodruff. *The Psychology of Teaching.* New York: Longmans, Green, 1951. [355]

Reference

N. L. Gage (ed.), *Handbook of Research on Teaching.* Skokie, Ill.: Rand McNally & Company, 1963.

CHAPTER 12

Test Items

1. Teaching is best defined as
   a. the process of facilitating student learning
   b. the process of implementing the school's curriculum
   c. the process of student–teacher interaction
   d. the promotion of student growth
   e. the transmission of knowledge and skills

2. The teacher's primary task is
   a. to act as guide and consultant to students as they learn
   b. to apply remedial help where indicated
   c. to ensure that the experiences incorporated into the school's program are truly productive of student growth
   d. to help the student develop effective learning skills
   e. to supply and supervise the setting in which learning takes place

3. Which of the following is *not* one of the teacher's major tasks in promoting learning?
   a. to forestall the development of faulty techniques and misinformation
   b. to give the learner moral support
   c. to help the student clarify what he is to learn and how
   d. to provide remedial help where indicated
   e. to set the objectives to be attained

4. The most effective guidance is that which
   a. attempts to give insight into the nature of the desired performance
   b. emphasizes errors to be avoided
   c. emphasizes errors to be corrected
   d. concentrates on giving the learner moral support
   e. is given in the early stages of the learning

5. Teacher guidance of the child's learning is most effective in
   a. eliminating errors after they have appeared
   b. clarifying complicated concepts
   c. maintaining student motivation
   d. preventing the development of bad habits
   e. promoting final proficiency in the learning of skills

6. Manual guidance of the child's learning of a skill serves its best purpose in
    a. cutting down the time necessary to achieve proficiency
    b. eliminating persistent bad habits
    c. giving him a kinesthetic feel of good performance
    d. introducing a complex skill
    e. putting the final touches on a complex skill

7. The one generalization that seems to apply to all forms of guidance of the child's learning is that
    a. continuous guidance should be provided throughout the learning
    b. generally speaking, the more guidance the teacher provides the better
    c. guidance can be overdone
    d. guidance should be concentrated on putting the final touches on a skill
    e. guidance should be introduced early

8. Learning curves serve the primary purpose of
    a. diagnosing impediments to progress
    b. identifying where the student needs to concentrate his efforts
    c. motivating the student to greater effort
    d. showing general progress
    e. showing plateaus where remedial work is needed

9. What is the shape of the learning curve?
    a. All complete curves begin slowly, accelerate, and finally taper off.
    b. All learning curves begin with a slow start.
    c. All learning curves eventually taper off.
    d. All learning curves gradually accelerate.
    e. Each learning curve has its unique pattern.

10. What is the major contribution of practice to learning?
    a. Practice consolidates previously acquired learnings.
    b. Practice gives the opportunity for learning to take place.
    c. Practice increases precision and smoothness in the learning of skills.
    d. Practice is a necessary and a sufficient condition for learning.
    e. Practice promotes insights into the nature of the content to be learned.

11. The feature common to all learning curves is
    a. a final deceleration
    b. a gradual acceleration

    c.   one or more plateaus

    d.   short-term fluctuations

    e.   a starting point relatively close to zero

12. Plateaus signal

    a.   the existence of bad habits interfering with progress

    b.   a failure to coordinate the various components of the learning task

    c.   a loss in motivation

    d.   the need for remediation

    e.   none of the above necessarily

13. Research into the relative effectiveness of group versus individuals in problem solving has generally shown

    a.   a combination of group and individual work superior to either alone

    b.   groups to be superior to individuals only when traditional groups are involved

    c.   groups superior to individuals in the total number of solutions obtained

    d.   groups superior to individuals in the quality of the solutions obtained

    e.   individuals superior to groups in per-capita output of solutions

14. The final limit in performance is generally dictated by _____ limits

    a.   materials

    b.   mechanical

    c.   methodological

    d.   motivational

    e.   physiological

15. The teacher's task in a group problem-solving situation is

    a.   to act as a resource person or consultant

    b.   to coordinate the efforts of the group

    c.   to guide student efforts along productive lines

    d.   to provide basic facts

    e.   to structure the problem so that a solution can be reached

16. People differ in skill proficiency primarily because they differ in

    a.   adequacy of instruction

    b.   aptitude

    c.   aspiration (motivational limits)

    d.   experiential background

    e.   physiological coordination

17. The most effective practice is that which
    a. comes early in the sequence, before bad habits are formed
    b. consists of the application of learning to more advanced learnings
    c. consists of specific drill on specific subskills
    d. is devoted to the final touches of high proficiency performance
    e. is oriented toward the elimination of bad habits

18. Research evidence on massed versus spaced practice has shown that
    a. the advantages of distributed practice tend to be registered at the expense of other learnings
    b. intermittent practice encourages errors as the result of disuse
    c. practice is most economical when concentrated in a few relatively long practice periods
    d. short practice periods tend to be best from the standpoint of immediate memory
    e. spaced sessions are best because they allow the learner to engage in surreptitious learning

19. The present consensus concerning the parts-versus-whole issue is that the whole method is best when
    a. the learner is relatively mature and knowledgeable
    b. the material can be divided into logical parts
    c. the material has an inherent structure
    d. the material is long and involved
    e. the material is of uneven difficulty

20. Massed practice seems to be best when
    a. long-range retention is not an issue
    b. motivation is low
    c. the material is not particularly meaningful
    d. the probability of erroneous response is high
    e. the quantity of material to be learned is large

21. The primary criterion in deciding whether to study by parts or by whole is
    a. the background the learner brings to the situation
    b. the degree of structure in the material
    c. the learner's experience with the two approaches
    d. the motivation the learner brings to the situation
    e. the relative uniformity of difficulty of the material

22. The relative ineffectiveness of the parts method stems primarily from
    a. the difficulty of integrating the parts after each has been learned
    b. the difficulty of relating the parts to previous experience

c.   its failure to capitalize on the continuity of the material
d.   the loss of motivation that is likely to occur
e.   its tendency to promote rote memory

23. Research concerning the relative effectiveness of recitation as against
     rereading of material suggests that
     a.   recitation is best after a basic grasp of the material is achieved
     b.   recitation is best
     c.   recitation is best only when it simulates the testing situation
     d.   rereading is best whenever the material has natural meaningful-
          ness and continuity
     e.   the results are equivocal; neither is "best"

24. The most effective method of presentation is
     a.   the classroom discussion
     b.   a combination of methods, depending on what is being taught
     c.   the demonstration
     d.   the lecture
     e.   none of the above; it really makes no difference; learning, not
          teaching, is what counts

25. The lecture-versus-discussion issue revolves primarily around
     a.   the characteristics of the students
     b.   the content being presented
     c.   the goals we set for ourselves
     d.   personal preferences of the students and their teacher
     e.   the relative effectiveness of the instructor in the use of each

26. Probably the greatest contribution of educational television to the
     educational enterprise has been
     a.   to highlight the need for a redefinition of the role and function of
          instructional materials and personnel
     b.   to increase the school's offerings at a minimal cost
     c.   to promote in pupils greater self-reliance and less dependency on
          the teacher
     d.   to provide inexpensive education to large groups of pupils
     e.   to stretch outstanding faculty members over more students

27. Accentuation is an instance of
     a.   functional fixity
     b.   perceptual distortion
     c.   perceptual sensitivity
     d.   psychological closure
     e.   tunnel vision

28. The best way for the teacher to improve the child's perception of a given lesson is
    a. to emphasize the details, which as a whole constitute the content of the lesson
    b. to highlight the crucial out from the trivial, the relevant from the irrelevant
    c. to keep the lesson short and oriented to the key ideas as unobscured by details as possible
    d. to provide adequate structure into which the details fit as a meaningful unit
    e. to provide exercises to sharpen listening and observational skills

29. Which of the following is most predictive of high proficiency in a motor skill?
    a. ability to withstand distraction
    b. basic aptitude
    c. motivation
    d. quality of instruction
    e. specific habits acquired in the earlier stages of learning

30. A factor whose operation is somewhat peculiar in the learning of psychomotor skills is
    a. the greater importance of the lower brain centers
    b. the immediacy of reinforcement
    c. the need for sensitivity to small cues
    d. obvious feedback and constant readjustment in response to feedback
    e. reliance on multimodal cues

31. Various recommended study habits are best conceived as
    a. deductions from learning theory
    b. empirically validated generalizations
    c. rules derived from basic psychological principles
    d. suggestions generally derived from common sense
    e. suggestions students tend to find effective

CHAPTER 13

Motivation
in the Classroom

Even though there is not complete agreement on the theoretical aspects of motivation, there is general consensus as to the importance of motivation for the complex human learnings of the kind with which the school is concerned. Unfortunately, teachers typically rely too heavily on aversive stimulation despite all that is known about its ineffectiveness and even its detrimental effects. Whereas no one denies that anxiety can have benefits in promoting certain types of effort, higher levels of anxiety have disruptive effects and result in avoidance, if not disorganized, behavior.

It is especially important to remember that each child has a relatively unique motivational structure, depending on the particular pattern of reinforcement to which he has been previously exposed. Although there is a certain basic common denominator here—e.g., the need for recognition, achievement, etc.—the means through which these needs are satisfied vary rather drastically. Lower-class children, for example, emerge with motivational patterns often quite different from those of their middle-class counterparts. Unfortunately, teachers, coming from the middle class and attempting to impart a curriculum developed by middle-class professionals and oriented to middle-class values, tend to have difficulty in taking into account the great diversity of motivational and value systems among children of different backgrounds. The successful teacher must be able to discern and to capitalize upon the unique features of each child's motivational complex; he must especially recognize that teaching methods and his own personality interact with the student's motivation. The problem is obviously complex—which makes it difficult for the teacher to provide appropriate reinforcement for each and every child in his care. We must also recognize that teachers differ in their ability to satisfy each child's needs within the context of the classroom setting. Robinson's article is a good example of what an imaginative teacher "who cares" can do. Keislar presents a different facet of the motivational problem, namely, the argument that, for certain classroom learnings at least, motivation as an operational concept is not particularly helpful.

Thomas E. Robinson

His Teacher Improved, Too *

Timothy was a talented youth, although as his English teacher I must confess that the mark I gave him at the end of each of the first two marking periods did not in any way reflect his inherent ability.

In the comments I penned on his report card, opinions were expressed concerning his indifference, his uncooperative attitude, and his lack of effort. When Tim's second report card was returned to me, I noticed that Tim's father had written in the space reserved for parents' reactions the pithy comment, "I am dissatisfied, too."

But the situation changed markedly in February. By chance I learned that Tim was interested in tennis. I asked him to stay after school, and in the conversation I mentioned some of the major tournaments I had seen.

Because of his interest, I invited him to my home on a Saturday afternoon to meet my eldest son, who had acquired some prominence as a local netster. When Tim left my home, after a demonstration of tennis strokes, he took with him a half-dozen books on court techniques and strategy.

Frequently thereafter he stayed after school to talk to me about his reading. He developed an eagerness to give expository talks to his classmates on his hobby. He wrote several papers on tennis ethics and the lessons taught by the lives of great net stars. His paper on tennis ethics he must have rewritten at least a dozen times before it was accepted by the school literary magazine.

I believe no one in the class read or wrote more than he did during the next six weeks. His classmates obtained a liberal education in the romance of tennis.

When I totaled his grades for his next report card, I was surprised to see the great advances he had made in his knowledge of and skill in English. When I inscribed his mark on his card, I wrote:

"Timothy has made rapid advances recently as a student, and I congratulate him."

Back came the father's response. "You give my son too much credit, sir. It is you who should be congratulated, for the rapid advances you have made recently as a teacher."

* From *NEA J.*, 41: 54, January 1952. By permission of author and publisher.

Evan R. Keislar

A Descriptive Approach
to Classroom Motivation *

Psychologists have generally accorded motivation a central position in the conceptual structure of the educative process. Yet as a concept, motivation is particularly unclear. This article proposes that, for certain types of classroom problems, motivation be discussed without recourse to the usual hypothetical constructs such as *motives* or *interest*.

Motivation is usually assessed by noting the kind and the amount of the learner's behavior: pupils who read a great deal are said to be interested or motivated in reading, students who study diligently are said to have a strong achievement motive, etc. To the extent that these motivational terms are inferred entirely from behavior, to use them to explain what caused the behavior is an exercise in circular reasoning: "We can tell Bill is interested in reading because he reads so much; his interest in reading is what causes him to read so much." As description of observable behavior, motivational terms possess considerable value: they are useful in predicting other behavior, for example. But they are of limited usefulness from the standpoint of controlling student behavior. It isn't very helpful for teachers to hypothesize: if I arouse my pupils' interest in arithmetic, they will do their problems regularly—if such interest can be identified only by the way the pupils act.

Since it is still necessary to clarify what must be done to "arouse" the interest, the teacher might just as well formulate a hypothesis which suggests what she must do to get the pupils to do their problems; she does not need to use the word "interest" at all. Motivational terms will have greater utility for education when they refer to antecedent as well as consequent conditions, for it is only through identifying the conditions which must occur before the child is motivated that we can achieve control of his behavior. These conditions are then said to have "stimulus control." The present report deals with three investigations in the development of such control.

(a) *Development of stimulus control of problem-solving behavior.* The first study attempted to conceptualize one process through which new

* Adapted and abridged from *J. teach. Educ.*, 11: 310–315, 1960. By permission of author and publisher.

incentives are developed. The hypothesis was that, if a neutral stimulus (a light–bell combination) is present when the child is reinforced for solving a variety of problems and is not present when he is not reinforced, then this stimulus will gain control of the problem-solving behavior, i. e., it will become an incentive. Twenty-two second-graders were rewarded for responding to a picture card *only when the light and bell were presented with the card*. In the testing situation, each child was shown a new card. For half the children, the light-and-bell stimulus was presented along with the card; for the other half, the card was presented alone. The group with the incentive present gave significantly more responses than the group operating without it; apparently the presence of a neutral stimulus previously associated with reinforcement in a variety of problems induces greater problem-solving ability in a new task. As an implication, it might be well for the teacher to realize that lack of interest on the part of pupils is simply an indication that the school setting is no incentive for them: If such children are provided with a wealth of appropriately administered reinforcements in the classroom setting, they will participate actively in school.

(b) *Learning sets*. A central "motivational" problem in education is that of getting children to change their behavior—i. e., to learn—as a consequence of being presented with a pattern of stimuli. This is often conceived as a matter of teaching students to "pay attention," to "study hard," to "concentrate," etc. A descriptive approach to motivation sees the above problem simply as one of developing stimulus control of a learning set. The general hypothesis of Experiments II and III was that a learning set is brought under the control of a stimulus through a program of selective reinforcement: If students exhibit this set in a variety of situations where a common distinctive stimulus is present and are reinforced for the appropriate learning, this stimulus will acquire control of the learning set. On the contrary, if subjects learn in a variety of situations where a distinctive stimulus is present but are not reinforced, this stimulus will lose control of the learning set; the students will simply remain unmotivated under this particular setting.

In Experiment II, each subject was shown a series of 48 information cards, after each of which followed either a blank card or a question card. Correct answers were rewarded. A green light was on when the information card was exposed if the pupil was to be questioned on this card; a white light was on when a blank card was to follow. The results of the testing situation showed the children learned significantly more when the information card was accompanied by the light previously associated with a test than they did from information presented with a light having no such association.

Experiment III dealt with the effect of knowledge of results (KR) on the learning set. The setting was the same as in Experiment II except that both the experimental and control conditions involved test questions. However, the students were rewarded for a correct answer to the test card only if the KR light had been on when the information card was presented. When the other information card was presented with the No-KR light, the pupils were never informed as to whether their answers were right or wrong. The students learned more under KR conditions, suggesting that not only is knowledge of results an important factor in the acquisition of specific knowledge but it can also strengthen a learning set.

(c) *Shaping of a learning set.* In Experiments II and III, the task was to develop stimulus control of a learning set; the pupils were taught *when* to learn. Experiment IV attempted to modify *what* was learned. By reinforcing students for learning certain kinds of things from the information cards and not others, learning sets can be shaped in a manner analogous to response differentiation. What students learn from their study in a given course is more likely to be influenced by reinforcement from course examinations than by its high-sounding objectives. The specific hypothesis was that students would learn better the kind of information for which they had been previously tested than they would the kind of information not previously tested. Each subject was presented with 22 paragraphs of pseudo-historical information containing three facts and three reasons for the event. Immediately after each paragraph, one half of the group was tested on the facts, the other half on the reasons. Correct answers were immediately rewarded. In the testing situations, all subjects were tested on both kinds of information. Each group tested significantly higher on the type of material on which they had previously been tested and reinforced; in other words, the learning set of these pupils in reading the paragraphs was altered by a previous program of differential reinforcement.

When students are shown the same film, given the same lecture, or taken on the same field trip, different students learn different things. This is often "explained" by saying that students differ in their "interests" and therefore "pay attention" to different things. But such language is of little value in making education more effective; it merely describes the phenomena we observe. It is far more fruitful, for purposes of controlling what students learn, to suggest that such learning sets have been shaped differently by virtue of different reinforcement histories.

Conclusion

This discussion of motivation has emphasized the stimuli in the presence of which the child is active or learns. But it has also stressed the fact that such stimuli function as they do because of prior reinforcements. The crucial aspects of motivation are therefore to be found in the systems of reinforcement which a school provides for pupils.

Comments

1. This is an interesting article, voicing some common objections to motivation as both a theoretical and an operational concept and, at the same time, presenting a reinforcement alternative developed along Skinnerian lines. Such a viewpoint places the learner in a relatively passive role and the teacher in a very active and crucial role as the manipulator of reinforcements through which the former learns. While it is true that what is reinforcing in a given situation is not independent of the learner's present self, that too is essentially a function of his previous reinforcement history, in which, again, *external manipulation was the primary agent.*

2. Some people would object to this arrangement whereby the subject's behavior is inevitably and relentlessly shaped to a predetermined end through a schedule of differential reinforcement. This in no way denies the author's basic premise that recognizing motivation in certain children is not very helpful; it certainly does not identify the antecedents of such a happy state as the basis for an operational program designed to induce similar "motivation" in the other members of the class.

That's What They Said

"When we speak of the motivation for learning, we are thinking not so much of the tricks that the teacher employs as of the basic drives within the child that impel him to learn."

> H. N. Rivlin. "The classroom teacher and the child's learning," *Amer. J. Orthopsychiatry*, 24: 776–781, 1954. [778]

"Never worry about *creating* motivation in children. Every child has a tremendous amount of motivation that he is eager to satisfy every hour of the day."

> Henry P. Smith. *Psychology in Teaching*. Englewood Cliffs: Prentice-Hall, Inc., 1954. [205]

"Try as we may we cannot *force* an unwilling learner to learn. We can make him go through the motions or even make him memorize the material we have prescribed, but we cannot force him to apply it to situations outside the classroom or to remember it after he leaves. Hence, the only thing we can attain through force or coercion is the mere shadow of learning, not any real change in behavior, self-concept, or experience."

> Henry C. Lindgren. *Educational Psychology in the Classroom*. New York: John Wiley & Sons, 1962. [262]

"It is not enough that we see that the learnings he attains will be important to him in the future. They must be important *now*."

> Henry P. Smith. 1954. Op. cit. [243]

"The late Harry Stack Sullivan, one of our outstanding psychiatrists, declared that the very worst method of educating children is to create anxiety in them. The second worst method, Sullivan added, is not to generate anxiety in children."

> Nathaniel Cantor. *The Teaching-Learning Process*. New York: Holt, Rinehart and Winston, Inc., 1946. [31]

"The job of the teacher is apparently that of keeping a nice balance between an ease of tasks that conveys no challenge and a difficulty of tasks that frustrates most of the group."

> E. R. Hilgard and D. H. Russell. "Motivation in school learning," in N. B. Henry (ed.), *Learning and Instruction*. 49th Yearbook, National

Society for the Study of Education, Part I. Chicago: University of Chicago Press, 1950. Pp. 36–68. [63]

"Most, if not all, of the motives which operate in school instruction have been learned. In other words, interest, motive, and purpose grow out of experience as much as does cognition."

> Ernest Horn. "Language and meaning," in N. B. Henry (ed.), *The Psychology of Learning*. 41st Yearbook, National Society for the Study of Education, Part II. Chicago: University of Chicago Press, 1942. Pp. 377–413. [393]

"In our eagerness to get children to learn the prescribed curriculum, we commonly forget that motivation for learning depends on the needs of the learner, not those of the teacher. As a consequence, we think of motivation as something the teacher does *to* the student—a kind of winding him up before pressing the button that starts him off in a learning experience."

> Henry C. Lindgren. 1962. Op. cit. [264]

"An educational institution is one of the few places where a client frequently tries to get as little as possible for his investment—or his parents' investment."

> Don Robinson. "Scraps from a teacher's notebook," *Phi Delta Kappan*, 47: 157, 1965.

"Interestingly enough, the students enter the classroom prepared to listen to the instructor, as a rule, in a negative way. Their general attitude may be expressed as follows: 'Here we are. Talk to us, and we'll do what we're supposed to do. Only please let us alone. Don't pick on us, don't ask any embarrassing questions. Just talk, and we'll take notes. Let us know when the exam comes around, we'll do a bit of cramming, go through our notes of your answers and we'll pass. Only please don't bother us. We don't know the stuff. That's what we're here for. Tell us.' "

> Nathaniel Cantor. 1946. Op. cit. [111]

"With few if any exceptions, all laboratory studies of learning would support the notion that the longer the subject works at learning, the more he will learn. Motivation in this broad sense, then, is of utmost importance in learning. It squares with the common-sense notion of the influence of motivation. . . . This does not mean that motivation influences directly the process of forming associations; motivation may simply maintain the subject in a situation so that factors which are responsible for learning can operate.

> Benton J. Underwood. "Laboratory studies of verbal learning," in E. R. Hilgard (ed.), *Theories of Learning and Instruction.* 63rd Yearbook. National Society for the Study of Education, Part I. Chicago: University of Chicago Press, 1964. Pp. 133–152. [145–146]

"In so far as the improvement of instruction is concerned, there is probably no substitute for the provision of a program of activities which enlist and expand the interests of children. When programs of this kind are provided in elementary schools, the need for obviously extrinsic devices will be slight or non-existent."

> G. Max Wingo. "Implications for improving instruction in the upper elementary grades," in N. B. Henry (ed.), *Learning and Instruction.* 49th Yearbook, National Society for the Study of Education, Part I. Chicago: University of Chicago Press, 1950. Pp. 280–303. [296]

"The most important characteristic of a favorable learning situation is a strong ego-involved drive on the part of the learner to acquire the various socially approved behavior patterns with which the school is concerned."

> Walter W. Cook. "What educational measurement in the education of teachers?" *J. educ. Psychol.,* 41: 339–347, 1950. [339]

"Much of modern curriculum-planning concerns itself with the structure of knowledge and with the kind of thinking that is divergent rather than convergent; when conditions are appropriate, motivation appears to take care of itself."

> Pauline S. Sears and Ernest R. Hilgard. "The teacher's role in the motivation of the learner," in E. R. Hilgard (ed.), *Theories of Learning and Instruction.* 63rd Yearbook. National Society for the Study of Education, Part I. Chicago: University of Chicago Press, 1964. Pp. 182–209. [189]

"A fact which few educators have ever really faced up to is that much significant learning simply cannot be acquired during the school years at all because it is totally unrelated to the needs and problems of school children. Every year we manage to distort, obscure, and otherwise mishandle a great deal of religion, philosophy, and literature by force-feeding it to children who haven't the foggiest notion of what it really means and whose only adequate defense lies in either total indifference or naive misinterpretation."

> William F. O'Neill. "Existentialism and education for moral choice," *Phi Delta Kappan,* 46: 48–53, 1964. [51]

"When love or acceptance at any price is sensed to be futile, the child can fall back on his nuisance value to be sure of not being neglected, and he may incorporate such nuisance traits into his structure. It is commonly regarded more threatening to be overlooked than to be punished."

> C. M. Anderson. "The self-image: A theory of the dynamics of behavior," *Mental Hyg.*, 36: 227–244, 1952. [233]

"One teacher was persuaded to abandon traditional methods of assign, test, mark. She tried a newer method the others were talking about —teacher–pupil planning, individual and group projects, and so on. Suddenly the class became alive. The pupils began asking *her* questions, and she didn't know the answers. It was terrible! Things couldn't go on that way. So pretty soon she got everything back in order again—assign, test, mark. And after that, some children were 'lazy.' "

> William C. Trow. "When are children ready to learn?" *NEA J.*, 44: 78–79, 1955. [79]

"It has been amazing to me how just one teacher can damage or destroy a child's enthusiasm for a given subject. . . ."

> William M. Simpson. "A parent looks at teaching," *J. sec. Educ.*, 38: 175–181, 1963. [176]

"The apathetic student, if he is at all affected by schooling, *receives* an education. To say that teachers must meet him more than halfway understates the case: They must block all exits and trap him into learning. They must be wonderfully inventive in catching his attention and holding it. They must be endlessly solicitous in counseling him, encouraging him, awakening him and disciplining him. Every professor has observed what Lounsbury once described as 'the infinite capacity of the undergraduate to resist the intrusion of knowledge.' "

> John W. Gardner. *Excellence.* New York: Harper & Row, Publishers, 1961. [94]

CHAPTER 13

Test Items

1. The main reason teachers have so much difficulty with student motivation is that
    a. the curriculum is typically remote from the students' immediate purposes
    b. they do not understand children and their dynamics
    c. they fail to capitalize on the social dynamics of the classroom
    d. the school typically makes demands on students beyond their ability to comply
    e. students naturally resist teacher efforts

2. What acceptance is there for the concept of motivation?
    a. All major theories of learning make motivation an essential condition for learning.
    b. All major theories of learning present motivation as an important component step in the learning process.
    c. The fact that learning results from the organism's goal-seeking behavior is a central theme of modern psychology.
    d. Cognitive theories make motivation a sufficient, although not a necessary, condition for learning.
    e. Motivation, in its broad sense, is characteristic of the associationistic theories of learning.

3. Incentives are best defined as
    a. attainable goals
    b. conditions or objects having need-satisfying possibilities
    c. conditions which energize the organism
    d. objects having positive valence in relation to a given need
    e. reinforcement-producing objects or conditions

4. Defined in its basic meaning, motivation in school is largely a matter of
    a. encouraging the child to learn effective ways to satisfy his needs within the framework of the school's operation
    b. helping the child develop new interests
    c. helping the child find schoolwork rewarding
    d. making the classroom a pleasant place to work

e.   providing the child with a systematic schedule of selective reinforcements

5.   The child's development of a particular motive (rather than another) is best explained on the basis of
    a.   the functional autonomy of certain drives
    b.   innate predispositions
    c.   the natural priority of certain needs
    d.   selective reinforcement
    e.   the teacher's skill at socializing the young

6.   The major difficulty the teacher encounters in motivating his class is that
    a.   the classroom setting presents many other attractions that compete for the students' attention
    b.   curricular demands are necessarily frustrating to some children
    c.   each individual presents a unique motivational pattern calling for a particularized approach
    d.   there are not enough rewards (e. g., good grades) to go around
    e.   too much of the school's motivational efforts revolves around the teacher's authority

7.   The teacher's greatest asset in motivating children is probably
    a.   his ability to make the subject matter clear and logical
    b.   his ability to organize school routine on an efficient basis
    c.   his ability to relate to and inspire children
    d.   his skill in adapting the curriculum to individual needs
    e.   his skill in manipulating incentives, both positive and negative

8.   The teacher's major decision with regard to the motivation of his students is
    a.   just how much anxiety can teachers allow
    b.   just what is the school to promote
    c.   just what "mix" of failure and success is optimal for pupil growth
    d.   just what use can be made of the classroom as a social group
    e.   to what extent can the curriculum be "adapted" to individual needs

9.   Interests in academic subject matter is best explained on the basis of
    a.   basic predispositions related to neuro-chemical balance
    b.   the inherent appeal of certain topics or subjects
    c.   previous experience with related materials
    d.   their relationship to the child's needs
    e.   transference from the teacher's (or the parents') enthusiasm

10. The difficulty in motivating lower-class children in the school is that typically
     a.   the curriculum is too difficult in relation to their ability
     b.   the school's menu is meaningless in relation to their background
     c.   their middle-class teachers do not understand them
     d.   they are lacking in the necessary experiential background
     e.   they find the classroom climate cold and rejecting

11. The curriculum presents a major obstacle to effective motivation in that
     a.   by its very orientation toward future competence, it presents an unnatural situation
     b.   it attempts to monopolize too much of the child's time and efforts, presumably at the expense of his more basic needs
     c.   it ignores individual differences in ability and interest
     d.   it is too remote from the child's basic purposes, goals, and needs
     e.   much of the content is outside the child's psychological structure

12. The most valid objection to extrinsic incentives in the sense of having the most common detrimental effect is that
     a.   they create emotional disturbances
     b.   they emphasize a boss–worker relationship between teacher and pupil
     c.   they exist only on a rationed basis, which predestines some students to frustration
     d.   they have self-extinction properties
     e.   they tend to supersede the real goals of education

13. A major weakness of extrinsic incentives is that
     a.   they are aversive in their basic orientation
     b.   they are extraneous to the motives of the learner
     c.   they are often achieved apart from the activity they are to sponsor
     d.   they promote undue anxiety
     e.   unless coupled with intrinsic incentives, they are relatively ineffective

14. A safe rule regarding the intrinsic–extrinsic issue is for the teacher
     a.   to avoid extrinsic incentives at all costs
     b.   to minimize the use of all incentives; a well-motivated child does not need them
     c.   to rely on a judicious balance between extrinsic and intrinsic incentives
     d.   to restrict the use of extrinsic incentives to high schools and colleges where students can understand their limitations
     e.   to use extrinsic incentives; intrinsic incentives (e. g., food) are rarely appropriate to the school situation

15. From the standpoint of increased pupil productivity, research has shown that
    a. intrinsic incentives are more effective than extrinsic incentives
    b. negatively valenced intrinsic incentives are more effective than their positively valenced counterparts
    c. negative incentives promote greater productivity but also more anxiety
    d. extrinsic incentives are typically superior
    e. neither is clearly or consistently superior to the other

16. Under what conditions is punishment "acceptable"?
    a. mild punishment used in connection with reward of improved behavior
    b. moderate punishment of the young child by his parents
    c. punishment designed to emphasize behavioral limits
    d. punishment of inadequate behavior having (inherent) self-reinforcement
    e. none of the above; punishment is never justified

17. The incentive with the greatest relative valence is probably
    a. food
    b. a function of the individual's current motivational structure
    c. pain
    d. social approval
    e. success in line with one's aspirations

18. Research on the relative effects of punishment as an incentive has shown that
    a. punishment has definite inhibitory effects
    b. punishment soon loses its effectiveness
    c. severe punishment given on rare occasions is more effective than mild punishment on a systematic basis
    d. severe punishment is notoriously ineffective and frequently harmful
    e. to be effective, punishment should be moderate to severe

19. Which of the following forms of punishment is potentially most dangerous?
    a. mild punishment as part of the teacher's disciplinary practices
    b. physical aggression by one's peers
    c. punishment alternated with reward
    d. punishment through natural consequences
    e. a punitive approach of children by their parents

20. Research has shown the most powerful need in human adults to be
     a. achievement
     b. belonging
     c. hunger
     d. a matter of the particular motive structure the individual has de-
         veloped
     e. sex

21. The most likely effect of repeated failure is that
     a. it causes a downgrading of the self-concept
     b. it creates a distraction which interferes with improvement
     c. it discourages the individual from trying and promotes subse-
         quent failure
     d. it interferes with realistic goal-setting
     e. it promotes personal and social maladjustment

22. Research on praise and reproof has shown
     a. reproof more effective than praise
     b. reproof more effective for boys than for girls
     c. both praise and reproof more effective than "no comments"
     d. praise more effective with the extrovert than with the introvert
     e. none of the above necessarily; there is no simple answer to the
         question

23. The most serious objection to competition is that
     a. failure leads to a personal sense of failure
     b. fear of failure discourages participation and thus promotes incom-
         petence
     c. fear of failure leads to anxiety
     d. it interferes with cordial social participation
     e. success is restricted to the few

24. Competition in school serves its greatest purpose by
     a. capitalizing on innate tendencies for the maximum actualization
         of the child
     b. generating the anxieties necessary for adequate socialization
     c. motivating students
     d. providing a basis for meaningful self-appraisal
     e. providing a basis for realistic goal-setting

CHAPTER 14

Retention
and Transfer of Training

The fact that education is, at least in large part, for future use places the dual problem of retention and transfer of training in a position of critical importance. We need to be concerned with the degree to which the materials and skills taught and learned at school are retained over time and used as the basis for both effective operation and further learning, and with the conditions which maximize both retention and transfer. Unfortunately, once again most of the research on memory and transfer have been conducted in the laboratory, often with animals or nonsense syllables—which, as Ausubel points out, tells us very little about its school-connected counterpart.

The explanation of forgetting has been under continuous review; the psychoanalytic concept of repression, for example, has been criticized by FitzGerald and Ausubel, who suggest that unfavorable attitudes toward controversial material probably have their effect through deterring the individual from building a background to which the new learning can be attached. The common view of interference has also undergone a rather major change: it now seems that, with meaningful materials, forgetting is best explained on the basis of *proactive* rather than *retroactive* interference. An important contribution to the psychology of retention is Ausubel's subsumption theory, which postulates that newly learned material will be recalled better at first if there exists in the individual's cognitive structure appropriate concepts to which the material can be associated. Later, however, the recall of newly learned material may be lost as it becomes obliterated by being integrated (i.e., subsumed) under this existing conceptual structure.

Research findings on forgetting are far from being unequivocal; to the extent that the degree of original learning seems to have emerged as the crucial determinant of retention—as it seems to be to a large extent in matters of readiness and transfer of training—we need to encourage relative mastery through testing and, perhaps more meaningfully, wherever possible, through practice in a real-life situation. This has obvious implications for curriculum construction and for the timing of education in the life span of the individual. Material which has no meaning for the individual in his present stage of development is not likely to be learned well enough to be remembered or used. It also seems likely that the retention of material taught in school would be enhanced if the curriculum maker achieved a better integration among the various aspects of the overall curriculum. We particularly need to emphasize effective storage as the key to effective retrieval.

The problem of transfer has been a prominent feature throughout the history of psychology; it is still a matter of primary current interest. The breakthrough in this area is the concept of learning sets as postulated by Harlow, who presents convincing evidence to the effect that probably the most important thing a person learns through experience in a multitude of learning experiences is *how to learn,* i. e., how to develop a set or orientation which enables him to deal more effectively with similar problems in the future. Such a concept has broad psychological as well as pedagogical implications. While it does not necessarily relegate the theory of identical components to the ashcan, in certain respects, at least, it constitutes a more usable way of conceptualizing transfer of training. Learning how to learn as an educational objective has particular significance in connection with the current knowledge explosion; Tyler discusses some of its implications for secondary schools.

David P. Ausubel

A Subsumption Theory of Meaningful Verbal Learning and Retention *

The present paper presents a comprehensive theory of cognitive organization and of long-term learning and retention of large bodies of meaningful verbally presented material. In the absence of such a theory, inappropriate explanatory principles have been uncritically extrapolated from experimental findings based on non-verbal or short-term, fragmentary, and rote learning. This theory is limited to the nature and conditions of meaningful verbal reception learning and forgetting; it deals only with problems of cognitive organization and interaction, i. e., with (a) systematic changes in the availability and identifiability of ideational materials as they interact with and are incorporated into existing cognitive structure, and (b) variables which increase or decrease the incorporability and subsequent availability of these materials. It does not cover less complex kinds of learning or such other forms of cognitive activity as non-verbal, rote, or discovery learning, which in the opinion of the writer, call for entirely different explanatory principles.

The principles governing the nature of meaningful verbal reception learning can be discovered only through engineering type research that actually takes into account the distinctive attributes of this phenomenon as it occurs in the classroom. We cannot simply extrapolate general principles derived from the laboratory study of qualitatively different and vastly more simple instances of learning. Since meaningful learning of verbally presented materials constitutes the principal means of augmenting the learner's store of knowledge, there is need for research into the fundamental variables involved.

Process Differences between Rote and Meaningful Reception Learning

There are good reasons to believe that rote and meaningfully learned materials are organized differently in consciousness and hence conform to quite different principles of learning and forgetting. First, meaningfully

* Adapted and abridged from *J. gen. Psychol.*, 66: 213–224, 1962. By permission of author and publisher.

learned material has been related to existing concepts in cognitive structure in ways which permit the understanding of various kinds of significant relationships. Most new ideational materials that pupils encounter in a school setting can be tied to a previously acquired background of meaningful ideas and information. In fact, the curriculum is deliberately organized to ensure that this will occur. Materials learned by rote, on the other hand, are discrete and isolated entities which have not been related to established concepts in the learner's cognitive structure; they may or may not be potentially meaningful to begin with. Because they are not anchored to existing ideational systems, they are much more vulnerable to forgetting.

These differences have important implications in terms of underlying learning and retention processes. Because they are essentially isolated from cognitive structure, rote materials are subject to the interference of *similar* rote materials learned immediately before or after. As a result, learning and retention of discrete rote units can be explained in such S–R terms as intra- and inter-task similarity, response competition, and stimulus or response generalization. The learning and retention of meaningful materials, by contrast, are primarily affected by their interaction with relevant subsuming concepts already established in cognitive structure.

The Subsumption Process in Learning and Forgetting

The model of cognitive organization for the learning and retention of meaningful materials proposed here assumes the existence of a cognitive structure that is hierarchically organized in terms of highly inclusive conceptual traces under which are subsumed traces of less inclusive subconcepts as well as traces of specific informational data. The major organizational principle, in other words, is that of progressive differentiation of trace systems of a given sphere of knowledge from regions of greater to lesser inclusiveness, each linked to the next higher step in the hierarchy through a process of subsumption. As new material enters the cognitive field, it interacts with and is appropriately subsumed under a relevant and more inclusive conceptual scheme. The very fact that it can be subsumed (i. e., related to established elements of the present cognitive structure) accounts for its meaningfulness and permits the perception of insightful relationships. If it were not subsumable, it would constitute rote material and form discrete and isolated traces.

The initial effects of subsumption—orienting, relating, and cataloging—facilitate both learning and retention. These preliminary operations are obviously essential for meaningful learning and retention, since the incorporation of new material into existing cognitive structure necessarily presupposes consistency with the prevailing organization. Furthermore, subsumption of the traces of the learning task by an established ideational system provides anchorage for the new material and thus constitutes the most orderly, efficient, and stable way of retaining for future availability. Hence, for a variable period of time, the recently cataloged subconcepts and informational data can be dissociated from their subsuming concepts and reproduced as individually identifiable entities.

Although the stability of meaningful material is initially enhanced by anchorage to relevant conceptual foci in the learner's cognitive structure, such material is gradually subjected to the erosive influence of the conceptualizing trend in cognitive organization. Because it is more economical and less burdensome to retain a single inclusive concept than to remember a large number of more specific items, the import of the latter tends to be incorporated by the generalized meaning of the former. When this second or obliterative stage of subsumption begins, the specific items become progressively less dissociable as entities in their own right until they are no longer available and are said to be forgotten.

This process of memory reduction to the least common denominator capable of representing cumulative prior experience is very similar to the reduction process characterizing concept formation. For the same reason that a single abstract concept is more manipulatable for cognitive purposes than a dozen diverse instances, the specific items of meaningful experience underlying an established conceptual entity tend to undergo gradual obliterative subsumption.

Learning and Forgetting

In reception learning, the distinctive attribute of both learning and forgetting is a change in the availability of the material. Learning represents an increase in availability; forgetting a decrease. Retention is largely a later temporal phase and diminished aspect of the same phenomenon or functional capacity, with later availability obviously a function of initial availability. This relationship between learning and forgetting is even closer for *meaningful* material. During the learning phase, new ideational material forms an interactional product with a subsuming focus in cognitive structure and is, to some degree, dissociable therefrom. Continued interaction, however, gradually reduces this dissociability of the new material until the interactional product is reduced to the least common denominator capable of representing the entire complex, i. e., to the subsuming concept itself. In rote learning, by contrast, cognitive interaction does not take place so that learning represents an increment in availability involving one discrete cognitive process while rote forgetting represents a loss in this availability due to interference from another discrete process set in motion shortly before or after learning.

Principal Factors Influencing Meaningful
Verbal Learning

An important variable affecting the incorporability and longevity of new meaningful material is the availability in cognitive structure of relevant subsuming concepts at an appropriate level of inclusiveness to provide optimal anchorage. Since it is highly unlikely that ideally relevant and proximate subsuming concepts are already available in cognitive structure to provide such optimal anchorage, it may be desirable to *introduce* appropriate subsumers and make them part of cognitive structure prior to the presentation of the learning task. These introduced subsumers would thus constitute efficient advance organizers or anchoring foci for the reception of new material.

A second important factor presumably affecting the retention of a meaningful learning task is the extent to which it can be discriminated from the established conceptual structure that subsumes it. If the distinguishable features of the new material is not clearly discriminable from stable subsuming foci, they cannot be adequately represented by the latter for purposes of memory and will not persist as dissociable entities identifiable in their own right. Conversely, anything that brings out the discriminability of new material from its presumed subsumer enhances its chances of retention. The longevity of new meaningful material is also a function of the stability and clarity of its subsumers. Ambiguous and unstable subsumers not only provide weak anchorage for related new materials but also cannot be easily discriminated from them.

Subsumption Theory versus Connectionism

Rote verbal learning and forgetting are adequately explained in terms of habit strength. The principal variable in rote forgetting, for example, is exposure to materials similar to but not identical with the learning task either before (proactive inhibition) or after (retroactive inhibition) the learning session. By contrast, because meaningful material interacts with subsuming concepts in cognitive structure, it seems more logical to define learning and forgetting in terms of the dissociability of the material from its subsumers at successive stages of the interactional process, with the major variables affecting retention being those mentioned in the previous section. The inapplicability of connectionist principles of proactive and retroactive interference to meaningful verbal material is clearly shown in experimental studies of retention: the short-term interference of similar elements (so basic to rote forgetting) is a relatively insignificant factor in the forgetting of meaningful material adequately anchored to established subsumers. In fact, retroactive exposure to material of the same ideational import as the learning passage but differing in specific content, sequence, and mode of presentation, is actually just as facilitating as repetition of the learning passage.

Comments

1.   The present article is a major contribution to the psychology of the learning and forgetting of meaningful learning; it is of special interest in view of the gradually increasing emphasis on meaningfulness, structure, and understanding. The author's concept of advance organizers (Ausubel, 1960) as the basis for optimal anchorage of new materials bears directly on the new emphasis on concept formation, abstraction, and generalization.

2.   Ausubel presents a strong case against the unwarranted use of principles derived from studies based on laboratory and nonsense materials to meaningful materials of the type with which the school is concerned. He postulates that conclusions from these studies have little to offer the teacher whose tasks deal with meaningful and complex verbal learning. The paper presents a sophisticated modern view of retention of major significance to educational practice: As Ausubel points out, extrapolation of findings from rote-learning studies has not only held back the improvement of verbal instruction but has also encouraged teachers to present meaningful materials in rote fashion.

Reference

Ausubel, David P. "The use of advance organizers in the learning and retention of meaningful verbal material," *J. educ. Psychol.,* 51: 267–272, 1960.

Ralph W. Tyler

The Knowledge Explosion: Implications
for Secondary Education *

The knowledge explosion is bound to have basic implications for the operation of the secondary school. Not only are new facts being discovered at an exponential rate but new discoveries change the meaning and implication of many of the "facts" previously "known." Memorizing a huge number of facts today will not provide an adequate education for tomorrow. Students who are crammed full in this way will find several years hence that they have a mixture of information and misinformation rather than adequate background to understand our changing world and to use its material, intellectual, and esthetic resources effectively. In order to deal effectively with the situation, the high school needs to:

(a)   Concentrate its major efforts on important tasks that it can do best. Skills like driver education can be picked up elsewhere; basic concepts and modes of inquiry in science, English, etc., on the other hand, must be carefully organized over time into systematic structure that will enable the student to reach a relatively high level of understanding. It is especially important for the school to provide learning opportunities in cases where the essential factors are not obvious to the observer; an understanding of history, for example, cannot be introduced directly in the ordinary activities of daily life.

(b)   Update its objectives, its contents, its emphasis, and its learning experiences. This is a joint enterprise involving scholars, scientists, teachers, experts in learning, administrators, etc.

(c)   Emphasize the concept of education as a process of continuing, lifelong learning; it is not possible for us to master in three years, twelve years, sixteen years, or any specified time, all that we need to learn. The secondary school must help its students develop the ability to learn and a continuing interest in learning.

(d)   Select and organize the content in such a way that these vast quantities of material can be understood and used effectively. Knowl-

* Adapted and abridged from *Educ. Forum,* 29: 145–153, 1965. By permission of Kappa Delta Pi, An Honor Society in Education, owners of the copyright.

edge is more than the simple accumulation of isolated items; it must be provided with structure so that it can be grasped.

(e)   Work out a better sequence of learning in the several fields. There is need to build the second year on the first, and the third on the second, etc. We must work out better sequences of courses from the elementary school to the high school so as to reach an increasingly higher level of learning.

(f)   Pay careful attention to efficient learning. This is a matter of enabling the student to see phenomena from relevant points of view, of gaining satisfaction from more effective behavior, of providing guidance in trying out new behavioral patterns, etc. We need to pay more attention to providing the conditions that will markedly increase the effectiveness with which learning takes place.

Comments

1.   These are obviously significant suggestions concerning a crucial issue; they deserve the serious consideration of educators responsible for the education of tomorrow.

2.   In a related article, Flanagan (1964) points out that, even though high-school enrollments have increased drastically over the past 50 years, very little change has taken place in the program of studies to which high-school students have been exposed. Fortunately, signs indicating a rapid change over the next few years are beginning to show. Flanagan also emphasizes the need for systematic research into ways of effecting substantial improvement in the secondary schools' program. He notes, for example, that, according to Project Talent, from 25 to 30 percent of ninth-graders already know more about many educational subjects than the average twelfth-grader; any attempt to provide the same educational activities and experiences on a gradewide basis is, therefore, going to be wasteful.

3.   Johnson (1967) notes that up to now research has played a very minor role in determining practices in secondary education; that the practitioner has emphasized reforming the school through innovations, many of which owe their success, partly if not wholly, to the Hawthorne effect; that the program of innovation has been rather opportunistic and uncoordinated; and that it has proceeded piecemeal without adequate coordination in relation to the overall purposes to be served by the school and without adequate research into its effectiveness. Since it is foolish to seek better ways of doing the wrong things, the current escalation of research activities must be accompanied by thorough attention to the aims of secondary education in the greatly altered context of the present.

4.   The idea of eliminating from the school's curriculum those activities which could be assumed by other social agencies while the school attends to its multifaceted responsibilities makes sense.

References

Flanagan, John C. "The implications of recent research on the improvement of secondary education," *Amer. educ. Res. J.*, 1: 1–9, 1964.

Johnson, Mauritz. "Research in secondary education," *Educ. Forum*, 41: 293–301, 1967.

That's What They Said

"If graduation marks the beginning and not the end of learning, then the goal in school must be learning how to learn. This means learning the basic method and content of learning. All students need to learn the three R's. Beyond this they all need to learn, but not necessarily the same things."

Don Robinson. "Scraps from a teacher's notebook," *Phi Delta Kappan,* 43: 344, 1962.

"Nearly everything that is now known was not in any book when most of us went to school: We cannot know it unless we have picked it up since."

Robert J. Oppenheimer. "The tree of knowledge," *Harper's Mag.,* 217: 55–60, 1958. [56]

"The traditional argument that one learns to understand the future by knowing the past has lost much of its validity. There is little precedent in the past for what our children face in the future. This fact is profoundly disturbing to many people and gives rise to the irrational demand from the far right that we continue to educate for life in a kind of world which has ceased to exist."

Arthur F. Corey. "Improvement of instruction," *Midland Sch.,* 49: 11–13, September–October, 1966. [11]

"The key to retrieval is organization or, in simpler terms, knowing where to find information and how to get there."

Jerome S. Bruner. "The act of discovery," *Harv. educ. Rev.,* 31: 21–32, 1961. [31]

"Our aim as teachers is to give our student as firm a grasp of the subject as we can and to make him as autonomous and self-propelled a thinker as we can."

Jerome S. Bruner. 1961. Ibid. [23]

"I am concerned with one additional dimension of educational objectives, namely, with what has been called the 'surrender value' of the curriculum. Five or ten years after the student has successfully attained the immediate objectives of the curriculum, what is he expected to retain? Should we not construct curricula with conscious attention to their surrender value, that is, to their long-term retention benefits?"

John B. Carroll. "School learning over the long haul," in John D. Krumboltz (ed.), *Learning and the Educational Process*. Skokie, Ill.: Rand McNally & Company, 1965. Pp. 249–269. [258]

"If we once admit the proposition that forgetting is determined by events filling a time interval, it immediately becomes apparent that the experimental designs for the study of transfer of training are also those for the production of forgetting. Negative transfer, then, is admitted to be one of the mechanisms of forgetting."

James Deese. *The Psychology of Learning*. New York: McGraw-Hill, Inc., 1958. [256]

"Yet, the fact is that the differences in retention are probably due entirely to differences in degree of learning attained in the ten acquisition trials. Indeed, if level of learning is equivalent before a retention interval is introduced, there is no evidence that *any* task variable (meaningfulness, intralist similarity, and so on) is associated with appreciable differences in rate of forgetting. Enormous differences in learning may be produced by task variables, but they produce small if any differences in rate of forgetting."

Benton J. Underwood. "Laboratory studies of verbal learning," in E. R. Hilgard (ed.), *Theories of Learning and Instruction*. 63rd Yearbook. National Society for the Study of Education, Part I. Chicago: University of Chicago Press, 1964. Pp. 133–152. [148]

"The convergence of such facts . . . has made the degree of learning emerge as the critical variable involved in retention. Such a conclusion, with its corresponding relegation of individual-difference variables to a very minor role, will be resisted. Indeed, it is resisted by those of us who have been investigating forgetting within the framework of an interference theory."

Benton J. Underwood. 1964. Ibid. [149]

". . . If slow and fast learners achieve the same degree of learning before the retention interval is introduced, there is no evidence that the rate of forgetting differs. A slow learner may appear to show more rapid forgetting than a fast learner in uncontrolled observations because the level of learning is higher for the fast learner."

Benton J. Underwood. 1964. Ibid. [149]

"The reason a person who is an expert in a given field can read a book and retain a lot after short study is not that he has a better memory but simply that he probably has better background and therefore has more hooks into which he can hang what he needs whereas a newcomer to the field must start from scratch."

> Norman L. Munn. *Psychology: The Fundamentals of Human Adjustment.* Boston: Houghton-Mifflin Company, 1961. [475]

"So long as we insist that children learn so much that is already obsolete to prepare them for a world that no longer exists, we are handicapping human intelligence and by so much are sabotaging our human potentialities."

> Lawrence K. Frank. "Four ways to look at potentialities," in Alexander Frazier (ed.), *New Insights and the Curriculum.* 1963 Yearbook. Washington: Association for Supervision and Curriculum Development, 1963. Pp. 11–37. [36]

"There is a danger of training scientists so narrowly in their specialties that they are unprepared to shoulder the normal and civic responsibilities which the modern world thrusts upon them. But just as we must insist that every scientist be broadly educated, so we must see to it that every educated person be literate in science. In the short run, this may contribute to our survival. In the long run, it is essential to our integrity as a society."

> John W. Gardner. *The Pursuit of Excellence.* Garden City, N.Y.: Doubleday & Company, Inc., 1958.

"The phenomenon of transfer is so pervasive that it is difficult to distinguish between research on transfer specifically and on learning in general."

> Herbert J. Klausmeier and J. K. Davis. "Transfer of learning," in Robert L. Ebel (ed.), *Encyclopedia of Educational Research.* New York: The Macmillan Company, 1969. Pp. 1483–1493. [1484]

"Virtually every mistake the pupil makes in interpretation is a 'reasonable' one, based on the application of some concept that has worked in the past and seems applicable here."

> Lee J. Cronbach. *Educational Psychology.* New York: Harcourt, Brace, and World, Inc., 1954. [291]

"The inadequacies of this theory (of identical components) are quite apparent. The problem is that of finding a substitute theory which can be of value in the designing of curricula and training programs."

Robert M. W. Travers. *Essentials of Learning.* New York: The Macmillan Company, 1963. [402]

Reference

Slamecka, N. J., and J. Ceraso. "Retroactive and proactive inhibition of verbal learning," *Psychol. Bull.,* 57: 449–475, 1960.

CHAPTER 14

Test Items

1. Retroactive inhibition is to proactive inhibition as
   a. forgetting is to learning
   b. forgetting is to transfer
   c. learning is to transfer
   d. negative transfer is to positive transfer
   e. transfer is to forgetting

2. What toll does forgetting take?
   a. Five to ten percent of a given high-school course may be forgotten over the summer vacation.
   b. Ten to twenty-five percent of a college course is forgotten in two years.
   c. A fair overall estimate might be fifty percent within a year.
   d. Knowledge of principles and their application may actually increase with time rather than decrease.
   e. It varies with such a large number of factors that no estimate can be made.

3. Forgetting is best explained on the basis of
   a. the deterioration of neurological processes
   b. inadequate initial learning
   c. the interference of prior or subsequent learnings
   d. the repression of conflicting materials
   e. the time factor

4. The most recent theory (explanation) of forgetting is
   a. the Law of Disuse
   b. the principle of proactive inhibition
   c. the principle of retroactive inhibition
   d. the principle of repression
   e. the Theory of Formal Discipline

5. Which is the *incorrect* association regarding views on forgetting?
   a. Ausubel—Subsumption theory
   b. Freud—Repression
   c. Muller and Pilzecker—Retroactive inhibition
   d. Underwood—Proactive inhibition
   e. none of the above; all are correct associations

6. The primary determinant of the degree of retention in school-connected materials is
   a. the degree of mastery of the original learning
   b. the intelligence of the learner
   c. the logical continuity of the material
   d. the method of measuring retention
   e. the time factor

7. Forgetting is best conceived as
   a. an elimination (liquidation, clearance)
   b. a loss
   c. a reinterpretation
   d. a reorganization (subsumption)
   e. a substitution

8. Probably the *least* fundamental of the concepts underlying the existence of the school is
   a. the application of learning
   b. learning
   c. problem-solving
   d. retention (nonforgetting)
   e. transfer of learning

9. Which of the following statements concerning retention is most accurate?
   a. The basic determinant of the degree of retention is the degree of
      mastery.
   b. The degree of retention is primarily a function of the similarity
      between learning and testing situations.
   c. The greater the similarity between two learning situations, the
      more they interfere retroactively and proactively.
   d. The more closely two learning situations follow one another, the
      more they reinforce each other.
   e. The more thoroughly a given lesson is learned, the more it will
      interfere with the retention of new (less learned) material.

10. Probably the most efficient means of ensuring a high level of long-
    term retention (say, to the final examination) is
    a. 50 percent overlearning
    b. 100 percent overlearning
    c. learning by wholes
    d. learning through discovery
    e. periodic reviews

11. Review is an effective way of dealing with forgetting inasmuch as
    a.   it brings about a more adequate structure to the material
    b.   it extends the period of active cerebration on the subject
    c.   it increases the number of opportunities for positive reinforce-
         ment
    d.   it promotes greater transfer to the testing situation
    e.   it restores what was lost

12. Generally speaking, the best form of review is
    a.   an attempt to cast the material into a different perspective
    b.   a program of selective restructuring of key concepts
    c.   recitation of the material
    d.   rereading of the material for ideas that may have been skipped
    e.   the use of the material as a stepping stone to more advanced
         work

13. Which of the following suggestions would *not* find support from the
    psychology of retention?
    a.   Effective learning; emphasis should be on mastery, meaningful-
         ness, structure.
    b.   Intent on memory; anticipating having to recall material is a good
         way of increasing mastery and retention.
    c.   Interference of learning; each unit should be presented as a unit
         separate from related ideas with which it might be confused.
    d.   Overlearning; the extra time pays extra dividends in greater in-
         sights and greater retention.
    e.   Periodic review; review is probably the most economical way of
         ensuring retention.

14. _____ is to retroactive as _____ is to proactive inhibition.
    a.   Ausubel; Underwood
    b.   Carmichael; Ausubel
    c.   forgetting; transfer
    d.   Muller; Underwood
    e.   Pilzecker; Ausubel

15. The school's function is changing from an emphasis on _____ to an
    emphasis on _____.
    a.   accumulation; application
    b.   knowledge; competence in acquiring knowledge
    c.   knowledge; problem solving
    d.   knowledge; skills
    e.   retention; transfer

16. Modern educational psychologists see the school's role in relation to transfer of training to be that of emphasizing
    a. basic concepts, principles, and skills
    b. generalizations and problem solving
    c. learning sets
    d. life-adjustment education
    e. vocational and socio-civic knowledge and skills

17. Which of the following statements *least* adequately represents the relationship between forgetting and transfer of training?
    a. Forgetting is simply a case of negative transfer.
    b. Forgetting and transfer are two ways of looking at the same continuum.
    c. Proactive facilitation is simply a case of positive transfer.
    d. Proactive inhibition is simply a case of negative transfer.
    e. Retroactive inhibition is simply a case of positive transfer.

18. Forgetting is best viewed as an instance of
    a. failure in positive transfer
    b. failure in understanding (meaningfulness)
    c. negative facilitation
    d. negative transfer
    e. nonlearning (or inadequate learning)

19. Current thinking concerning transfer of training favors
    a. the concept of transposibility
    b. Harlow's concept of learning sets
    c. the theory of formal discipline
    d. stimulus and response generalizations
    e. Thorndike's theory of identical components

20. The degree of transfer from a given educational experience is primarily a function of
    a. the learner's grasp of the relevant fundamentals
    b. the overall IQ of the learner
    c. the readiness of the learner for that particular experience
    d. the teacher's handling of the subject
    e. the transfer inherent in the subject matter

21. Which of the following is *not* a correct association?
    a. Ausubel: advance organizers, theory of subsumption
    b. Harlow: learning sets, learning how to learn

    c.   Thorndike: identical components, laws of learning
    d.   Osgood: transfer of training, retention
    e.   Underwood: retroactive inhibition, stimulus generalization

22.   The most crucial factor in ensuring the transfer value of education is
    a.   adequacy in basic skills (e. g., writing, reading)
    b.   intellectual curiosity and openness to experience
    c.   meaningfulness of the content
    d.   relevance in relation to the learner's goals and purposes
    e.   the use of discovery as a method of teaching

23.   The most comprehensive view of transfer centers around the concept of
    a.   discrimination
    b.   openness to experience (a positive self-concept)
    c.   response generalization
    d.   stimulus generalization
    e.   stimulus substitution

24.   The *least* effective way to promote transfer is to emphasize
    a.   broad learning sets
    b.   facts and skills
    c.   a positive self-concept
    d.   principles and generalizations
    e.   skills in problem solving

25.   The transfer difficulties experienced by the dull child in school have their origin in
    a.   his inadequate grasp of the material
    b.   his lack of orientation toward the transfer possibilities of the material he learns
    c.   his lack of readiness
    d.   his poor study habits
    e.   his tendency toward extensive forgetting

26.   The degree of transfer from a given educational experience is most nearly proportional to the extent
    a.   to which one teaches and learns with transfer in mind
    b.   of the disciplinary value of the subject matter content
    c.   of its practical (vocational) significance
    d.   to which its complete mastery is achieved
    e.   to which it is carried to the level of generalization and abstraction

27. The fact that students who study Latin in high school tend to be good students in college shows that
    a. anyone who survived three years of Latin is probably a good student
    b. Latin facilitates vocabulary development
    c. Latin has superior transfer value
    d. studying Latin calls for the development of effective study habits
    e. none of the above is necessarily true; the findings are based on an ex post facto design that is totally incapable of interpretation

28. Research into the transfer value of high-school subjects to intellectual development suggests that
    a. classical subjects promote greatest transfer
    b. the social studies have actually greater transfer than the sciences and mathematics
    c. transfer is a function of intelligence, not methods or contents
    d. the transfer value of a given subject is a function of the standard of achievement that is required (e.g., the degree of mastery), not the subject matter per se
    e. the transfer value of a subject is a function of the way it is presented, not of its content per se

CHAPTER 15

The Higher Mental Processes

The school in a democratic society has a major responsibility for helping its students develop the meanings and the problem-solving skills that will enable them to function effectively as future citizens. The fact that reasoning is predicated upon information means that, by the very nature of its curriculum, the school necessarily contributes to thinking, reasoning, or problem solving. However, information simply accumulated is not much of a foundation for effective reasoning; the school must help children not only to learn but also learn how to use what they have learned. The concept of learning sets, considered in the previous chapter, has particular meaning in this connection. We have come to accept transition and change as a fundamental characteristic of our culture; the fact that we can no longer even approximate the problems our students will face in the future and the information they will need makes training in how to learn all the more imperative. This new emphasis on meaningfulness and understanding together with the concept of learning sets provides us with the only hope of dealing with the future. Unfortunately, far too much of the school's emphasis in the past has been on the transmission of established "knowledge"; with the rapidly changing status of knowledge, this is no longer possible. Our mode of operation must change; the school must now concern itself with providing basic information and basic skills but especially with developing the ability to seek new answers. Also relevant in this connection are the concepts of self-actualization, openness to experience, and the various factors of a general nature which contribute to effective citizenship. The current emphasis on discovery, sponsored by such writers as Bruner, has relevance in this connection. Even though not necessarily more effective with regard to the teaching of any given unit— and certainly not more effective with regard to the teaching of all units— the discovery method may have certain important transfer benefits from the standpoint of later citizenship.

On the other hand, it is easy to overestimate the reasoning ability of children. As Almy points out, we must avoid superimposing our adult model on children's thinking. To the extent that a prerequisite to effective reasoning is a foundation of valid and meaningful information, the child needs, first of all, concrete experiences. However, to be useful in reasoning, these experiences must be generalized and an important aspect of education consists of helping children form precise concepts and meanings and to organize subject matter into conceptual structure at their own level of understanding. This emphasis on concept development as a series of substeps leading to mastery and conceptual clarity is an important feature of programed instruction. Of particular relevance in this connection are Weir's article on the learning of meanings in the present chapter and, of course, Bayles' article on learning as the development of insight presented in Chapter 11. Also of special significance is Bruner's "Learning and Thinking," in which he emphasizes how the operation of the classroom can be made more effective by "leaping the barrier from learning into thinking."

We also need to be concerned with creativity, which until recently has been badly neglected. On the other hand, there has been an unwarranted tendency to emphasize creativity by downplaying "convergent" thinking, traditional intelligence, and other presumably nondivergent processes. As Thorndike points out, creativity is itself a pretty global term. An even stronger criticism of the tendency to downplay traditional IQ is presented by McNemar (see Chapter 9). Neither of these articles denies the need for concern over the way in which creativity can be fostered and, of course, the need for full awareness of the way it can be destroyed by the very nature of the orientation of the school toward authoritarianism, convergence, conformity, and conventionality.

Jerome S. Bruner

Learning and Thinking *

One of the principal objectives of learning is to save us from subsequent learning. When we learn something, the objective is to learn it in such a way that we get a maximum of travel out of what we have learned. If the principle of addition has been grasped in its generic sense, it becomes unnecessary to learn multiplication, for in principle multiplication is only repeated addition. Learning something in a generic way is like leaping over a barrier, on the other side of which is thinking. When the generic has been grasped, we are able to recognize new problems as exemplars of old principles we have already mastered.

There are two interesting features in generic learning. One of them is *organization;* the other is *manipulation.* If we are to use our past learning, we must organize it in such a way that it is no longer bound to the specific situation in which the learning occurred. For example, it would have been possible for Galileo to have published a handbook of the distances traversed per unit time by falling bodies. Such tables, cumbersome though they might have been, would have contained all the necessary information for dealing with free-falling bodies. Instead, Galileo had the inspiration to reorganize this welter of information into a highly simplified form. You recall the compact expression $S = \frac{1}{2}gt^2$; it not only summarizes all possible handbooks but organizes their knowledge in a way that makes manipulation possible.

A significant aspect of the human mind is its limited capacity for dealing at any one moment with diverse arrays of information. We must, therefore, condense this information to that having general significance.

A simple formula that can regenerate the distance fallen by any free body, past or future, is under these conditions highly nutritious for its weight. Good organization achieves the kind of economical representation of facts that makes it possible to use the facts in the future. Sheer brute learning, noble though it may be, is not enough. Facts simply learned without a generic organization are the naked and useless untruth.

These principles do not apply only to science, mathematics and the social studies. To use an example from mythology, consider the slaying of

* Adapted and abridged from Jerome S. Bruner, "Learning and thinking," *Harv. Educ. Rev.,* 29: 184–192, Summer 1959. Copyright © 1959 by President and Fellows of Harvard College.

the Medusa by Perseus who had to rely on the reflection of his polished shield to guide his sword in order to avoid being turned into stone: Beneath the story, beneath all great stories, there is a deeper metaphoric meaning. It occurred to me that the polished shield might symbolize all of the devices by which we are able to take action against evil without becoming contaminated by it. I do not wish to hold a brief for my interpretation of the Perseus myth. But I would like to make one point about it.

Man must cope with a relatively limited number of plights—birth, growth, loneliness, the passions, death, and not very many more. I would urge that a grasp of the basic plights through the basic myths of art and literature provides the organizing principle by which knowledge of the human condition is rendered into a form that makes thinking possible, by which we go beyond learning to the use of knowledge. I am not suggesting that Greek myths are better than other forms of literature. I urge simply that there be exposure to, and interpretation of, literature that deals deeply with the human condition. I have learned as much from Charley Brown of *Peanuts* as I have learned from Perseus. The pablum school readers, stripped of rich imagery in the interest of "readability," stripped of passion in the erroneous belief that the deeper human condition will not interest the child—these are no more the vehicles for getting over the barrier to thinking than are the methods of teaching mathematics by a rote parroting at the blackboard.

I should like to consider now some conditions in our schools today that promote and inhibit progress across the barrier from learning to thinking. I should point out in advance that I am not very cheerful on the subject.

(a) The Passivity of Knowledge-getting

I have been struck during the past year or so, sitting in classrooms as an observer, by the passivity of the process we call education. The emphasis is upon gaining and storing information, gaining it and storing it in the form in which it is presented. We carry the remainder in long division so, peaches are grown in Georgia, transportation is vital to cities, New York is our largest port, and so on. There is little effort indeed which goes into the process of putting the information together; into finding out what is generic about it. Algebra is not a set of rules for manipulating numbers and letters except in a trivial sense. It is a way of thinking, a way of coping with the drama of the unknown. It is an enriching strategy, algebra, but only if it is grasped as an extended instance of common sense.

(b) Episodic Curriculum

Much of the learning in our classrooms is atomistic and episodic; children learn one fact here, one fact there. This sort of curriculum is made up of separate units, each a task unto itself. "We have now finished addition; let us now move to multiplication." I do not wish to make it seem as if our present state of education is a decline from some previous Golden Age. For I do not think there has ever been a Golden Age in American public education. The difference now is that we can afford dross less well than ever before. The volume of positive knowledge increases at a rapid rate. Atomizing it into facts-to-be-filed is not likely to produce the kind of broad grasp that will be needed in the world of the next quarter-century.

(c) The Embarrassment of Passion

Also objectionable is the way the curriculum material is presented in the context of ideal adjustment. The story of Columbus, for example, simply leaves out the essential truth—the fanatical urge to explore in an age of exploration, the sense of an expanding world—presumably on the premise that such "pablum" accounts touch more directly on the life of the child.

What is this "life of the child" as seen by text writers and publishers? It is an image created out of an ideal of adjustment, an ideal which has little place for the driven man, the mythic hero, the idiosyncratic style. Its ideal is mediocentrism, reasonableness above all, being nice. Such an ideal does not touch closely the deeper life of the child. It does not appeal to the dark but energizing forces that lie close beneath the surface. The Old Testament, the Greek Myths, the Norse legends—these are the embarrassing chronicles of men of passion. They were devised to catch and preserve the power and tragedy of the human condition—and its ambiguity, too. In their place, we have substituted the noncontroversial and the banal.

(d) The Quality of Teachers

I do not wish to mince words. The educational and cultural level of the majority of American teachers is not impressive; on the whole, they do not have a good grasp of the subject matter that they are teaching. This leaves us with a small core of experienced teachers. Do we use them to teach the new teachers on the job? No. The organization of the school with respect to utilization of talent is something short of imaginative. I would urge, and I believe that educators have taken steps in this direction, that we use our more experienced teachers for on-the-job training of less experienced, new teachers.

The task of improving American schools is not simply one of technique; it is a deeper problem, one that is more philosophical than psychological or technological in scope. What do we conceive to be the end-product of our educational effort? The training of well-rounded human beings to be responsible citizens, while a worthy objective, has not always led to happy results, for much of what we have called the embarrassment of passion can, I think, be traced to this objective, so too the blandness of the social studies curriculum. This ideal, sadly, has also led to the standardization of mediocrity by a failure of the schools to challenge the full capacity of the talented student. The new competition occasioned by such factors as the technical progress of the Soviet Union has rekindled our awareness of excellence. Perhaps the fitting ideal for such a situation is, the active pragmatic ideal of leaping the barrier from learning into thinking. It matters not *what* we have learned. What we can *do* with what we have learned: this is the issue.

Comments

1.   The article deals with a crucial issue; our schools have concentrated on the more tangible, but, in a sense, the more mechanical and trivial aspects of education—perhaps because this is what is emphasized in our tests and examinations. The present emphasis on excellence may well accentuate, rather than alleviate, this problem.

2.   The content of the article is such as to warrant considerable thought—particularly in relation to the views presented by such phenomenologists as Combs, Kelley, Maslow, and Rogers. It raises again the apparent difficulty involved in getting an education that is both personally meaningful and academically adequate.

Millie Almy

Wishful Thinking about Children's Thinking *

Public criticism of the school has focused attention on the process of thinking. In this concern, the educator is joined by the psychologist, the scientist, the mathematician, as well as the linguist, each representing a different perspective. However, if this concern is to be reflected in the more effective training of children to think, there is need to reconcile these viewpoints and thus avoid the inclination to think wishfully, rather than realistically, about the way they think. The difficulty lies in the fact that adults tend to assume that the thinking of children basically parallels their own. In fact, many of the principles of educational practice rest on the false assumption that children and adults think alike.

The process of education would be considerably simplified if children, once having acquired speaking vocabularies resembling those of adults, also shared with them similar ways of explaining and viewing the world. But this overlooks important limitations in the thinking abilities of children. This does not imply that the curriculum of the elementary school should be a matter of intellectual pablum, for the problem is not that children are unable to cope with ideas, but rather that they apprehend them in ways that are characteristic of their level of development. We don't want to postpone opportunities for thinking, for there is nothing wrong with injecting substantial content into the curriculum; the danger lies in not recognizing that each level of development contributes its own special understanding of that content.

Misconceptions as to the nature of the child's thinking are relatively common. Wishful thinking on the part of teachers is readily noted in their willingness to accept glib answers, when all along they know that his ability to give the expected answer may actually mask understandings that are quite different from those they expected. Scientists also engage in wishful thinking when they assume that whatever approach leads to effective thinking in their discipline will probably apply equally well to other disciplines.

Piaget's Views

Particularly enlightening in this connection is Piaget's study of the development of logical "operations," i.e., ways of getting information

* Adapted and abridged from *T. C. Rec.* 62: 396–406, 1961. By permission of author and publisher.

from the world of reality into the world of thought. During infancy, the child is capable only of direct action on his world. Later, he internalizes his actions and is able to carry them out symbolically. But it is not until he is also able to cancel or "reverse" them mentally (i.e., to be aware of a previous thought) that he can comprehend the world in the way the adult does. Not until this point can the adult hope to teach him the most elementary concepts of physics or mathematics. Similarly, it is not until he can mentally handle potentiality or possibility as effectively as reality that he can comprehend mathematics or physics in abstract terms.

The child's logical development proceeds from a stage of *intuitive thought* to a stage of *concrete operations* and finally to a stage of *formal operations*. It is only in this final stage that genuine abstract thinking becomes possible; up to that point, the child cannot deal with possibilities except by actual trial and error. Only then can he examine the consequences of various combinations of factors in a systematic and orderly fashion.

Piaget's views have been supported by numerous studies. Reichard et al., for example, found the child's thinking to proceed from a concretistic level in which he classifies objects on the basis of non-essential (incidental) features; to a functional level where the classification is based on use; and finally to an abstract level making its appearance somewhere around the age of 10. The challenge put to the educator by such studies of the development of thinking processes is that of ascertaining, on the one hand, the level at which the children can think, and, on the other, the level of thinking the material presented demands if it is to be understood.

Teaching children at the intuitive level presents a special problem; they are too involved in the perceptions of the moment to be able to deal logically with the interrelationships among the various aspects of their experiences. Children today have a much greater and varied background of experiences than their parents; yet, for all their verbal facility, they are restricted in their ability to think conceptually about these experiences. At the kindergarten level, for example, they still think largely on a perceptual level, and what the teacher wishfully labels "concepts" are in reality the child's names and labels for personal experiences.

A source of difficulty in understanding the nature of the child's thinking is the failure to distinguish adequately between *concepts* as "abstractable, public, essential forms," as viewed by the scientist, and *conceptions* as "individual mental images and symbols," as viewed by the child. Since the child's ability to solve a problem revolves crucially around the array of meanings he brings to the situation, the curriculum must be based on a foundation of meaningful experiences. However, it is equally important to remember that, for the solution of certain problems, the application of meanings other than those that are public and abstract is a hindrance to efficient solution. There comes a time when the concrete is no longer enriching. In mathematics, for example, the child cannot indefinitely perform calculations with counters, beads, etc. Numbers and their relationships must eventually be dealt with abstractly. In physics, the notions that some objects float and others sink, followed by the awareness that objects of equivalent size may have different weights, must eventually be replaced with the abstract idea of specific gravity as a quantifiable relationship.

Inhelder has suggested devoting the first two years of school to a series of exercises in basic logical operations, e. g., addition, multiplication, etc. She suggests that such a pre-curriculum might be effective in building up the intuitive and inductive understandings that might form the basis for formal instruction. Actually such an approach may promote little more than memorization and automatic repetition of the correct responses, and provide little in the way of real experiences. Furthermore, it seems to involve a high degree of formality hardly compatible with current American educational philosophy.

In the long run, the important contributions of the kindergarten and possibly even the first grade to later intellectual development may lie as much in the nurture of the normal child's curiosity and zest for learning as in the early exercise of incipient logical thinking. The encouragement of keen observation, furtherance of the awareness of the properties and the actions of objects that make up his world, and the development of a vocabulary adequate to describe them, all appear to be appropriate educational goals. Indeed, if the children in the exploratory study, particularly those coming from lower socio-economic backgrounds, provide a good example, such goals may sometimes take priority over the early promotion of "concrete operations."

Our emphasis on the intellectual and the cognitive must not cause us to overlook the emotional. The distortion of thinking as a result of emotions is particularly clear in the case of children with learning difficulties. Eleven year olds who according to Piaget's theory should be able to function logically are often unable to understand the problems, much less cope with them. Their anxieties tie them down so closely to their immediate perceptions that they cannot deal effectively with complex relationships. Thinking cannot be considered apart from the other aspects of the developing personality. The mind has an entity in the person. To comprehend a child's mind adequately is to know him and those who are like him. It is to know how he views the world and what is meaningful to him.

Comments

1.   The theme of Almy's article is well stated in her final statement. When the teacher is indeed wise, he does not bid his students enter the house of wisdom but, rather, leads them to the threshold of their own minds. The teacher can help in this development of the child's thinking

but, Almy points out, it is still possible to overestimate, perhaps wishfully, the extent of his influence.

     2. Whereas everyone is quite eager to improve the child's thinking, the traditional approach of having children work through adult problems to adult solutions is open to serious question as to its effectiveness. There is undoubtedly need to synchronize our teaching procedures with the child's present level of development in critical thinking.

Edward C. Weir

The Meaning of Learning
and the Learning of Meaning *

Recent concern over both the process and the goals of teaching and learning has focussed on (a) methodological approaches to helping students discover, analyze, and test ideas which can be used to solve problems and to explain and order phenomena, and (b) the organization of the curriculum around the underlying structure of the various subject areas. It is not our intent to disparage this "new" focus in educational thought; we are most heartily receptive to any effort which conceives of the human entity as an awareness and a seeking after meaning, a disposition to order and to control experience. Such efforts are especially fortuitous at this particular time when the behavior of the rat is seriously being proposed as the model for explanations of human behavior and technological and curricular gadgetry as the nostrum for the ailments of education.

However, while concentrating on the development of a logisticalistic methodology for teaching and learning, we may overlook the *person* who is to teach and the *person* who is to learn. We need to remind ourselves of the ultimately *subjective* nature of thinking and learning, of knowledge and meaning. Principles of logic do not objectively exist; they exist only in *persons* who understand, accept, and use them in their thinking and learning. Knowledge exists in someone knowing. Concepts exist in someone conceptualizing. Meaning is not objectively *in* the universe; it exists in a particular individual *person's* awareness as he perceives his own identity and relatedness. Reflective thinking, which is an attribute of the highest order of human behavior, obviously can only occur in persons who are *subjectively* disposed and able to think reflectively. Critical examination of one's beliefs and behavior is not merely an exercise in logic; it is an operation requiring a high degree of psychological competence. By the same token, the reflective teacher is not merely a logician; he is a *person* who is able to function reflectively as a person within the intricate complex of meanings and motivations, dreams and disappointments, hates and hopes and fears and loves that exist in the persons he is to teach. If he is to teach —that is, if he is to help his students to grow in their ability to function

* Adapted and abridged from *Phi Delta Kappan,* 46: 280–284, 1965. By permission of author and publisher.

reflectively—it is important that he have competence in logic and that he have profound intimacy with the structure of his subject. However, it is at least of equal importance that he be the kind of human being who can relate personally to his students in such a way that they become psychologically free to create themselves, to engage themselves fully and courageously in the hazardous project of examining and reconstructing the meaning of their own living.

A man is an idea; he is what he perceives himself to be and what he perceives himself as becoming. An idea is a man; it comes into being as a man discovers it or creates it and employs it in shaping the essence of his living. Translated into a concept of learning, this statement means that an individual has learned when he integrates into himself a new meaning, a meaning that has such personal significance in his awareness that the quality and direction of his existence are in some way different than they were before. What do we mean by "meaning"? We suggest a subjective definition: *Meaning is the order imposed upon experience by the individual as he becomes aware of the interrelationships between the self and the phenomena encountered in his experience.* When I say, "Now *that* really *means* something!" I am actually saying that the fact or event has significance for *me,* that it fits in or perhaps reinforces my way of looking at things, that it somehow serves what I conceive to be the purposes of *my* thinking and doing. My statement indicates that I have a fairly sharp awareness of how I should relate my own behavior to this fact or event.

It is true that the order I imposed on a given experiential situation may be objectively illogical, completely or partially out of conformity with reality. I may completely or partially misinterpret the relationship the event or object has with my goals and values, so that my behavior, as a result, will be seen by others to be inappropriate. But it is the relationship *I* see, the order *I* impose, and to me, therefore, my behavior will seem quite appropriate—until such time as my pattern of meanings takes on a new and perhaps more realistic configuration. Herein, of course, lies the task of education—*to help the young to discover and take into themselves increasingly more realistic and encompassing meanings with concomitantly increased efficiency of behavior.* Rigorous application of principles of logic, together with understanding of the fundamental structure of organized knowledge, are essential in the development of a pattern of subjective meaning that is consistent and whole, but one must also be psychologically consistent and whole if he is to recognize the inappropriateness of his perceptions of reality.

Meaning is present in some degree in all learning; conversely, if the individual can find no meaning in a situation, he will learn nothing in that situation. In the case of the child touching the hot stove, we can infer from the consistency of his subsequent avoidance behavior that the stove has taken on for him a new meaning. He not only discriminates the stove from the other objects in the room, but also generalizes so that he is able to behave appropriately with respect to the stove when he encounters it again. The world has become a little more meaningful; he has learned and his living, therefore, becomes a little more efficient.

All learning involves an increase in the learner's store of personal meanings or a shift or re-patterning of perceptual structure and is accompanied or followed by relevant changes in behavior. A situation must mean something to the individual if he is to respond to it. Psychologically, it is impossible for him to react to a situation that means nothing to him, and if he cannot respond to a situation, he obviously cannot learn from it. According to Hartmann (1942) ". . . no experience or stimulus is ever meaningless or valueless in a strict sense. It may have little meaning, a distorted meaning, or an ugly meaning, but anything that affects a person and provokes a reaction from him cannot be strictly devoid of meaning. . . . An experience with zero meaning is psychologically nonexistent. Rote learning, the curse of all inadequate instruction, defines one end of the meaning continuum and 'logical' or 'systematic' learning the other; but absolutely it is present all along the line."

This "meaning continuum" is a useful device. It helps to explain learning which occurs in situations which are seemingly meaningless, such as the acquisition of motor skills or arbitrary associations through procedures of drill and rote memorization. Actually, if we look carefully at these situations we find that some degree of cognitive activity *is* involved, some degree of meaning, some association, form, or order is imposed by the learner. In learning nonsense syllables, for example, the student invariably imposes some order on the material in order to learn it. Furthermore, the more meaningful the learner's behavior, the more effective the learning will be.

When attempting to evaluate the effectiveness of learning, we usually refer to two criteria: Has the learning significantly affected the learner's behavior? And will the learner be able to use the learning in life situations other than that in which the learning has occurred? Actually, if any learning at all has taken place, there is some effect, however inconsequential, on the learner's behavior; there will be some degree of transfer, however transitory. It is true that his having learned may have little or any effect on his basic patterns of thinking and living, and further that he may find little use for the facts in other life situations. The student who has been exercised in logic may be able to repeat the procedure in analyzing generalizations and problems on an examination. He has learned that much; but if he does not perceive the applicability of the procedures to *his* problems and *his* explanations of existence, the learning remains superficial.

The point is that learning ranges along a continuum of effectiveness, with the position of a given learning situation on the continuum a function of the transferability of the learning and of the effect of the learning on the individual's behavior, and these, in turn, a function of personal meaning-fulness. It will be recalled that in our definition of meaning, we empha-sized the individual's awareness of the interrelationships *between the self and the phenomena encountered in experience.* Such self-identification with phenomena is necessary not only in a learning situation; it is equally necessary in a transfer situation. The individual must see that the new situ-ation has relationship to his own self-concept, to his own life purposes, val-ues, and interests. He must *see* the applicability of his learning in a new situation, and he must *want* to make the transfer.

In summation, what we have been saying is that learning is the self-incorporation of meaning into the subjectivity of the learner. The more deeply personal the meaning acquired through a learning experience, the more effective and lasting the learning will be. If allowances are made for the "intuitive hypothesis," the processes of systematic thinking are proba-bly productive of the most highly dependable and fruitful meanings. We need to remember, however, that learning occurs only to the extent that these processes are internalized into the personality structure of the learner as an integral part of a way of living.

Comments

1.   The author's emphasis on personalized meaning finds sup-port in the writings of Combs, Kelley (*Education for What Is Real*), Rog-ers, and other phenomenologists. As Weir points out, this is not to detract from the importance of the cognitive structure of knowledge or the process of systematic thinking, but rather to caution against overlooking the per-sonal component of the equation.

2.   Unfortunately, too much of our current "education" is coldly academic and divorced from personal meaning and involvement. As a consequence, it has little effect on the student's behavior outside of the examination.

Reference

Hartmann, G. W. "The field theory of learning and its educational conse-quences," in N. B. Henry (ed.), *Psychology of Learning.* 41st Yearbook, National Society for the Study of Education, Part II. Chicago: Uni-versity of Chicago Press, 1942. Pp. 165–214.

That's What They Said

"A student solves a problem when his initial state of confusion ends in understanding. If his initial state is understanding, he is not confronted with a problem. If the terminal state is confusion, the student has not solved the problem."

> William J. Pauli. "Confusion and problem solving," *Clearing House,* 35: 79–82, 1960. [79]

"Research and theory seem to show one thing clearly. Reflective thought is called into play *only in the presence of problems which are of genuine concern to the learner.* The failure of most schools to stimulate reflective thought very likely can be accounted for by their failure to organize instruction so that children encounter concrete problems with which they have great concern to deal. The whole pattern of instruction in the upper elementary school commonly has been pitched at 'studying about,' and children have rarely had the opportunity to engage in reflection and inquiry, which the presence of actual problematic situations stimulates."

> G. Max Wingo. "Implications for improving instruction in the upper elementary grades," in N. B. Henry (ed.), *Learning and Instruction.* 49th Yearbook, National Society for the Study of Education, Part I. Chicago: University of Chicago Press, 1950. Pp. 280–303. [287]

". . . There is not adequate theoretical recognition that all which the school can or need do for pupils, so far as their *minds* are concerned (that is, leaving out certain specialized muscular abilities), is to develop their ability to think."

> John Dewey. *Democracy and Education.* New York: The Macmillan Company, 1916. [179]

"By virtue of language and logic, thinking takes on a dimension in man different from that of the cat in the box. Man is a language-using creature; this fact opens to him spheres of experience not given to other creatures. A point so obvious might go without saying were it not for the fact that the epithets 'merely verbal' and 'verbalism' have dulled the edge of understanding where language and logic are involved in teaching and learning. The plain fact is that without language, nothing can be taught or learned about the past, nor about things removed from immediate observation. The laws of science can be learned only through language and retained in symbolic form alone. Without language the scientific method could not progress beyond the scramblings of the cat in the box. An adequate theory of control over our thinking will acknowledge the central role of linguistic behavior."

> B. O. Smith. "Logic, thinking, and teaching," *Educ. Theory*, 7: 225–233, 1957. [228]

"A constant source of misunderstanding and mistake is indefiniteness of meaning. Because of vagueness of meaning we misunderstand other people, things, and ourselves; because of ambiguity we distort and pervert. Conscious distortion of meaning may be enjoyed as nonsense; erroneous meaning, if clear-cut, may be followed up and got rid of. But vague meanings are too gelatinous to offer matter for analysis and too pulpy to afford support to other beliefs. They evade testing and responsibility. Vagueness disguises the unconscious mixing together of different meanings, and facilitates the substitution of one meaning for another, and covers up failure to have any meaning at all. It is the aboriginal logical sin—the source from which flow most bad intellectual consequences."

> John Dewey. *How We Think*. Boston: D. C. Heath and Company, 1933. [159–160]

"Human energy is never more extravagantly wasted than in the persistent effort to answer conclusively questions that are vague and meaningless. Probably the most impressive indictment that can be made of our educational system is that it provides the student with answers, but it is poorly designed to provide him with skill in the asking of questions that are effectively directive of inquiry and evaluation. It teaches the student to 'make up his mind' ready or not, but it does not teach him how to change it effectively."

> Wendell Johnson. *People in Quandaries*. New York: Harper & Row, Publishers, 1946. [55]

"I certainly do not deny that everyone can think whatever he pleases or even that everyone has the right think as he pleases. But the assertion that everyone is entitled to his opinion usually is intended to say that everyone's opinion is equally valuable. This view ignores the fact that the mark of an opinion is that it can be right or wrong. However, the right to be wrong is a political right and not an intellectual prize or heritage. To assert that wrong opinions are equally as valuable as right opinions is at least self-contradictory, and a sure way of perpetuating ignorance."

> A. Nemetz. "On the teacher," *Educ. Res. Bull.*, 35: 154–163, 1956. [158]

"Engaging in discussion without having defined terms is an exercise in futility."

> William H. Burton et al. *Education for Effective Thinking.* New York: Appleton-Century-Crofts, 1960. [182]

"Where all think alike, no one thinks very much."

> Walter Lippmann

"When two people think alike, one is unnecessary."

> Oscar Wilde

"Our job is to educate free, independent and vigorous minds capable of analyzing events, of exercising judgment, of distinguishing facts from propaganda, and truth from half-truths and lies, and—in the most creative of them at least—of apprehending further reaches of truth. It is also our responsibility to see that these minds are imbedded in total persons who will stand with faith and courage, and always, too, in thoughtful concern for others."

> Nathan Pusey. *The Age of the Scholar.* New York: Harper & Row, Publishers, 1963. [16]

"One may argue, as Toynbee does, that a society needs challenge. It is true. But societies differ notably in their capacity to see the challenge that exists. No society has ever so mastered the environment and itself that no challenge remained; but a good many have gone to sleep because they failed to understand the challenge that was undeniably there."

> John W. Gardner. "Renewal in societies and men," cited in Gordon I. Swanson, "International education: Its claims on ingenuity," *Phi Delta Kappan,* 47: 215–219, 1965.

". . . we should be misled if we were to believe that the symbolic operations of a computer are carried out *in the same way* as are human cognitive reactions. A digital computer system can simulate many aspects of behavior but it is not for that reason a valid model of a behaving system."

> Karl U. Smith and Margaret F. Smith. *Cybernetic Principles of Learning and Educational Design.* New York: Holt, Rinehart and Winston, Inc., 1966. [437]

"A tremendous body of experimental evidence can be marshalled to support the hypothesis that learning proceeds much more rapidly and is retained much longer when that which is learned possesses meaning, organization, and structure."

> Glenn M. Blair. "Are learning theories related to curriculum organization?" *J. educ. Psychol.*, 39: 151–166, 1948. [164]

"Often teachers organize their courses too well, offering them neatly packaged and predigested, thus robbing the students of the thoughtful experience of doing some of the organizing for themselves."

> Don Robinson. "Scraps from a teacher's notebook," *Phi Delta Kappan*, 43: 343, 1962.

"The high focus on intelligence may have had the undue influence of keeping the creative and other types of high level talent from being freed and developed. Instead, we should conceive of students as thinkers and producers and creators rather than solely as learners or, in the worst extreme, as merely recorders or memorizers, (spongeheads) and regurgitators."

> Calvin W. Taylor. "Many-sided intelligence," *Childh. Educ.*, 39: 364–366, 1963. [365]

"The most common complaint that I have heard concerning our college graduates in these positions is that while they can do assigned tasks with a show of mastery of the techniques they have learned, they are much too helpless when called upon to solve a problem where new paths are demanded."

> J. P. Guilford. "Creativity," *Amer. Psychol.*, 5: 444–454, 1950. [446]

"I am convinced that we do teach some students to think, but I sometimes marvel that we do as well as we do. In the first place, we have only vague ideas as to the nature of thinking. We have little actual knowledge of what specific steps should be taken in order to teach students to think."

> J. P. Guilford. 1950. Ibid. [448]

"In education we tend to turn out conformists, stereotypes, individuals whose education is 'completed,' rather than freely creative and original thinkers."

> Carl R. Rogers. "Toward a theory of creativity," *ETC: Rev. gen. Sem.*, 11: 249–260, 1954. [249]

"Our conclusions at this point, then, are as follows: The evidence we have reviewed points to the discouraging inference that procedures designed to assess creativity have in fact not revealed a dimension of individual differences that, on the one hand, is cohesive and unitary, and, on the other, is relatively distinct from intelligence."

> Michael A. Wallach and Nathan Kogan. *Modes of Thinking in Young Children.* New York: Holt, Rinehart and Winston, Inc., 1965. [23–24]

"One cannot learn order, system, and discipline without some violence to freedom and spontaneity, nor can one indulge in spontaneity without sacrificing some orderliness. The trick is to learn to live with a degree of ambiguity and be comfortable with it, without abdicating all standards."

> Don Robinson. "Scraps from a teacher's notebook," *Phi Delta Kappan,* 50: 125, 1968.

"The American tradition has always dictated that it is far better to debate an important matter without settling it than to settle it without debating it."

> Don Robinson. "Scraps from a teacher's notebook," *Phi Delta Kappan,* 44: 385, 1963.

"My own impression, based on my observation of a good many generations of students, is that the conventional undergraduate curriculum in psychology is about as culture-bound as any curriculum could be. I am regularly appalled by the innocent unthinking dogmatism with which students accept the psychology they have been taught as though it had been handed down on a tablet from Mount Sinai. They have learned to be critical, it is true, but only in the sense that they are uncomfortable about a statement which lacks a confidence level or an observation reported without a control group."

> Robert B. MacLeod. "The teaching of psychology and the psychology we teach," *Amer. Psychol.,* 20: 344–352, 1965. [346]

"I am not advocating that we attempt to create a generation of young rebels. It should be possible to teach appreciation for those things of the past that are good as well as to encourage students to see how things might have been better."

> J. P. Guilford. Special address cited by George G. Stern. "Measuring noncognitive variables in research on teaching," in N. L. Gage (ed.), *Handbook of Research on Teaching.* Skokie, Ill.: Rand McNally & Company, 1963. Pp. 398–447.

"For students the three R's of Restraint, Rote Memory, and Regurgitation must be replaced by inquiry-centered activities—activities that help students to ask meaningful questions about a real situation in which they find themselves, to seek information on which to base conclusions, to act on the basis of the conclusions reached, and to evaluate the results of the action in relation to the predicted outcomes. Critical thinking, inquiry, and self-directiveness must be made part of the curriculum."

> Eugene Howard. "The I.D.E.A. plan for innovative schools," in Richard R. Goulet (ed.), *Educational Change: The Reality and the Promise.* New York: Citation Press, 1968. Pp. 192–200. [194]

"1. Everything thou doest must be useful. 2. Everything thou doest must be successful. 3. Everything thou doest must be perfect. 4. Everyone thou knowest must like thee. 5. Thou shalt not prefer solitude to togetherness. 6. Remember concentrated attention and keep it holy. 7. Thou shalt not diverge from culturally-imposed sex norms. 8. Thou shalt not express excessive emotional feeling. 9. Thou shalt not be ambiguous. 10. Thou shalt not rock the cultural boat."

> Stanley Krittner. "The ten commandments that block creativity," *Gifted Child Quart.*, 11: excerpts, 144–151, 1967.

CHAPTER 15

Test Items

1. Problem solving entails
    a. the development of effective problem-solving skills
    b. the grasping of new complex relationships
    c. the identification of causal relationships among phenomena
    d. mastery of the formal steps of scientific reasoning
    e. the reorganization of experience with respect to a problem situation

2. The third step in Dewey's formulation of the scientific method is
    a. application of the results
    b. formulation of the hypothesis
    c. generalization
    d. identification of the problem
    e. review of the literature

3. The hypothesis is best seen as
    a. a basic principle
    b. a guide to research
    c. a postulate from theoretical premises
    d. a proposition to be tested
    e. a tentative generalization or conclusion

4. Which of the following is the most crucial factor underlying ability to derive fruitful hypotheses?
    a. a critical skeptical attitude
    b. imagination, originality, flexibility
    c. training in scientific problem solving
    d. training in syllogistic reasoning
    e. a strong intellectual and experiential background

5. The best way of promoting effective problem solving in children is to provide them with
    a. experience in the use of discovery method of learning
    b. exercises in scientific problem solving
    c. a good background of related experience
    d. meaningful questions within their framework of concern
    e. training in science and the other classical subjects

6. The chief reason for inadequacies in the reasoning of children is
    a. their incomplete mental development
    b. their insensitivity to the existence of problems
    c. their lack of objectivity
    d. their lack of proficiency in the use of research techniques
    e. their lack of relevant experience

7. The greatest impediment to successful problem solving in school is that
    a. children are limited in dealing with real-life problems by their lack of experience with real life
    b. children have difficulty in coordinating group problem-solving processes
    c. the curriculum tends to center around adult problems which are relatively artificial
    d. individual differences preclude the choice of a problem meaningful to all
    e. real problems do not fit into the artificial fragmentation of the curriculum and of the school day

8. How familiar should one be with previous research on a given topic?
    a. thoroughly; this is the only way he can be effective
    b. somewhat; in order to avoid major blunders
    c. to a limited extent; no problem is ever the same
    d. not at all; it places the investigator in a mold away from the solution
    e. it depends; it usually helps a little

9. A crucial prerequisite for effective group problem solving is
    a. experience as a "traditioned" group
    b. freedom from domination
    c. group cohesiveness
    d. individual commitment to group goals
    e. a wide diversity of talents

10. Failure in communication usually stems from
    a. the arbitrary nature of language
    b. the confusion of unnecessary details
    c. the direction in mind-set in the receiver
    d. failure of the speaker to express his ideas correctly
    e. lack of synchronization of background

11. The factor most detrimental to the cultivation of effective problem solving on the part of school children is
    a. the relative ineffectiveness of problem-solving techniques in the hands of children

b.   the school's overemphasis on authority and the "right" answer

c.   the school's overreliance on "looking up" answers

d.   the teacher's overenthusiasm in solving the children's problems for them

e.   the wide range of individual differences in problem-solving ability

12.   The first consideration in effective problem solving is for the teacher to see that the class

a.   has access to resource materials and resource people

b.   has adequate cohesiveness and skill in working together

c.   has a problem of both psychological and academic significance to them

d.   has the required background knowledge

e.   has sufficient guidance in devising an adequate problem-solving strategy

13.   What is the best statement of the relation of facts to effective problem solving?

a.   Facts are a necessary but not sufficient condition for effective reasoning.

b.   Facts are simply the means to the clarification of a problem area.

c.   Facts simply provide hypotheses which, when verified, constitute the solution.

d.   Facts per se are useless; they must be generalized and organized into a meaningful storage and retrieval system.

e.   When fully organized in relation to the problem, facts automatically provide the solution.

14.   The aspect of problem solving most amenable to improvement is

a.   the child's willingness to seek meaningful answers to problems

b.   the child's ability to define and clarify the issue into a problem capable of solution

c.   the child's experiential background

d.   the development of formal reasoning skills

e.   the removal of anxiety leading to functional fixity

15.   The major strength of the problem-solving approach to teaching stems from the fact that

a.   it capitalizes on the child's natural curiosity

b.   it constitutes a more effective approach to learning

c.   it permits adapting the curriculum to individual differences in ability and interest

d.   it provides practice in meaningful democratic citizenship

e.   it takes advantage of the group situation for maximum individual and group productivity

16. Research into the relative merits of discovery versus traditional approach to teaching suggests that
    a. discovery leads to less effective learning and retention but more adequate transfer
    b. the discovery method tends to be more effective
    c. discovery promotes greater learning, retention, and transfer only insofar as it stimulates the expenditure of greater effort
    d. the evidence favors the traditional approach
    e. traditional teaching constitutes a more systematic and dependable approach to the attainment of basic educational objectives

17. For maximum learning effectiveness, the content of the discussion should first of all
    a. allow the free expression of any and all opinions
    b. be accurate in its basic details
    c. be as complete and thorough as time will permit
    d. emphasize total participation and consensus rather than achievement of the whole truth
    e. be meaningful to the child at his level of insight

18. The greatest impediment to the child's grasp of academic content is
    a. the ambiguous nature of symbols
    b. failure in memory of relevant background data
    c. inadequate reading and listening skills
    d. lack of common background between "sender" and "receiver"
    e. lack of intelligence

19. Fuzziness of meaning in school children is primarily caused by
    a. the difficulty of most academic concepts
    b. inadequacies in their intellectual and experiential background
    c. the lack of persistence and their willingness to be satisfied with a "general idea"
    d. the lack of relevance of schoolwork to their purposes and goals
    e. the overly bookish nature of our schools

20. Verbalism refers to
    a. presentation of complicated material in advance of the necessary maturation
    b. reliance on an unnecessarily high level of abstraction
    c. the unnecessary "invention" of hypothetical constructs when reference could more logically be made to actual objects
    d. the use of symbols for which there is no adequate referent in the learner's cognitive structure

e. the use of verbal symbols when data are best represented non-verbally

21. The most dependable way to ensure understanding in school children is for the teacher
   a. to concentrate on clarity of presentation
   b. to delay the introduction of topics until readiness is achieved
   c. to emphasize principles and generalizations rather than facts
   d. to keep the vocabulary load at reasonable levels
   e. to provide them with a good background of systematic knowledge

22. The greatest single approach to increasing meaning in classroom learning is for the teacher
   a. to postpone the introduction of difficult concepts
   b. to provide experiential background
   c. to promote vocabulary development
   d. to stress effective study habits, e.g., outlining
   e. to stress thorough mastery of content

23. Meaningfulness in the classroom is best promoted by
   a. the accumulation and organization of experience
   b. emphasis on clarity in presentation
   c. the postponement of difficult concepts
   d. the promotion of intellectual development
   e. the simplification of vocabulary

24. The most dependable way to ensure that the child generalizes his experiences is
   a. to have the children apply the knowledge to similar situations
   b. to have the generalization formulated by two or three of the group leaders
   c. to have the teacher present them with a correct version of the generalization
   d. to help the children formulate their own generalizations in their own words
   e. to reach the generalization through group discussion

25. Concepts are best conceived as
   a. abstractions from experience
   b. hypotheses
   c. symbols designed to label experience
   d. theoretical constructs
   e. verbal nomenclature used for clarity of communication

26. Creativity differs from problem solving primarily from the standpoint of
    a. the contribution of experiential background
    b. the nature of the solution
    c. the mental equipment involved
    d. the number of people who can participate
    e. the potential benefits to society

27. The closest parallel between the steps of the thinking and the creative process is
    a. felt need—preparation
    b. hypothesis—incubation
    c. insight—illumination
    d. problem—hypothesis
    e. proof—verification

28. Creativity is best seen in the theoretical setting provided by
    a. Guilford
    b. Köhler
    c. Osgood
    d. Spearman
    e. Thorndike

29. Creativity is to problem solving as
    a. divergent thinking is to convergent thinking
    b. inspiration is to experience
    c. intuition is to aptitude
    d. nonintellectual factors are to intellectual factors
    e. talent is to intelligence

30. That IQ has greater predictability of academic success than any measure of creativity is largely a function of
    a. the more basic nature of intelligence
    b. the relatively greater accuracy of IQ tests
    c. the relative incompatibility of the creative child in the school
    d. the relative lack of motivation of the creative child in formal educational experiences
    e. the traditional nature of our current classroom operation

31. Probably the most unique characteristic of the creative child is
    a. his immaturity, eccentricity, and narrowness
    b. his independence of social constraints
    c. his lack of social sensitivity

d. his nonconformity in moral values
e. his willingness to tolerate ambiguity and to take chances

32. The two major factors basic to creative productivity are
a. freedom from anxiety and freedom from social constraints
b. freedom from social constraints and tolerance for ambiguity
c. inadequate socialization and a sense of individual identity
d. openness to experience and intellectual honesty
e. psychological safety and psychological freedom

33. The most important factor in promoting creativity in the classroom is
a. an atmosphere of novelty and unorthodox operation
b. an emphasis on proper form and effective techniques designed to promote superior performance
c. an emphasis on self-expression as an aspect of the need for achievement
d. a permissive nonevaluative atmosphere
e. a systematic emphasis on quality performance

34. Probably the greatest deterrent to the development of creativity in the classroom is
a. the child's need for peer and adult approval
b. an insistence on conformity to adult standards
c. the overregimentation of the school's program
d. overemphasis on objective evaluation
e. the traditional nature of the curriculum

35. A major reason for the shortage of truly creative teachers is that
a. coordination of the school's efforts demands uniformity in operation
b. creative teachers are typically dismissed because of their failure to "communicate" with the more conventional students
c. creativity is stifled by current (noncreative) teacher-education programs
d. the job requirements preclude the exercise of originality
e. truly creative people are discouraged from becoming teachers

36. The greatest support for the present convergent IQ stems from
a. empirical evidence as to its consistency
b. its endorsement by such authorities as Terman
c. its usefulness as an index of adequacy relative to the traditional classroom
d. its usefulness as an index of problem-solving ability
e. theoretical considerations related to innate capacity

CHAPTER 16

Measuring Academic Achievement

Although the appraisal of the results of one's efforts must necessarily be an integral part of any enterprise, testing in the schools has always been a rather marginal operation. Not only are teachers not particularly qualified in tests and measurements but, more fundamentally, the fact that they continue in their present unsophistication suggests that they are not aware of—or, for that matter, concerned over—their shortcomings in what is necessarily a most critical aspect of teaching. Testing goes on without a clear conception of the purposes to be served and how this is to be accomplished. The results of poor tests are accepted uncritically as the basis for awarding grades, devising honor rolls, promoting or failing students, etc. —all of which constitute pretty serious decisions to the youngsters involved. It is safe to suggest that teachers simply do not bring to testing the effort, the thought, the insight, and the competence that they bring to other phases of the teaching function. Rarely is testing made a sufficiently integral part of the teaching–learning process, the way it is in programed instruction, for example—which, as Adkins points out, might have B. F. Skinner qualify as the sponsor of the century's most comprehensive testing movement. This is apparently true of testing in general; Anastasi, for example, while addressing herself to the current revolt against testing, emphasizes the need to have testing fit more clearly into the framework of the psychological purposes of the situation in which it is being used.

Years ago, teachers operated without regard to individual differences in ability, background, or interest; if the pupil did not learn, he was lazy —or stupid; at least it was his fault. Even today, many teachers operate on the premise that any failure to achieve is the student's failure; they need to recognize that testing is a crucial responsibility, far more instrumental in determining what will be studied and learned than their high-falluting objectives. It can be equally potent in the damage that it can cause in terms of negative attitudes, deflated self-concepts, lost motivation, etc. All of which suggests that testing might well be the last thing teachers would want to slough off.

On second thought, it might be that grading is more the whipping-boy than the culprit. Certainly, the school needs to know what progress students are making toward the objectives it has selected. If the idea is blunted by poor tests, carelessly administered, and the results used to the detriment of the child—if testing is allowed to distort the real goals of education—the blame must lie with the more fundamental aspects of the way the school operates rather than with the tests per se. We might ask, for example, what priority does the typical teacher-education program give tests and measurements in its professional education sequence? Even the experts are under fire; how can we assume that proficiency in testing is something that teachers come by naturally? And the solution is not in eliminating testing—whether of academic achievement or of intelligence— for what will we use instead? The fault lies not so much with our tests as with our current educational philosophy. Only as we reorient our goals to more meaningful education, can we turn to devising different and better tests. Glaser, for example, points to rather obvious inadequacies in the norm-referenced orientation of current academic testing. In a more general frame of reference, Anastasi associates the current anti-test movement to the relative dissociation of much of today's testing from its legitimate psychological content.

Dorothy C. Adkins

Measurement in Relation to the Educational Process *

The measurement of change in the learner as an integral part of the educational process can be assumed to involve the following steps: (a) Defining behavioral goals or objectives. This implies knowledge of the abilities of the prospective learner to reach alternative ends. (b) Planning curricular materials and teaching methods. Again this implies adapting content and method to the learner's present level of readiness. (c) Predicting the degree to which the objectives can be achieved. It implies careful consideration of the goals, the content, and the teaching techniques in relation to the learner's background. (d) Applying the teaching method. The teacher needs to be alert to deviations from expected progress and ready to make the necessary adjustments in goals, content, or teaching technique. (e) Testing achievement. This generally implies a control group as a means of isolating irrelevant factors so that the contribution of the teaching and learning process to student progress can be unequivocally assigned. (f) Defining new behavioral objectives in the light of how well the old ones were met.

The ultimate purpose of psychological measurement is to predict future behavior; there would be little purpose in administering a test if we did not believe that in some way present performance is predictive of future performance. Awareness of the fundamental purpose of educational tests as predictors rather than merely as evaluative devices should lead to a revision of the measuring devices themselves, of the curriculum, and of the teaching method.

Pressey, for example, notes that less than half of the material covered in tests at the end of typical high-school and college courses is remembered after one year and about one-quarter after two years. A repetition of such an experiment in almost any field would yield equally sobering results. The basic difficulty may be that the materials were not adequately mastered in the first place; even though the advantages of some degree of overlearning have been well known since Ebbinghaus' work in 1885, the need for adequate mastery is not sufficiently emphasized in teaching practice. We need to teach each learner to the mastery level those materials that he is capable of really mastering by suitable teaching methods and

* Adapted and abridged from *Educ. Psychol. Measmt.*, 18: 221–240, 1958. By permission of author and publisher.

with more or less continuous appraisal based on tests of defined educational objectives. The remedy is not simply to multiply the use of tests, but rather to ensure that tests are clearly integrated into the entire educational process.

The educational process is expensive, to the society that supplies the dollar and to the learner who contributes the time. Our educational system demands radical improvement. Consider, if you will, the hundreds of hours that are devoted to instruction in English by the time a person becomes a college senior. Then ponder his inability to write; reflect upon the ineptitude of the typical college student in solving the most elementary equation or even in adding a column of figures; recall the idiosyncrasies in spelling that confront you in personal correspondence; contemplate the current reading hub-bub, by no means without foundation, and shudder at the prevalent superstition and gullibility of the American public.

This is not a criticism of individual teachers or of the teaching profession. It is an indictment of an educational system within which teachers operate and which is so firmly entrenched by long tradition that no single teacher or group of teachers or school can hope to resist it. We know that widespread individual differences exist in any given class. Yet, with notable exceptions, every child is given identical assignments, exposed to essentially the same teaching methods for the same amount of learning time, and tested occasionally by identical tests. Teachers are well aware that the amounts learned under such conditions will vary markedly, and achievement tests commonly reveal wide ranges of ability. So inured are we to these differences that their very presence provides a clue to the validity of the test.

As a result, the poorer students are forced to endure repeated failure which, besides being highly questionable as a motivational approach, is likely to have blighting effects upon his personality development. The more capable student, on the other hand, is not helped either; he experiences success too easily and is not provided with training in meeting situations requiring exertion.

Along what lines lies a solution, short of providing a private tutor for every child? The first major need is for extensive curricular revisions, in the direction of a large number of learning units scaled according to difficulty within subject-matter areas. The next step would be to develop mastery tests for each unit. These would be entirely different from the tests commonly administered at the end of a unit of instruction, in which the teacher is disappointed if he cannot observe wide individual differences. Rather, the learner would be expected to persist at curricular units of a given difficulty level until he had achieved a standard degree of mastery, at which time he would be ready for the next higher level.

Note some of the features of such an educational plan. The learner is not assigned content entirely beyond his current ability level; nor is he wasting time on materials absurdly easy for him. He rarely experiences failure. The questionable luxury of not exerting effort is disallowed. The learner competes always at his own ability level; he is not exposed to content for which he lacks prerequisites. He becomes well acquainted with his limitations as well as with his strengths. His degree of mastery of what he is learning is continuously appraised, so that at all times both he and his teachers know exactly how he is progressing.

This approach will accentuate rather than reduce individual differences. It will also make possible more precise reporting on such test differences to prospective employers or higher educational institutions. In 1984, we may be able to say to an employer or to a university that John Doe has mastered mathematics unit 1728, English grammar 642, spelling 1021, physics 305, and so on. We need to get away from an educational system geared to presenting identical doses of pablum to be partially digested within a uniform allotment of time; instead we need to devise a program in which the student proceeds at his own rate on material geared to his ability level, with a record of his progress constantly available to him and to his teacher. Some attempts in this direction have been made by Thurstone, Skinner, and Dressel. In all cases, the aim is to develop an integrated approach to evaluation and teaching. In fact, evaluation differs from instruction only when the primary purpose is that of passing judgment on the achievement.

Comments

1.   The article presents programed instruction, as advocated by Skinner, as an answer to this problem of the effective integration of measurement into the teaching–learning process. If his plans fully materialize, posterity may consign his pigeons to extinction and pay homage to him chiefly as the sponsor of the century's most massive measurement movement. This is indeed a commendable feature of programed instruction.

2.   The idea of a student's grade as a matter of the number of units over which he has complete mastery constitutes an interesting way of looking at educational measurement. Skinner postulated, for example, that complete mastery of each step along the way would insure readiness for the next step so that the only things that would differentiate the bright from the dull would be the speed at which they covered the units.

3.   In a related article, Trow (1966) makes a strong plea for a shift from norm-referenced to criterion-referenced grading. (See also Glaser, 1963; pp. 393–395 of this volume.)

Reference

Trow, William C. "On marks, norms, proficiency scores," *Phi Delta Kappan*, 48: 171–273, 1966.

Anne Anastasi

Psychology, Psychologists, and Psychological Testing *

"It is the main thesis of this paper that psychological testing is becoming dissociated from the mainstream of contemporary psychology. Those psychologists specializing in psychometrics have been devoting more and more of their efforts to refining the techniques of test construction, while losing sight of the behavior they set out to measure. Psychological testing today places too much emphasis on testing and too little on psychology. As a result, outdated interpretations of test performance may remain insulated from the impact of subsequent behavior research. It is my contention that the isolation of psychometrics from other relevant areas of psychology is one of the conditions that have led to the prevalent public hostility toward testing" [p. 297].

Among the many reasons for the current anti-test revolt, the one that has received the greatest amount of attention is that psychological tests constitute an invasion of privacy. While this objection relates primarily to personality measures, it also applies to any kind of test or observation designed to provide information about the individual that he would prefer not to divulge. There is no easy solution here, although an immediate consideration would be the relevance of the information sought to the purpose for which it is being sought. "For example, the demonstrated validity of a particular type of information as a predictor of performance on the job, in question, would be the important factor justifying its ascertainment" [p. 297].

There is also the problem of confidentiality; professional ethics would demand that the transmission of test data to another person be permissible only when the individual is told at the outset of such intended use of his test results. A major difficulty here is that of possible misinterpretation in the process of communication. Also of concern is the impact which knowledge of test results can have on the individual and his associates, particularly in view of prevailing misconceptions concerning test. "Suppose, for example, that an IQ is regarded as a broad indicator of the individual's total intelligence, which is fixed and unchanging and of genetic origin" [p. 298].

A third major criticism of tests has centered on test content. Our critics have frequently attacked individual items out of context; they have also made "much of the fact that multiple-choice items are sometimes misunderstood and that they may occasionally penalize the brilliant and erudite student who perceives unusual implications in the answers" [p. 289]—all of which simply implies that tests are not perfect. But then, neither are the alternative assessment procedures—grades, essay examinations, interviewing techniques, etc.

Tests have also been blamed for objectionable features of the criteria they are designed to predict. Objective tests of scholastic aptitude have been criticized for their alleged tendency to select unimaginative college students; personality tests are said to select executives who are conformists, etc. "Insofar as these criticisms may be true, they are an indictment, not of the tests but of the criteria against which selection tests must be validated. If we were to ignore the criteria and choose less valid tests, the persons thus selected would merely fail more often in college, on the job, or in other situations for which they were selected. Predictors cannot operate as instruments of criterion reform" [p. 298].

Another common criticism is that psychological tests are unfair to the culturally disadvantaged, an argument which makes no sense. "To criticize tests because they reveal cultural influences is to miss the essential nature of tests. Every psychological test measures a sample of behavior. Insofar as culture affects behavior, its influence will and should be reflected in the test. Moreover, if we were to rule out cultural differentials from a test, we might thereby lower its validity against the criterion we are trying to predict. The same cultural differentials that impair an individual's test performance are likely to handicap him in school work, job performance, or whatever other subsequent achievement we are trying to predict" [p. 299].

A sixth objection is that tests foster a rigid, inflexible, and permanent classification of individuals. This objection is typically levelled at "intelligence" tests, particularly when used on a culturally disadvantaged group, an objection obviously involved in the decision to discontinue the use of group IQ tests in the New York City public schools. This relates to the misconception of the IQ as a measure of innate capacity and the corresponding criticism of "intelligence tests" for their susceptibility to environmental differences. "The critics fail to see that it is these very differences in environment that are largely responsible for individual differences in qualifications or readiness for job performance, job training, and educational programs" [p. 300]. To ignore these differences in present developed abilities is to risk placing the individual in a position of likely failure.

A final category of objections directed at intelligence tests charges that, "because of their limited coverage of intellectual functions, intelligence tests tend to perpetuate a narrow conception of ability. . . . This is but one more reason for discarding the label 'intelligence tests' as some psychologists have been advocating for several decades" [p. 300].

"It is apparent that all seven classes of objections to psychological testing arise at least in part from popular misconceptions about current testing practices, about the nature of available tests, and about the meaning of test scores. Nevertheless, psychologists themselves are to some extent responsible for such misinformation. Nor is inadequate communication with laymen and members of other professions the only reason for such prevalent misinformation. It is my contention that psychologists have contributed directly to the misinformation by actively perpetuating certain misconceptions about tests" [p. 300].

So far, the anti-test revolt has been discussed chiefly from a professional point of view; it might be profitable to consider current objections to testing from the standpoint of the science of psychology. While the invasion of privacy and the confidentiality of test results are matters of professional responsibility and ethics, the other five categories of criticism involve important substantive matters. "Although the very essence of psychological testing is the measurement of behavior, testing today is not adequately assimilating relevant developments from the science of behavior. The refinements of test construction have far outstripped the tester's understanding of the behavior the tests are designed to measure" [p. 300].

Psychologists often display considerable confusion as to specifically what the IQ is supposed to mean. Another source of difficulty is the strange notion of "innate intelligence." Although every psychologist "would undoubtedly agree that what an individual inherits is not intelligence in any sense, but certain chemical substances which after innumerable interactions with each other and with environmental factors, lead eventually to different degrees of intelligent behavior" [p. 301]. Yet the notion of the IQ as a measure of innate intelligence, of potential for intellectual development, of hereditary intellectual capacity still persists. Similar misconceptions concern other forms of testing, e.g., personality assessment, where again the psychometrician is often "so deeply engrossed in the technical refinement of his specialty that he loses touch with relevant development in other psychological specialities" [p. 302].

Another aspect of the problem is to be found in the built-in inertia of tests. Not only does it take years to devise a test, develop adequate norms, and establish its validity, but the effectiveness of a test is likely to increase markedly as more and more data are accumulated from research involving its use in different contexts. A third source of difficulty is the undue willingness on the part of test makers to accede to popular demands for shortcuts and quick and easy answers. Furthermore, the gap between testing and psychological science is likely to be even wider when tests are used by members of other professions, who are more likely to find out about the existence of a new test than to become conversant with the psychological developments pertaining to insightful interpretation of its results.

Comments

1. The point that tests achieve an existence of their own apart from their original purpose—a sort of functional autonomy—is well taken. Tests are often administered on a routine basis with very little thought given to the question: What return is John to receive from his investment in taking the test? Unfortunately, the reaction of the public to abuse tends to be an across-the-board rejection of tests, to the detriment of all concerned.

2. It is also true that current instruments in some of the more significant areas are still very crude.

3. The prevalence of misconceptions concerning the nature of what our tests really measure—after 50 years of testing—is rather discouraging. In a related article, Dyer (1961) agrees that misuse of test data actually makes them somewhat of a menace to education.

Reference

Dyer, Henry S. "Is testing a menace to education?" *N. Y. State Educ.*, 49: 16–19, 1961.

Robert Glaser

Instructional Technology
and the Measurement of Learning Outcomes *

"The scores obtained from an achievement test provide primarily two kinds of information. One is the degree to which the student has attained criterion performance. . . . The second . . . is the relative ordering of individual students with respect to their test performance" [p. 519]. Underlying all achievement measurement is the notion of a continuum of knowledge ranging from zero to complete proficiency. The distinction between these two kinds of information lies in the standard used as a reference: the former is criterion-referenced and depends on an *absolute* standard of quality; the second is norm-referenced and depends on a *relative* standard (see Flanagan, 1951; Ebel, 1962).

Norm-referenced measures need not have reference to criterion behavior. "They tell that one student is more or less proficient than another, but do not tell how proficient either of them is with respect to the subject-matter task involved" [p. 520]. This is useful in correlating performance with aptitude, etc., but it raises questions with respect to the purposes of achievement measurement. "We need to behaviorally specify minimum levels of performance that describe the least amount of . . . competence the student is expected to attain, or that he needs in order to go to the next course in the sequence" [p. 520].

Another major consideration is that achievement performance, besides providing information about the characteristics of the individual's present behavior, can also provide information about the conditions or instructional treatment which produced that behavior. The first discriminates among individuals, the second discriminates among treatments. "Achievement tests used to provide information about *individual* differences are constructed so as to maximize the discriminations made among people having specified backgrounds and experience. . . . On the other hand, tests used primarily to provide information about differences in treatments need to be constructed so as to maximize the discrimination between

* Adapted and abridged from Robert Glaser, "Instructional technology and the measurement of learning outcomes," *Amer. Psychol.*, 18: 519–521, 1963. Copyright 1963 by the American Psychological Association and reproduced by permission.

groups treated differently and to minimize the differences between the individuals in any one group. Such a test would be sensitive to the differences produced by instructional conditions. For example, a test designed to demonstrate the effectiveness of instruction would be constructed so that it was generally difficult for those taking it before training and generally easy after training" [p. 520].

This is accomplished through the proper selection of test items. In constructing an achievement test to differentiate among *individuals* at the end of training, it would be necessary to select from a large sample of items relating to curriculum objectives those that discriminate among individuals so as to maximize the distribution of scores. On the other hand, a test constructed for the purpose of assessing *group* rather than *individual* differences would retain items responded to correctly by all members of the post-training group but answered incorrectly by students not yet trained; items showing substantial variability within either the pre- or the post-training group would be unacceptable. "In brief, items most suitable for measuring individual differences in achievement are those which will differentiate among individuals all exposed to the same treatment variable, while items most suitable for distinguishing between groups are those which are most likely to indicate that a given . . . instructional treatment was effective" [p. 521].

In summary, achievement and criterion measurement has frequently cast itself within the framework of the predictive, correlational aptitude test "theory" which has dominated test development to date. ". . . many of us are beginning to recognize that the problems of assessing existing levels of competence and achievement and the conditions that produce them require some additional considerations" [p. 521].

Comments

1.   This article describes a problem which has not received adequate consideration to date. It has a bearing on all aspects of research in which achievement test scores serve as the basis for hypothesis testing and may well contribute to the number of nonsignificant differences typically found in the literature.

2.   The practitioner would perhaps feel more comfortable to see that a given teaching method leads to superior performance on a regular test of academic achievement rather than on a test specifically designed to bring out intergroup differences.

References

Ebel, Robert L. "Content standard test scores," *Educ. psychol. Measmt.,* 22: 15–25, 1962.

Flanagan, John C. "Units, scores, and norms," in E. F. Lindquist (ed.), *Educational Measurement*. Washington: American Council on Education, 1951. Pp. 695–763.

That's What They Said

"Evaluation has no meaning except as it is a process of attempting to determine to what extent a school is realizing the aims and objectives it has set for itself. When the aims and values which govern the operation of the school are clearly defined, teachers and administrators are ready to collect data from all possible sources to appraise their efforts, but, until this clear definition is achieved, evaluation is apt to be only a mechanical and meaningless gathering of unrelated facts."

> G. Max Wingo. "Implications for improving instruction in the upper elementary grades," in N. B. Henry (ed.), *Learning and Instruction*. 49th Yearbook, National Society for the Study of Education, Part I. Chicago: University of Chicago Press, 1950. Pp. 280–303. [302]

"The aims of education in any school should determine the nature of the evaluation program in that school."

> Julian C. Stanley. "ABC's of test construction," *NEA J.*, 47: 224–226, 1958.

". . . the 'good' child is *not* one who is resourceful, explorative, able to act freely on the basis of his own ideas, experimentally-minded, spontaneous in his behavior, but rather to judge by reporting practices and administrative codes, prompt, obedient, dependable, curious, thrifty, and appropriately attentive to personal cleanliness, neatness, and standards of dress and appearance."

> Nora Weckler. "Individual differences and school practices," *Educ. Lead.*, 18: 307–314, 1961. [311–312]

"In general, I've come to the conclusion (there are exceptions, of course) that the ease and accuracy with which any educational outcome is measured is in direct proportion to its unimportance. That is, the easy items to measure accurately are the ones which make least difference whether they are measured or not."

> Edwin J. Brown. "Some of the less measurable outcomes of education," *Educ. psychol. Measmt.*, 2: 353–358, 1942. [354]

"When any outcome of education is claimed to be important but unmeasurable, inquire concerning the clarity with which it has been defined.

If an operational definition is possible, the outcome can be measured. If not, its claim to importance cannot be verified."

> Robert L. Ebel. "The relation of testing programs to educational goals," in Warren G. Findley (ed.), *The Impact and Improvement of School Testing Programs.* 63rd Yearbook, National Society for the Study of Education, Part II. Chicago: University of Chicago Press, 1964. Pp. 28–44. [36]

"What is needed is a little 'enlightened skepticism' toward measurements. We should realize that educational measurements are not 'yardsticks,' as they are in the physical world."

> Henry C. Lindgren. *Educational Psychology in the Classroom.* New York: John Wiley & Sons, Inc., 1962. [414]

"Why are schoolmen so insistent upon the importance of tests, measurements, and evaluations and so reluctant to be evaluated themselves? Why are they so gung-ho about having every kind of activity evaluated but their own?"

> Don Robinson. "Scraps from a teacher's notebook," *Phi Delta Kappan,* 47: 456, 1966.

"There is little basically wrong with the concept of grading. The notion of measuring achievement and maintaining standards of excellence accords with our ideas of encouraging and rewarding achievement. What is wrong is the limited nature of most testing and grading. Too often tests and grades are equated with pat learning, with convergent thinking and unimaginative regurgitation."

> Don Robinson. "Scraps from a teacher's notebook," *Phi Delta Kappan,* 48: 248, 1967.

"The most natural and commendable thing in the world is for the student to devise the most effective strategy for passing the course; that is his job. It is the teacher's responsibility to devise the strategy for ensuring that passing the course symbolizes learning or doing whatever is supposed to have been learned or done. Whenever students succeed in bypassing the learning while passing the course, they are roundly criticized for not appreciating their opportunities. This may be so, but the heaviest criticism should fall on the teacher who permits them to pass when they don't deserve to pass."

> Don Robinson. 1967. Ibid.

". . . Most marking systems are undesirable forms of motivation in that they stem from the authority of the teacher or principal rather than from the relationship between skill, attitude, or information acquired and the motivational system of the pupil. They are often dangerous also in that they limit outstanding success to the few and, if based on actual achievement, condemn a large group of children to continual frustration and defeat in school."

> Ernest R. Hilgard and D. H. Russell. "Motivation in school learning," in N. B. Henry (ed.), *Learning and Instruction*. 49th Yearbook, National Society for the Study of Education, Part I. Chicago: University of Chicago Press, 1950. Pp. 36–68. [58]

"The future of measurement in teacher education will depend largely on the extent to which excellence is emphasized in education. If intellectual excellence becomes the primary goal, measurements will be used increasingly in all aspects of the selection and education of prospective teachers. Research leaves little doubt that tests and measurements can help education toward excellence, if that is where educators want it to go."

> Robert L. Ebel. "Measurement applications in teacher education: A review of relevant research," *J. teach. Educ.*, 17: 15–25, 1966. [24]

"Despite their limitations and imperfections, despite the occasional misuses and despite the criticisms, reasonable or unreasonable, educational measurements have established themselves as versatile, indispensable tools of effective education. They are likely to be used more widely and more wisely in the future than they have been in the past."

> Robert L. Ebel. "Measurement in education," in Robert L. Ebel (ed.), *Encyclopedia of Educational Research*. New York: The Macmillan Company, 1969. Pp. 777–785. [781]

"Whereas it might be nice for a child with an IQ of 90 to know that he is not college material, it is not the purpose of the report card to advise him of this fact."

> Jerome M. Seidman. *Readings in Educational Psychology*. Boston: Houghton Mifflin Company, 1955. [325]

References

Fishman, J. A., and P. I. Clifford. "What can mass testing do for—and to—the pursuit of excellence in American education?" *Harv. educ. Rev.*, 34: 63–79, 1964.

Gulliksen, Harold. "Measurement of learning and mental abilities," *Psychometrika*, 26: 93–107, 1961.

CHAPTER 16

Test Items

1. Which of the following is generally not part of the school's regular testing program?
   a. academic achievement
   b. intelligence
   c. personal and social adjustment
   d. sociometric status
   e. special aptitude

2. The school's testing program should operate primarily for the benefit of
   a. prospective employers
   b. the pupil
   c. the school
   d. society (protection against incompetence)
   e. the teacher

3. The greatest danger of misuse of academic test data is that
   a. they create anxiety
   b. they discourage students from doing their best
   c. they lead to the neglect of other important aspects of education
   d. they serve to separate the sheep from the goats
   e. they supersede the true objectives of education

4. Which of the following is not a legitimate use of pupil academic test data?
   a. adjusting the curriculum to pupil background
   b. determining grade placement of pupils and of curricular contents
   c. determining the relative status of individual pupils
   d. evaluating teacher effectiveness
   e. maintaining academic standards

5. Tests of academic achievement should be primarily seen in the context of
   a. counseling
   b. learning
   c. promotion–retention
   d. reporting
   e. school administration

6. Probably the most important single benefit of the academic testing program to the child accrues from
   a. appraising his progress so as to plan his further growth
   b. consolidating his learning
   c. identifying areas of difficulty that could become cumulative
   d. motivating him to greater (or continued) effort
   e. satisfying his need for competition as the basis for realistic self-identification

7. What to include in a given course examination (if it is to be valid) is primarily a function of
   a. the accuracy with which the various components can be measured
   b. the emphasis given in class to the various components in the course
   c. the instructor's judgment as to what is important and measurable
   d. the objectives of that particular course
   e. the various emphases incorporated in the basic text

8. The list of objectives is to the table of specifications as
   a. the goals of instruction are to the mechanics of testing
   b. the validity of the course is to the validity of the test
   c. the validity of the test is to its reliability test
   d. the validity of the test is to the distribution of scores it yields
   e. what is "teachable" is to what is "testable"

9. The primary determinant of the true objectives of a specific course is
   a. the goals envisaged by the curriculum maker
   b. the interests of the students
   c. the nature of available teaching aids
   d. the nature and the coverage of the test
   e. the teacher's emphasis in class

10. Deducting marks from a pupil's score on a course examination for misspelled words is justified
    a. always; spelling is an important academic skill
    b. never; it destroys the validity of the test
    c. never; it overbalances the objectives of the school toward the mechanical aspects of education
    d. only when the words in question are part of the objectives of the course
    e. only when reported as a separate score

11. The most important criterion of a good test is
     a. its difficulty
     b. its discrimination
     c. its reliability
     d. its usability
     e. its validity

12. The more reliable a test is,
     a. the greater its predictive value
     b. the greater its validity
     c. the greater the homogeneity of the scores it provides
     d. the more difficult it is to "fake"
     e. the smaller the chance fluctuations in the repeated testing of a given individual

13. The major advantage of a standardized test lies in
     a. its general high quality
     b. its norms
     c. its reliability
     d. its usability
     e. its validity

14. The primary point of distinction between a standardized and a teacher-made test is
     a. the availability of norms
     b. its commercial availability
     c. its relative overall quality
     d. its relative validity
     e. the standardization of administration procedures

15. Whether to use an objective or an essay test relates primarily to
     a. the content to be covered
     b. the number of students to be tested
     c. the objectives to be appraised
     d. the pupils' familiarity with each
     e. the teacher's preference

16. The greatest weakness of the essay-type examination lies in
     a. the cost and labor of construction
     b. its inability to isolate the factor of verbal fluency
     c. its relative lack of validity
     d. its relative unreliability
     e. its wasteful use of the testing period

17. The major advantage of the objective-type test lies in
    a. its ability to measure certain objectives that cannot be evaluated by essay tests
    b. its ability to sample widely
    c. its ease of construction and scoring
    d. the interpretability of the scores it yields
    e. its validity

18. Which of the following statements concerning the speed-versus-power issue is most correct?
    a. Power tests make better use of the testing period.
    b. Power tests provide a better sampling of the course content.
    c. Speed tests are more valid.
    d. Speed tests tend to register higher reliability.
    e. The trend is toward short speed tests.

19. Which of the following is *not* generally recognized as a derived score?
    a. achievement quotient (AQ)
    b. educational quotient (EQ)
    c. grade equivalent
    d. intelligence quotient (IQ)
    e. percentiles

20. Measurement is to evaluation as
    a. absolute standards are to relative standards
    b. objective is to subjective
    c. scores are to norms
    d. a score is to an interpretation
    e. psychometrics are to philosophy

21. Measurements in education are typically on
    a. a derived score scale
    b. a displaced cardinal scale
    c. a percentile rank scale
    d. a raw score scale
    e. an absolute ordinal scale

22. The major advantage of derived scores over raw scores is that
    a. they have greater validity
    b. they permit the absolute comparison of individuals in a given group
    c. they permit direct conversion into grades
    d. they provide a wider distribution of scores
    e. they relate to a known distribution

23. Which of the following is *not* an accepted rule for good academic test construction?
    a. Avoid ambiguous or trick questions.
    b. Give options whenever possible.
    c. Have a variety of test instruments and test items.
    d. In essay examinations avoid global questions.
    e. Keep the difficulty of the items such that the average student obtains a score of 50 percent of maximum.

24. Which of the following statements is correct?
    a. A child cannot have an EQ and an AQ over 100.
    b. A child cannot have an IQ and an AQ of less than 100.
    c. A child cannot have an EQ below 100 and an AQ above 100.
    d. A child cannot have an AQ below 100 and an EQ above 100.
    e. Only a child of IQ = 100 can have an EQ of 100 and an AQ of 100.

25. Which of the following statements is *not* correct?
    a. A child with an AQ of 120 and an EQ of 80 is a bright under-achiever.
    b. A child with an AQ of 100 and an EQ of 120 is bright.
    c. A child with an AQ of 100 and an EQ of 100 is of average intelligence.
    d. A child can have an AQ, an EQ, and an IQ all above 100.
    e. A child whose EQ is greater than his AQ has an IQ above 100.

26. Grading in a professional school has, as its primary purpose,
    a. the diagnosis of student difficulty
    b. the evaluation of professional training
    c. the guidance of the learner's efforts
    d. the prescription of remedial steps
    e. the protection of society

27. Probably the major objection to grades in public school is that
    a. they are misleading as indicators of pupil growth
    b. they create anxieties that interfere with effective learning
    c. they distort the school's overall goals
    d. they interfere with the development of a healthy self-concept
    e. they interfere with the development of effective teaching procedures

28. Self-grading is basically objectionable in that
    a. children are not psychologically ready for self-evaluation
    b. it eliminates the motivational value of grading
    c. it is in violation of the school's responsibility
    d. it results in systematic distortion of the grades actually deserved
    e. none of the above; its benefits outweigh its limitations

29. The modern consensus regarding grading is that
    a. formal grading should be discontinued below high school
    b. the most adequate basis for grading is the performance of a relevant comparison group
    c. the S–U system is a simple and effective approach to grading and reporting
    d. self-evaluation constitutes the soundest solution to the grading and reporting problem
    e. when grading on the curve, 7 percent of the students in any one group should be failed

30. All things considered, probably the best approach to reporting student progress to the parents at the junior and senior high school level is
    a. the form letter
    b. the parent–teacher conference
    c. the pupil self-report
    d. the traditional academic-effort-citizenship grade with relevant comments
    e. home visitation by teachers or counselors

PART IV

The Child
and His Adjustment

CHAPTER 17

Attitudes and Character Development

Psychology, as the study of human behavior, is more fundamentally concerned with just who, just what kind of a person, is doing the behaving. This has been the basic theme of *The Psychology for Effective Teaching,* as emphasized in its orientation toward the self-concept, self-actualization, openness to experience, child-rearing practices, socialization, emotional and social maturity, and, in the present section, attitudes, values, and personal and social adjustment. This is not to minimize the importance of cognitive and intellectual development, learning, retention and transfer, etc., for they too are obviously fundamental to the effective and successful operation of the individual.

While recognizing the obvious importance of positive attitudes and values in the overall educative process, educators are typically uneasy about the subject. This is understandable: First of all, they have not been particularly effective in promoting such outcomes—at least if we are to judge from the current turmoil in matters ranging from student dissent, the new morality, and other aspects of the current generation gap. More fundamentally, the ambivalent feelings of society toward "juvenile offenders" —whether in matters of narcotics, sexual freedom, or civil disobedience and campus riots—might just suggest that we are not too sure of our own values. We seem rather confused as to what we are trying to accomplish, if anything, beyond fighting a defensive war. We are, for example, repelled by the thought of indoctrination and "enforcement," this despite the constant, if not systematic, attempts on the part of teachers, parents, and society in general to do precisely that in matters of honesty, integrity, democracy, law-abidance, not to mention just plain conformity. It might be, in fact, that our very ambivalence at both the verbal and the behavioral level is at the very root of the problem of "hypocrisy" and "irrelevance" with which adult middle-class society is being charged. Meanwhile, we might want to consider just what values and attitudes these youthful dissenters are being "taught" by default, if not through deliberate teaching. The "success" of the Soviets, as described by Bronfenbrenner, (and previously the "success" of the Nazis) in generating a set of attitudes and values according to prescription might be worth considering in this connection.

The school—along with society at large—apparently needs to define with greater clarity just what it really believes and just how it is to "teach" this important aspect of education. It would make sense, for example, to think that, only as we replace our present emphasis on social and ethical standards as abstract and arbitrary taboos and limitations to behavior by a corresponding emphasis on their positive foundation and opportunity for young people to realize the benefits of these standards in their personal lives, can we expect youth to abide by these moral "standards" of our society. Because of the importance of early child-rearing, parents are necessarily in Position No. 1. We have noted, for example, the importance of maternal warmth in the development of dependency as a prerequisite for effective socialization. Nevertheless, teachers also play a sensitive role because of their strategic position as models and mentors to all the children of all the people throughout the period of their formative years. How they see their role in this important aspect of the overall education of the child has not received the attention it deserves. Nor has the school been particularly successful: Four years of college have only minor influence in molding the attitudes of college students, at a time when presumably they might be highly susceptible to such influence. Perhaps, current student involvement is causing colleges to recognize that education that does not touch the individual, that is not "relevant" and ego-involving, is not an education at all. By the same token, the schools have tended to promote a morality at the level of irrational-conscientious conformity to rules for the sake of rules. Such a morality is not going to endure in our present society; but then perhaps it was not much of a morality anyway!

In addition to Bronfenbrenner's discussion of the Soviet system of character education, this section presents important papers by Gayer on making morality operational and by Neff on the need to avoid placing morality in the realm of certainty and immutability. Heald presents a strong defense of middle-class values; they certainly need clarification and extension but any attempt to shift to lower-class values in order to be "relevant" with respect to today's youth may turn out to be a bad bargain. The last article, by Hill, presents the acquisition of values from the standpoint of learning theory—one more instance that the better part, if not all, of psychology can be approached from the standpoint of the psychology of learning.

Urie Bronfenbrenner

Soviet Methods of Character Education: Some Implications for Research *

"Every society faces the problem of the moral training of its youth. This is no less true of Communist society than of our own. Indeed, Communist authorities view as the primary objective of education not the learning of subject matter but the development of what they call 'socialistic morality.' It is instructive for us in the West to examine the nature of this 'socialistic morality' and the manner in which it is inculcated, for to do so brings to light important differences in the ends and means of character education in the two cultures" [p. 550].

Soviet methods of character training are the direct reflection of the teaching of one man, Anton S. Makarenko, the Soviet "Dr. Spock" in matters of moral upbringing. Makarenko developed his ideas and methods over a lifetime of practical work with young people going back to the early 1920s when he headed a rehabilitation program for children made homeless by the civil war. In time, he was able to generate in his wards such a sense of group responsibility and commitment to the work program and code of conduct he had laid out for the collective that his commune became recognized throughout the Soviet Union for its high morale and discipline and for the productivity of its farms. His theories and teachings have since become accepted as the basis for Soviet educational practices; his influence extends throughout the Communist world.

Underlying Makarenko's approach is the view that the parents' authority over the child is a matter of delegation by the state and that duty to one's children is simply a specific instance of one's broader duty to Soviet society. His basic thesis is that optimal personality development can occur only through productive activity in a series of social collectives—first the family, then the school, the neighborhood and other community settings— whose primary function is to develop socialistic morality through a careful regimen of activities mediated through group criticism, self-criticism, and group-oriented punishments and rewards.

* Adapted and abridged from Urie Bronfenbrenner, "Soviet methods of character education: some implications for research," *Amer. Psychol.*, 17: 550–564, 1962. Copyright 1962 by the American Psychological Association and reproduced by permission.

A special feature of Soviet training is its strong orientation toward competition—competition in the classroom, competition between classrooms, competition between schools, etc.—a fact clearly recognizable in the Soviet concept of rivalry among nations, rivalry among social systems, etc. From the first grade on, the teacher emphasizes, "Let's see which row can sit the straightest." As a consequence, the children soon develop responsibility not only for their own behavior but also for that of their comrades who collectively determine the achievement of the row. Records are kept for each row from day to day; grade charts are displayed in the school. Posters and pennants identify the winners; rewards are given. The grade each child gets depends on the performance of his group, so that helping others becomes a matter of self-interest: "Today, Peter helped Kate and, as a result, the group did not get behind." In the case of negative behavior, group pressure is enlisted in condemning the infraction; again the emphasis is on the detrimental effect of such behavior on the group's success.

At first, the teacher sets the standards but soon—even in the first grade—monitors are provided for each row and, by the third grade, the children are encouraged to criticize themselves. The parents are also expected to report on their child's behavior at home and, in keeping with the Soviet view of the subsidiary role of the home, a representative of the commune visits each home to observe. The influence of the home will be minimized further, as the Soviet Union is now moving in the direction of providing boarding schools where children will be entered as early as three months of age, with parents visiting only on weekends. This will mean that children from the first year of life will be spending their formative years in collective settings, exposed continuously to the influences of collective socialization.[1]

Comments

1.   We see in the Soviet educational system—as we did in the Nazi regime—a total commitment of the nation's educational and social resources to the development and support of its political ideologies. Character education in the Soviet Union is primarily a socio-political enterprise. Psychologically speaking, this probably makes sense; if that's what you want, that's how to do it. From a sociological and philosophical point of view, such an approach would conflict with our democratic way of life; Americans would be inclined to think that this persistent indoctrination would hardly promote the kind of flexible morality we would favor.

[1] The article presents a number of research possibilities provided by the sharp contrast between American and Soviet views on such matters as the role of the family in child-rearing, the emphasis on competition and group structure, etc. These will be omitted here in the interest of brevity.

2.   The political–ideological emphasis of Soviet character formation is brought out in two related articles (Schlessinger, 1964; Malkova, 1964). Schlessinger, for example, points out how posters, statues, etc. erected everywhere under government auspices provide evidence of the regime's all out commitment to the task of indoctrination to communistic values. With the state-controlled communication media, the individual is constantly exposed—at home, at school, at work and at play—to the official doctrine of the state. The avowed purpose of Soviet institutions as well as the Party is the promotion of complete dedication to Marxism. From the early grades, children are encouraged to engage in socially useful work in the collectives; whole classes of students after school closes travel to the northern regions or to the steppes to volunteer their labor for the common good. The emphasis placed on the glory of labor as the basis of communist society is reflected in such Communist slogans as "One for all, all for one," "From each according to his abilities, to each according to his work." There is a strong attempt to instill a sense of responsibility and concern for the common good in the attainment of Soviet goals—which is, of course, essential to the survival of the system.

3.   It is interesting to note that all three articles present morality almost exclusively in the sense of the development of socialistic citizenship; they all ignore questions of integrity, honesty, etc.—which apparently are incidental, if not irrelevant. Correspondingly, it would seem that the Soviets have been more successful in the development of total commitment to Soviet communism than they have in the development of morality; crime exists, for example (its existence is deplored—and blamed on American influence). They have not been particularly successful in overcoming the desire for individual gain, nor have they been able to eliminate religion, despite considerable effort. In short, they have developed a higher level of commitment to the state than to the more common values—which is presumably what one might expect.

References

Malkova, Zoya. "Moral education in the Soviet schools," *Phi Delta Kappan*, 46: 134–138, 1964.

Schlessinger, Ina. "Moral education in the Soviet Union," *Phi Delta Kappan*, 46: 72–75, 1964.

Nancy Gayer

On Making Morality Operational *

The school is inevitably involved in moral education; its responsibility is to find out more about it and improve it so that it will result in a moral people, where "moral" is not to be equated with adherence to a repressive, rigid, narrow code of behavior, but rather where the concept of morality is taken broadly to include freedom and innovation, liberation and progress, rationality, and discipline. We first need to determine what values and moral outlooks naturally permeate our educational activities and in what manner they are being promoted. Then we shall be in better position to decide what values the school *ought* to teach.

There are many ways of deliberately teaching moral values: (a) direct effort—e.g., the teacher lectures or leads a discussion on why one ought to be honest; (b) example—e.g., the teacher influences pupils to be trustworthy by consciously being a model of reliability; (c) intended by-product—e.g., the teacher in using problem-solving techniques to teach a subject also instills in his pupils an appreciation of critical thinking; (d) training—e.g., the children become democratic as a result of specifically developed and guided experiences in self-government; and (e) discovery—e.g., the teacher uses role-playing procedures to help pupils examine and understand their own values.

There are also a number of unconscious, unplanned, or linguistic approaches in which largely unintended and unnoticed transmission of values occurs from the logical function of language. Unplanned instruction comes about in the very act of speaking, whether one is actually talking about values or not. In cases such as truth telling, cleanliness, or honesty, our habitual uses of language are working on our side in that the values embedded in these words and usages are the ones we want the young to have anyway.

But there are also cases in which language is working against our interests and where, therefore, it is important to become aware of what we are saying and doing in order to prevent damage. The word "may," for example, is made ambiguous by the way it is used in the classroom—with undesirable consequences. While appearing to be giving the child a choice,

* Adapted and abridged from *Phi Delta Kappan,* 46: 42–47, 1964. By permission of author and publisher.

all too often teachers use expressions of freedom for eliciting non-choice responses and follow them by actions which belie the true meanings of the words. They thus violate the big concepts of freedom, choice, and responsibility. When the teacher says "You *may* line up, children," she really means "You *must* line up" as any child who takes the word *may* at its literal meaning will soon find out. We are so accustomed to swaddling commands in the soft garments of requests that it may be forgotten that "You may" does not even make a request. It offers a choice; it gives an option to do otherwise.

How is Robbie to deal with the teacher's "You may play on the jungle gym today"? Does this mean that he is to play on the jungle gym and nowhere else? Or that the jungle gym is one of the places he can play? He can respond by looking to see what the others are doing and follow the pack—which, of course, sows the seeds of other-directedness. He can play it safe by going to the jungle gym, or he can take "may" literally as indicating a choice, thus earning the reputation of being anti-social, stubborn, or not-quite-bright.

Observe, however, that he is not likely to be called *disobedient*. That term went out with the coming of the mythology surrounding the democratic classroom. The same conceptual framework which has led to the use of "may" for "must" also disguises the use of obedience as a behavior criterion. "Disobeying" implies the existence of a rule, command, or order. One is not disobedient if there is nothing to disobey. Within a frame of reference where teacher-made rules and teacher orders are thought to be undemocratic, a disobedient child is an implicit reflection on the teacher. She has not been "democratic." Far better to shift the onus on the pupil by calling him "uncooperative." His offense thus is against the group and not against an "authoritarian" teacher, guilty by virtue of the nature of the child's crime.

Using "may" for "must" helps to perpetuate a widespread and pervasive myth among American teachers that they don't give orders and that doing so is undemocratic. Such beliefs are unwarranted. They are relics from an unrealistic and misconceived educational theory which envisages the teacher as sort of a grown-up peer member rather than as a person in charge. Giving orders is an integral part of almost any leadership function; when we clothe what we actually command in the vocabulary of choice, we violate the truth just as much as if we were to tell our pupils that the earth is flat. Both of these verbal acts are deceptions about reality.

Using "may" to mean both "may" and "must" makes it difficult for children to learn the all-important distinction between what they are allowed to choose to do or not to do and what is not left up to them to decide. Actually, the damage is not in being told what to do but in having the *telling* disguised. Pupils are not so much deceived by the teacher's stratagem as enlightened in respect to the real authoritarianism lurking beneath the sweetness and light. Realistic moral education should sharpen and not blur the distinction between the permissive and mandatory and thus prepare the pupil for living in a world in which he will find both positive laws enjoining or forbidding certain courses of action and areas where he is expected to exercise responsible choice. This is the essence of moral freedom.

We want pupils to develop into autonomous moral agents, but we should keep in mind that the areas in which we can permit them to exercise their judgment without restriction are circumscribed by values which are too basic to relax. If this seems to conflict with our democratic presuppositions, it is because we confuse authoritarianism with authority— because we misconstrue as authoritarianism the authority of leadership which inevitably goes with positions of responsibility. It is not rules as such which constitute authoritarianism, but rules arbitrarily and unjustly formulated and enforced. The teacher who says, "Clean up because I tell you to" is being overtly authoritarian, just as the teacher who says, "You may clean up now" is covertly so. But the teacher who says, "Clean up, so that our classroom will be nice for tomorrow" is giving a reason why it is desirable to behave in a certain way. And this is a crucial difference between arbitrary and rational leadership, between good and bad ways of exercising control over others.

It is not always necessary to give reasons for a request; in routine cases the pupils already know the reasons. However, teachers must be *prepared* to justify their orders, rules, or requests, as well as to volunteer their reasons at the relevant times. The reasons must be sound, and, ideally, the person to whom they are addressed should be given every practical opportunity to offer counterarguments. But the nature of even the most democratically administered authority is such that when neither party is persuaded of the rightness of the other's view, the decision of the one in authority prevails, for that is what is meant to be "in authority." This is not authoritarianism, rather a nonauthoritarian exercise of authority.

Teachers need to be aware of what values are being inculcated through the use of language, for only then can they decide which of these values are basic and mandatory. These can then be explained to the pupils and their enforcement justified in rational terms. We can also extend as much as possible the area in which we invite the pupil to use his own judgment. In this way we can avoid the familiar paradox of moral education by combining both the teaching of positive values and the teaching of independent critical reflection. Moral reflection in the classroom is just a shadow of the real thing unless it leads up to actions in which the pupil has a genuine free choice. If the answer which pupils are to give to the question of what the standards of classroom behavior should be is predetermined by the teacher, the pupils can't help but catch on to the strategy and feed back the expected answer. This isn't a sample of real moral re-

flection; it isn't education for the burden of real moral choice and for the
responsibility of choosing and justifying one's own actions.

Teachers frequently get elementary school pupils to volunteer the
very rules they themselves would have made. I have yet to see among these
"pupil-made" rules, "If someone hits first, it is all right to hit back." No
sensible teacher can include such a rule, since children are not allowed to
fight each other. The fault lies in pretending that the teacher has not used
the pupil as a ventriloquist's dummy to give voice to her own intended
rules and to con her pupils into thinking that they ought to obey these rules
because they made them up themselves. And this in the name of anti-au-
thoritarianism! This is no preparation for autonomous rule making. Teacher-made rules against physical aggression can be explained without authoritarian overtones and without intellectual dishonesty. Teachers should not
ask pupils to make up rules in any domain in which they are not prepared
to accept whatever the pupils list; difficulty can be avoided by circumscrib-
ing clearly with mandatory rules the area of freedom the children are allowed. The pupils can then be encouraged to make their own rules and
choices within this area of freedom, but these must be genuine and not in-
duced by manipulation.

When the teacher says to Robbie that he should obey the rules because he and his friends made them up, it isn't only that the teacher is
being dishonest but that this isn't a good enough reason for Robbie. They
aren't his rules and he knows it. If she had said, "Do it because I say so,"
he *would* have a good enough reason, even though she was being authoritarian, because *she is the teacher.* If she had said, "Do it because we will
have a much better time if we obey the rules, and the rules are good ones,
the result of much thought and experience on my part," Robbie would
have a reason for obeying them twice-over, once because a recognized authority says he has to, then again because a recognized authority says
there's happiness ahead in following these rules.

As pupils grow older they may come to question society's basic values. This is the time when rational explanation by teachers becomes even
more crucial, for it is unlikely that pupils will challenge all the values at
once. They will have internalized most of them, even as you and I.
Pupil–teacher arguments will be conducted in terms of other values, and
pupils will learn how moral differences arise within the framework of general standards accepted by both sides.

It is the outcome of such moral arguments that is productive of innovation and progress, stability and sanity in an ever-changing world. Education for such a world must be education for the exercise of genuine moral
responsibility under conditions of genuine moral freedom. Such is the task
and obligation of the school, and the moral responsibility of its teachers.
"Morality" need not be a nasty word. But it needs to be made operational
for the here and now, and for all of us who live in it.

Comments

1. This is a thought-provoking article whose implications permeate the whole of our social and ethical relationships, particularly in these times of student protest and other attacks on the "phoniness" of the "establishment." These are the days of truth—in which pious answers are no longer acceptable.

2. Our apparent dread of being authoritarian might profitably be reviewed in the light of the Soviet character education program as described by Bronfenbrenner in this chapter (see also Ausubel in Chapter 19). Furthermore, whereas there can be disagreement as to what values a given society *ought* to emphasize, there can hardly be disagreement regarding the obligation to use the tools made available to us by modern science to increase the efficiency with which we promote whatever values we decide are desirable. (See Rogers, 1961, Chapter 1 of this volume, in this connection.)

Frederick C. Neff

Education and the Cult of Certainty *

Our present generation is faced with a problem which the teaching profession can no longer safely or sensibly ignore. I refer to the question of whether we ought to foster notions of rigidity and certainty in respect to truth and morality, or whether we would be better to nurture attitudes of flexibility and caution in such matters. It is at once a philosophic and practical problem—philosophic because it requires a grappling with theoretical and scientific principles, and practical in that it penetrates to the very core of human affairs.

To be trained to believe that ours is a fixed, static world, where truth and goodness lie idle and immutable, and later to discover that we are living in an active, changing world, where every concept is open to modification and improvement, must be for the sensitive individual a startling experience, for it demands a considerable overhauling of belief and some painstaking scrutiny.

Are we really educating when we neglect to incorporate change as an integral part of our procedures? Can we afford to teach what we are teaching as certain knowledge? Perhaps most important of all, can any teacher who is seriously concerned with cultivating moral standards take for granted that answers are all that is needed and that criticism, discussion, and process are never to be engaged in?

The position that the teacher actually has a moral obligation to search with students for satisfactory answers to questions of right and wrong is receiving increasing support from respected thinkers in the field. It is relatively easy to find precepts that have already been laid down. One can do little more with them than to memorize and apply them. But the quest for the good life—the quest for God, if you will—is a distinctly moral undertaking. And the very heart of this quest lies in *process*—in probing, discussing, evolving, pondering, criticizing, refining, and improving.

It is only when all the facts are in that we will be able to say that an assertion is finally and irrevocably true (and maybe not even then). To say at this early stage of human history that nothing that is now believed could possibly be altered or supplanted becomes a bit irreverent.

* Adapted and abridged from *Phi Delta Kappan,* 39: 168–170, 1958. By permission of author and publisher.

Insofar as theory guides practice and moral precepts spill over into conduct, the problem with which we are faced is significantly more than a philosopher's dilemma. If my moral codes mean anything at all, then they have a bearing upon how I shall behave in my teaching, in my business transactions, toward my family and friends, and in my political decisions. In fact, the significance of belief can *only* be measured by how we behave. Those who hold that things are either right or wrong, that people are either good or bad, reveal a dangerous inflexibility in their behavior. It is rarely, if ever, that an idea could be considered as either all right or all wrong. Nor are people either all good or all bad.

For better or for worse, the cult of certainty appears to have had its day. It was a child of the flat earth, of mechanism, of determinism, and of scholastic and Aristotelian logic. In place of certainty, we might cultivate a proper degree of caution; instead of indulgence in complacency, we would do well to humble ourselves before the tasks that lie ahead; and in place of administering answers that are final, we might address ourselves to a quest for truth, and righteousness, and justice that may yield undreamed of pinnacles of human decency.

Comments

1.   The import of this article warrants serious consideration by anyone delegated responsibility for the moral and character development of youth; old answers are no longer accepted simply because they are old. As our world changes, morality must undergo some change; as the problems change, the answers should also change. Youth—and not only the hippies—is looking for meaningful answers. Perhaps more than ever, we need to be more concerned with answers that do not get questioned than with questions that do not get answered.

2.   Rarely can our answers be final. Rarely can an issue be stated in terms of a right-or-wrong dichotomy. We do our students—and the cause of morality—no service by constructing our moral training program on the good guys/bad guys specifications of the TV westerns.

James E. Heald

In Defense of Middle-
Class Values *

Increased educational concern for the culturally deprived has been attended by innuendoes to the effect that something is inherently wrong with middle-class values. Scientists, sociologists, and educators have charged that teachers with middle-class values must change these values if they are to succeed in educating the lower-class child. Presumably only by laying aside their middle-class values can the slum-area teachers expect to become effective. In fact, it would seem that all society might be better off for the loss of such a restrictive set of values.

Were they to scrap their middle-class values in order to become effective, what value system would teachers substitute therefor? Although the critics do not define the new value structure for teachers which would assure their effectiveness, three possibilities suggest themselves: (a) teachers can accept the values of another class; (b) they can reject middle-class values without replacement (this would seem a psychological impossibility); and (c) they can replace their current value system with a new one, nature yet undetermined.

Before we proceed to make our schools more nearly in conformity with the cultural and behavioral patterns of the lower class, it might behoove us to examine the values supporting middle- and lower-class cultural and behavioral patterns. According to Havighurst and Taba (1949), members of the middle class value: (a) civic virtue and community responsibility; (b) cleanliness and neatness; (c) education as a potential for solving social problems; (d) education as a preparation for adulthood; (e) good manners; (f) honesty in all things; (g) initiative; (h) loyalty . . . (n) thrift. In contrast, members of the lower class value honesty, responsibility, and loyalty, all when friends and neighbors are involved; on the other hand, they condone stealing and dishonesty, they are less restrained in acts of aggression and in sexual activity, they view juvenile delinquency as normal behavior, and feel little compulsion to stay in school. These, then, are the value systems at issue; teachers are told to exchange their orientation from the first set to the second in order that the education of the culturally de-

* Adapted and abridged from *Phi Delta Kappan,* 46: 81–83, 1964. By permission of author and publisher.

prived be improved. Such a movement would place the school in a position of attempting to stand for the moral and the legal while condoning the immoral and the illegal. It would overlook the fact that behavior improves as expectations increase. To condone dishonesty, unrestrained sexual activity, and juvenile delinquency as acceptable behavior is to establish conditions conducive to having such behavior remain normative. To expect humans to rise above such behavior is to offer hope for changing behavior which is considered immoral and judged illegal.

One of the most serious indictments made about middle-class values concerns the inflexibility and rigidity associated with the structure itself. A member of the middle class *must* be of a particular value pattern to be acceptable; deviations from this perceived pattern of acceptability is cause for peer rejection. This is not just and deserves its criticism. But rigidity of structure per se is not sufficient reason for rejecting the values attached thereto. Rigidity alone cannot be inherently evil unless one accepts as a basic tenet that every good is flexible. In fact, to carry moral flexibility forward is to remove guilt and simultaneously to destroy human conscience—with frightening consequences.

To assess the relative merits of the value systems under consideration, a comparison might be drawn against the Hebraic–Christian ethic as a system so secure that whatever may have been the original source of sanction, the insights have been thoroughly validated by the long experiences of mankind (Counts, 1952). The precepts embodied in this Hebraic–Christian ethic include: (a) Every man is precious because he is unique. (b) Man is a moral creature in a moral order. (c) There shall be a brotherhood of equality and essential unity among the races of mankind. (d) There shall be no privileged castes or orders and no man shall exploit another or his property. (e) For the protection of human society, man is to do justice, be generous, show mercy, be honest, be truthful, etc.

When examined in the time-honored light of such an older ethic, the values revered by the American middle class take on new luster. Middle-class values are acceptable as guides to the conduct of teachers engaged in the education of the culturally deprived. They are not all-encompassing, but their weakness lies not in what they include but rather in what they omit. Therefore, the new value structure proposed for consideration incorporates all of the middle-class values and the high expectations attached thereto, but, in addition, gleans new values of even higher order: (a) there shall be value in treating all persons as beings of supreme worth; (b) there shall be value in living as a brother to men of all races, creeds, and social positions; (c) there shall be value in actively working for improvement in all social arrangements affecting the lives of men; and (d) there shall be value in striving to make good prevail in the family, the community, the nation, and the world. It is not a matter of condemning middle-class values, or even reorienting them, but rather of recognizing their lack of inclusiveness and of expanding them to the point where the entire class, including its teachers, can find value and pleasure in improving the culture, the education, the morality, and the social usefulness of the deprived, the impoverished, the destitute, and the abandoned.

Comments

1.	The author does not imply that we can afford to reject the child who, because of his background, does not conform to our middle-class value system. We must recognize that before we can convert anyone to the pinnacles of morality, we must be able to engage with him in meaningful dialogue and this usually necessitates starting at a point somewhat short of ultimate perfection. The ultimate goal may lie in the direction of expanded middle-class values; the means, on the other hand, may require some degree of initial compromise.

2.	The problem is perhaps not so much the system of values to which American society subscribes as the extent to which these values become truly operational in the lives of its members. The lofty ideals which even the middle class presumably espouses are not always evident in its work-a-day interaction: "We ain't living half as good as we already know how!"

References

Counts, George. *Education and American Civilization.* New York: Teachers College, Columbia University, 1952.

Havighurst, Robert J., and Hilda Taba. *Adolescent Character and Personality.* New York: John Wiley & Sons, Inc., 1949.

Winfred F. Hill

Learning Theory and the Acquisition of Values *

Despite its importance and considerable interest on the part of psychologists, sociologists, educators, and others, the process by which a child acquires the values of his culture is still relatively obscure. A major problem here is that "this area of research has become a battleground of conflicting terminology, with one term having a multiplicity of half-distinct meanings, and what appears to have the same meaning having a multiplicity of different labels" [p. 317]. Three terms are of particular interest in this connection: *identification, introjection,* and *internalization.* All involve some relationship between an individual, i.e., a subject (S) and another person or personalized entity, i.e., a model (M), such that S's behavior is in some way patterned after M's. The use of these three terms in the literature suggests that several processes are involved with no generally accepted conventions for labeling them. The present writer believes that clarity would be served by abolishing all three terms from the technical vocabulary of personality development, and, on the premise that these processes are learning processes, to substitute therefor the vocabulary of learning.

"This approach involves treating human learning in a socio-cultural environment in the same terms, at least for a first approximation, as animal learning" in the laboratory environment with the social rewards and punishments applied to humans considered "equivalent to the food pellets and electric shocks used with rats. Similarly, social roles can be considered the equivalent of mazes which must be learned in order to obtain the rewards and avoid the punishments" [p. 318]. While human beings constitute a far more variable environment than laboratory hardware, yet "since most of the theory in this area is concerned with the adaptation of S to a relatively constant human environment (i. e., the culture), this should not prove a serious stumbling block" [p. 318]. In addition, this approach treats values simply as inferences from overt behavior—an assumption which presents no insurmountable difficulty. In view of the above considerations, an attempt to study the acquisition of values as a branch of learning theory appears justified.

* Adapted and abridged from Winfred F. Hill, "Learning theory and the acquisition of values," *Psychol. Rev.,* 67: 317–331, 1960. Copyright by the American Psychological Association, and reproduced by permission.

Kinds of Reinforcement

While theorists are by no means unanimous as to the value of reinforcement terminology, there is little question that the consequences of an act influence its subsequent occurrence (the empirical law of effect). Three kinds of reinforcement might be distinguished as the basis for analyzing the learning of values:

(a) Primary Reinforcement

"Primary" reinforcement refers to "the effects not only of innate physiological reinforcers but also of those social reinforcers which play a primary role in human motivation. Presumably the positively reinforcing effects of attention and praise or the negatively reinforcing effects of criticism, ridicule, and rejection are at least partly learned, but the nature of the learning process is obscure and, at the present level of analysis, it seems preferable to treat praise for a human as comparable to food for a rat" [p. 319]. One particular kind of learning mediated through "primary" reinforcement is the development of a generalized tendency to imitate others, i.e., a tendency for S to pattern his behavior after that of M, not only when M is present but also in his absence.

(b) Secondary Reinforcement

Also involved is secondary reinforcement; because of stimulus generalization, duplication by the child of his parents' patterns of speech, facial expressions, gestures, etc. should be rewarding to him, so that he may be expected to show some of the same mannerisms as his parents. This same process is capable, "at least in principle, of being adapted to the more general and more significant values as well" [p. 321].

(c) Vicarious Reinforcement

In addition, some important human learnings seem to call for vicarious reinforcement, involving the generalization of reinforcing effects from others to oneself, and thus learning from the reinforcers which others receive. The reinforcement of M of a given act performed by M is also reinforcing to S. Furthermore, stimulus generalization occurs not only from M's behavior to S's but also from one act of M to another, so that, "if M is frequently reinforced, S should find it rewarding to resemble M in general, including the imitation of some of M's behaviors which S has never seen rewarded" [p. 321].

Traditionally, *identification, introjection,* and *internalization* might be applied to any or all of the learning processes described above. The need for the rather subtle distinctions among them stems from the possibility of conflict: conditions might be such as to have one of these processes produce one kind of behavior while another produces quite different behavior. A common conflict, for example, is between "the tendency to imitate Ms whom S is directly reinforced for imitating (e.g., well-behaved children) and the tendency to imitate Ms whom S perceives as successful (e.g., tough kids)" [p. 322]. The use of a single inclusive term, e.g., *identification,* would obscure the relevant variables in such a conflict situation.

There is no special merit to the classificatory scheme presented here; the discussion simply attempts to show "how the terminology of learning theory can be applied to processes of value acquisition as described by personality theorists. This not only serves as a step toward the integration of the two areas of study, but also suggests the probable usefulness of employing such independent variables as . . . delay of reinforcement, distribution of practice, and discriminability of stimuli in the study of value acquisition" [pp. 322–323]. The remainder of the present discussion concerns the application of this kind of thinking to the development of conscience.

Conscience

Sears et al. (1957) identify three criteria underlying the operation of conscience in young children: resistance to temptation, self-instruction to obey the rules, and evidence of guilt over transgressions. The analysis of these diverse response patterns from a learning theory approach follows:

(a)   Resistance to temptation may be viewed simply as avoidance learning. Although children presumably can learn to respond to more abstract cues than animals, there is no reason to regard learning to avoid certain behaviors as fundamentally different in the child than in the rat. It would follow that factors effective in animal avoidance learning would also be among the most appropriate for studying in connection with the development of conscience in children. The greater certainty of punishment, for example, might be expected to produce inhibitions which would be more complete in the short run but also less persistent once punishment is permanently withdrawn.

(b)   "Sears, Maccoby and Lewin's second criterion of conscience, self-instruction, obviously makes the human case different from the animal case, but it does not introduce any new motivational principle. It is natural that a person learning an avoidance, like a person learning any other difficult response pattern, should give himself verbal instruction, especially since verbal coaching by others is so important in the learning of social prohibitions" [p. 324].

(c)   The third criterion, *guilt* at violations of prohibitions, is complex in that it often involves the seeking of punishment: "The person who has transgressed, rather than trying to avoid punishment . . . , actually seeks out the authority, confesses, and receives his punishment with apparent relief. . . . Were it not for these phenomena of punishment-seeking and self-sacrificing restitution, it would be easy to dismiss guilt as merely the kind of fear associated with anticipation of . . . punishment. As it is, the existence of guilt serves as an argument for regarding conscience as something more than the sum of all those avoidances which have moral significance in one's culture" [pp. 324–325].

"Sears, Maccoby and Lewin found that the development of conscience . . . was greater in those children whose parents used love-oriented forms of discipline . . . than in those whose parents used 'materialistic' forms of discipline. . . . This is consistent with a widely held view that the acquisition of parental values occurs most fully in an atmosphere of love. . . . It is possible, however, that this finding may be due, not to love-oriented discipline as such, but to other characteristics of discipline which are correlated with it" [p. 325].

"The various forms of punishment commonly applied to children probably differ markedly in the temporal relations and the reinforcement contingencies involved. Physical punishment is likely to occur all at once and be over quickly, while punishment by deprivation of objects or privileges is likely to be either for a fixed period of time or for as long as the disciplinarian finds convenient. Discipline by withdrawal of love, on the other hand, probably much more often lasts until the child makes some symbolic renunciation of his wrongdoing, as by apologizing, making restitution, or promising not to do it again. The child is deprived of his parents' love . . . for as much or as little time as is necessary to get him to make such a symbolic renunciation. When he has made it, he is restored to his parents' favor. On repeated occasions of transgression, punishment by withdrawal of love, and symbolic renunciation, the child may be expected not only to learn the renunciation response as an escape from parental disfavor but eventually also as an avoidance . . . response. Thus, if the wrongdoing is not immediately discovered, the child may anticipate his parents' impending disfavor by confessing in advance and making the symbolic renunciation" [p. 326].

"The result of this hypothesized sequence of events is that the child makes a verbal response which is in effect an instruction to himself not to repeat the wrongdoing. The next time temptation comes, he is more likely to make this verbal response before transgressing. Although this does not guarantee that he will not transgress, it is likely to reduce the probability. If he succumbs to temptation, he is more likely to confess before being caught and thereby avoid the temporary loss of his parents' love. Thus if the above reasoning is correct, all three criteria of conscience should be present to a greater degree in the child who has been disciplined in this fashion than in other children. According to the present hypothesis, however, this is due to the fact that punishment continues until the child makes a symbolic renunciation, rather than to the fact that it involves the withdrawal of love. If physical chastisement or loss of privileges are used in the same way, the same outcome is predicted" [p. 326].

"A possible weakness of this hypothesis is that the child might learn a discrimination between the symbolic and the actual avoidances, so that he would develop a pattern of violating parental standards, immediately confessing and apologizing, and then transgressing again at the next hint of temptation. If forgiveness is offered freely and uncritically enough, such a pattern presumably does develop. . . . However, if the parents' discrimination keeps up with the child's so that the latter cannot count on removing all of the parents' disfavor with a perfunctory apology, the efficacy of this kind of discipline should be at least partially maintained" [p. 326].

The fact that reasoning with the child, for example, shows a higher relation to conscience than do two of the three love-oriented techniques suggests that the crucial factor in those techniques associated with conscience may not be love-orientation as such but something else connected with it. It is predicted that conscience is more closely related to the parents' tendency to make termination of punishment contingent on symbolic renunciation, i. e., to response contingencies, than to love-orientation per se.

It would be particularly enlightening to compare evidences of conscience of the same people while in kindergarten and later in life when they are no longer under the direct influence of their parents. While predictions from learning theory on this topic are by no means unambiguous, two lines of reasoning suggest themselves:

(a)   The first line of reasoning concerns the fact that response tendencies based on fear undergo a greater weakening as a result of the removal of cues associated with changes in stimulus conditions than do response tendencies based on other drives. This implies that, as the distance of the disciplinarian increases, discipline based on fear would lose its efficacy more quickly than discipline based on reward, so that, "of two otherwise equal inhibitions learned in childhood, . . . one based on the threat of losing rewards would be more effective later in life than the one based on fear-provoking threat of punishment" [p. 328]. Furthermore, because of the likely persistence of the child's desire to continue receiving love from his parents, "discipline by withdrawal of love in an atmosphere of warmth might therefore be even more effective than other forms of discipline involving the denial of reward in producing persistent avoidances" [p. 328].

(b)   The other line of reasoning argues for the persistence of conscience associated with the process through which a symbolic renunciation of wrongdoing terminates punishment. Partial reinforcement underlies all forms of discipline, since punishment depends on the parent's moods, on the social situation, and, of course, the child's being caught. The child may also avoid punishment by confessing and apologizing, although, in such cases, the discerning parent learns not to accept the apology, and the child is punished anyway so that he has to make a more convincing symbolic renunciation than before in order to terminate the punishment. He soon learns that punishment can be avoided only by the actual avoidance of wrongdoing. However, if after a period of obedience, he once more transgresses and confesses, he is more likely not to be punished—which starts the cycle of extinction and reconditioning of the avoidance response on a reinforcement schedule in which only part of the transgressions are punished. While the effects of such partial reinforcement in retarding extinction is admittedly problematic, the following hypotheses deserve consideration: (a) "That discipline by deprivation . . . has more persistent effects than discipline by noxious stimulation . . ."; (b) "that where the child is taught to confess and apologize for his transgressions, avoidance behavior will go through cycles of extinction and reconditioning"; and (c) "that punishing only part of the child's transgressions results in more persistent long-range obedience than does punishing all of them" [p. 329].

Comments

1.	Hill's integration of learning and personality theory represents a significant attempt at parsimony. His analysis of the acquisition of values from the standpoint of learning theory might be expected to simplify (as well as standardize) terminology, encourage more precise study, and bring to bear on the problem of values and personality development, the extensive literature on the psychology of learning. The issue is, of course, whether learning theory can indeed accurately explain all that is involved in the acquisition of values.

2.	The fact that this analysis is based on reinforcement along associationist lines is interesting in the light of the fact that personality development is more typically considered in a cognitive framework. The attempt to cross-reference various areas of psychology is commendable.

Reference

Sears, Robert R., et al. *Patterns of Child Rearing.* New York: Harper & Row, Publishers, 1957.

That's What They Said

"The end of learning is not only a skill or knowledge but also the acquisition of motives, attitudes, and interests which serve individual, educational, and social needs."

> Howard L. Kingsley and Ralph Garry. *The Nature and Conditions of Learning.* Englewood Cliffs: Prentice-Hall, Inc., 1957. [206]

"The effort to force the child to agree that an act of cheating was very bad when he does not really believe it . . . will only be effective in encouraging morally immature tendencies toward expedient outward compliance. In contrast, a more difficult but more valid approach involves getting the child to examine the pros and cons of his conduct in his own terms (as well as introducing more developmentally advanced considerations)."

> Lawrence Kohlberg. "Moral education in the schools: A developmental view," *Sch. Rev.,* 74: 1–30, 1966. [25]

"If one asks a child, 'Is it very bad to cheat?' or 'Would you ever cheat?' a child who cheats a lot in reality is somewhat more likely to give the conforming answer than is the child who does not cheat in reality. This is because the same desire to 'look good' on a spelling test by cheating impels him to 'look good' on the moral-attitude test by lying."

> Lawrence Kohlberg. 1966. Ibid. [6]

The *only* method that works in favor of mature, dependable character is first to give people—whether children or adults—reason to feel an *incentive* to behave ethically; and then guide them intelligently, patiently, and with growing freedom to make and test their own decisions. This may work; *none* of the other methods of child rearing, or of reformation, breeds more than unthinking, rigid compliance at best—and many methods breed savagely hostile revenge behavior."

> Robert F. Peck and Robert J. Havighurst. *The Psychology of Character Development.* New York: John Wiley & Sons, Inc., 1960. [192]

"No objective evidence, in other words, for any 'should' or 'ought' or 'must' in the realm of value can be produced. When men prescribe values to their fellows, according to this philosophy, they are simply manifesting their own subjective preferences. They wish that others agreed with their own value-judgments, and so they issue imperatives. They tell others that these things 'ought' to be valued, which they themselves hold dear, often invoking the sanctions of society to enforce their demands."

> L. A. Larrabee. *Reliable Knowledge.* Boston: Houghton Mifflin Company, 1955. [502]

"Our censure should be reserved for those who close all doors but one. The surest way to lose truth is to pretend that one already wholly possesses it."

> Gordon W. Allport. *Becoming.* New Haven: Yale University Press, 1955. [17]

"The teacher is constantly and unavoidably moralizing to children, about rules and values and about his students' behavior toward each other. Since such moralizing is unavoidable, it seems logical that it be done in terms of consciously formulated goals of moral development. As it stands, liberal teachers do not want to indoctrinate children with their own private moral values. Since the classroom social situation requires moralizing by the teacher, he ordinarily tends to limit and focus his moralizing toward the necessities of classroom management, that is, upon the immediate and relatively trivial behaviors that are disrupting to him and to the other children. Exposure to the diversity of moral views of teachers is undoubtedly one of the enlightening experiences of growing up, but the present system of thoughtlessness as to which of the teacher's moral attitudes or views he communicates to children and which he does not leaves much to be desired."

> Lawrence Kohlberg. 1966. Op. cit. [17–18]

"To put Dewey's criticism more bluntly, both conventional character-education classes or preaching and conventional moralizing by teachers about petty school routines are essentially 'Mickey Mouse' stuff in relationship to the real need for moral stimulation of the child. To be more than 'Mickey Mouse,' a teacher's moralizings must be cognitively novel and challenging to the child and they must be related to matters of obvious, real significance and seriousness."

> Lawrence Kohlberg. 1966. Ibid. [22]

"We must decide what is truly important and concentrate on things that really matter. If it is too much to expect many teachers to be able to change their goals and values very much, this reminder to select those that really matter is still worth sounding, for we teachers may yet wield some influence with our students. We may yet help young people to think seriously about what is worth spending their lives thinking about."

Don Robinson. "Scraps from a teacher's notebook," *Phi Delta Kappan,* 48: 416, 1967.

"After a class discussion or seminar it is not so important to discover how many persons have changed their opinion about the issue under discussion as it is to discover how many have learned to hold their opinion at a deeper level of understanding."

Don Robinson. "Scraps from a teacher's notebook," *Phi Delta Kappan,* 47: 102, 1965.

"Since one is never obligated to do the impossible, and since all that is possible is not necessarily obligatory, the value question is more than a search for means to given ends. Both ends and means are transformed by expansions and contractions in the sphere of possibility. For example, the fight against cancer and vaccination for smallpox were not objects of moral obligation for Socrates, but they are for us. The abolition of poverty, overpopulation, pollution of air and water, and the abatement of ignorance are all matters of our obligation, because the power is clearly available for their accomplishment. Once technology makes social justice possible, we cannot get by with good intentions."

Harry S. Broudy. "Art, science, and new values," *Phi Delta Kappan,* 49: 115–119, 1967. [116–117]

"I am not suggesting that professors take advantage of their positions to impose their own morals and views on students; but I am suggesting that colleges have an obligation to create a climate where moral commitments to values are seriously examined and seriously respected so that a student is given the opportunity to enter life with whole being. I am not suggesting that we resist change because it creates problems; but I am suggesting that we strive to obtain a quality that is vitally pressing in today's academic scene; namely, the ability to maintain faith in essential humanistic values while joyfully adapting to new ways of receiving them, of preserving them, and of teaching them to the mod generation."

Patricia R. Plante. "Morality and the mod student," *Lib. Educ.,* 53: 466–475, 1967. [475]

"In short, college can contribute to the growth of a student's values only when it penetrates to the core of his life and confronts him with fresh and often disturbing implications which are different from those which he and his society have taken for granted. This can hardly occur as a by-product of a curricular assembly-line. It requires a highly personal relationship that is warm, considerate, and at the same time, mutually aggravating."

Philip Jacob. "Does higher education influence student values?" *NEA J.*, 47: 35–38, January 1958.

"If the object of education is the improvement of man, then any system of education that is without values is a contradiction in terms. A system that seeks bad values is bad. A system that denies the existence of values denies the possibility of education."

Robert M. Hutchins

"If a liberal education does not result in personality change, it has not been liberal and it has not been education. During your years in college, you will learn about dealing with ambiguity and uncertainty. Things will no longer seem so black or so white, and you will become able to accept grays—although you may not be particularly comfortable with them. Your college years will produce a willingness on your part to change and accept change and an openness of mind which many of you do not possess now. You will become disciplined enough to accept the compelling quality of new evidence which really forces you to change your mind."

Dean Robert J. Wert (Stanford). Cited in *Phi Delta Kappan,* 46: 210, 1965.

"But since man is a moral creature with a conscience, he has had to justify his inhumanity to man. And since man is also ingenious, he has never in this respect had any difficulty."

Samuel Tenenbaum. *Why Men Hate.* Philadelphia: Ruttle, Shaw & Wetherhill, 1947. [13]

"In recent years, it has been generally accepted that two complementary assumptions are necessary concerning human behavior if we are to give adequate description of this behavior. These are the assumptions of determinism and the assumption of free will. The research minded psychologist feels that he must assume determinism in order to establish a science of human behavior. In this position he sets himself up in opposition to the philosopher who feels he must assume freedom of choice if he is to establish an ethic, a system of good and bad, right and wrong in human behavior. When accepted independently of each other as complementary descriptions, each assumption is legitimate and proper. Nevertheless, many persons suffer from a mild type of mental anguish when of necessity we shift from one construct to the other. It will be my thesis in this comment to suggest that we can eliminate such mental anguish by eliminating the use of the free will assumption altogether. I suggest that all behavior be considered determined regardless of whether we are setting up a science of behavior or an ethical system."

William C. Budd. "Is free will really necessary?" *Amer. Psychol.*, 15: 217–218, 1960. [217]

"There is no better foundation for citizenship than learning in our schools and our communities to respect the rights and differences of others, whether they be differences of race, or religion, or opinion. Without such tolerance, neither our freedom at home nor peace in the world can long be secure."

Arthur J. Goldberg

CHAPTER 17

Test Items

1. Attitudes are best conceived as a form of
   a. conditioned response
   b. emotion
   c. ideal
   d. motivational predisposition
   e. perceptual predisposition

2. Attitudes are of special importance inasmuch as
   a. once formed, they are highly resistant to change
   b. they form the very substance of the self-concept
   c. they have a direct bearing on personal and social adjustment
   d. they permeate all aspects of emotional behavior
   e. they screen the flow of experience feeding the individual's growth

3. Ideals and values differ from attitudes in that
   a. they are more definite and specific but less intense
   b. they are more stable
   c. they exert a more compelling influence on a wider segment of one's behavior
   d. they exist at a higher level of cognitive awareness
   e. they involve a higher element of abstraction and generalization

4. Attitudes develop through
   a. association supported by a schedule of selective reinforcement
   b. deliberate cultivation as part of early socialization
   c. a process of conditioning
   d. the restructuring of the perceptual field
   e. a process of learning involving any and all of the above

5. Attitudes differ from ideals primarily in that
   a. they are more likely to exist at the subconscious level
   b. they are more likely to lead to action
   c. they are more specific to a given situation or object
   d. they are of greater social significance
   e. they have a greater affective component

6. Probably the most significant determinant of the attitudes the child develops toward the school is
   a. the adequacy of the co-curricular program

b.   the attitudes of the home
c.   the emotional climate of the classroom
d.   the suitability of the curriculum
e.   the teacher's personality

7.   The first consideration in dealing with children of the lower classes
     is for the teacher
     a.   to adapt the curriculum to their background and their needs
     b.   to help them achieve peer acceptance
     c.   to inculcate middle-class values necessary for success in school
     d.   to minimize the emphasis on formal standards of achievement
          and conduct
     e.   to understand them as individuals

8.   The resistance of attitudes to change is primarily explained on the
     basis of
     a.   functional autonomy
     b.   intermittent reinforcement
     c.   the pivotal position which attitudes hold in the total personality
     d.   their long-standing history
     e.   spontaneous recovery

9.   The major influence on the child's development of attitudes is
     a.   the church and other character-development agencies
     b.   the community (including mass media)
     c.   the home
     d.   the peer culture
     e.   the school

10. Probably the most effective way of changing attitudes is
     a.   to give insight into the self (rather than insight into the problem
          itself)
     b.   to modify the self-concept to allow for the change in attitude
     c.   to mount a deliberate hard attack on the position to be changed
     d.   to provide a systematic logically coherent case for the change
     e.   to provide the individual with a sense of security as the basis for
          openness to experience

11. Which of the following is *not* characteristic of the prejudiced person?
     a.   He displays a self-concept relatively closed to experience.
     b.   He has a narrow phenomenal field.
     c.   He is close-minded.
     d.   He is intolerant of ambiguity.
     e.   He seeks safety in "loads" of information—which he distorts.

12. The effectiveness of group discussion in changing attitudes stems primarily from
   a. the greater ability of the group to impose its views on its members
   b. the human tendency to go along with one's peers
   c. the more careful consideration of both sides which group discussion promotes
   d. the more convincing case that can be obtained through group discussion
   e. the personal commitment to action which group decision encourages

13. Which of the following is *not* more effective in changing attitudes than its opposite?
   a. emphasizing the threat involved in the present position
   b. presenting both sides of an issue
   c. using an approach congruent with the setting of the reference group
   d. using a popular speaker to present the point of view
   e. using a powerful prestige figure to present the issue

14. The consensus regarding the indoctrination of school children in the values of our society is that
   a. it is acceptable only when done in a subtle incidental manner
   b. it is both desirable and essential to the survival of our way of life
   c. it should be restricted to encouraging full discussion of issues so that the evidence will prevail
   d. it violates democratic principles
   e. the question is not whether the school should but rather with respect to what and how can it be made effective

15. An important prerequisite to the proper indoctrination of school children is
   a. having a program specifically designed to bring attitude changes
   b. having teachers totally dedicated to society's basic values
   c. having the school exemplify the basic values of our society
   d. helping students develop skills in group problem solving
   e. helping students identify with the school through providing a wholesome school climate

16. The basic contributor to prejudice is
   a. group identification and cohesiveness
   b. imitation

c. personal insecurity and the need to protect oneself
d. the natural resentment toward strangers
e. repressed hostility

17. Which of the following is *not* characteristic of the authoritarian personality?
    a. He is basically undemocratic in his behavior.
    b. He is insecure.
    c. He is a radical and an agitator.
    d. He is rigid and moralistic.
    e. He projects his shortcomings onto others.

18. The major fallacy in prejudice is
    a. arriving at a conclusion without benefit of adequate information
    b. assigning negative characteristics to a given individual on the basis of irrelevant class designation
    c. ordering individuals into incorrect classifications
    d. overgeneralizing to all members of a given group the traits that characterize only a few
    e. rejecting individuals simply because they belong to an out-group

19. Character is most fundamentally defined by
    a. consistency in matters of moral and ethical behavior
    b. conformity to the social code
    c. the level of morality characteristic of one's behavior
    d. the orientation of the self-concept
    e. the way the individual typically satisfies his needs

20. Prejudice is best eliminated by
    a. emphasizing tolerance as a basic tenet of democracy
    b. encouraging discussion on the dynamics of behavior
    c. encouraging frequent association with members of the victim set
    d. encouraging openness to experience by providing personal security
    e. helping the victims eliminate their objectionable characteristics

21. The major influence in effective character development is
    a. an innate need for social approval
    b. an innate sense of right and wrong
    c. the individual's basic need to experiment
    d. selective giving and withdrawing of love as a means of fostering early dependency
    e. selective punishment as part of the socialization process

22. Which of the following is *not* one of the Peck–Havighurst compo-
    nents of maturity of character?
    a. ego strength
    b. hostility–guilt
    c. moral stability
    d. social sensitivity
    e. superego strength

23. Javet in Victor Hugo's *Les Miserables* fits the _____ character pat-
    tern.
    a. amoral
    b. conforming
    c. expedient
    d. irrational–conscientious
    e. rational–altruistic

24. The expedient individual differs from his amoral counterpart in that
    a. he has a more adequately internalized system of values
    b. he is basically more moral
    c. he is less concerned with social approval and social constraints
    d. he is less irresponsible but more mercenary
    e. he is more totally motivated by concern over self-gratification

25. Our present ineffectiveness in helping children develop meaningful
    system of values stems primarily from
    a. the cold scientific valueless orientation of modern psychology
    b. the conflict in values among various components of the social
        order
    c. conflicting theories concerning the development of values
    d. the difficulty of providing reinforcement of a sufficiency and con-
        sistency necessary for effective learning
    e. failure to undertake moral training in early years when children
        are pliable

26. Values are best conceived as
    a. a broad spectrum of ideas and motives subscribed to by the social
        order
    b. an orientation toward theological matters
    c. generalized attitudes toward matters of ethical and moral con-
        cern
    d. internalized concepts of right and wrong
    e. the code of behavior through which the self is expressed

27. Sound moral development is primarily a matter of
    a. commitment to morality for morality's sake

b. the development of anxiety over moral transgressions
c. the development of enlightened self-interest and commitment to social welfare
d. the development of sound moral habits
e. internalization of the socio-moral code

28. Morality is defined in terms of
    a. behavior deliberately selected with full awareness of its social implications
    b. behavior guided toward the social welfare
    c. behavior in compliance with the moral code, e.g., law-abidance
    d. conscience development
    e. social sensitivity and social adequacy

29. Conscience stems from
    a. fear of external punishment
    b. habits of compliance instilled in youngsters
    c. the actualization of the self
    d. the internalization of the social code
    e. the satisfaction/frustration of one's needs

30. The major criticism of Piaget's postulations regarding the development of morality is with regard to
    a. the age at which the various stages are said to occur
    b. the discontinuity implied in his stages
    c. the order in which his stages are sequenced
    d. the rigidity he assigns to the earlier stages of morality
    e. the underemphasis on environmental influences

31. The rational–altruistic personality is best identified with
    a. self-actualization
    b. self-sacrifice
    c. social conformity
    d. social responsibility
    e. unyielding morality

32. Authoritarian child-rearing (strict unquestioned discipline) tends to lead to
    a. an amoral character pattern
    b. an expedient character pattern
    c. a high level of social sensitivity
    d. an irrational–conscientious character pattern
    e. none of the above

CHAPTER 18

Personal and Social Adjustment

Another critical aspect of individual functioning in which the school's responsibility is second only to that of the home is personal and social adjustment. Not only is the adjustment of its pupils, in itself, a major component of the school's overall educational objectives but, even more important, by virtue of its continuous contact with all the children of the nation, the school is automatically a major agent in the adjustment—or the maladjustment—of America's future citizens. We must remember, for example, that for some children schooling is a particularly anxiety-producing experience on a relatively permanent schedule. The results may very well be both personal and social maladjustment. We must also remember, however, that the task of the school is not so much that of the prevention of maladjustment as it is one of personality development—one of promoting emotional security, a greater openness to experience, a more adequate perception of self and of reality, i.e., one of promoting self-actualization on the part of all its pupils.

The teacher—the procedures he uses, the standards he enforces, the emotional climate he promotes—is unavoidably a, if not *the*, major factor in the school's contribution to the adjustment, or maladjustment, of school children. As Davidson and Lang point out, the way the child perceives his teacher and his teacher's perception of him constitutes a critical element of the classroom environment. The problem is complicated by the phenomenal nature of perception, which introduces a self-compounding feature that makes it difficult to deal with the alienated child, for example. The problem is complicated further in the case of the child from the lower class by the very fact that his teachers are typically middle class, with a world of perception, concepts, attitudes, and competencies totally unlike that of the world which is reality to him. The gap pervades all aspects of teacher–pupil interaction and precludes mutual understanding and meaningful dialogue. By the time his early deficiencies are compounded by year after year of inappropriate education, the cumulative inadequacies obviously defy easy remediation.

In the first article in this chapter, Mallick and McCandless question the cathartic value of aggression; it seems that catharsis may actually increase, rather than decrease, aggression. Grimes and Allinsmith, on the other hand, report a relationship between personality factors (compulsivity and anxiety) and school achievement. Finally, Kliebard expresses concern that watered-down versions of the curriculum to accommodate the culturally disadvantaged may actually freeze their inadequacies to a relatively permanent status; his arguments have an important bearing on recent trends toward adapting the curriculum and teaching methods to the needs and learning styles of these youngsters.

S. K. Mallick and B. R. McCandless

A Study of Catharsis of Aggression *

A common belief in psychological circles is that aggressive "acting out" behavior reduces aggression and hostility. Play therapy, for example, operates on the "hydraulic" notion that allowing the frustrated, angry, hostile child to behave aggressively serves to reduce his hostility and aggression. Unfortunately, the research evidence concerning catharsis as an aggression-reducing mechanism is not particularly convincing. The present study undertakes to test the following hypotheses: "(1) Angry aggression directed toward an inanimate object is not cathartic; (2) aggression, unmotivated by anger or hostility, has no cathartic effect but may, instead, lead to an increase in aggressive responses, particularly in a socially permissive atmosphere; (3) positive and reasonable verbal interpretation of a frustrating situation has cathartic value in that it reduces hostility toward the frustrator; (4) verbal aggression against a frustrator of the same sex does not reduce the hostility toward him . . . ; and (5) United States girls, presumably because of cultural forces, will show less open aggression than boys. However, in a permissive situation where privacy is assured, sex differences in open expression of aggression will be reduced" [p. 592].

Study I

In the first study, third-grade children were assigned at random, five boys and three girls to each of six treatment conditions in a 2 x 3 x 2 factorial design, involving two treatments (frustration and nonfrustration), three types of interpolated activity (shooting a play gun at targets on which were drawn figures of a boy, a girl, a man, a woman, a cat, or a dog; shooting at targets blank except for a bull's eye; and solving simple arithmetic problems); and two sexes. In addition, two sixth-grade children, a boy and a girl, acted as confederates. The first phase of the study lasted five minutes and involved the subject in five moderately simple block-construction tasks; he was to get a nickel for each task completed during the time limit. In the frustration condition, the confederate "inadvertently and clumsily" prevented the subject from completing any of the tasks; he also

* Adapted and abridged from S. K. Mallick and B. R. McCandless. "A study of catharsis of aggression," *J. Pers. Soc. Psychol.,* 4: 591–596, 1966. Copyright 1966 by the American Psychological Association, and reproduced by permission.

added a predetermined set of sarcastic remarks for good measure. In the nonfrustration condition, the confederate helped the subjects complete the assigned tasks. This was followed by a second, or activity interpolation, phase lasting eight minutes.

"In the third phase, each subject was shown his partner sitting outside the experimental room with his hands in contact with electric wires which were apparently attached to a shock apparatus installed in the experimental room. The experimenter casually reminded each subject in the frustration condition of the confederate's uncooperative behavior and told him that he could 'get even' by pushing the button, thus administering shocks (which would not hurt the frustrator very much, but would make him uncomfortable). They were further told that the frustrator would not know who was shocking him" [p. 593]. The number of shocks given to the confederate was taken as a measure of hostility. Subjects in the nonfrustration treatment were also shown the confederate and told that they could shock him if they wanted to and that he would not know who had shocked him. "Frustrated subjects manifested greater hostility than nonfrustrated subjects, but neither the sex of the subject or the type of interpolated activity resulted in differences in the amount of hostility shown" [p. 593].

Study II

In the second study, third-grade children were assigned at random, six boys and six girls to each of five experimental conditions. Again, a sixth-grade boy or girl acted as confederate. The experimental conditions in the frustration and nonfrustration situations were similar to those of Study I, except that the subjects in the frustration situation were given five nickels in advance with one nickel forfeited for each failure. At the end of this phase, each subject was asked to rate his confederate on a simple five-step "like–dislike" scale.

"The second eight-minute experimental phase for one group each of frustrated and nonfrustrated subjects consisted of shooting guns at a target on which was placed a picture of an 11-year-old child of the same sex. The second pair . . . (one frustrated, one nonfrustrated) engaged in social talk . . . with the experimenter. . . . The third frustration group was administered social talk plus interpretation . . . to the effect that the frustrator was sleepy, upset, and would probably have been more cooperative if the subject had offered him two of the five nickels. At the end of the second phase, each subject was asked to check the like–dislike rating scale of his/her confederate" [p. 593]. In Phase III of Study II, the subject was shown a response box and told that "the experimenter would go to an adjoining room and ask the confederate to do the same set of block-building tasks the subject had done. The subject could slow the older sixth-grader's work by pushing one button, or help him by pushing the other" [p. 593].

The hostility criterion score was the number of times the slowing button was pushed.

For both the aggressive play and the social talk treatments, the frustrated subjects obtained substantially higher aggression scores than their nonfrustrated counterparts but the aggression scores for these two treatments did not differ significantly from each other. The subjects to whom interpretation of the frustrator's behavior was given produced significantly fewer aggressive responses than the children in the two other frustration groups. Like–dislike ratings showed the three frustration groups disliking their confederate much more than the nonfrustrated groups, but there was no difference among the three frustration, or between the two nonfrustration, groups. Only in the frustration condition did girls admit to less dislike of their confederate than their male counterparts. With regard to the interpolated activity, social talk and aggressive play did not reduce the subject's dislike of the confederate but the interpretation (interpolated) condition did.

Study III

Study III is an exact replica of Study II except that only half the subjects in each treatment condition were asked to rate their confederate. The results showed the total aggression scores for subjects who had been pretested with the like–dislike rating scale to be significantly greater than those of subjects who had not been pretested, suggesting that "being asked to 'consider your enemy' may actually intensify the expression of aggression toward him" [p. 595]. The remainder of the findings of Study III agree rather closely with those of Study II.

Discussion

The principal hypotheses, namely, that "aggression without anger lacks cathartic value but that aggressive play in the presence of a permissive adult may lead to an increase in aggression" [p. 596] were supported in all three of the studies. "Taken together, the findings suggest that aggressive play, with or without previous frustration, has no cathartic value" [p. 596]. The hypothesis that reasonable positive interpretation of the frustrating situation has a cathartic effect was strongly supported by the data of Studies II and III. On the other hand, verbal expression of aggression does not seem to have a cathartic effect on aggression directed toward the frustrator; if anything, it appears to have the opposite effect. Contrary to expectation, in a permissive situation where they cannot be detected, girls tend to behave just as aggressively as boys, but their like–dislike ratings suggest less hostility than boys.

Comments

1. This throws interesting light on the concept of blowing off steam, gripe sessions, etc. Unless accompanied by some degree of interpretation, such activities may actually intensify negative feelings rather than reduce them. It is, of course, rather likely that mobs are incited to violence by rehearsing their alleged grievances.

2. The long-standing hydraulic model of personality adjustment is related to the concept of homeostasis; it assumes that aggressive behavior helps to reduce the tensions accumulating from the inevitable conflicts and frustrations of social living. It bears on the recommended mental health principle favoring emotional expression over emotional repression. The present study would seem to suggest that such expression should be along constructive lines.

Jesse W. Grimes and Wesley Allinsmith

Compulsivity, Anxiety, and School Achievement *

Among the many possible causes of reading retardation, some, such as physical handicaps or low intelligence, are obvious; others are more subtle. Research suggests, for example, an interaction between student characteristics and teaching methods, so that classroom procedures that are effective for some children may prove deleterious to the progress and development of others.

There are two major schools of thought with respect to the teaching of reading in first grade, each presumably leaning on psychological principles. One initiates reading instruction through the systematic presentation of sounds and their letter symbols. The child, using this "phonics" method, learns that word symbols are built in an orderly manner from their letter elements. In contrast, in the look-and-say approach, the child is taught to recognize whole-word configurations and to develop a sight vocabulary through repetitive exposure to a gradually expanding number of words. These two methods involve different degrees of structure. The phonics method, with its reliance on rules, systematic arrangements, and relative certainty in word-identification, is highly structured. The whole-word method, on the contrary, particularly in the earlier stages, is relatively unstructured. The fact that some children appear to learn more readily through one approach while other children seem to make better progress through the other suggests a possible interaction between student characteristics and method of teaching. The present study investigated the possible interaction of anxiety and compulsivity with these two methods of teaching initial reading.

The compulsive person tends to have an exaggerated need for exactness and order. He can be described as relatively rigid, preoccupied with small details, inhibited in spontaneity, conforming, perfectionistic and intolerant of ambiguity. While this description applies in marked degree only to disorganized personalities (or to periods of stress), compulsive tendencies can be noted in many children who are clinically within the normal range. It seems logical to predict that the structured phonics approach would facilitate the reading progress of highly compulsive children, who

* Adapted and abridged from *Merrill-Palmer Quart.,* 7: 247–271, 1961. By permission of author and publisher.

would see the whole-word approach, by contrast, as disorganized and un-systematic. In the same way, the highly anxious person tends to perceive a greater degree of threat in a variety of situations; Noll (1955), for example, found that highly anxious subjects had difficulty adjusting to new learning situations but that, having mastered a series of tasks aiding in the structuring of the succeeding tasks, they performed as well as or better than their non-anxious controls. We can then hypothesize that the anxious child learning to read through the highly structured phonics approach will make greater progress than similar children taught by the unstructured whole-word method. In other words, the structured phonics approach will favor both the anxious and the compulsive child learning to read.

Research Procedures

The subjects came from two city school systems, one of which initiated reading through a systematic phonics program; the other used the whole-word approach, followed by incidental phonics late in the first grade. Socio-economic status was controlled by selecting certain schools within the two school systems in order to provide equal proportions of children from upper lower- and lower middle-class neighborhoods. The two school districts differed in emotional climate, with the phonics group reflecting a more authoritarian classroom atmosphere and a more traditional curriculum. The study was conducted at the third-grade level and involved 156 children from 24 classrooms on the look-and-say approach and 72 children from 8 classrooms on a phonics schedule. The degree of compulsivity of the children was determined through a specially-devised rating scale in which parents were asked to describe the child's typical behavior in situations providing an opportunity for the latter to display tendencies toward perfectionism, irrational conformity to rule, orderliness, punctuality, and need for certainty. Anxiety was assessed by means of the *Children's Anxiety Scale*. The criterion of school achievement was the composite of six subtests of the *Stanford Achievement Test:* paragraph meaning, word meaning, spelling, language, arithmetic computation and arithmetic reasoning.

Results

As predicted, the highly compulsive children scored significantly better in the structured setting than they did in the unstructured classroom. (See Figure 1.) They also did a little better than the low compulsives in the look-and-say classroom, perhaps because their need to organize led them to induce some degree of structure and achieve in spite of the lack of inherent direction. In other words, the compulsive child perhaps tends to accentuate those elements of a lesson which aid him in systematizing his work.

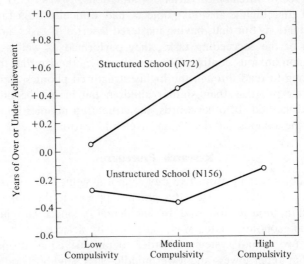

FIGURE 1

*Graph of Test Results Showing Mean School Achievement
of Children Categorized as to Compulsivity*

Also as predicted, the highly anxious children in the unstructured classes scored more poorly than both their high anxious counterparts in the structured classes and their low anxiety counterparts in the unstructured classes. (See Figure 2.) On the other hand, they performed up to par in the structured classrooms. The most striking aspect of the interaction

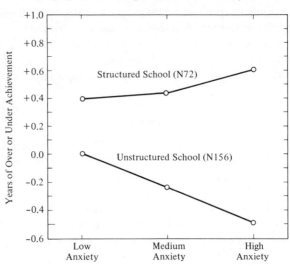

FIGURE 2

*Graph of Test Results Showing Mean School Achievement
of Children Categorized as to Anxiety*

between personality and method is the marked decrement in performance suffered by the highly anxious children in the unstructured schools, presumably, according to the theory proposed here, because of the perceived threat that persists unabated for the anxious child in an ambiguous environment. Because of their structure, the symbols the child is asked to learn in the phonics approach, on the other hand, are simple; this reduces the threat and increases his power of discrimination. Apparently, academic challenge in the structured setting creates an optimum of stress so that the child with high anxiety is able to achieve because he is aroused to an energetic state without becoming confused or panicked.

When the school systematizes the learning experiences for highly anxious children in accordance with their need for orderliness, their anxiety is facilitating and it may well be that teachers need to be less concerned with allaying anxiety for these children on the assumption that, by so doing, they are providing better learning conditions, and simply be more concerned with teaching in a manner that allows these children to make optimal use of their existing anxieties. This does not mean that the phonics approach is superior to the look-and-say approach of teaching reading for all children; it simply suggests that many grade-school children might be helped by a more formal structure in their early school learnings.

Comments

1.   The authors postulate that structure in the method of teaching accounts for the superior achievement among highly compulsive and highly anxious children. They consider alternative explanations but find that a number of logical considerations suggest that these alternatives do not constitute as parsimonious an explanation as does the degree of structure of the teaching method. They note that the grouping of children on the basis of homogeneity of personality characteristics in relation to teaching methods might be in order. This is again the argument as to the extent to which the school needs to adjust its instructional procedures to the idiosyncrasies of the learner's style of learning. Perhaps there is a need for reducing their anxieties to constructive levels so that they can eventually adapt to a variety of teaching styles. A high degree of structure (concomitant with other techniques) would be particularly reassuring and beneficial in a remedial program where structure might be used concomitantly with therapy in allaying fear. On the other hand, it should be remembered that any specially created benign environment should probably come equipped with the means for weaning students away from itself.

2.   The study did not consider all aspects of the situation, of course; the authors point out, for instance, that the children in the unstructured school seemed better socially adjusted; this might be due to the classroom climate rather than the teaching method per se.

3.   In a related article, Neel (1959) reports that authoritarian persons encounter difficulty in learning material which is ambiguous or which deals with a humanitarian philosophy but they do not experience difficulty in learning factual material. It would seem logical to expect that, where a choice exists (as in college), the highly structured personality would seek out courses that are well structured (e. g., mathematics) and would avoid the less structured humanities and social sciences.

References

Neel, Ann F. "The relationship of authoritarian personality to learning: F-scale scores compared to classroom performance," *J. educ. Psychol.*, 50: 195–199, 1959.

Noll, J. O. "An investigation of the relation of anxiety to learning and retention," *Diss. Abstr.*, 15: 1916, 1955.

Herbert M. Kliebard

Curriculum Differentiation for the
Disadvantaged *

Within the past several years, educators have experienced one of their periodic reawakenings to the fact that a portion of our school population is poor, that poverty may bring with it cultural deprivation, and that this cultural deprivation, in turn, may have some effect on success in school. The question asked is essentially the same: What should we do about it? One's initial impulse is to transform the school into an employment agency, medical and dental clinic, social service agency, and nutritional center so as to eliminate as quickly as possible all traces of the difficulty. In the past, the "whole child" slogan has been used to justify this humanitarian attack on the problem. Fortunately, in recent years, there has been a gradual recognition that the school is just one agency of society, and that like other agencies of society, its functions are limited. But even if one resists the generous impulse to remake the world, one is still confronted with the same question: What should we do about it?

In general, the response on the part of professional educators may be seen as taking three forms: compensatory education, instructional adaptation, and curriculum differentiation. These three approaches are not mutually exclusive, and it may be difficult to draw the boundaries among them absolutely, but there may be some merit in considering each independently. It is with curriculum differentiation that I am most concerned, but let me begin by briefly discussing the first two.

The most obvious concrete expression of compensatory education is remedial teaching of some type. This is not an especially imaginative approach to the problem of educating the disadvantaged, but it is certainly an appropriate one in many cases. In every normal population there will be those who, for one reason or another, need more specialized instruction than others. With respect to the disadvantaged, the need for remedial education is usually greater given the alienation and disaffection that slum conditions breed. A more creative and probably more effective form of compensatory education is represented by a program like Project Head

* From Herbert M. Kliebard, "Curriculum differentiation for the disadvantaged," *Educ. Forum,* 32: 47–54, 1967, by permission of Kappa Delta Pi, An Honor Society in Education, owners of the copyright.

Start, which attempts to use recent research on the disadvantaged in an effect to anticipate certain problems which are liable to occur as a result of a deprived environment. Thus, an effort is made to fill certain gaps in the experience of very young children so that the normal expectations of the first few years of schooling will not be unrealistic for this group.

The second approach involves the recognition that in teaching the disadvantaged, one must occasionally adapt teaching method to the classroom conditions that prevail in disadvantaged schools. It may be necessary, for example, to proceed at a slower pace than under conventional conditions. This differs from curriculum differentiation in that the course of study, the content of the courses, and the expectations on the part of the teacher remain essentially the same as for conventional classes. Only the method is modified. Levine, in a recent article, cites evidence to show that, in terms of the child-rearing patterns of lower-class and middle-class families, disadvantaged children may not react to permissiveness in the classroom in the same way that middle-class children do. He suggests therefore that in teaching students who are socially and culturally disadvantaged, it may be necessary to create a more structured classroom environment than would normally be the case. He recommends, for example, that "Definite rules should be introduced and enforced at the beginning of the school year. The teacher should stand ready to provide close direction at every stage, no matter how small, of every classroom activity" (Levine, 1966). This kind of instructional adaptation, from my own experience in teaching disadvantaged youth (and apparently from Dr. Levine's), is often necessary for a teacher's survival.

Many educators concerned with the problem of educating the disadvantaged, however, want to go further than just compensatory education like Project Head Start and instructional adaptation of the type described by Levine. They want to adapt the *curriculum* specifically for this group; that is, they want to provide a different set of courses, or at least greatly modified content, for the underprivileged. The usual argument is that these students are simply not equipped to cope with the so-called "academic" studies that characterize most curricula, and that they are furthermore (by virtue of their impoverished backgrounds) not in a position to profit from such a curriculum in later life. One expression of such a point of view is the notion that teaching standard English usage to working-class children is a waste of time. The argument that this skill may be necessary for social and economic mobility is considered to be either invalid or unimportant (Sledd, 1965). As a general rule (the argument goes), it is incumbent on us as educators to devise programs that reflect the natural inclination of the disadvantaged to the concrete and the directly functional. Although "academic" subjects are not eliminated entirely, they are relegated to an inferior status as a kind of necessary evil. This is justified as a way of recognizing the diverse character of our school population.

Consider, for example, the following argument:

> The traditional concern of American schools has not been simply with academic prowess—admirable though that may be; its goal has been the over-all education—vocational, cultural, academic, economic, and social—of *all* the youngsters of *all* the people, whose talents, interests, and needs reflect the diversity of a free, multigroup society. When curriculum-makers, perhaps at the prodding of vested pressure groups, inaugurate certain courses and water down or delete others in order to favor the incipient Latin scholar at the expense of the potential draftsman, they are tampering, not merely with the curriculum, but with a fundamental precept of the American way of life, viz., the intrinsic worth of every citizen, and his right to prepare for and engage in a legitimate vocational pursuit commensurate with his capacity to do so. (Neff, 1964)

A fundamental curriculum doctrine underlies the position taken here, a doctrine common to many educators who are trying to cope with the problem of educating disadvantaged youth in our schools. It is that "certain courses," the so-called "academic" ones like history, mathematics, and science, are appropriate only for "the incipient Latin scholar" or (to give that term its broadest connotation) those who will one day earn their living from academic pursuits.[1] Any attempt to teach such courses to the "potential draftsman" is taken to be part of an effort to fit him into a narrow intellectual mold. The assumption implicit in this argument is that "academic" subjects are somehow nonpractical, that they are concerned with rarefied abstractions of interest only to a small segment of the school population. Closely identified with this position is the more fundamental assumption that the curriculum is to be planned mainly with reference to a "legitimate vocational pursuit," and it is on these grounds that one must decide the question of what identifiable groups of students are to take what courses of study.

When one applies these precepts to the question of what to do with disadvantaged youth, the answer is obvious:

> Among the so-called underprivileged youth of our country the meaning of life is usually earthy—it is defined largely in terms of job opportunities and bread-and-butter values. Life assumes meaning in so far as airy abstractions are kept to a minimum and jobs are or will be available that are commensurate with training and ability. The line between present training and future placement had best be kept taut, lest the teen-ager lose interest and become discouraged. (Neff, p. 408)

In other words, in adapting the curriculum for underprivileged youth, one must (in contrast with programs for, let us say, privileged youth) design

---

[1] Indeed, one cannot give that term a literal interpretation since there are no high-school programs which are specifically designed to produce Latin scholars, and it would be a rare thing for Latin to be a required subject in a modern public high school.

the program so as to minimize "airy abstractions" and maximize what is immediately practical and potentially profitable in terms of the job market. Stating this proposition in more general terms, the main organizing principle for curriculum planning, especially with references to the disadvantaged, is job placement.

This argument is sometimes taken a step further. No only are members of a given group, such as the disadvantaged, uninterested in intellectual matters, they are (as a group) actually incapable of pursuing an "academic" curriculum.

> In being overly concerned with "intellectualism" we have pretended that every learner is a nice, obedient, diligent, bright, interested boy or girl—a story-book Dick or Jane. We have been urged to put aside such trivial concerns as health, preparation for earning a livelihood, and home problems, and instead to cultivate disembodied "minds," which once trained, are supposed to enable their possessors to cope with every type of problem with equal ease. We have allowed an intellectual elitism gradually to displace education for vocations and common life pursuits despite the fact that, according to James B. Conant, only about fifteen per cent of our high-school population are equipped to partake of and to profit from a strictly academic brand of education. (Neff, p. 410)

The implications are clear. The child who is disadvantaged because of his cultural, social, or family environment is really of a different breed. Not only has he no cultural aspirations, but he has little or no academic ability. All he thinks about is getting a job and making money, and the school exists to facilitate the achievement of these aims. Why waste time teaching him mathematics or literature or science when he obviously is not fitted for it and, besides, that kind of curriculum is for potential Latin scholars, not ordinary human beings. The crowning irony is that all this is justified in terms of attention to individual differences and a humane attitude toward the underprivileged.

Although the case for curriculum differentiation usually appears in this guise, it frequently has the effect of cutting off the children of the poor from their traditional avenue for social mobility. In support of this position, there is sociological and psychological evidence that children from working-class homes, on the whole, score lower on achievement and intelligence tests than do children of the middle-classes. Of course they do! The real question is not whether they score lower or higher, but whether the schools should, through their curricula, become an agency for perpetuating social class differences, or whether schools should continue to act as the major vehicle for social mobility in our democratic society. "Individualizing" the curriculum on the basis of such factors as environment, economic or social class, and even ability must not become a way of placing students into "case groups" which effectively serve to limit educational opportunity.

With the most humane motives, we lump together the disadvantaged, the unintelligent, the mechanically talented, the racial minorities, and the so-called non-college bound, and *we systematically cut them off from the intellectual resources of their culture by designing a curriculum for them which minimizes intellectual content.* We rigorously exclude this group from the mainstream of intellectual life and then piously decry the lack of rationality in decision-making at the personal and national levels. We do not have the honesty to admit that we have botched the job of putting our youth in touch with the intellectual resources of our culture and instead have tried to cover this failure with a dubious doctrine which asserts that this can be accomplished with only a small proportion of the school population.

It is interesting that some key spokesmen for the disadvantaged, like Kenneth Clark, will have nothing to do with such a doctrine. Quite the opposite. In reporting on his experiences with ghetto schools, Clark argues cogently against the notion that "children from working-class cultures . . . need not only a different approach in the educational process, but a different type of education from that provided for children from middle-class families" or even that "children from deprived communities bring into the classroom certain psychological problems that are peculiar to their low socio-economic status and that interfere with the educational process in the classroom" (Clark, 1965). Assumptions such as these, Clark argues, are essentially alibis for failing in the task of educating the disadvantaged. It is from assumptions such as these that we arrive at one of the most vicious of self-fulfilling prophecies, the one that goes something like this: Children from low socio-economic groups cannot cope with academic subject matter. We must, therefore, remove, or at least water down, the academic content of the curriculum in order to allow for this deficiency. Then, when disadvantaged youth fail to give evidence of intellectual interest or achievement, this is regarded as proof of the original assumption. Thus, the differentiated curriculum for the disadvantaged simply becomes a vehicle for effectively stratifying social-class lines.

But the case for differentiated curricula for different groups has had some powerful advocates over the course of the history of American education. It may be that it has become over the years a dominant position among educationists although the justifications for holding that position have varied. One of the early expressions of that position was set forth by G. Stanley Hall in the debate that raged around the turn of the century over the report of the Committee of Ten. The Committee, under the chairmanship of Charles W. Eliot, chose not to recommend differentiated curricula in secondary schools. Although four courses of study were suggested, none was designated as distinctively appropriate either for college or for "life." In attacking the Committee's view that preparation for life was also preparation for college, Hall spoke of the "great army of incapables" that was now invading the high school. (Hall, 1904) Obviously, one had to provide for them a radically different curriculum which took into account their presumed inability to cope with even the modern school subjects for which the Committee of Ten sought academic respectability. Then, too, the profoundly pessimistic doctrine that the "masses" are inherently incapable of rational thought and intellectual development was couched in the language of individual differences and concern for the underprivileged.

The case for differentiated curricula took on a somewhat different aspect in the early part of this century when the doctrine of social efficiency held sway. Under the leadership of such men as Ross L. Finney, David Snedden, and Charles Hughes Johnston, the case for differentiated curricula was proposed in terms of the efficiency with which these curricula prepared one for his presumed social role. The purpose was to design "distinctive curriculums definitely planned with reference, not to each pupil's personal needs primarily, but with reference to the different educational requirements of special groups of pupils—curriculums based upon social rather than necessarily vague psychological considerations." (Johnston, 1964) In this way the differentiated curriculum was essentially a device for insuring that each individual filled his proper niche in the social order.

This case was put even more bluntly in Ross Finney's *A Sociological Philosophy of Education,* especially the chapter called, "Followership and the Duller Intellects." Here Finney attacks the position that, "Every citizen . . . ought to be encouraged to the utmost to think for himself," a position he attributes to James Harvey Robinson and "Doctor John Dewey." Instead, he argues, that "if leadership by the intelligent is ever to be achieved, followership by the dull and ignorant must somehow be assured." In support of his position, Finney goes on to say that those with I.Q.'s below 99 + are incapable of "cogitations of any great social fruitfulness" and that our hope lies not in "the intellectual independence of the duller masses but in their intellectual dependence." Dewey's profound mistake, according to Finney, was in exalting "the independent thinking of the average citizen as the means of saving democracy." (Finney, 1929) Although Finney's case was presented in terms of I.Q. level and not social class, the social implications are obvious.

Whether the case for differentiated curricula is argued in terms of psychological differences, social efficiency, or the inability of disadvantaged youth to cope with academic subject matter, the effect on the school program is essentially the same. Certain groups, historically defined in different ways, are isolated from the mainstream of our cultural heritage on the grounds that they are ill equipped to cope with such abstruse matters. For these groups we are asked to design curricula which will result in "followership" or perhaps in getting and keeping a job. To act on the premise that all normal youth have the capacity for intellectual competence in the modern world becomes a form of "intellectual elitism," a denial of their right to be educated for a vocation or for "common life pursuits."

What is the alternative insofar as the disadvantaged are concerned? The alternative is to use whatever means are at our disposal, through compensatory education and instructional adaptation, to see to it that the genuine disadvantages with which certain children may start life do not become permanent handicaps. Sharply differentiated curricula for such groups, however, would seem to have the effect of perpetuating disadvantages rather than overcoming them.

Since opposition to differentiated curricula is probably a minority position among educationists and one that has been subject in the past to charges ranging from unrealism to cruelty, I should be careful to describe what this position does *not* imply as well as what it implies:

1. It does *not* mean that the high school as an institution should abandon responsibility for developing marketable skills, particularly for those students who will receive no further training or education. It *does* mean that school subjects for all students can be justified on grounds other than vocational aspiration. Getting and holding a job is obviously an important element in one's life, and a good education takes this into account. But every man is more, far more, than a job holder, and anyone who interprets education primarily in terms of one's vocational ambitions has a tragically limited view of the educational enterprise.

2. It does *not* mean that students ought to be denied the opportunity to exercise some choice in what they will study. It *does* mean that the student should exercise this choice on the basis of *individual* interest and ability and not because he has been labeled as belonging to a certain group. To assign students to tracks, whether they are called college-preparatory, general, and vocational, or robins, bluebirds, and sparrows, is a poor way indeed to take into account the many manifestations of individuality.

3. Most of all, it does *not* mean that disadvantages, whether attributable to poverty or any other source, should be ignored. It *does* mean that the disadvantaged must have the same opportunity to develop intellectual competence that everyone else has. Even under our much imitated system of universal education in the most prosperous society the world has ever produced, we still offer our citizens essentially one opportunity only to become initiated into the world of ideas. In a world where ideas and intellectual competence are increasingly prized, we rarely allow a second chance. If that chance is not taken in the period of childhood through adolescence it is, for all intents and purposes, lost. Nothing could be more inimical to the American Dream than a system of schooling which acts to

deny a segment of our population that one opportunity to participate in the cultural mainstream of modern society.

The schools have a special responsibility to those in our society who, through prejudice, poverty, or adverse social conditions, have been denied access to our society's cultural resources. It is a flat admission of failure to interpret that responsibility in terms of the narrowly vocational. No one would question that to teach truly disadvantaged children to think and to use knowledge effectively is an extraordinarily difficult task, but the American experiment in mass quality education is still too new to be abandoned.

Comments

1. The question raised by this article is as timely as it is important. With the modern view of ability as something one develops as a result of interaction with the environment, there is no excuse for denying certain children the opportunity for growth and later personal and vocational success. Let us not underestimate human potentiality. As Tyler (1959, see 255) points out, every decision we make places another constraint on our later freedoms and later achievements. The question of assigning a student to a course in practical mathematics rather than algebra is not to be taken lightly when this can be the beginning of a long series of consequences revolving around the differences between eligibility and non-eligibility for college, for example. Vernon (1958) raises a similar question regarding the British system of allocating students to an academic or a vocational program at the beginning of high school.

2. The question of learning styles (Riessman, 1966, 309) and cognitive styles (Kagan, 1966, 135) is another dimension of the same problem. While it is perhaps true that certain children learn better one way than another, might we be on safer ground to expect them to develop the ability to profit from a variety of approaches rather than to cater to their current style of learning? By allowing them to restrict themselves to their peculiar style of learning, are we also allowing them to cut themselves off from later adequacy in meeting the demands of the mainstream culture?

References

Clark, Kenneth R. *Dark Ghetto.* New York: Harper & Row, Publishers, 1965.
Finney, R. L. *A Sociological Philosophy of Education.* New York: The Macmillan Company, 1929.
Hall, G. S. *Adolescence.* New York: Appleton-Century Crofts, 1904.
Johnston, C. H. "Curriculum adjustments in modern high schools," 1914. Quoted in E. A. Krug. *The Shaping of the American High School.* New York: Harper & Row, Publishers, 1964.

Levine, D. U. "Differentiating instruction for disadvantaged children," *Educ. Forum,* 30: 144, 1966.

Neff, F. C. "Let them eat cake," *Educ. Forum,* 28: 405–410, 1964.

Noll, J. O. "An investigation of the relation of anxiety to learning and retention," *Diss. Abstr.,* 15: 1916, 1955.

Sledd, J. "On not teaching English usage," *Engl. J.,* 54: 701, 1965.

Vernon, Philip E. "Education and the psychology of individual differences," *Harv. educ. Rev.,* 28:91–104, 1958.

That's What They Said

"The concept of personality does not lend itself to concise description, for it corresponds to no single or simple attribute of human life. Personality does not depend on one or a few characteristics only, but upon the interplay of practically all of an individual's qualities. Physical structure, chemical functioning, learned motives, and habits of adjustment all contribute to personality, and not as separate entities but as interacting aspects of an organized system."

> Laurance F. Shaffer and Edward J. Shoben. *The Psychology of Adjustment.* Boston: Houghton Mifflin Company, 1956. [310]

"No person has an unlimited amount of energy available and the anxious child invests so much of his energy in his problems that there is little left over to conduct the ordinary affairs of life."

> Robert F. Peck and James V. Mitchell. *What Research Says to the Teacher.* No. 24. Washington: American Educational Research Association, 1962. [15]

"It is because man is maladjusted that he is unique in Nature. From his maladjustment—evident in the chasm between aspiration and capacity, vision and performance—spring all the distinctively human activities: scientific inquiry, artistic creation, philosophical speculation, and—the supporting condition of them all—historical experience."

> M. V. C. Jeffreys. *Personal Values in the Modern World.* Baltimore: Penguin Books, Inc., 1968. [125]

"They are not a different *kind* of people; they simply present more extreme forms of quite ordinary behavior. 'Everyone's queer but thee and me'—and we wouldn't know about ourselves, of course. In a sense, there are no 'crazy' people—there are only 'crazy' ways of behaving. And we all behave in those ways more or less."

> Wendell Johnson. *People in Quandaries.* New York: Harper & Row, Publishers. 1946. [12]

"Misfits are the unfortunate souls who never have the good luck to find the niche in which they might excel and who lack the initiative to create one."

> Don Robinson. "Scraps from a teacher's notebook," *Phi Delta Kappan,* 45: 357, 1964.

"In the not-too-distant future, the motivational and emotional conditions of normal life will probably be maintained in any desired state through the use of drugs."

> B. F. Skinner. "The control of human behavior," *Trans., New York Academy of Sciences,* 17: 547–551, 1955. [549]

"The trouble with the younger generation is that they are growing up to be no better than their parents."

> Henry C. Lindgren. *Educational Psychology in the Classroom.* New York: John Wiley & Sons, Inc., 1956. [153]

"Everybody has his potential breaking point at any given time in his life. A personality defect may go unrecognized until the individual is called upon to face some challenge which unduly taxes his personal resources. Then the inadequacy is rudely exposed."

> Wayland F. Vaughn. *Personal and Social Adjustment.* New York: Odyssey Press, 1952. [3–4]

"Some timid souls would rather read about life than participate in living. Probing into dusty tomes in a library may serve as a retreat from the headaches of society, providing at one and the same time isolation and the prestige of scholarship."

> Wayland F. Vaughn. 1952. Ibid. [60]

". . . personality change appears to be very difficult for those who think it is difficult, if not impossible, and much easier for those who think it can be done."

> David C. McClelland. "Toward a theory of motive acquisition," *Amer. Psychol.,* 20: 321–333, 1965. [322]

"The neurotic type of individual demonstrates how a person proceeds to make a failure out of living. He guarantees his own unhappiness by following certain patterns of behavior which are fundamentally maladjustive: evading responsibilities, making excuses for himself, losing self-confidence, going around with a chip on his shoulder, using illness to win sympathy, resorting to tricks to get his own way, indulging in self-pity to protect his self-esteem."

> Wayland F. Vaughn. 1952. Op. cit. [20]

"The remark about the New England conscience, that it doesn't stop you from doing what you want to do but it does take all the fun out of it, sums up in a nutshell the psychology of the 'neurotic compromise.' The neurotic knows very well that he is not supposed to do something. He goes ahead just the same, then suffers the consequences when his superego gets after him. After paying the penalty, he repeats the prohibited pleasure and pays for it again with remorse. This circle of events can go on indefinitely."

> Wayland F. Vaughn. 1952. Op. cit. [305–306]

". . . The child who fails to find satisfaction for his organic, emotional, or social needs must find ways of reconciling these failures with the necessity of maintaining his self-respect. If he is unable to achieve essential recognition because he has been unable to attain his goal, he then is compelled to devise some means of restoring and protecting his ego. It becomes intolerable to sit by and admit his incapacity. It may be impossible to ignore his defeat, but at least it must be made plausible, unavoidable, or reasonable in the eyes of himself and others."

> Henry Beaumont and F. G. Macomber. *Psychological Factors in Education.* New York: McGraw-Hill, Inc., 1949. [265]

"The greater 'freedom' which boys are allowed in the sphere of sex and in other spheres (such as fighting and other expressions of hostility) may to a large extent be an illusion. If along with a greater appearance of outward freedom there still is a tendency toward self-blame, then the outer freedom merely invites trouble. To the extent that moral codes, in their practical interpretation, but not in their personal implications, make it easier for a boy to exploit his desires and to express his resentments, such codes make it harder rather than easier to be a boy. Stated more figuratively, greater freedom to sin, without greater freedom from scruple aroused by sin, is not a very beneficial kind of freedom.

"So, the male child, while allowed more freedom in some ways, does not have the immunity that should go with freedom if it were complete, and he may have more on his conscience."

> Arthur T. Jersild. *Child Psychology.* Englewood Cliffs: Prentice-Hall, 1954. [264]

"The student who gives up says it's not worthwhile; he doesn't try; he is the one we fail. He may be the one shrewd enough and strong-willed enough to know that all this is meaningless for him. In failing him (and if we have no alternative program we must fail him) we are merely labeling him as a non-conformist."

> Don Robinson. "Scraps from a teacher's notebook," *Phi Delta Kappan,* 42: 269, 1961.

"The education of the young is always one generation out of date. We can only educate by the standards of our own generation, not by those of the next."

Don Robinson. "Scraps from a teacher's notebook," *Phi Delta Kappan*, 45: 474, 1964.

"It is not easy to abandon traditional ideas and methods in favor of a more enlightened approach to delinquency. Unfortunately, it is more satisfying emotionally to punish a youthful delinquent than to spend a great deal of time, patience, and energy in understanding and working with him. The policy of patience and understanding does not go down well with citizens who want immediate action."

Henry C. Lindgren. 1962. Op. cit. [490]

"In other words, the behavior of the parents of delinquent children is such as to alienate their offspring rather than to draw them closer. The social tragedy of this state of affairs lies in the fact that the parents are not only distinctive persons; they are the representatives of society to the developing youngster. In learning that their parents are unfair, unencouraging, and unloving, delinquents act as if they had also learned that the world in general is unfair, unencouraging, and unloving. It can accurately be said that these children have learned to want to be *unlike* their parents. More technically, they have learned motives that are at variance both with their community and with their own long-term happiness. This unfortunate motivational learning has occurred through the mediation of undesirable models, the parents, who have inadequately represented society at large to their growing children. The 'home curriculum' may not have been planned but it is startlingly effective.

"Against this instance of social learning, it may be asked what the teacher represents. Of what is she a model?"

Edward J. Shoben. "Viewpoints from related discipline: Learning theory," *T. C. Rec.*, 60: 272–282, 1959. [273]

"There is a general rule about parents: The less mother knows what to do with a child, the better she knows what the father should do. This applies equally for the relationship between teacher and parents. If the teacher were able to deal effectively with her pupils, she would not need to complain about the lack of cooperation on the part of the parents."

Rudolf Dreikurs. *Psychology in the Classroom.* New York: Harper & Row, Publishers, 1968. [9]

"Understanding the causes of delinquency alone will not solve the difficulty, but there is no use discussing the role of the schools until there is some understanding of the nature of the trouble. It is not a profound observation, but it is probably basic to note that delinquency, like swollen tonsils, is a symptom more than it is a cause. If we as educators have little opportunity to treat the disease—if our role is limited to giving aspirin—then we ought to know it, and we ought to make it clear that we know."

> Stanley Elam. "Editorial," *Phi Delta Kappan*, 39: 161, 1958.

"It is rather futile for the juvenile court to attempt to deal constructively with the truancy problem until the school curriculum has been modified to fit the child. . . ."

> M. E. Kirkpatrick and T. Lorge. "Some factors in truancy," *Ment. Hyg.*, 19: 610–618, 1935. [618]

"The lower-class child is 'systematically punished' for what he *is* and not for what he *does*. It is therefore impossible for him to learn what behavioral patterns are instrumental in obtaining reward or in avoiding punishment."

> W. W. Charters. "The social background of teaching," in N. L. Gage (ed.), *Handbook of Research on Teaching*. Skokie, Ill.: Rand McNally & Company, 1963. Pp. 715–813. [735]

"The machine now has a high school education in the sense that it can do most jobs that a high school graduate can do, so machines will get the jobs because they work for less than a living wage. A person needs fourteen years of education to compete with machines."

> Secretary Willard Wirtz. Cited in *Phi Delta Kappan*, 46: 354, 1965.

"Why must schoolmen continue to toss around the slippery figures relating attendance to employment and income? One of ten who did not finish high school is unemployed while only one of fifty high school graduates is jobless. What does this prove? Surely not that if everyone finished high school unemployment would disappear."

> Don Robinson. "Scraps from a teacher's notebook," *Phi Delta Kappan*, 46: 414, 1965.

CHAPTER 18

Test Items

1. The concept of personal and social adjustment pertains primarily to
   a. human effectiveness
   b. need satisfaction
   c. personal and social productivity
   d. personal happiness
   e. self-actualization

2. Adjustment refers to
   a. the adequacy of the behavior patterns through which the individual typically satisfies his needs
   b. freedom from overreliance of the usual "adjustment" mechanism
   c. the relative absence of conflict and self-defeating behavior
   d. the relative absence of tensions and anxieties
   e. the relative success of the individual in coping with situational demands

3. Adjustment is best visualized as
   a. a condition or state
   b. a goal
   c. an ideal
   d. an incentive
   e. a process

4. An adjustment situation involving two alternatives each with its attraction and its repulsion value would be known as _____ conflict.
   a. a double approach–avoidance
   b. an ambivalence
   c. an approach–approach
   d. an approach–avoidance
   e. an avoidance–approach

5. Anxiety differs from fear in that
   a. it is more intense and devastating
   b. it is more likely to lead to inappropriate behavior
   c. it is more localized as to object of focus
   d. it is more pervasive and longer-lasting
   e. it is more readily alleviated

6. The most common outcome of anxiety is
   a. experimental neurosis
   b. functional fixity
   c. personal maladjustment
   d. phobia
   e. restriction of the perceptual field

7. Dollard is to Barker as
   a. aggression is to regression
   b. displacement is to repression
   c. fixity is to fixation
   d. frustration is to hostility
   e. neurosis is to psychosis

8. Frustration–aggression is to Dollard as
   a. adjustment mechanisms is to Shaffer
   b. behavioral rigidity is to Maier
   c. deterioration of constructive activity is to Barker
   d. learning is to Thorndike
   e. regression is to Freud

9. Which is the *incorrect* association?
   a. Barker—regression
   b. Dollard—aggression
   c. Freud—repression
   d. Horney—displacement
   e. Maier—functional fixity

10. The development of adjustment is best approached from the standpoint of
   a. character formation
   b. the drive-reduction theory
   c. frustration theory
   d. learning theory
   e. socialization

11. The adjustment patterns most likely to lead to maladjustment are those that
   a. are essentially effective
   b. are highly effective
   c. are partially effective
   d. are totally ineffective
   e. produce definitely noxious results

12. The quality of the individual's adjustment depends on the consequences of his behavior. Which of the following is *not* correct?
    a. Behavior in violation of the social code that leads to satisfaction
    also leads to delinquency.
    b. Behavior that leads to systematic reward also leads to adjustment.
    c. Ineffective behavior leads to further trial.
    d. In (a) above, if the individual has internalized the social code,
    such behavior will lead to guilt.
    e. Partially effective behavior leads to maladjustment.

13. The crucial feature of personality is
    a. the balance of one's assets and liabilities
    b. the dependability of one's reactions
    c. the integration of one's assets and liabilities into a functional
    organism
    d. the special characteristics that set one apart as an individual
    e. one's adjustment–maladjustment balance

14. Which of the following is generally *not* considered a basic dimension
of personality?
    a. affective
    b. cognitive
    c. moral
    d. personal
    e. social

15. Which is the *incorrect* association of personality theory and its sponsor?
    a. learning theories—Hilgard
    b. learning theories—Sheldon
    c. personality dynamics—Lewin
    d. self theory—Rogers
    e. trait theories—Cattell

16. The primary factor involved in school dropout is
    a. the gap between pupil ability and academic demands
    b. incompatibility between student and the peer culture
    c. the lack of orientation of the home and community to the value
    of education
    d. the negative view of the school characteristic of the lower-class
    child
    e. the unsuitability of the school's curriculum

17. Which of the following theories of personality, in one form or another, is probably most widely accepted in modern psychology?
    a. developmental theories
    b. learning theories
    c. phenomenological theories
    d. role theories
    e. trait theories

18. Probably the most acceptable definition of maladjustment is in terms of _____ view.
    a. medical
    b. pathological
    c. the self-actualizing
    d. social functioning
    e. statistical

19. Which of the following is not a basic dimension of personality adjustment?
    a. the affective
    b. the cognitive
    c. the personal
    d. the phenomenological
    e. the social

20. Probably the major symptom of maladjustment is
    a. a general tendency to evade the problems of life
    b. hysterical symptoms
    c. immaturity
    d. persistent anxiety and feelings of insecurity
    e. repressed hostility

21. The well-adjusted person is characterized primarily by
    a. drive, leadership, and effectiveness
    b. freedom from conflict
    c. personal integration and openness to experience
    d. sensitivity to social pressures and conformity to social constraints
    e. spontaneity, decisiveness, and zest

22. Adjustment mechanisms are
    a. habits maintained through functional autonomy
    b. learned behavior patterns used in response to environmental demands
    c. need-satisfying reactions
    d. personality disorders
    e. symptoms of maladjustment

23. Defense mechanisms are to withdrawal mechanisms as
    a. adjustment is to maladjustment
    b. aggression is to response
    c. compensation is to hysteria
    d. lying is to rationalization
    e. protection is to reaction formation

24. Which of the following is *not* a pair from the standpoint of belonging to the same classification?
    a. compensation—sublimation
    b. fantasy—regression
    c. hysteria—phobia
    d. procrastination—reaction formation
    e. projection—rationalization

25. A distinguishing feature of phobia (as opposed to fear) is
    a. chronic repetitive behavior
    b. displacement
    c. hysteria
    d. reaction formation
    e. repressed guilt

26. Which of the following is the best statement of the quality of a given adjustment mechanism?
    a. Adjustment mechanisms are undesirable only when they introduce greater problems than they solve.
    b. Adjustment mechanisms are neither good nor bad apart from who uses them and why.
    c. Adjustment mechanisms are bad only when they close off the avenues to experience.
    d. The basic orientation is whether they serve overall personal and social purposes.
    e. The question of adjustment/maladjustment is primarily a matter of degree.

27. The task of helping individual children achieve effective behavior falls primarily on
    a. the counselor
    b. the parents
    c. the peer group
    d. the school psychologist
    e. the teacher

28. The major cause of juvenile delinquency is
    a. failure to identify with the positive forces of the social order
    b. failure to internalize social values
    c. ineffective early child-rearing practices
    d. the misorientation of the value system of the peer culture
    e. unsuitable curricular demands

29. Which of the following is *not* characteristic of the juvenile delinquent?
    a. high leadership potential
    b. hostility, defiance and lack of commitment to dominant social values
    c. inability to foresee the consequences of one's behavior
    d. a mesomorphic body-build
    e. personal maladjustment

30. The most significant aspects of the pupil's overall development are probably best appraised through
    a. objective tests
    b. psychiatric examination
    c. questionnaire responses
    d. sociometric techniques
    e. teacher observation

31. Juvenile delinquency is best approached from the standpoint of
    a. character (conscience) development
    b. the deterring effects of punishment
    c. the development of a positive self-concept
    d. the innate predisposition to misbehavior as part of the problem of establishing one's identity
    e. the redirection of motivation through selective reinforcement

32. Which is the *incorrect* statement of the effect of various home climates on personality development?
    a. The authoritarian home produces either compulsive overachievers or rebellious children.
    b. The overly permissive home produces irresponsible children with weak consciences.
    c. The overprotective home produces immature, insecure, jealous children.
    d. The overstrict home produces blind conformists with a high degree of repressed hostility.
    e. Permissive parents have spoiled, dependent, and insecure children.

33. Generally speaking, the aspect of pupil appraisal of greatest overall significance to his long-range welfare is his
    a. academic status and progress
    b. attitudinal structure
    c. intellectual competence
    d. motivational structure
    e. social sensitivity

CHAPTER 19

Mental Health
in the Classroom

Although the primary responsibility for the mental health of the child lies with the home and although all of society must share in this responsibility, operationally a good share of the burden must necessarily fall upon the school as part of its overall educational function. Actually, the school is in a strategic position here; not only is it easier to promote positive growth through challenging educational experiences than to reverse self-defeating behavioral patterns through therapy but, by providing continuous opportunity for reality testing, the school is in an ideal position to promote self-identification and positive behavior modification. The school's task is to capitalize on meaningful curricular experiences adequately fitted to individual differences as well as on the social setting of the classroom as its two major allies in promoting personal growth. Yet, the mental health function is typically assigned to the school on the basis of default on the part of other social agencies and, in view of the increased demands on the school, an attempt might be made to have these other agencies assume part of the burden, e.g., provide more adequate referral services and other facilities that would expedite the operation of the school and minimize the frustration of teachers who, despite obvious lack of qualification, invariably find themselves having to function as therapists. On the other hand, it is undoubtedly the teacher who plays the major role in determining whether school experiences will be profitable, neutral, or even harmful to children, individually and collectively, for it is he who sets the tone of the four-way interaction between teacher, learner, curriculum, and method; it is he who sets the emotional climate of the classroom through which children will find either self-fulfillment or, on the contrary, self-destruction.

The first paper in this chapter is by Beilin who finds that teachers now have a better understanding of the mental health implication of pupil problem behavior than did their earlier counterparts. But then, in the second article, Hoyt reports that, contrary to what one might logically expect, a teacher's knowledge of the characteristics of his pupils is not reflected in the latter's greater adjustment or academic achievement. At the operational level, Davidson and Lang point to the importance of teacher–pupil interaction as a factor in promoting wholesome pupil self-perception. Finally, in a more general article, Ausubel points to a number of misconceptions underlying current mental health practices in our schools.

Harry Beilin

Teachers' and Clinicians' Attitudes toward the Behavior Problems of Children *

Wickman's *Children's Behavior and Teachers' Attitude* (1928) showed a sharp contrast between the seriousness attributed by teachers and mental hygienists to the behavior problems of elementary school children: mental hygienists expressed greatest concern over withdrawal and other forms of nonsocial behavior, whereas teachers attached greatest seriousness to the problems relating to classroom management. The present report reviews the literature over the thirty years since the publication of Wickman's study.

Wickman had teachers from thirteen schools and two additional teacher groups enrolled in graduate study rate fifty items of undesirable pupil (problem) behavior, then had thirty mental hygienists rate the same problem behaviors. The instructions to teachers stressed present problems and the seriousness of the difficulties created by them. With clinicians, on the other hand, the instruction emphasized relevance of the problem behavior for *future* adjustment and though "seriousness" and "difficulty" were retained, the focus was on the clinical significance of the behavior.

The principal results can be summarized as follows:

(a)   Teachers were most concerned with aggressive behavior, inattention to school tasks, and behavior which violated their standards of morality. They were much less concerned with behavior indicative of social and emotional maladjustment not directly interfering with school routine. Mental hygienists, by contrast, were concerned over withdrawing and other nonsocial behavior and minimized the seriousness of anti-social behavior and violations of school rules.

(b)   A correlation of .11 was found between the rankings of the 50 behavior problems by mental hygienists and those by the total sample of teachers.

(c)   Boys were more frequently than girls associated with behavior problems. Teachers preferred the less active, more compliant be-

* Adapted and abridged from Harry Beilin, "Teachers' and clinicians' attitudes toward the behavior problems of children," *Child Devel.*, 30: 9–25, 1959. Copyright 1959 by the Society for Research in Child Development, Inc., and reproduced by permission.

havior of girls to the more aggressive behavior of boys. For teachers, then, desirable behavior took on the distinguishing characteristics of "girl behavior."

A number of objections to Wickman's findings and interpretations have been presented. Watson, for example, questioned whether the views of the mental hygienists toward the behavior problems of children can be considered an adequate criterion. He also pointed out that there has been too ready an acceptance of a causal relationship between withdrawal behavior in childhood and maladjustment in adulthood, a relationship which certainly had not been proved in 1928 and is perhaps even now relatively inconclusive. A large number of studies have been conducted duplicating or in some way modifying Wickman's original study. These studies suggest that lack of uniformity in the directions to the two groups contributed to the differences in their ratings. However, even when identical directions are given, differences still remain; there are also differences between elementary and secondary teachers as to their agreement with clinician judgment.

The studies reviewed agree that boys are more likely than girls to be identified as behavior "cases"—presumably because girls are more likely to comply with expected behavioral patterns. As Wickman suggests, teachers tend to be disturbed by behavior which interferes with their teaching. More pertinent, there is evidence to show that in the 30 years since Wickman's study, teacher attitudes have undergone substantial changes so that they approximate more closely those of clinicians. There is also some possibility that clinicians have tempered their evaluations as well.

Teacher–clinician differences in viewpoint as to the severity of behavior problems undoubtedly reflect differences in function. The prevailing philosophy of education in 1927, "whether explicit or implicit, was oriented to the training of intellectual skills." The teacher must remain task-oriented; the clinician, by contrast, is adjustment-oriented. Under the circumstances, it seems unrealistic to expect teachers' attitudes to coincide with those of clinicians. The teacher has a vital role in the socialization of the child. She is, after all, a culture carrier and to some extent a parental surrogate. There is no question that the teacher needs to be aware of withdrawing and other undesirable personality characteristics. What is questioned is the need for the teacher to concern herself with them to the same extent and in the same way as the clinician.

Comments

1.   This is an important synthesis of a number and variety of studies on the mental hygiene orientation of teachers. The fact that there is greater convergence in viewpoint between teachers and clinicians is en-

couraging; perhaps complete agreement is not to be expected as long as teachers remain teachers and therapists remain therapists. While clinicians can afford to think in terms of the long run, teachers have to maintain reasonable classroom decorum here and now and, in so doing, at times make the mistake of favoring withdrawal behavior and of suppressing overtly aggressive (symptomatic) behavior without thought of the consequences. Nor has it been established that clinician judgment is the ultimate criterion of teacher "enlightenment" as to the severity of problem behavior in children.

2.   In a repetition of the Wickman study, Stouffer (1952) concluded that the behavior problem child in school in 1952 was still, as he was 25 years before, identified chiefly by annoying, disorderly, irresponsible, aggressive, untruthful, and disobedient behavior. Teachers of today, however, are not so oblivious to behavior indicative of social and emotional maladjustment.

3.   It should also be noted that awareness of the Wickman study by today's teachers probably predisposes them to give clinically oriented (but invalid) responses. Another complication is that reported by Goldfarb (1963) who found that, while teachers can properly rank as to severity various behavior problems when presented as abstract concepts, they are not as competent in dealing with their behavioral counterparts. Apparently, teachers have been adequately instructed as to the correct ranking of behavioral problems but they cannot be relied upon to correctly diagnose for possible referral the severity of actual cases.

References

Goldfarb, Allan. "Teacher ratings in psychiatric case finding—Methodological considerations," *Amer. J. public Health,* 53: 1919–1927, 1963.

Stouffer, George A. "Behavior problems of children as viewed by teachers and mental hygienists," *Ment. Hyg.,* 36: 271–285, 1952.

Wickman, E. K. *Children's Behavior and Teachers' Attitudes.* New York: Commonwealth Fund, 1928.

Kenneth B. Hoyt

A Study of the Effects of Teacher Knowledge of Pupil Characteristics on Pupil Achievement and Attitudes toward Classwork *

Concern over individual differences existing in the classroom is meaningful only in terms of the actions which are taken as a consequence. This has prompted certain educators to insist that teachers be familiar with the characteristics of their pupils. The advisability of providing teachers with information concerning their pupils can be investigated only from the standpoint of the effects of such knowledge on the latter's achievement and relationships with the teacher.

The experiment was conducted over a period of six months with eighth-grade students in two junior high schools, further divided into six groups on the basis of sex and three levels of ability. The experimental variable consisted of three levels of information regarding students: (a) No-Information (N): teachers were simply given the names of their pupils; (b) Test-Score (TS): teachers were given their pupils' IQ and Cooperative Achievement test scores; (c) Test-Plus-Other-Information (TO): teachers had test scores plus other information; in addition, they were encouraged to discover all they could about their pupils.

Teacher knowledge of pupil characteristics did not by itself result in increased pupil achievement in mathematics, social studies, or English. This was true of the overall group and each of the six subgroups. On the other hand, there was a definite tendency for increases in teacher-knowledge of pupil characteristics to be associated with improved attitudes towards teachers; this improvement was not significantly related to sex or ability.

Comments

1.   This is one of a number of studies challenging the basic premise that the more teachers know about their pupils as individuals, the

* Adapted and abridged from Kenneth B. Hoyt, "A study of the effects of teacher knowledge of pupil characteristics on pupil achievement and attitudes toward classwork," *J. Educ. Psychol.*, 46: 302–310, 1955. Copyright 1955 by the American Psychological Association and reproduced by permission.

more effective they will be in teaching them. Research has given this premise only tentative and partial support; in some studies, the results have been nil. As suggested by Gage (1958), the onus of proof now lies with those who insist that teachers know their pupils. On the other hand, the apparent humanizing effect reflected in improved pupil attitudes may well justify the time and effort teachers expend in knowing more about their pupils.

2.   To the extent that testing and other techniques of pupil appraisal involves a considerable outlay, more definitive results might have been anticipated. The need for more meaningful data and for their more fruitful utilization is definitely indicated.

3.   It must be noted that, unless one knows exactly what specific "treatment" goes with that particular combination of pupil characteristics, he might as well treat all students alike rather than treat them differentially on the basis of false premises. It would seem that either we are not appraising the crucial student characteristics with adequate precision or we lack the insights and skills necessary to adapt our procedures to the characteristics of individual students as we have discovered them to be.

Reference

Gage, N. L. "Explorations in teachers' perceptions of pupils," *J. teach. Educ.,* 9: 97–101, 1958.

Helen H. Davidson and G. Lang

Children's Perceptions of Their Teacher's Feelings toward Them Related to Self-Perception, School Achievement, and Behavior *

The purpose of the study can be stated in terms of three basic hypotheses: There is a positive relationship between the children's perception of their teachers' feelings toward them and (a) the children's own perception of themselves; (b) their academic achievement; and (c) desirable classroom behavior. The subjects were 89 boys and 114 girls from Grades 4, 5, and 6 of above-average ability in reading but of diverse socio-economic status. The procedure involved successive administrations of a 35-adjective checklist, with the children responding first in terms of "My teachers think I am" and secondly in terms of "I think I am."

The results yielded strong support for all three hypotheses: The children's perceptions of their teachers' feelings toward them were significantly related to their perceptions of themselves, their academic achievement, and their classroom behavior. Among some of the other findings, the girls rated the teachers' feelings toward them as more favorable than did the boys. These findings are in line with the expectations derived from the literature. They are also in line with logic, especially in view of the overlapping among the variables: The ratings of achievement and of classroom behavior by the teachers and the children's perception of their teachers' feelings toward them are likely to have a common basis in the teachers' actual attitudes toward the children in question.

Comments

1.   The fact that the lower half of the group in reading ability was eliminated because of the difficulty of the checklist would tend to attenuate any relationship actually present.

2.   The fact that nine out of the ten teachers who did the ratings were women is probably not independent of the less favorable ratings

* Adapted and abridged from Helen H. Davidson and G. Lang, "Children's perceptions of their teacher's feelings toward them related to self-perception, school achievement, and behavior," *J. exper. Educ.*, 29: 107–118, 1960.

given the boys as to their teachers' feelings. There is evidence to suggest that women teachers (perhaps all teachers) do indeed treat girls better both in the feelings they display and their ratings of achievement and behavior.

       3.   Teachers need to be aware of the effects the feelings they communicate to children (perhaps unconsciously) have on the latter's self-concept.

       4.   The article should be consulted for a good discussion of the construction and validation of the instrument. Although the discussion is possibly more relevant in a course in tests and measurements, the fact that the results of any study cannot be any better than the instruments on which they are based makes the understanding of what constitutes an adequate instrument fundamental to any consideration of research data.

David P. Ausubel

Some Misconceptions Regarding Mental Health Functions and Practices in the School *

The school has undeniable responsibility with regard to mental health and personality development simply because it is the place where children spend a good part of their waking hours, where they perform much of their purposeful activities, where they obtain a large share of their status, and interact significantly with adults, agemates, and the demands of society. Nevertheless, inasmuch as the mental hygiene role of the school has been so often oversold and misrepresented, I would like to discuss some of the more serious misconceptions about mental health functions and practices in the school setting.

The Primary Responsibility of the School

We need to recognize that the primary and distinctive function of the school in our society is not to promote mental health and personality development but rather to foster intellectual growth and the assimilation of knowledge. The school does have important responsibilities with regard to the social, emotional, and moral aspects of pupil behavior but certainly not the primary responsibility. Its role in intellectual development, on the other hand, is incontrovertibly primary. Furthermore, much of the school's legitimate concern with interpersonal relations in the classroom stems not merely from interest in enhancing healthful personality development as an end in itself but rather reflects an appreciation of the negative effects which an unfavorable social and emotional school climate has on academic achievement, motivation to learn, and attitudes toward intellectual inquiry.

The Selection and Evaluation of Teachers

Educators have tended to overvalue the mental health implications of teacher–pupil relationships and the personality attributes of the teacher and to undervalue his intellectual functions and capabilities. Despite recent trends, placing ability to get along with people ahead of professional com-

* Adapted and abridged from *Psychol. Sch.,* 2: 99–105, 1965. By permission of author and publisher.

petence is self-evidently a dangerous state of affairs where professional personnel in any field of endeavor are concerned. The principal criterion in selecting and evaluating teachers should not be the extent to which their personality characteristics conform to the theoretical ideal but rather their ability to organize and present subject matter effectively, to explain ideas clearly, and to stimulate and competently direct pupil learning activities.

The Limits of Normality

Some educators exaggerate the seriousness and permanence of the effects on mental health of minor deviations from the norms of desirable hygienic practices. There is every reason to believe that a wide margin of safety is the rule, both in physical and mental health; within fairly broad limits, many different kinds of teacher personality structure and ways of relating to children are compatible with normal mental health and personality development in children. In general, children are not nearly as fragile as we profess to believe.

The Cult of Extroversion

We have succumbed to the cult of the warm, outgoing, amiable, and extroverted personality and have tended to regard any deviation from this standard as axiomatically undesirable from a mental hygiene standpoint. There is absolutely no evidence that teachers who happen to be shy and introverted impair their pupils' mental health, even though they may conceivably be less popular as individuals than their extroverted colleagues. In the same way, the pupil who is unpopular because of temperamental shyness or strong intellectual interests is not necessarily maladjusted or inevitably fated to become so.

The Effects of Authoritarianism

Many educators have uncritically accepted the premise that only democratic teacher–pupil relationships are compatible with normal mental health and personality development. Yet there are many examples of authoritarian western cultures (Germany, Italy, Switzerland) in which all the indices of mental health and mature personality development compare very favorably with those prevailing in America. It is obviously not authoritarianism per se that has damaging consequences but rather the incongruity between authoritarian practices in home and school and the general pattern of interpersonal relations in the culture at large. Children in an authoritarian home and school environment can satisfactorily internalize adult personality traits and mature attitudes toward authority provided that (a) personal, social, and working relationships among adults are similarly authoritarian, and (b) adults generally make as stringent demands on themselves as they do on young people. In Germany and Switzerland, where the latter conditions prevail, authoritarianism in school and home has few adverse effects on mental health and personality development.

In New Zealand, on the other hand, authoritarianism in the home and secondary school does have serious effects because it contrasts sharply with the egalitarian and generally relaxed character of adult social and vocational life. While the teenager who obtains a job or joins the Armed Services is treated like an adult, his secondary school counterpart is treated like a child and subjected to discipline which is stricter, more rigorous, and more restrictive than when he was in primary school. Under these circumstances, adolescents feel unjustly treated. Attributable at least in part to this incongruous authoritarianism of the secondary school are many immature attitudes toward authority displayed by New Zealanders who, on the one hand, tend to defer excessively to the opinions of authority figures and to overconform to their dictates, and, who, on the other hand, display a puerile defiance and an irresistible impulse to reject traditional values out-of-hand, to take outrageously extreme positions, and to shock the sensibilities of conventional folk with sacrilege, profanity, and the desecration of revered symbols. Moreover, because of resentment toward a discriminatory type of authoritarianism and over-habituation to external controls, many secondary school pupils fail to internalize recognized social norms and individual restraints. Hence, they feel quite justified in violating rules and asserting themselves when authority turns its back.

Distortions of Democratic Discipline

Proponents of democratic classroom discipline believe in imposing the minimal degree of external control necessary for socialization, personality maturation, conscience development, and emotional security. Discipline and obedience are not regarded as ends in themselves but only a means to these latter ends, which are expected to follow naturally in the wake of friendly and realistic teacher–pupil relationships. The democratic discipline is as rational, nonarbitrary, and bilateral as possible. It provides explanations, permits discussion, and invites the participation of children in the setting of standards where they are qualified to do so. Above all, it implies respect for the dignity of the individual and repudiates the use of sarcasm, ridicule, and intimidation and harsh, abusive, and vindictive forms of punishment.

These attributes of democratic classroom discipline are obviously appropriate in cultures where social relationships tend to be egalitarian. This type of discipline also becomes increasingly more feasible as children become older, more responsible, and more capable of understanding and formulating rules of conduct based on concepts of equity and reciprocal obligation. But contrary to what the extreme permissivists would have us believe, democratic school discipline does not imply freedom from all external constraints, standards, and direction, or freedom from discipline as an end in itself. And under no circumstances does it presuppose the elimination of all distinctions between pupil and teacher roles, or require that teachers abdicate responsibility for making the final decisions in the classroom.

Many educational theorists have distorted the ideal of democratic discipline by equating it with an extreme form of permissiveness. According to one widely held doctrine, for example, only "positive" forms of discipline are constructive and democratic. It is asserted that children must be guided only by reward and approval; that reproof and punishment are authoritarian, repressive, and reactionary expressions of adult hostility which leave permanent emotional scars on children's personalities. What the theorists conveniently choose to ignore, however, is the fact that it is impossible for children to learn what is *not* approved simply by generalizing in reverse from the approval they receive for behavior that is acceptable. There is good reason to believe that acknowledgment of wrongdoing and acceptance of punishment are part-and-parcel of learning moral accountability and developing a sound conscience. Few, if any, children are that fragile that they cannot take deserved punishment in stride.

A second distortion of democratic discipline is reflected in the popular notion that there are no culpably misbehaving children in the classroom, but only culpably aggressive, unsympathetic, and punitive teachers; that if children misbehave, one can implicitly assume that they must have been provoked beyond endurance by repressive and authoritarian classroom discipline. Similarly, if they are disrespectful, then the teacher, by definition, must not have been deserving of respect.

These distortions of classroom democracy are used to justify the commonly held belief among educators that pupils should not be reproved or punished for disorderly or discourteous conduct. I can only say that I am sufficiently old-fashioned to believe that rudeness and unruliness are not normally desirable classroom behavior in any culture. When such misconduct occurs, I believe pupils have to be unambiguously informed that it will not be tolerated and that any repetition of the same behavior will be punished. This action does not preclude in any way either an earnest attempt to discover why the misbehavior occurred, or suitable preventive measures aimed at correcting the underlying cause. But, by the same token, the mere fact that the pupil has a valid psychological reason for misbehaving does not mean that he is thereby absolved from moral accountability or rendered exempt from punishment.

Still another related distortion of democratic discipline is reflected in the proposition that it is repressive and authoritarian to request pupils to apologize for discourteous behavior or offensive language. Apology is the most civilized and effective means mankind has yet evolved for protecting human dignity from affront. In a democratic society, nobody is that important that he is above apologizing to those persons whom he has wrongfully offended. Everybody's dignity is important—the teacher's as well as the pupil's; it is no less wrong for a pupil to abuse a teacher than for a teacher to abuse a pupil.

In seeking to correct these undesirable permissive distortions of classroom democracy it would be foolhardy to return to the equally undesirable opposite extremes of authoritarianism. Democratic school discipline is still an appropriate and realistic goal for education in a democratic society. It is only necessary for us to discard the previously mentioned permissivist doctrines masquerading under the banners of democracy and behavioral sciences and to restore certain traditional values that have been neglected in the enthusiasm of extending democracy to home and school. First, we must stop equating permissiveness with democratic discipline and realistic adult control and guidance with authoritarianism. We should cease instructing teachers that it is repressive and reactionary to reprove or punish pupils for misconduct or to have them apologize for offensive and discourteous behavior. We should also stop making teachers feel guilty and personally responsible for all instances of misconduct and disrespect in the classroom.

We should refrain from misrepresenting our personal biases as the indisputably-established findings of scientific research. The available evidence merely suggests that in a democratic cultural setting, authoritarian discipline has certain undesirable effects—*not* that the consequences of laissez-faire permissiveness are desirable. In fact, research suggests that the effects of extreme permissiveness are just as unwholesome as those of authoritarianism. In a school situation, a laissez-faire policy leads to confusion, insecurity, and competition for power among pupils. Assertive pupils tend to become aggressive and ruthless, whereas retiring pupils tend to withdraw further from classroom participation. The child who is handled too permissively at home tends to regard himself as a specially privileged person. He fails to learn the normative standards and expectations of society, to set realistic goals for himself and to make reasonable demands on others. In his dealings with adults and other children he is domineering, aggressive, petulant, and capricious.

Finally, teachers' colleges should terminate the prevailing conspiracy of silence about the existence of disciplinary problems in the schools. Although discipline is the one aspect of teaching that the beginning teacher is most worried about, he receives little or no practical instruction in handling this problem. Due respect for the facts of life suggests that prospective teachers today not only need to be taught more realistic propositions about the nature and purposes of democratic discipline, but also require adequately supervised, down-to-earth experience in coping with classroom discipline.

Comments

1. The article makes a good deal of sense; while it does not prescribe specific alternatives, it at least sets straight some of the premises from which constructive classroom practices can evolve.

2. There is a great deal of confusion on the part of those in authority—parents, teachers, school administrators, law enforcement officers, our society in general—on how to assert themselves in the face of campus disorders, looting, vandalism, riots, and open defiance of law and order. The article by Bronfenbrenner (1961; Chapter 3) regarding the strong orientation of American parents toward permissiveness in child-rearing is interesting in this connection.

That's What They Said

"I have a strong belief that every learner should feel better, more able to cope with unknown vicissitudes more courageously at the end of a class than he did at the opening. If he feels worse, less able and less courageous, then the class has damaged him, rather than helped him. If this is oft repeated, then he is on his way to the human scrapheap."

> Earl C. Kelley. "The place of affective learning," *Educ. Lead.,* 22: 455–457, 1965. [457]

"When we speak of mental hygiene in the schools, we are not thinking of the teacher as standing between his pupils and their otherwise inevitable collapse."

> H. N. Rivlin. "The role of mental health in education," in N. B. Henry (ed.), *Mental Health in Modern Education.* 54th Yearbook, National Society for the Study of Education, Part II. Chicago: University of Chicago Press, 1955. Pp. 7–28. [13]

"Let there be no doubt that the pupils' learning to read, compute, and communicate is a responsibility of the school today just as it has ever been. The mental hygiene viewpoint merely emphasizes that this responsibility can best be carried out by recognizing that the 'whole child' goes to school—that learning is not simply a matter of mental activity."

> Harold W. Bernard. *Mental Hygiene for Classroom Teachers.* New York: McGraw-Hill, Inc., 1952. [87]

"It is in connection with the academic and social life of the school that many children have their most poignant experiences of failure, humiliation, and rejection."

> Arthur I. Gates et al. *Educational Psychology.* New York: The Macmillan Company, 1949. [104]

"In our adult-centered culture, we are inclined to think of children's behavior as something that should be brought into line with adult standards as soon as possible. Even though this attitude runs the risk of creating resistance to learning, it leads us to insist on the teacher domination of the learning situation."

> Henry C. Lindgren. *Educational Psychology in the Classroom.* New York: John Wiley & Sons, 1962. [318]

"For the majority of children the most effective mental health benefits they can derive from school is through the intrinsic quality of educational experience rather than by some sort of therapeutic regime that is grafted onto school life."

> Viola W. Bernard. "Teacher education in mental health," in Morris Krugman (ed.), *Orthopsychiatry in the School.* New York: American Orthopsychiatric Association, 1958. Pp. 184–203. [186]

"Probably the most important single contribution that the school can make to its students is to see that the emotional climate of the classroom is wholesome."

> H. N. Rivlin. 1955. Op. cit. [14]

". . . some matters have so intimate a bearing on the mental health of school children that attention to them is warranted. One of these is the 'complex,' which many teachers seem to have, that every question raised in class must be answered. To make it even more difficult, a teacher often feels that the answers must be phrased in the exact words that he had in mind when the question was asked."

> Harold W. Bernard. 1952. Op. cit. [201]

"Teachers are as susceptible to error as anyone, and perhaps more susceptible to the error of thinking they are not."

> Don Robinson. "Scraps from a teacher's notebook," *Phi Delta Kappan,* 47: 102, 1965.

"School should be a place where pupils can make mistakes without excessive risk; where they can experiment, try things out, test themselves, test ideas and feelings and impulses."

> Don Robinson. "Scraps from a teacher's notebook," *Phi Delta Kappan,* 49: 411, 1968.

"Making jobs available to people who have little interest in work, little belief in its rewards, and no skills, produces the paradox of continued unemployment together with labor shortage. We are thus in the unfortunate position of sitting on a powder keg and not knowing how to defuse it.

"The very existence of masses of chronically unemployed and unemployable youth testifies to the continued failure of counseling and guidance as professions and as a body of social institutions to meet the need."

> Jesse E. Gordon. "Project Cause, the federal anti-poverty program, and some implications for sub-professional training," *Amer. Psychol.,* 20: 334–343, 1965. [334–335]

"All discussions of mental health in the schools lead back to the personality and competence of the teacher."

> Ruth Strang. "Mental health," in Chester W. Harris (ed.), *Encyclopedia of Educational Research*. New York: The Macmillan Company, 1960. Pp. 823–835. [830]

"The occupation of teaching is unique with respect to need-fulfillment. It can afford opportunities for an altruistic, beneficent, and constructive kind of need fulfillment. It can unfortunately provide a setting for relatively vicious, destructive, and neurotic kinds of satisfactions."

> Robert F. Peck and James V. Mitchell. "What research says to the teacher," No. 24. *Mental Health*. Washington: American Educational Research Association, 1962. [20]

"A teacher is, by the very nature of his work, denied clear-cut, indisputable proof of his effectiveness."

> Robert H. Snow. "Anxieties and discontents in teaching," *Phi Delta Kappan,* 44: 318–321, 1963. [318]

"Teachers are inclined to set high standards for themselves. They are likely to be people who never quite achieve what they expect of themselves—that is, there tends to be a gap between their self-ideal and their self-concept. Therefore, when they find themselves the focal point of criticism, their sense of failure and guilt is heightened. A probable result of these pressures is the relatively high proportion of neurotic symptoms to be found in the teaching profession."

> Henry C. Lindgren. *Educational Psychology in the Classroom*. New York: John Wiley & Sons, Inc., 1956. [488]

"If the school is to promote healthy self-understanding and self-acceptance rather than serve only as a place where some of the symptoms of unhealthy self-regard are displayed, it will be necessary to re-examine the whole conception underlying our grade placement system, our standards, our so-called norms of achievement. It will be necessary to try to distinguish more rigorously than we have done in the past between competition that may be regarded as a sign of health and life and that which is a symptom of neurosis."

> Arthur T. Jersild. *In Search of Self*. New York: Teachers College, Columbia University, 1952. [92–93]

CHAPTER 19

Test Items

1. The increasing rate of mental illness in America is probably due pri-
    marily to
    a. better reporting
    b. our greater willingness to seek psychiatric help
    c. the increased percentage of old people in our population
    d. the increased tensions associated with an industrialized society
    e. the various crises that characterize our present society

2. Which is the most correct statistic of the incidence of mental illness in
    America?
    a. half a million mental patients at any one time in the nation's
        mental institutions
    b. in any given year, over half a million Americans receiving out-
        patient psychiatric care
    c. one of every 10 accidents having its roots in personality disorder
    d. one out of every four hospital beds occupied by people whose
        difficulty is primarily psychogenic
    e. some 10 percent of the adult population with criminal records

3. The most serious aspect of mental difficulty in terms of overall loss
    to American society is the high incidence of
    a. crime and delinquency
    b. general human ineffectiveness
    c. marital problems
    d. neurosis
    e. psychosis

4. The social agency in best position to deal with the nation's mental
    health problem is probably
    a. the medical profession
    b. the psychological profession
    c. the school
    d. society in general
    e. sociological and social case work personnel

5. The social agency having the greatest effect on the nation's mental
    health is
    a. the clinical profession
    b. the communication media

c. the home
d. the pediatric profession
e. the school

6. Mental hygiene in the school operates primarily through
   a. the academic curriculum
   b. the classroom and its teacher
   c. the guidance department
   d. its referral system
   e. a systematic program of pupil development

7. The first prerequisite to the mental health of the school child is
   a. ability to do satisfactory schoolwork
   b. a congenial peer group
   c. a genuine desire for self-improvement
   d. a good home base
   e. a suitable curriculum

8. The school's major contribution to the mental health of its children is most likely to be made within the framework of
   a. its diagnostic and referral services
   b. its guidance department
   c. the need-satisfaction possibilities of its academic program
   d. its social (sociometric) operation
   e. its teaching function

9. Mental hygiene as it operates in the classroom is best conceived as
   a. a body of knowledge and skill in its application
   b. a point of view relating to a wholesome classroom climate permeating every aspect of its operation
   c. a program of co-curricular activities designed to promote self-realization
   d. a systematic program dedicated to the self-realization of each individual student
   e. a systematic program of positive character development

10. The teacher's main responsibility with regard to mental hygiene in the classroom is
    a. to concentrate on the effective presentation of subject matter
    b. to provide each child with security and acceptance
    c. to provide the class with a meaningful curriculum
    d. to be sensitive to pupil needs
    e. to be thoroughly familiar with the symptoms of maladjustment

11. To be effective, the guidance and mental hygiene emphasis of the classroom must
    a. operate as an "advisory" program to the academics
    b. operate as a separate program independent of the other aspects of school
    c. be organized into a formal system of operation
    d. parallel and supplement but yet maintain separate identity from the academic program
    e. be totally integrated into and operate through the school's "educative" program

12. The teacher's major contribution to pupil mental health is for him
    a. to accept each child for what he is
    b. to be ever alert to the symptoms of maladjustment
    c. to lend a sympathetic ear to children having difficulty
    d. to see that the school does not aggravate the child's adjustment problem
    e. to see that school is for each child a meaningful and need-satisfying experience

13. The child in the school in greatest psychiatric danger is
    a. the aggressive competitive child
    b. the mischievous prankster
    c. the nonconformist
    d. the quiet "model" child
    e. the troublemaker

14. A common mental health hazard created by women teachers is for them
    a. to discourage aggressiveness on the part of boys and to encourage withdrawal on the part of girls
    b. to encourage defiance by unreasonable demands
    c. to insist on relatively complete conformity and submission
    d. to make children emotionally dependent upon them
    e. to squelch all symptoms of maladjustment, e. g., anger

15. The primary criterion in evaluating the mental health aspects of classroom discipline is:
    a. Are our regulations in keeping with natural pupil needs?
    b. How much "immature" behavior is part of normal growing up?
    c. Just how much pupil misbehavior is caused by the teacher's behavior?
    d. Just what causes children to behave as they do?
    e. To what extent are children learning self-discipline?

16. Which of the following is not a feature of autocratic discipline?
    a. It aggravates the "cause" of the original misbehavior.
    b. It feeds the teacher's ego and is therefore reinforcing.
    c. It promotes a high level of pupil productivity and is therefore reinforcing.
    d. It promotes resistance and precludes the development of mutual pupil–teacher respect and acceptance.
    e. It works at the superficial levels and is therefore reinforcing to the teacher.

17. The best overall interpretation of the Wickman study and subsequent studies on the same topic is that
    a. the assumption that teachers must agree with clinicians would be more correct if reversed
    b. it is difficult for this type of research to provide valid results
    c. teachers and clinicians cannot operate from the same point of reference
    d. teachers don't know what constitute real mental health hazards
    e. teachers tend to be more concerned with classroom decorum than the long-term development of the child

18. The greatest weakness of the Wickman study is that
    a. it assumed that teachers and clinicians ought to agree
    b. clinician ratings were assumed to be the standards
    c. it did not cover all behavior symptoms
    d. it was based on a relatively small number of cases
    e. the two groups were given different directions

19. The most serious mental health hazard in the school is probably
    a. its inability to cope with individual differences in ability
    b. its emphasis on discipline geared to the maintenance of classroom decorum
    c. the lack of a cohesive peer structure
    d. the teacher's inability to relate effectively with each of his pupils
    e. the unsuitability of the curriculum for a sizable minority of the students

20. The most significant precondition for a mentally healthy classroom atmosphere is
    a. a compatible peer group
    b. a competent, well-organized, well-adjusted teacher
    c. a curriculum meaningful from the standpoint of pupil goals, needs, and purposes
    d. an adequate referral system
    e. a relative, if not total, freedom from competition and coercion

21. Mental hygiene, education, and guidance differ in that
    a. education, in its true sense, encompasses both guidance and mental hygiene
    b. education refers to the acquisition of academic material
    c. guidance is geared primarily to long-range planning
    d. mental hygiene, education, and guidance, all proceed toward the same goals in much the same way
    e. mental hygiene is concerned almost exclusively with the avoidance of mental illness

22. Estimates suggest that _____ percent of teachers in the field are in need of psychiatric help.
    a. two
    b. five
    c. ten
    d. twenty
    e. forty

23. Probably the best suggestion for the maintenance of the positive mental health of the classroom teacher is
    a. for administrators to improve working conditions, e. g., reduce class load
    b. for the community to raise salaries so as to attract the better teachers
    c. for each teacher to assume responsibility for his own mental health
    d. for the principal to make all-around teacher growth and teacher morale an item of top priority in his administration
    e. for the state to upgrade certification standards

24. The mental health of the teacher is of major concern because of its effects on
    a. the academic success of his students
    b. his effectiveness as a person
    c. the efficient operation of the school
    d. the mental health of his students
    e. the public image of the school

25. The principal can contribute most to teacher mental health by
    a. eliminating such hazards as traditional grading, reporting, etc.
    b. emphasizing teacher morale and welfare
    c. improving teacher competence through systematic supervision
    d. freeing teachers from unnecessary chores and overloads

e. giving teachers moral support in conflicts with pupils and parents

26. What effect does teacher maladjustment have on pupil adjustment?
   a. The evidence as to the effect of teacher adjustment on pupil adjustment is controversial and equivocal.
   b. Maladjusted teachers produce maladjusted pupils.
   c. Maladjusted teachers who are aware of their problems have a decidedly beneficial effect on the mental health of their pupils.
   d. The only effect of teacher maladjustment on pupil adjustment is to aggravate the problems of the already damaged child.
   e. Teacher adjustment affects pupil adjustment only in preschool and primary grades.

27. The classroom under a "supportive" teacher is characterized by
   a. academic productivity
   b. efficient "routine" operation
   c. emotional attachment
   d. emphasis on character formation
   e. a student-centered curriculum

28. Which of the following is *not* one of the findings of research on teacher characteristics (e.g., Barr, Heil et al., Ryans)?
   a. Greatest pupil initiative is associated with teachers who are relatively lacking in organization and responsibility.
   b. Maladjusted teachers tend to have maladjusted students.
   c. The more information teachers have about their students the more effective they can be in helping them.
   d. Students known as "strivers" do equally well under all kinds of teachers.
   e. Systematic, responsible teachers tend to have docile classes.

29. All in all, the greatest mental health hazard facing the classroom teacher is
   a. the constant association with immature minds
   b. disappointment over inability to promote pupil progress or even to see such progress
   c. the heavy work load, large classes, low pay, and other adverse conditions
   d. monotony and loss of enthusiasm
   e. the petty and persistent teacher–pupil, teacher–administrator conflicts

30. Probably the most effective means of improving the mental health of the teaching profession is
    a. to eliminate mental health hazards, e. g., grading
    b. to improve the teacher's overall professional competence
    c. to improve teacher–pupil–administrator relationships by improving communication among them
    d. to improve the working conditions of teachers
    e. to select mentally stable prospective teachers

31. The primary responsibility for the teacher's mental health lies with
    a. the certification agencies
    b. the community
    c. the principal and school administrators
    d. the school counselor and psychologist
    e. the teacher himself

32. A major mental health hazard in teacher–administrator relationships is
    a. the administrator's overconcern with routine at the expense of the essentials of pupil growth
    b. the administrator's tendency toward autocratic rule as a means toward efficient school management
    c. the basic employer–employee relationship itself
    d. a lack of appreciation of their common role
    e. a lack of (or breakdown in) effective communication

PART V

Synthesis

CHAPTER 20

The Modern Classroom— *A Psychological Reorientation*

The school occupies a clearly strategic position with regard to the future of America and, indeed, of the world; it may even determine whether our culture will survive in these times of social unrest. Such an awesome responsibility may be more than the school is prepared for, or even capable of fulfilling. Nor is the situation helped by the fact that the school operates within the framework of a society characterized not only by serious conflicts and turmoils of its own but also by a tendency to pile on endless, often self-contradictory, demands for the school to be all things to all men, while, all along, lending only limited support to requests for improved facilities, reduced class loads, referral services, and other prerequisites to effective operations. Yet the primary responsibility is indeed ours, for this is the service we have contracted to provide. Excuses are never substitutes for accomplishments. Our task is twofold: First, we need to generate greater clarity as to the goals to be achieved. We seem to agree that helping the child "learn how to learn" is a more defensible form of education for tomorrow's world than is the accumulation of knowledge for knowledge's sake. What kind of a balance in emphasis might we strike between education as cognitive development and education of the individual along the lines of responsible citizenship, openness to experience, and other aspects of self-actualization? Secondly, we need to generate greater clarity as to the means for attaining the goals we have selected. The two articles selected for this section emphasize the need to relate the curriculum to the goals and purposes of the student. Corey presents a number of basic considerations in designing a curriculum for student development, while McKeachie compares the effectiveness of the student-centered and the instructor-centered approaches to teaching at the college level.

Stephen M. Corey

Designing a Curriculum for Student Development *

While everyone recognizes that in designing the secondary school curriculum we must take into account the needs and interests of adolescents,
there is no consensus as to the emphasis to be given thereto. Some feel that
the concerns of adolescents should be given top priority; others argue that,
while these concerns are important, they are apt to be ephemeral and transitory and that the major focus should be on the cognitive aspects of the
cultural heritage.

It is exceedingly fortunate that few high-school teachers and administrators claim, as do many university professors, that knowledge of subject
matter is all that is necessary for good teaching. Extensive familiarity with
academic content is a necessary, but not a sufficient, condition for effective
high school instruction. Sufficient conditions obtain only when there is
added to the teacher's mastery of subject matter a sympathetic understanding of the personal needs, interests, and wants of adolescent boys and girls.
Unless both types of competency characterize high school instruction, pupils will learn very little of benefit to them.

This does not mean that teen-agers are unique. Everybody in the
world learns only when he believes his learning will enable him to get
something that he personally wants. This fact is frequently lost sight of in
schools because they do not represent voluntary learning organizations in
the sense that an adult education program is usually voluntary. Rarely
does an adult educator state explicitly, or even imply: "We will give them
what is good for them whether they like it or not." If such an attitude were
acted upon, adult students would simply stay away. High school is different though; while, strictly speaking, high school students can also stay
away, the consequences are so unpleasant that a school must literally be
intolerable before youngsters will do so.

Compulsory education is not an unmixed blessing. It sometimes acts
as a deterrent to the improvement of the curriculum. As long as society requires that pupils attend a particular school, one excellent test of its value
is precluded, the natural test of the worth of any activity, namely, the

* Adapted and abridged from *N.A.S.S.P. Bull.*, 32: 101–110, 1948. By permission of author and publisher.

number of people who voluntarily choose to participate in it. Schools suffer from the sickness that is apt to characterize any monopoly.

Designing a curriculum that takes into account the developmental needs of adolescents requires that we learn a great deal about them. This is difficult learning; for one thing our age stands in our way. Teachers and administrators need to learn as much as they can about teen-age boys and girls; they need to study the psychology of adolescence, to recall their own adolescence, to study their pupils, etc. One of the major responsibilities of any secondary school is to help adolescent boys and girls achieve such developmental tasks as adjusting to their developing bodies, working out new relationships with their age-mates, particularly in the area of sexual adjustment, and developing more mature relationships with their parents and other adults. Boys and girls must become men and women. They must develop self-reliance, a sense of responsibility, and independence. They must learn to live on their own. They need practice trying to work out their destinies, and they must be permitted to suffer the consequences of their mistakes; or at least most of them.

I never visit a secondary school and watch the boys and girls mill through the corridors as they go from class to class without feeling humble in my ignorance as to what really is going on in their minds. I feel so often that the gap between them and me is almost unbridgeable. On the other hand, I know of no better exercise for a secondary school teacher or administrator than to work hard at the job of trying to find out what it is boys and girls value and think important. It is only through such understanding of adolescents that teaching can be made vital and meaningful; it is only through such understanding that the curriculum can actually be designed and built for student development.

Comment

The article is self-explanatory and to the point: It would be difficult to take issue with its basic thesis.

W. J. McKeachie

Student-Centered versus Instructor-Centered Instruction *

"Even psychologists have their stereotypes. And for most of us, 'student-centered' and 'instructor-centered' are stereotypes. With 'student-centered' we associate the halo terms of democratic, permissive, insight, affective, and student growth. 'Instructor-centered' brings to mind the terms authoritarian, Fascistic, knowledge for its own sake, and content-centered. In our psychological sub-culture, the mere labels in our title stack the deck against any one who attempts to defend the instructor-centered point of view" [p. 143].

Goals

The instructor-centered teacher sees himself as ultimately responsible for determining goals; the student-centered teacher, on the other hand, sees the goals determined cooperatively by the students and the instructor. There is also a difference in the types of goals toward which the two methods are oriented: The instructor-centered approach emphasizes "the traditional goals of a liberal education. It attempts to create an interest in 'knowledge for its own sake.' The primary goal is to teach students to think. The instructor may be interested in attitudes, but they are the attitudes of the scientist toward his subject matter, not social attitudes" [p. 144]. The student-centered instructor, by contrast, tends to emphasize affective goals and he is likely to be unhappy with having to rely heavily on course examinations as the criterion of the success of his efforts. There is, on the other hand, considerable overlap between the goals emphasized in the two teaching orientations.

Methods of Teaching

Other basic differences between the two approaches include a much higher degree of student participation and group cohesiveness in the stu-

* Adapted and abridged from W. J. McKeachie, "Student-centered versus instructor-centered instruction," *J. educ. Psychol.,* 45: 143–150, 1954. Copyright 1954 by the American Psychological Association, and reproduced by permission.

dent-centered approach, a greater feeling on the part of the student that he can influence his own fate, and a greater amount of time devoted to personal experiences.

Experimental Evidence

Despite the controversy over the years and the numerous studies on the subject, there has been no resolution of the problem. This does not mean that every one can go his own way and teach any way he pleases. "Personally, we are not willing to go quite so far, but certainly none of us should exclaim with horror: 'His classes are instructor-centered' " [p. 148]!

One of the reasons for our inability to reach a conclusive answer is that "student-centered" means different things to different people. An even more important reason is "that we have been lumping together more variables than we can handle with our experimental designs" [p. 148]. Nonetheless, some clarity is beginning to emerge. Smith and Johnson found the student-centered procedure to produce higher scores on tests of reasoning ability and creativity. "Furthermore, all research on the problem seems to agree that . . . student-centered teaching results in little decrement to the learning of facts (provided the classes have textbooks and tests are based on the texts)" [p. 149].

The problem of grades apparently presents the greatest obstacle to the success of the student-centered method: Students tend to prefer a directive method of teaching which makes clear what they have to do in order to pass the course. Judging from theoretical premises, "one would predict that the effect of instructor permissiveness would depend on whether or not the group possessed the skills necessary to achieve their goals. In a new group, the effect of instructor permissiveness may depend on the presence or absence of individuals . . . who have had previous experience in working in democratic groups. If the instructor retains control of rewards, permissiveness with respect to the means to the goal (such as assignments, classroom activities, etc.) may simply increase the ambiguity of the situation for the student and reduce student learning" [p. 150].

Comments

1.   This is but one of a series of studies conducted at the University of Michigan on student-centered versus instructor-centered teaching at the college level. See McKeachie (1963).

2.   The role of examinations in this connection is interesting. If the student's worth is to be judged on his performance on a test, his need to know what he will be evaluated on leads him to prefer the teach-

er-directed method where requirements and relative emphases are more clearly defined.

3.   In a similar study involving a graduate course in the psychology of child development, Rasmussen (1956) found no difference between students in instructor-centered and student-centered classes in test achievement. However, the members of the student-centered sections estimated that "they had learned more, that what they had learned would be of more practical use to them, that more attitude change had taken place as a result of the course, and that the classes had been more interesting," all differences significant at the .01 level. There was no significant difference, on the other hand, between the two groups in the amount of studying done in child psychology or in the use of the text as a reference during the six-month period following the class.

References

McKeachie, W. J. "Research on teaching at the college and university level," in N. L. Gage (ed.), *Handbook of Research on Teaching,* Skokie, Ill.: Rand McNally & Company, 1963. Pp. 1118–1172.

Rasmussen, Glen R. "An evaluation of a student-centered and instructor-centered method of conducting a graduate course in education," *J. educ. Psychol.,* 47: 449–461, 1956.

That's What They Said

"The present state of affairs of education in the United States has one heartening aspect. At long last, the potency of the school as a social institution is being recognized. Yet there is an almost frightening quality in the degree to which our effectiveness as a society, our progress as a nation, are currently perceived as dependent upon the relative excellence of our system of schooling."

> Barbara Biber. "Learning–teaching paradigm integrating intellectual and affective processes," in Eli M. Bower and William G. Hollister (eds.), *Behavioral Science Frontiers in Education*. New York: John Wiley & Sons, Inc., 1967. Pp. 115–155. [115]

"Education must make good on the concept that no child within our society is either unteachable or unreachable—that whenever a child appears at the doors of our schools he presents a direct challenge to us and to all our abilities. . . . For education, the question is not the environment that children bring to the school from the outside, but the environment the school provides from the inside."

> Francis Keppel. Cited in *Phi Delta Kappan,* 45: 302, 1964.

"The objectives of education, we have maintained, are not the mere acquisition of subject matter, such as geography, social science, algebra, and so on. This content may become the means for the growth of a pupil *if it makes a real difference in the way he meets problems.*"

> Nathaniel Cantor. *The Teaching-Learning Process*. New York: Holt, Rinehart and Winston, Inc., 1946. [203–204]

"Curriculum theorizing to date is best described as abstract speculation; curriculum research as 'dust bowl' empiricism; and curriculum practice as rule of thumb guesswork (often a wet thumb at that, held aloft to test the direction of the prevailing breeze)."

> John I. Goodlad. "Curriculum: The state of the field," *Rev. educ. Res.,* 30: 185–198, 1960. [195]

"An excellent example of the fruitless search for one grand method is that which sought to show that learner-centered instruction was superior to teacher-centered instruction. . . . Like many other efforts to locate the instructional pot of gold, the learner-centered method turned out to be an ill-defined, unspecified, and unreplicable collection of methods. The results of its use show a normal distribution of outcomes."

Lawrence M. Stolurow. "Model the master teacher and master the teaching model," in John D. Krumboltz (ed.), *Learning and the Educational Process*. Skokie, Ill.: Rand McNally & Company, 1965. Pp. 223–247. [225–226]

"Much educational practice is now based almost exclusively upon the idea that man has to be prodded or moved into action by an external force or stimulus. This notion that man is at the mercy of the external forces exerted upon him has led to a system of education that seeks to provide the forces necessary to move students from inertia to prescribed activity. The organism has been seen as a sort of inert mass of protoplasm or object to be molded—made into something."

Arthur W. Combs. *Perceiving, Behaving, Becoming*, 1962 Yearbook. Washington: Association for Supervision and Curriculum Development. 1962. [84]

"Our society can ill afford to waste a large proportion of the talent and other resources inherent in our population by holding on to ineffective educational procedures."

Ernest A. Haggard. "Learning: A process of change," *Educ. Lead.*, 13: 149–156, 1955. [150]

"In bygone days there was much talk of a student-centered curriculum as opposed to a content-centered curriculum, and the triumphant cliché was: 'I don't teach history; I teach students.' Whoever said that did not know much about English syntax and was probably a very poor teacher."

Robert B. MacLeod. "The teaching of psychology and the psychology we teach," *Amer. Psychol.*, 20: 344–352, 1965. [347]

"In short, the choice of instructor-dominated versus student-centered discussion techniques appears to depend upon one's goals. The more highly one values outcomes going beyond acquisition of knowledge, the more likely that student-centered methods will be preferred."

W. J. McKeachie. "Research on teaching at the college and university level," in N. L. Gage (ed.), *Handbook of Research on Teaching*. Skokie, Ill.: Rand McNally & Company, 1963. Pp. 1118–1172. [1141]

"People can learn, to be sure, from situations where they are treated as passive sponges, but this is pretty inefficient learning. It is a horse and buggy approach to a twentieth century problem. We can no longer afford the luxury of such inefficiency."

> Arthur W. Combs. 1962. Op. cit. [71]

"One of the shortcomings of traditional education is that it does not get the student sufficiently involved in a personal sense. The traditional concept of the student is that of an individual who passively absorbs the learning the teacher pours into him. Since we are beginning to realize that worthwhile and useful learning does not occur in this way, we have tried to develop techniques and approaches that will get children involved in the educational process."

> Henry C. Lindgren. *Educational Psychology in the Classroom.* New York: John Wiley & Sons, Inc., 1962. [336–337]

"We may teach with machines, with television, with teams of pre-professionals, para-professionals, and post-professionals, with overhead projectors and underhand methods, scientifically or artistically, and logically or illogically, but our efforts may all seem a bit foolish to our critics and more than ridiculous to our captive subjects if what we teach and what we reward, immediately or in Heaven, is something that makes little difference in the youth's struggles to attain self-regard and to attain acceptance from those who count in his world."

> Joseph Leese. "Highlights of research on teaching and learning," *High Sch. J.*, 45: 314–320, 1962. [319–320]

"When American schools are able to replace such techniques with *natural incentives, creative ability, realistic problems, freedom of choice, free play of cause and effect, allowance for mistakes and their inevitable results, and dependence on reward of what is accomplished,* American youth will be forever free from intellectual domination by dictators. What is more, they will be free to live and act fully in their own world, and will have the skills necessary to do so."

> A. D. Woodruff. *The Psychology of Teaching.* New York: Longmans, Green, 1951. [516]

"What we become tomorrow will be determined by the choices which we make today—what we become as a nation, what we develop in terms of schools, and what we produce as the kinds of persons coming from our schools."

> Gardner Murphy. *Human Potentialities.* New York: Basic Books, 1958. Paraphrased by Gordon N. Mackenzie in Alexander Frazier (ed.), *Freeing Capacity to Learn.* Fourth Research Institute. Washington: Association for Supervision and Curriculum Development, 1960. [6]

"It makes a great deal of difference . . . how we go about dealing with children if we believe they are fundamentally opposed to us or if we believe that they are basically seeking the same ends we are. We do not behave the same way toward our friends as we do toward our enemies."

Arthur W. Combs. 1962. Op. cit. [86]

"The fundamental business of the school at any level is to arrange matters so that children experience certain situations which are potentially educative and which children would not be likely to have unless they were deliberately provided by some agency or institution."

> G. Max Wingo. "Implications for improving instruction in the upper elementary grades," in N. B. Henry (ed.), *Learning and Instruction.* 49th Yearbook, National Society for the Study of Education, Part I. Chicago: University of Chicago Press, 1950. Pp. 280–303. [282]

"It may be that when teachers object to lack of integration in the newer methods [of instruction or classroom organization], they are referring to integration from the standpoint of the teacher, overlooking the fact that, in the final analysis, integration must be supplied by the student. It is the *student's* frame of reference that really counts in learning, not the teacher's."

Henry C. Lindgren. 1962. Op. cit. [310]

"The difficulty with the traditional approach to education is that its proponents tend to think that the educational problem has been solved if a teacher who is well grounded in subject-matter is placed in charge of a classroom. Traditionalists tend to be preoccupied with *teaching* rather than with *learning.*"

Henry C. Lindgren. 1962. Ibid. [294]

"As long as our schools persist in attempting to direct the child into activities which do not provide him with opportunities for immediate self-enhancement, children will show great ingenuity in avoiding these activities. They must do so in order to concentrate on their immediate personal problems, which are the only things important to them."

> Arthur W. Combs and Donald Snygg. *Individual Behavior.* New York: Harper & Row, Publishers, 1959. [370]

". . . the curriculum actually found in the school is too often a planned exercise in inertia instead of a confrontation with reality."

> Chris Buethe. "A curriculum of value," *Educ. Lead.,* 26: 31–33, 1968. [31]

CHAPTER 20

Test Items

1. Which of the following is the fundamental problem underlying educational practice?
    a. What adaptation should be made for individual differences?
    b. What are the real goals of education?
    c. What part of today's vast knowledge can we expect to teach?
    d. Who should be educated?
    e. Who should teach?

2. Significant education is perhaps best defined in
    a. ability to deal with materials of increased academic and cognitive complexity
    b. improved performance on some valid test of academic achievement
    c. increased insights into the self
    d. increased openness to experience
    e. increased vocational competence

3. The true essentials of education are best achieved through emphasis on
    a. academic competence
    b. democratic attitudes
    c. intellectual development (including creativity)
    d. personal growth
    e. social adjustment

4. The essentials of education are best defined in terms of
    a. academic content
    b. effective problem-solving skills
    c. self-actualization
    d. social adequacy
    e. vocational competence

5. The major indictment against today's school is probably
    a. its dominant authoritarianism
    b. its lack of clarity as to what its major goals and responsibility might be
    c. its overall inefficiency in accomplishing whatever it is trying to do

    d.   its overemphasis on the academics at the expense of overall pupil growth

    e.   the unsuitability of its curriculum and its operational practices for a large minority of its students

6.   The trouble with modern education is that

    a.   the concept of *school* as we know it is becoming progressively more irrelevant

    b.   the current curriculum is often irrelevant to today's world

    c.   the school is forced to teach all children regardless of their adequacy or motivation

    d.   for the school to operate as well as it used to is no longer good enough

    e.   the shortage of teachers has brought into the profession a large number of misfits

7.   The inefficiency of our schools is probably most clearly due to

    a.   the failure of teachers to operate according to the principles of psychology

    b.   the imposition by society of impossible demands and restrictions on the operation of the school

    c.   the lack of agreement as to what the school can and cannot do

    d.   overemphasis on the verbal, the abstract, and the technical

    e.   the relative divorce of the school's operation from the real world of the child's psychological space

8.   Philosophy is to psychology as

    a.   goal is to content

    b.   ideals are to attainables

    c.   long-term goals are to short-term goals

    d.   product is to process

    e.   teaching is to learning

9.   The major argument against education as a preparation for life is that such an education

    a.   is typically by definition out of phase with the child's current purposes

    b.   fails to take into consideration the child's present level of readiness

    c.   is prescribed in advance and therefore cannot capitalize on the opportunities of the situation

    d.   relies on the curriculum maker's ability to anticipate student interest

    e.   is difficult to synchronize with the child's evolving interest and purposes

10. With regard to the curriculum, psychology is primarily concerned with
    a. the appropriateness of the curriculum in relation to the major objectives of education
    b. the choice and use of the curriculum in promoting pupil growth
    c. the compatibility of curricular demands and pupil needs
    d. the content of the curriculum
    e. the logical continuity of curricular units

11. Ideally, the school's curriculum should comprise
    a. all educative experiences
    b. all positively educative experiences
    c. those experiences which are maximally productive of pupil growth
    d. those experiences which are primarily academic in nature
    e. a random sampling of the culture's major achievements

12. The curriculum should
    a. be life
    b. be like life
    c. be a preparation for life
    d. be an improvement on life
    e. be a selection and concentration of productive life experiences

13. The weakness of the teacher-centered approach stems primarily from
    a. its inability to capitalize on the spontaneous interests and purposes of the group
    b. its inability to deal with the motivational problem except through aversive control
    c. its inability to generate in the child the necessary readiness and perspective in an adult topic
    d. its inability to relate to the child's present purposes
    e. its general orientation toward adult goals and reliance on adult direction

14. The critical criterion in the selection of the curriculum is
    a. its contribution to academic and cognitive development
    b. its cultural significance
    c. its disciplinary (transfer) value
    d. its significance in terms of the child's goals and purposes
    e. its teachability at the particular grade level

15. The major impetus for curriculum change typically comes from
    a. general community (general public, PTA) demands
    b. leadership by noneducationist professionals
    c. pressures by minority pressure groups
    d. professional leadership based on professional insight
    e. state and regional accrediting agencies

16. The basic issue between the teacher-centered and the student-centered curriculum is
    a. the contents to which each best applies
    b. the degree of structure of the material
    c. their philosophical premises
    d. their relative amenability to evaluation
    e. their relative effectiveness

17. The primary basis of distinction between progressive and traditional education lies in differences in
    a. their assumptions as to the nature of the child
    b. the content of their curriculum
    c. the theories of psychology to which they subscribe
    d. the sequence in which the curriculum units are presented
    e. the scope and continuity of curricular experiences

18. Which of the following is *not* a basic contrast between the traditional and experience curriculum?
    a. curriculum centered in the past versus curriculum centered in the present and future
    b. curriculum with fixed outcomes required of all versus curriculum with flexible outcomes varying from person to person
    c. outcomes evaluated by formal testing versus outcomes assumed to occur as natural results of worthwhile experiences
    d. program controlled by the teacher versus program controlled by the students
    e. topics selected in advance by experts versus topics developed from spontaneous interests of the group

19. In the student-centered approach, the teacher is primarily
    a. a backstage instigator and organizer
    b. a diagnostician and evaluator
    c. a lecturer and comptroller
    d. a motivator and facilitator
    e. a resource person and consultant

20. A major limitation of the student-centered method is
    a. its disregard of the fundamental knowledge of the culture
    b. the ease with which it can be oriented in meaningless directions
    c. the fact that much of the curriculum does not fit such an approach
    d. its oversensitivity to student whims
    e. its potential lack of continuity

21. The teacher-centered approach deals with the motivational problem by relying primarily on
    a. the appeal inherent in a well-chosen curriculum
    b. the child's natural desire for growth
    c. secondary reinforcement, e. g., teacher approval
    d. the suitability of the curriculum in relation to individual pupil needs
    e. various types of aversive controls and teacher coercion

22. The primary weakness of an overuse of the student-centered approach is
    a. the anxieties its flexibility is likely to cause the insecure child
    b. its excessive reliance on the passing interests and whims of immature children
    c. its failure to provide for adequate mastery of the fundamentals
    d. the lack of continuity in the "education" it promotes
    e. the relatively incomplete grasp of curricular content which pupil projects are likely to promote

23. The strongest rebuttal against the criticism that the student-centered curriculum lacks logical organization is that
    a. organization is achieved *after* the material has been learned
    b. organization cannot begin until there is considerable knowledge to organize
    c. organization lies in the learner, not in the content
    d. organization to be meaningful must be phenomenological rather than absolute
    e. children's thinking is not logical, but rather illogical

24. The major reason for the inefficiency of the traditional teacher-centered curriculum is that
    a. it calls for pupil adaptation to the curriculum rather than the reverse
    b. it is difficult to relate it to the goals and purposes of children
    c. it fails to capitalize on group processes as a means of promoting pupil development

d. it incites resistance and negative attitudes, which must then be combatted by endless countermeasures
e. the unsuitability of its goals and demands promotes misbehavior and apathy

25. The strongest argument against the teacher-centered approach is
a. its failure to capitalize on social and democratic benefits of the classroom
b. the inappropriateness of its curriculum to many of its students
c. its lack of adaptability to individual differences in pupil readiness
d. the passivity and dependency attitudes it tends to promote
e. its relative disregard of the more significant aspects of education

26. The effectiveness of the student-centered approach revolves around
a. its greater adaptability to individual differences
b. the greater competence of the teachers it attracts
c. its greater emphasis on the fundamentals
d. its lack of predetermined objectives
e. the greater meaningfulness of its curriculum in relation to student purposes

27. The greatest advantage of the student-centered approach stems from
a. its adaptability to individual differences
b. the ego-involvement it tends to generate
c. its inbuilt sources of satisfaction of pupil needs
d. its more effective use of group dynamics
e. its orientation toward meaningful real-life experiences

28. The principal difference between the teacher-centered and the student-centered approach to teaching is in
a. the adequacy of the grasp of the fundamental they promote
b. the amount of learning they promote
c. the grade level at which each can be used most advantageously
d. the kind of learning they promote
e. the kind of teacher and pupil for which each is better suited

29. The primary defense against the disintegration of the student-centered approach into a pursuit of the frills and the futile is
a. the child's basic need to grow in significant directions
b. the enthusiasm generated by success
c. the challenge inherent in complex material
d. the reality demands inbuilt in any group project
e. the school's standardized testing program

30. The comparison of the teacher-centered versus pupil-centered approach has shown
    a. the student-centered approach to be more effective in the more intangible but also more functional and significant learnings
    b. the student-centered method to be superior simply because of the more adequate teachers it attracts
    c. the teacher-centered method to be more effective because it places the adaptation of the curriculum to individual differences directly under the teacher's control
    d. the teacher-centered method to be more effective because of its more dependable method of dealing with the motivational problem
    e. the teacher-centered method to be superior because of its logical organization of curricular material

31. The most valid conclusion as to the relative merits of the student-centered and teacher-centered approach to teaching is that
    a. they are equally good in the hands of equally competent teachers
    b. their relative effectiveness simply revolves around the choice of a criterion
    c. their relative effectiveness revolves around the competence of the teachers each attracts
    d. the student-centered method is generally more effective in promoting the more systematic and significant aspects of education
    e. a combination of the two is undoubtedly better than either one alone

32. The most significant of the following arguments against the student-centered approach is
    a. the excessive demands it makes on teacher ingenuity, competence, and security
    b. the excessive demands it makes on student initiative, originality, and self-direction
    c. its failure to provide for pupil growth in such areas as critical thinking, democratic leadership, and effective communication
    d. its ineffective use of teacher and pupil time
    e. its orientation toward *pupil* problems rather than the adult problems the child will face in life

33. Pupil preference as to the student-centered versus teacher-centered issue is primarily a function of
    a. the competence of the teacher with each
    b. the nature of the subject matter

   c.   past experience with each
   d.   the type of course examination expected
   e.   the relative maturity of the learner

34. Which of the following is *not* one of the basic concepts from which the present text introduces educational psychology?
   a.   anxiety as the basis for effective personal and social functioning
   b.   enlightened self-interest as the basis for effective social relationships
   c.   the importance of maternal warmth in the development of effective socialization
   d.   the meaningfulness of the curriculum in relation to the learner's needs, purposes, and background
   e.   openness to experience as a prerequisite to self-actualization

35. The teacher's major responsibility for effective education is for him
   a.   to facilitate the acquisition of academic material
   b.   to promote a healthy and productive classroom climate
   c.   to provide the setting and the opportunity for students to learn
   d.   to inspire children toward the dominant values of our society
   e.   to serve as a model with whom children can identify

Autoinstructional Devices

Programed instruction represents the application of learning theory, laboratory procedures, and modern technology to the improvement of classroom instruction. In the few years since Skinner's original article on "teaching machines" (Skinner, 1954; see p. 37 this book) programed instruction has been the subject of extensive discussion and considerable research into various aspects of its effectiveness. Its apparent advantages include: (a) greater individualization of instruction and greater diversification of the curriculum at minimal cost; (b) increased responsibility placed on the shoulders of the learner, thus eliminating one of the greatest obstacles to learning; (c) complete mastery leading to optimal readiness for the next step, and (d) more efficient learning resulting from immediate feedback. Probably its greatest contribution to the educational enterprise has been to cause educators to reexamine the total educational process and to sequence learning experiences more systematically. A particularly commendable feature of programed instruction is that it makes testing an integral part of the teaching–learning process. Finally, by taking over the mechanizable routine of teaching, programed instruction relieves the teacher to tend to the more human aspects of teaching. As teachers, we need to recognize both the potentialities and limitations of programed instruction and to keep "teaching machines" in proper perspective. The following paper by Hilgard presents an excellent discussion of the psychological rationale of autoinstruction.

Ernest R. Hilgard

Teaching Machines and Programed Learning: What Support from the Psychology of Learning? *

Programed learning presents the possibility of a relatively different method of instruction and of providing a new look at the process of learning itself. It derives support from such established principles in the psychology of learning as the following:

(a) It recognizes *individual differences* by beginning where the learner is and by permitting him to proceed at his own pace.

(b) It requires that the learner be *active.*

(c) It provides immediate *knowledge of results.*

(d) It emphasizes the organized nature of knowledge by requiring continuity between the easier (earlier) concepts and the harder (later) ones.

(e) It provides *spaced review* in order to guarantee a high order of success.

(f) It reduces anxiety because the learner is not threatened by the task: he knows that he can learn and is learning, and gains the satisfaction that this knowledge brings.

On the other hand, we must realize that a general principle of learning can never be tagged to a practical procedure as a validation of that procedure; any successful instructional device must agree with learning principles but psychological principles do not tell us what to do in practice. This is why we need educational as well as psychological research.

If, through teaching machines, we free the teacher of the drudgery of straightforward instruction in the imparting of information and questioning about facts, computations, etc., the teacher will then have time to do the things that he can do better than any machine. The hope is that the machine will permit the teacher to devote himself to the essential task of inspiring, stimulating, and encouraging students to feel a sense of their own significance in the scheme of things, to see themselves as creative individu-

* Adapted and abridged from *NEA J.* 50: 20–21, November 1961. By permission of author and publisher.

als who can set tasks for themselves and can achieve at a level that will increase their self-respect and give them a favorable self-image. The machine will help so far as the student's competency in routine achievement is concerned but the teacher will still have many opportunities for recognizing and rewarding individuality, initiative, and creativity.

By relieving the teacher of much that is routine, the teaching machine will permit the teacher to attend to the promotion of effective problem solving, divergent thinking, effective group participation. If much of the *science* of teaching is taken over by the machine, the *art* of teaching will again come into its own, residing where it should, in the teacher as a person.

Comments

1. Programed instruction has probably made its greatest contribution to the cause of education by forcing educators to reexamine the nature of the learning process and the role of the various components of the educational machinery.

2. Hilgard lays to rest the fear that machines will displace teachers; on the contrary, teaching machines will permit teachers to become "teachers" in the most significant and meaningful sense of the word.

That's What They Said

"Scarcely any area of human activity has been more resistant to scientific analysis and technological change than education."

B. F. Skinner. "Teaching machines," *Sci. Amer.*, 205: 91–102, 1961. [91]

"For the writer, an appealing alternative is to allocate to automatic devices whatever fundamental learnings appear not to require interposing the human teacher between learner and robot. Teaching machines might be housed in schools but it is conceivable that they could be provided to homes by the state and used by entire families in the process of self-education. Schools freed from routine burdens would now be forced to create programs scarcely imagined today."

John I. Goodlad. "Individual differences and vertical organization of the school," in N. B. Henry (ed.), *Individualizing Instruction*. 61st Yearbook, National Society for the Study of Education, Part I. Chicago: University of Chicago Press, 1962. Pp. 209–238. [237–238]

"A crucial new concept introduced by Skinner was the idea that any educational subject matter could be regarded as an accumulative repertoire of behavior which could be analyzed logically and behaviorally into a number of small 'steps' representing increments of successive approximation to final mastery."

A. A. Lumsdaine. "Educational technology, programed learning and instructional science," in E. R. Hilgard (ed.), *Theories of Learning and Instruction*. 63rd Yearbook, National Society for the Study of Education, Part I. Chicago: University of Chicago Press, 1964. Pp. 371–401. [383]

". . . Skinner and most others associated with programing developments emphasized the three characteristics . . .—namely, frequent response, immediate correction or confirmation, and progression at an individual rate."

A. A. Lumsdaine. 1964. Ibid. [382]

"The rather complete control of learner behavior and the feedback to the programmer provided by the continuous record of student response yielded by auto-instructional programs should afford the most promising vehicle yet developed for the analytical experimental study of variables affecting human learning and for the incorporation of research findings into improved instruments for practical instruction."

A. A. Lumsdaine. "Experimental research on instructional devices and materials," in Robert Glaser (ed.), *Training Research in Education.* Pittsburgh: University of Pittsburgh Press, 1962. Pp. 247–294. [253]

"Teachers should be trained in programing techniques so that they can prepare their materials to fit their specific needs. Such training is generally useful in that it provides insights into good teaching procedures and the nature of meaningful learning."

Karl U. Smith and Margaret F. Smith. *Cybernetic Principles of Learning and Educational Design.* New York: Holt, Rinehart and Winston, Inc., 1966. [328]

"As it looks today, the development of automatic teaching promises to be a repetition of the sad history of, for instance, intelligence testing and projective testing, where the number of uncritical and intuitive 'applications' far outweighs the number of experimental investigations into the basic nature of intelligence and imagination."

Jan Smedslund. "Educational psychology," *Ann. Rev. Psychol.,* 15: 251–276, 1964. [266]

"Moreover, if objective items are permitted to replace write-in responses to a large extent, then at one stroke, autoinstruction will be enormously facilitated and made more incisively effective. The prediction is ventured that in a few years the rejection of the objective item by Skinnerian programmers will be seen as one of the most odd and perverse episodes of American psychology. The writer has *no* evidence that, with meaningful autoinstructional matter, wrong alternates mislead or discriminative tasks aid *only* discriminative learning—or that, using such items, they may not be few and incisive rather than many and dull-easy. As it is, programing may be saddled for ten years with voluminous, clumsy, thousand-frame, write-in programs soon to be discarded, but with one more mark against psychologists as theory-bound and impractical."

Sidney L. Pressey. "Autoinstruction: Perspectives, problems, potentials," in E. R. Hilgard (ed.), *Theories of Learning and Instruction.* 63rd Yearbook, National Society for the Study of Education, Part I. Chicago: University of Chicago Press, 1964. Pp. 354–370. [368–369]

"The computer-based system appears to be the most efficient way of coping with the task of individualizing instruction. It can store the requisite information and the various decision rules that are differentially called upon to produce a program which each student requires."

Lawrence M. Stolurow. "Model the master teacher and master the teaching model," in John D. Krumboltz (ed.), *Learning and the Educational Process*. Skokie, Ill.: Rand McNally & Company, 1965. Pp. 223–247. [239]

APPENDIX

Test Items

1. Probably the greatest contribution of "teaching" machines to the cause of education is in the area of
   a. clarifying the nature of the teaching–learning process
   b. freeing the teacher to take on some of the more significant aspects of teaching
   c. increasing the school's offerings at minimal cost
   d. providing remedial and diagnostic services
   e. replacing inadequate teachers

2. The major impetus underlying the "invention" of teaching machines came from
   a. educators' urgent need to cope with individual differences
   b. the eminent success of the Skinner box in the training of animals
   c. psychologists' concern over the use of aversive control in the classroom
   d. public concern over teacher shortage in relation to a rapidly expanding population
   e. Skinner's concern over classroom inefficiency

3. Skinner's major criticism of classroom learning concerns
   a. the disorganized schedule of presentation of subject matter
   b. the failure to provide sufficient systematic schedule reinforcement
   c. the gaps and inadequacies in the mastery of content
   d. the inadequate breakdown of concepts into subcomponents
   e. the wasteful use of teacher time and talent

4. The primary practical benefit of the use of teaching machines in the framework of the overall operation of the school is that
   a. it enables the learner to concentrate his efforts on the material he does not know
   b. it frees the teacher to deal with the more personally meaningful aspects of teaching
   c. it keeps the class together by providing for remedial and make-up work
   d. it makes for more resistant learning by its greater adherence to recognized principles of the psychology of learning
   e. it reduces the time necessary to master a given learning task

525

5. The feature of autoinstructional devices that probably contributes most to their effectiveness is that
    a.   they build up concepts component by component
    b.   they involve the learner in his own learning
    c.   they make unlimited provision for individual differences
    d.   they provide immediate feedback of the learner's responses
    e.   they streamline academic content

6. Which of the following features of the teaching machine concept is most psychologically significant in terms of its effectiveness?
    a.   It has inbuilt review and application exercises.
    b.   It makes learning an active ego-involving process.
    c.   It precludes error (bad habits, misconceptions, etc.).
    d.   It promotes complete mastery and hence an ever-ideal level of readiness.
    e.   It provides optimal adaptation to individual differences.

7. The most psychologically significant principle underlying the concept of the teaching machines is that
    a.   it continually challenges the learner at his optimal level of readiness
    b.   it makes the learning an active process
    c.   by promoting mastery, it promotes effective retention and transfer
    d.   it provides an ideal way of dealing with individual differences
    e.   it provides immediate and continuous feedback

8. The major weakness of the teaching machine as a teaching device is
    a.   its lack of adaptability to individual differences
    b.   its mechanical nonhuman nature
    c.   the relatively low quality of most programs
    d.   the restricted range within which it can function
    e.   its rigidity in the presentation of content

9. The major point at issue between Skinner's linear programing and Crowder's branching programing is
    a.   the extent to which learning involves insight
    b.   the frequency and immediacy of feedback
    c.   whether or not "guessing" should be allowed
    d.   whether to devise or to select the answer
    e.   the size of the steps and the likelihood of error

10. In the final analysis, the major limitation of all teaching machine hardware stems from
    a.   their inflexibility and inability to provide review, skipping, emphasis, etc.

   b.   the lack of compatibility between different programs and different machines

   c.   their limited capacity

   d.   their relative cost and quick obsolescence

   e.   their slow, tediously repetitive approach to concept presentation

11.   The most valid criticism of autoinstructional devices is that
   a.   they are mechanical and impersonal
   b.   they cannot teach originality and creativity
   c.   they dissect content into meaningless components
   d.   their effectiveness is strictly a pinball "Hawthorne" effect
   e.   they tend to standardize and mechanize the process of education

12.   A major danger in the wholesale use of teaching machines is that of
   a.   the mechanization and narrowing of the process of education
   b.   the nationwide standardization of the curriculum
   c.   the orientation of the child away from human interaction
   d.   the orientation of education toward limited (mechanical) objectives
   e.   reliance on gadgetries for motivational purposes

13.   The key to "shaping" behavior is
   a.   drive-reduction
   b.   learner insight as to the goal
   c.   learner restlessness and curiosity
   d.   perceptual reorganization
   e.   selective reinforcement

14.   The major issue of the linear and branching controversy is
   a.   the objectives and contents for which each is designed
   b.   the relative merits of covering materials slowly and methodologically versus covering more material with less mastery
   c.   the relative reinforcement value of many tiny reinforcements
   d.   the relative validity of the associative versus cognitive theories of learning
   e.   the role of errors in efficient learning

15.   Crowder and Skinner would agree that
   a.   errors per se are undesirable
   b.   the ideal programing is that which promotes error-free performance for even the slowest student
   c.   the learning units should be arranged in a set sequence to be followed by all students (albeit at different rates)
   d.   the student should devise his own answers
   e.   the use of programed instruction is restricted to the teaching of factual material

Final Examination

1. Educational philosophy is to educational psychology as
   a. academic content is to teaching procedures
   b. deliberation is to research
   c. objectives and goals are to results
   d. theory is to practice
   e. values is to methods

2. Research attempts to derive
   a. direct one-to-one cause-and-effect relationships between variables
   b. functional relationships among variables
   c. hypotheses as to the cause of observed phenomena
   d. hypothetical constructs as explanations of empirical phenomena
   e. relations of concomitance among variables

3. The greatest single factor underlying the conflicts and contradictions in the results of educational experimentation is
   a. the complexity of educational variables
   b. failure to provide adequate experimental control
   c. the free will of human subjects
   d. the lack of competence and/or integrity of the investigators
   e. the nonamenability of educational variables to scientific determination

4. Harlow's studies suggest that the basic ingredient underlying the development of love is
   a. contact comfort
   b. innate (instinctive) predispositions
   c. maternal display of love toward the infant
   d. nursing (conditioning)
   e. successful peer contacts

5. The major complicating problem in the determination of teacher effectiveness probably is
   a. the choice of a criterion
   b. the nature of teaching as an art, rather than a science
   c. the number of combinations of teacher traits involved in effective teaching

    d.   the personal characteristics of the teacher

    e.   the unevenness of teacher performance

6.   The primary purpose served by theories of learning is

    a.   to disprove erroneous generalizations

    b.   to point out the inconsistencies in educational practice

    c.   to provide hypotheses to be tested

    d.   to provide structure for empirical findings

    e.   to structure research

7.   The clearest example of teaching as a science is that presented by

    a.   Lewin's modification of attitudes through group decision

    b.   Osborne's concept of brainstorming

    c.   Skinnerian conditioning

    d.   the promotion of reasoning and problem-solving ability

    e.   the teaching of reading through phonics

8.   Educational practice based on field theory would stress

    a.   analysis

    b.   group dynamics

    c.   meaningfulness

    d.   perceptual relativism

    e.   practice

9.   The key concept in cognitive theory is

    a.   learning

    b.   motivation

    c.   perception

    d.   reinforcement

    e.   the self

10.   A major objection to the current theories of learning is

    a.   the circularity of their "explanations"

    b.   their inadequacy as a guide to educational practice

    c.   their incompleteness

    d.   their lack of empirical foundation

    e.   their relative inconsistency

11.   "Shaping behavior" is a term used primarily in

    a.   behaviorism

    b.   classical conditioning

    c.   Freudian psychoanalysis

    d.   functionalism

    e.   instrumental conditioning

12. According to phenomenologists, whether a person's behavior is intelligent or stupid depends on
    a. his intelligence
    b. his previous habits
    c. the adequacy of his perception of the situation
    d. the relative strength of his motives
    e. the relative valence of the alternatives

13. Motives are best conceived as
    a. dependent variables
    b. empirical truths
    c. hypothetical constructs
    d. instinctive behavioral predispositions
    e. mediating factors

14. Motives differ from drives in that
    a. they are generally less insistent
    b. they are less resistant to extinction
    c. they are more complex
    d. they are psychological rather than biological
    e. they involve an element of learning

15. What is the most convincing argument against the drive-reduction theory of motivation?
    a. Certain motives are clearly innate, e. g., a chick's fear of hawks.
    b. The drive reduction theory is negatively oriented.
    c. Learning takes place in situations where no drive is being satisfied.
    d. The organism seeks stimulation rather than relief from stimulation.
    e. The organism reacts even when its needs are fully satisfied.

16. Functional autonomy is probably best explained on the basis of
    a. an unconscious desire to preserve the self
    b. partial reinforcement
    c. the resistant nature of early responses
    d. the self-perpetuating nature of habit
    e. the substitution of drives

17. Emotional security is best promoted through
    a. an atmosphere of unconditional love and unconditional acceptance
    b. a permissive home environment in which the child is free to chart his course with a minimum of interference

    c.   consistency in child-rearing practices

    d.   love-oriented child-rearing practices

    e.   strict child-rearing practices in which reward and punishment are applied with firmness and consistency

18.   Cognitive dissonance is most directly related to

    a.   a breakdown in the consistency associated with the self-concept

    b.   incongruity between the observed and the expected

    c.   the disparity between the cognitive and the affective components of a given experience

    d.   the distortion of reality to protect the self-concept

    e.   the unpleasant feeling associated with negative emotions

19.   By reference to the self-concept, the self ideal is most adequate when

    a.   it is approximately at the level of the self-concept

    b.   it is pegged slightly below the self-concept

    c.   it shows a slight positive discrepancy

    d.   it shows a substantial positive discrepancy

    e.   none of the above; the self-ideal need bear no consistent relation to the self-concept

20.   The factor most responsible for the consistency of the self-concept is

    a.   consistency in the environment

    b.   the functional autonomy of habits

    c.   the innate basis of its development

    d.   the individual's inability to attend to all stimuli

    e.   selective perception

21.   Which would suffer least under conditions of anxiety?

    a.   ability to improvise

    b.   alertness to details

    c.   clarity of judgment

    d.   creativity

    e.   skilled performance

22.   The basic premise of the concept of *becoming* is that

    a.   guidance is generally necessary for maximal growth

    b.   the individual needs to be activated by an external force if he is to attain his potential

    c.   the individual invariably mobilizes his potential for self-actualization

    d.   the individual will actualize himself if we but eliminate the obstacles toward his growth

    e.   there is an all-pervasive force impelling people toward growth

23. The common way of dealing with anxiety is
    a. to keep the perceptual field at a low level of differentiation
    b. to redouble one's efforts to deal with the situation
    c. to rationalize away the conflict
    d. to repress the object of reference
    e. to transfer the anxiety to some organ

24. The "secret of success" of the person in the process of becoming is
    a. a broad experiential background
    b. a high asset-to-liability balance
    c. a history of past success
    d. a realistic self-concept
    e. openness to experience

25. The self-ideal (level of aspiration) is set largely with reference to
    a. any convenient group standards
    b. norms based on a significant group
    c. one's ability
    d. one's motivational state
    e. one's self-concept

26. Probably the most educationally significant shift in viewpoint in recent years is
    a. the broadening of the scope of intellectual capacity
    b. the postponement of formal instruction as a means of ensuring readiness
    c. the rejection of the previous belief in the relative immutability of readiness
    d. the relative rejection of limits of human capacity
    e. the shift to training through conditioning as a means of circumventing inherited limitations

27. The strongest evidence of the need for early training in development comes from the studies of
    a. Harlow and his co-workers at Wisconsin
    b. Hebb and his co-workers at McGill
    c. McGraw; Gesell and Thompson
    d. Riesen; Von Senden
    e. Spitz, Bowlby, Ribble, and others

28. The key to the success of early training lies in
    a. emphasis on complete mastery as you go along (e.g., automated instruction)
    b. pretraining (readiness) exercises

     c.   systematic reinforcement (e.g., Skinnerian conditioning)
     d.   the adaptation of methods
     e.   the promotion of earlier maturation

29.   The major cause of infantile mortality, feeblemindedness, deformity, and other abnormalities is probably
     a.   abnormalities of the genes caused by radiation
     b.   birth injuries
     c.   dietary deficiency of the mother during pregnancy
     d.   inherited tendencies
     e.   lack of prenatal care

30.   The male sperm cell contains
     a.   48 chromosomes
     b.   46 chromosomes
     c.   23 chromosomes
     d.   any number of chromosomes from 45 to 48 (with deviations generally associated with abnormality)
     e.   a variable number of chromosomes (with no special meaning or effect)

31.   Individual differences in physical and psychological traits among school children are best conceived in terms of
     a.   differences in rate of maturing
     b.   a continuum ranging from, say, very tall to very short
     c.   a dichotomy; e.g., tall and short
     d.   a normal distribution ranging from, say, very tall to very short
     e.   an overall interval which can be divided into a number of arbitrary classes

32.   The significance of physical growth lies primarily in its effects upon
     a.   adjustment and mental health
     b.   physical health
     c.   other aspects of growth
     d.   the self-ideal
     e.   the reactions of others

33.   The more advanced levels of psychomotor proficiency depend primarily upon
     a.   motivation
     b.   general motor coordination
     c.   readiness
     d.   specific aptitudes
     e.   the adequacy of underlying skills

34. In appraising the physical status of public school children, the feature that stands out most strikingly is
    a. the parallelism in pattern of physical growth from child to child
    b. the rigid maturation-controlled nature of physical growth
    c. the smoothness of physical growth
    d. the uniformity in sequence in the development of physiomotor capabilities
    e. the wide difference among children of any given age

35. The fact that there is a gradual increase in height and weight from one generation to the next is best explained on the basis of
    a. higher mortality among the physically inadequate
    b. progressively improved environmental conditions, e. g., foods, vaccines
    c. progressively more adequate prenatal care
    d. selective reproduction (higher rate of reproduction among the physically adequate)
    e. stretching exercises due to greater interest in physical adequacy

36. Motor development derives its major psychological significance from the standpoint of
    a. the development of physical health and well-being
    b. the development of motor proficiency
    c. the promotion of related aspects of development
    d. the satisfaction of needs and the development of the self-concept
    e. social acceptance and reputation among peers

37. Socialization is best conceived as a deliberate program oriented toward
    a. the attainment of social competence and social sensitivity
    b. the development of conscience
    c. the indoctrination of youth into the mores and values of the social order
    d. the internalization of social constraints
    e. the molding of the child to the adult image

38. What constitutes a fear- or anger-producing situation is primarily a function of
    a. the individual's adequacy relative to the danger of the situation
    b. the individual's past habits
    c. the individual's self-concept
    d. the intensity of the stimulus
    e. the threat involved as interpreted by the individual

39. Anger in young children is most often caused by
     a. frustration of physiological needs, e.g., hunger
     b. habit
     c. interference (e.g., adult restrictions or personal incompetence)
     d. provocation or attack by others
     e. the need to assert themselves

40. The danger in promoting strong patriotism is that
     a. it automatically implies intolerance and rejection of out-groups
     b. it calls for an objectionable degree of indoctrination
     c. it often causes the individual to put group loyalties ahead of personal growth
     d. it often results in narrow provincialism
     e. it often transfers to less desirable groups or causes

41. Emotional maturity in its optimal sense is most equivalent to
     a. the concept of becoming (self-actualization)
     b. freedom from strong emotions (especially of a negative nature)
     c. love of mankind (charity)
     d. personal adjustment
     e. restraint of emotional involvement

42. The physiological changes accompanying an emotion tend to be
     a. a cause of mental and physical breakdown
     b. a handicap to survival in situations calling for clear thinking
     c. a handicap in situations calling for strength and stamina
     d. a help to survival
     e. a hindrance to the survival of modern man

43. Socialization is best developed through child-rearing practices which are
     a. guilt-producing in the case of infractions
     b. love-oriented
     c. object-oriented
     d. strict (and if necessary, punitive)
     e. systematic

44. Modern psychologists see leaders as
     a. emergent reflections of group needs
     b. extroverts who often exploit the group for self-aggrandizement
     c. molders of the destiny of mankind
     d. people possessed of a variety of leadership qualities
     e. persons possessed of social sensitivity and a willingness to serve

45. The major determinant of the success of group work is
     a.   the acceptability of the leader to all factions
     b.   the adequacy of communication
     c.   the commonness of basic purposes and goals
     d.   the diversity of talents in relation to the diversity of tasks to be
          performed
     e.   the experience of the group in acting as a group

46. The "effectiveness" of democratic group processes in promoting the
     school's purposes depends primarily upon
     a.   the cohesiveness of the group
     b.   the democratic orientation of the teacher
     c.   the meaningfulness of the group's goals
     d.   the way we define our function
     e.   the willingness of the school to abide by group decisions

47. Discipline is best when it is
     a.   developmental
     b.   permissive
     c.   preventive
     d.   supportive
     e.   therapeutic

48. The primary outcome of autocratic control in school is
     a.   apathy
     b.   dislike for school
     c.   docility
     d.   internalization of social constraints
     e.   rebellion

49. Intelligence is best viewed as
     a.   a hierarchy of intellectual functions
     b.   innate capacity
     c.   potential revealed through intelligent behavior
     d.   problem-solving ability
     e.   verbal aptitude

50. The measurement of intelligence of infants is complicated by
     a.   difficulties in the area of motivation (rapport)
     b.   the gradual shift with the years in the abilities which constitute
          intelligence
     c.   the sensorimotor nature of infant tests
     d.   the unreliability of infant tests
     e.   the unavailability of adequate norms

51. Guilford classified the human intellect according to
    a. divergent and convergent thinking
    b. innate and acquired abilities
    c. primary and secondary mental abilities
    d. processes, materials, and products
    e. specific and general factors

52. An accelerative IQ pattern is associated with
    a. the feminine sex role
    b. a high N Ach
    c. inappropriateness of the norms
    d. intellectual curiosity
    e. invalidity or unreliability of tests

53. The child's language at the age of three is described by Piaget as
    a. animistic
    b. autistic
    c. ego-centric
    d. socio-centric
    e. syncretic

54. The clearest sex differences exist with respect to
    a. artistic (creative) talent
    b. linguistic facility and clerical aptitude
    c. mathematical reasoning and computation
    d. personal adjustment and social sensitivity
    e. scientific orientation

55. Retaining students in a given grade is probably best justified on the basis of
    a. greater academic adequacy on the part of the students retained
    b. increased homogeneity among students in a given grade
    c. the beneficial effects of permitting the student some success at his level
    d. the maintenance of scholastic standards
    e. the motivational value of the threat of failure and retention

56. Sex differences in motor proficiency is primarily a function of
    a. competition of other interests
    b. differences in opportunity to practice
    c. innate differences in aptitudes in question
    d. physical strength and stamina
    e. social pressures (e.g., sex roles)

57. The greatest degree of independence is likely to be found among
 a. the IQ's of pairs of individuals selected at random
 b. the various abilities of elementary school students
 c. the various academic aptitudes of college students
 d. the various aspects of creativity
 e. the various psychomotor and intellectual aptitudes of adults

58. Probably the most "neglected" child in the classroom is the _____ child.
 a. creative
 b. dull
 c. gifted
 d. handicapped
 e. lower-class

59. The reinforcement effects of the "reward" of a given response is typically a function of
 a. the applicability of the law of effect in this particular instance
 b. the learner's awareness of being rewarded
 c. the "magnitude" of the reward
 d. the "motivation" of the learner
 e. the timing of the reward in relation to the response

60. Which of the following statements regarding learning is most correct?
 a. All changes in behavior represent learning.
 b. Learning always involves a change in behavior.
 c. Learning always involves goal-directed behavior.
 d. Learning is invariably the consequent of stimulation.
 e. Learning necessarily implies some degree and form of motivation.

61. The effectiveness of a given teaching–learning technique is primarily a function of
 a. the characteristics of the learner in relation to the complexity of the material
 b. the learning styles of the individual students
 c. the nature of the material to be taught
 d. the priority given to various educational objectives
 e. the teacher's experience with the technique

62. The feature most peculiar to psychomotor learnings (in contrast to verbal learnings) is
 a. their greater dependency on competent initial instruction
 b. their greater reliance on relevant "aptitudes"

    c.   their greater susceptibility to the development of bad habits

    d.   their independence of cognitive factors

    e.   their relative permanence

63.   The teaching effectiveness of audio–visual devices lies primarily in

    a.   the "change of pace" they offer

    b.   the generally higher quality of the instruction they provide

    c.   their greater ability to reach children who do not read well

    d.   their greater emphasis on charts, diagrams, pictures, etc.

    e.   the motivational appeal of "gadgets"

64.   The greatest weakness of the problem-solving approach to classroom operation is

    a.   the difficulty of execution

    b.   its relative inflexibility

    c.   its relative inadequacy for dealing with problems significant to students

    d.   its relative slowness

    e.   its susceptibility to allowing gaps to develop in the student's knowledge

65.   The distinction intrinsic–extrinsic pertains to

    a.   the adequacy of the goal-object in satisfying the need in question

    b.   the degree of clarity of the goal-object being sought

    c.   the primary-versus-secondary nature of the motives in operation

    d.   the relation of the goal-object to the need

    e.   the valence strength of the goal-object

66.   Long-continued failure generally _____ the individual's level of aspiration.

    a.   causes an upgrading of

    b.   causes a downgrading of

    c.   causes either an unrealistic upgrading or downgrading of

    d.   has no effect on

    e.   has random effects on

67.   The true determinant of human behavior is

    a.   the attractiveness of available incentives

    b.   the functional autonomy of past habits

    c.   the intensity of the frustration of one's needs

    d.   the net vector strength of the multiplicity of motives operating in the situation

    e.   the valence of available goals

68. As a means of discouraging inadequate behavior,
    a. mild punishment is effective but potentially harmful
    b. mild punishment is potentially effective and harmless when used in combination with reward
    c. punishment is basically ineffective but relatively harmless
    d. punishment is ineffective and generally harmful
    e. severe punishment is invariably ineffective and harmful

69. The critical factor in the degree of retention / forgetting of academic material is apparently
    a. its inherent organization and structure
    b. the degree of mastery
    c. the learner's intellectual caliber
    d. the learner's background of relevant information
    e. the method used in acquisition

70. The degree of retention of complex ideational material is determined primarily by
    a. the adequacy of the reinforcements provided
    b. the cognitive structure inherent in the material
    c. the degree of mastery of the material
    d. the nature of subsequent learnings
    e. the readiness of the learner

71. Retention and transfer are primarily a function of
    a. the adequacy of the instruction (presentation)
    b. the adequacy of the learning
    c. the motivation of the learner
    d. the nature of the material
    e. the readiness (intelligence) of the learner

72. The highest stage in Piaget's classification of concept development is
    a. concrete operations
    b. formal thought
    c. intuitive thought
    d. preconceptual thought
    e. sensorimotor operations

73. Effective transfer is most adequately promoted by emphasis on the promotion of
    a. a high degree of motivation
    b. a high level of mastery
    c. effective data retrieval

    d.   effective learning skills

    e.   transfer consciousness

74. The greater resistance to forgetting of psychomotor skills (over ideational learnings) is best explained on the basis of

    a.   overlearning

    b.   their greater meaningfulness

    c.   their kinesthetic as well as psychological basis

    d.   their inherent motivational appeal

    e.   their direct association with the satisfaction of basic physiological needs

75. From the standpoint of information as a prerequisite for reasoning and problem solving, the key concept is

    a.   classification

    b.   reorganization

    c.   retention

    d.   retrieval

    e.   storage

76. The most effective way of promoting effective problem solving in the classroom is

    a.   to emphasize the steps of the scientific method

    b.   to help pupils select meaningful problems

    c.   to guide their thinking along logical lines

    d.   to maintain a complete hands-off policy

    e.   to structure the problem through well-placed questions to be answered

77. The problem-solving approach to teaching is probably most effective from the standpoint of promoting

    a.   a democratic orientation

    b.   changes in attitudes

    c.   the acquisition of facts and information

    d.   the development of problem-solving ability

    e.   the quick resolution of problems

78. Thorndike is to trial and error as

    a.   Guthrie is to reinforcement

    b.   Köhler is to insight

    c.   Pavlov is to stimulus (and response) generalization

    d.   Skinner is to purpose

    e.   Watson is to introspection

79. Research has shown that, in contrast to the traditional teacher-directed approach, discovery generally promotes
    a. more efficient acquisition, retention, and transfer
    b. less effective acquisition but greater retention and transfer
    c. less retention and transfer but more effective acquisition
    d. less transfer but more efficient acquisition and greater retention
    e. results not clearly better nor worse apart from the particular situation

80. Probably the greatest deterrent to the promotion of thinking and reasoning in the classroom is
    a. lack of emotional detachment on the part of children
    b. overemphasis on the right answer
    c. overemphasis on memorization rather than understanding
    d. the use of objective tests
    e. underemphasis on knowledge as the foundation for reasoning

81. To be educationally profitable, generalizations achieved in the classroom should be
    a. clearly delimited
    b. free from difficult vocabulary
    c. individually meaningful
    d. logically simple
    e. scientifically precise

82. The greatest impediment to meaningfulness in the classroom lies in the area of
    a. clarity of presentation
    b. experiential background
    c. intellectual immaturity
    d. problem-solving skills
    e. pupil motivation and study habits

83. The greatest single "cause" of failure in communication is
    a. incorrect mind-set on the part of the receiver
    b. inadequacies in vocabulary (of both sender and receiver)
    c. lack of communality in background
    d. overemphasis on symbolism (as opposed to the tangibles)
    e. reliance on the accumulation of facts rather than on reasoning

84. The greatest factors underlying creativity are
    a. experience and cognitive clarity
    b. flexibility and intelligence
    c. intellectual curiosity and motivation

    d. motivation and perseverance
    e. psychological freedom and psychological safety

85. The decision as to whether to deduct for misspelled words in a test
    in history revolves around
    a. teacher preference
    b. the nature of the test
    c. the objectives of the course
    d. the scope of the test
    e. the seriousness of the error from the standpoint of effective
        writing

86. Test performance is best interpreted
    a. against the teacher's (subjective) standards
    b. against the student's previous performance
    c. in relation to the performance of a meaningful comparison group
    d. on an absolute basis
    e. on the basis of norms

87. The main advantage of the essay over the objective test is
    a. its ease of construction
    b. its greater validity
    c. its measurement of reasoning, interpretation of data, and other
        higher mental processes
    d. the insight it provides into the student's mental processes
    e. the more adequate studying which it promotes

88. Grading on the curve can be justified on the premise that
    a. adequacy of performance is always relative
    b. education should be oriented to enabling each person to make
        most of his potentialities
    c. grades are an important means of motivating students
    d. it makes grading an objective process and eliminates favoritism
    e. the use of the normal curve gives grading a sound mathematical
        basis

89. The general reaction of psychologists regarding self-grading has been
    one of
    a. caution concerning its impracticality
    b. caution concerning its unreliability
    c. indifference; it is no worse nor better than the present system
    d. overall endorsement
    e. rejection for reasons of invalidity related to personal bias

90. The strongest argument against grades is that
    a. the anxiety they promote interferes with effective learning
    b. they are frequently unfair; they are always unreliable
    c. they cannot possibly serve as an index of all the school is trying to do
    d. they often supersede the true goals of education and cast education into a secondary role
    e. they are often used by teachers as weapons to control students

91. The primary influence in the development of attitudes in the child is/are
    a. the emotional experiences one undergoes
    b. the gang
    c. the home
    d. the peer group
    e. the school

92. The antischool attitudes of lower-class children are best accounted for on the basis of
    a. conditioning to unhappy experiences in school
    b. deliberate indoctrination by the peer group
    c. imitation of the attitudes of the family and peer group
    d. the unsuitability of the school's program for these children
    e. the view of the school as an authority figure

93. According to Piaget, moral realism is to moral relativism as
    a. allegiance to moral standards based on social benefits is to blind allegiance to segmented aspects of morality for morality's sake
    b. "Behavior is good as it complies with rules" is to "Behavior is good as it serves human social needs"
    c. "Rules are sacred" are to "Rules are a matter of mutual agreement"
    d. "Rules stem from authority" are to "The severity of violations as a matter of the extent of damage"
    e. "Transgressions are to be punished by the authority whose rules have been broken" are to "Transgressions are to be punished through retaliation by the victim"

94. Prejudice is most closely associated with
    a. ignorance
    b. imitation
    c. insecurity
    d. group loyalty
    e. victimization and persecution

95. The most convincing argument against the use of direct indoctrination of children is that
    a. education should concern itself with how rather than what to think
    b. it is undemocratic
    c. to be effective, indoctrination must operate on a 24-hour-a-day basis
    d. unless determined and relentless, it will simply lead listeners to crystallize their current attitudes
    e. unless skillfully done, it may actually antagonize and have the opposite effect

96. The suggestion that teachers must know their students if they are to be effective in directing them
    a. has generally been shown in the area of both personal development and academic achievement
    b. has generally been shown in the area of personal development but not in academic achievement
    c. has generally been shown in academic achievement but not in personal development
    d. has sometimes been shown in one or the other but not consistently
    e. has not been shown in either personal development or academic achievement

97. Most definitions of normality suffer from the same limitation, namely
    a. they are oriented toward the absence of abnormality
    b. they do not provide rigid lines of demarcation
    c. they equate normality with average
    d. they make anxiety the point of departure
    e. they overlook the concept of values

98. Personality is best visualized as
    a. a matter of one's reputation among his fellowmen
    b. one's personal and social adjustment
    c. one's assets and liabilities as integrated to make the person who and what he is
    d. the sum total of one's assets and liabilities
    e. the way one affects his fellowmen

99. Personality develops primarily as a result of
    a. the enforcement of precepts and rules in early life
    b. identification with significant persons
    c. imitation
    d. maturation
    e. selective reinforcement

100. That a given individual should display consistency in the kind and quality of the adjustments he makes follows directly from
    a. the consistency of the environmental demands impinging upon him
    b. the functional autonomy of all habits
    c. the limited number of behavioral patterns of which the individual is capable
    d. the individual's closing off his avenues of stimulation whenever change is threatened
    e. the need to protect the self

101. According to Peck and Havighurst's classification, expedient is to conforming as
    a. allegiance to moral standards based on their social benefit is to blind allegiance to segmented aspects of morality for morality's sake
    b. disregard of social implications is to overconcern for social expectations
    c. disregard for moral connotations is to rigid compliance to the moral code
    d. irrational–conscientious is to rational–conscientious
    e. selfish concern for social consequences is to concern only for the rule as internalized

102. The major impediment to effective mental health in the school is
    a. the heterogeneity of its student population
    b. the lack of clinical training on the part of school personnel
    c. the relative maladjustment of the teachers
    d. the strong authoritarianism that typically pervades pupil–teacher relationships
    e. the unsuitability of the curriculum as a vehicle for pupil need satisfaction

103. Women teachers typically mishandle boys (from a mental hygiene point of view) by
    a. attempting to repress outward displays of aggression
    b. enforcing unnecessary conformity and compliance
    c. giving them more responsibility than they can handle
    d. making academic demands for which they are not ready
    e. subjecting them to curricular content that is unduly "feminine" in its orientation (e.g., literature)

104. The greatest mental hazard to boys and girls attending high school today is probably
    a. the authoritarian climate of the average classroom
    b. the gap in phenomenal field between teachers and pupils
    c. the hostility of the peer group to certain "isolates" and "rejects"
    d. the unfair and vindictive discipline that prevails in many classrooms
    e. the unsuitability of the curriculum to a large number of pupils attending the school

105. What is the relationship between education, guidance, and mental hygiene?
    a. Education is academic; guidance is personal; mental hygiene is clinical.
    b. Education is the most comprehensive.
    c. Guidance is but a subaspect of mental hygiene.
    d. They are, for all intents and purposes, synonymous.
    e. They are similar in scope, but slightly different in purpose.

106. A fundamental issue in the criticisms of education is
    a. the effectiveness with which we achieve whatever goal we have set
    b. the importance of facts and skills
    c. the legitimacy of influencing the lives of youngsters
    d. the pursuit of excellence at the expense of the dull child
    e. what constitutes the true goals of education

107. The curriculum is best conceived as
    a. any educative experience
    b. a sequence of experiences designed to promote academic competence
    c. a sequence of experiences selected to promote pupil growth and development
    d. the academic content provided for a given grade
    e. the course of study or syllabus of the school

108. The crux of the progressive—traditional controversy is whether
    a. learning should be a matter of "discovery" or of "absorption"
    b. social skills are more important than academic competence
    c. teaching should emphasize projects or lectures
    d. the organization of the curriculum should be psychological or logical
    e. transfer of training occurs in appreciable amounts

109. The greatest weakness of the experience curriculum approach is
     a. inadequacies in the student's grasp of the fundamentals
     b. its lack of concern for the all-around growth of the child
     c. its lack of provision for training children in doing things even though unpleasant
     d. the gaps it allows in the education of the child
     e. the ineffectiveness of learning arising from the fragmentation of the curriculum

110. The effectiveness of the pupil-centered approach stems largely from
     a. its greater reliance on pupil initiative and assumption of responsibility
     b. its greater provision for individual differences
     c. its organization of learning activities into a broader and less artificial framework
     d. its more effective use of the group as an educative influence
     e. the greater ego-involvement of students in its activities

Answers to Test Items

Chapter 1

1.	b	6.	d	11.	e	16.	e	21.	e
2.	b	7.	d	12.	d	17.	e	22.	e
3.	e	8.	c	13.	c	18.	e	23.	e
4.	c	9.	d	14.	a	19.	b		
5.	d	10.	e	15.	b	20.	e		

Chapter 2

1.	d	6.	c	11.	e	16.	c	21.	c
2.	a	7.	b	12.	d	17.	b		
3.	d	8.	c	13.	c	18.	b		
4.	d	9.	e	14.	a	19.	a		
5.	b	10.	b	15.	e	20.	d		

Chapter 3

1.	b	7.	c	13.	d	19.	d	25.	a
2.	e	8.	e	14.	b	20.	e	26.	d
3.	b	9.	c	15.	d	21.	b	27.	e
4.	b	10.	b	16.	d	22.	e		
5.	d	11.	a	17.	c	23.	a		
6.	a	12.	d	18.	e	24.	e		

Chapter 4

1.	e	6.	e	11.	c	16.	d	21.	d
2.	b	7.	d	12.	e	17.	c	22.	a
3.	e	8.	b	13.	b	18.	a	23.	d
4.	b	9.	d	14.	e	19.	d	24.	b
5.	c	10.	e	15.	c	20.	c		

Chapter 5

1.	b	6.	a	11.	d	16.	c	21.	c
2.	d	7.	e	12.	c	17.	a		
3.	a	8.	e	13.	b	18.	b		
4.	a	9.	a	14.	e	19.	a		
5.	c	10.	c	15.	c	20.	d		

Chapter 6

1.	e	5.	c	9.	e	13.	a
2.	d	6.	e	10.	d	14.	a
3.	a	7.	c	11.	c	15.	a
4.	a	8.	a	12.	d	16.	b

Chapter 7

1.	a	8.	a	15.	a	22.	a	29.	b
2.	a	9.	c	16.	a	23.	b	30.	d
3.	a	10.	d	17.	a	24.	c	31.	a
4.	a	11.	b	18.	b	25.	d	32.	b
5.	d	12.	a	19.	d	26.	b		
6.	d	13.	d	20.	e	27.	d		
7.	c	14.	e	21.	b	28.	b		

Chapter 8

1.	a	10.	e	19.	a	28.	c	37.	b
2.	d	11.	e	20.	d	29.	a	38.	e
3.	e	12.	c	21.	b	30.	c	39.	b
4.	b	13.	b	22.	e	31.	a	40.	b
5.	b	14.	c	23.	d	32.	b	41.	b
6.	c	15.	e	24.	c	33.	c		
7.	c	16.	d	25.	d	34.	b		
8.	a	17.	a	26.	c	35.	d		
9.	d	18.	e	27.	e	36.	b		

Chapter 9

1.	a	7.	e	13.	a	19.	b	25.	c
2.	c	8.	c	14.	d	20.	d	26.	b
3.	e	9.	b	15.	d	21.	e	27.	d
4.	d	10.	b	16.	e	22.	e	28.	a
5.	e	11.	c	17.	b	23.	d		
6.	c	12.	a	18.	c	24.	d		

Chapter 10

1.	e	7.	c	13.	c	19.	e	25.	b
2.	a	8.	d	14.	c	20.	b	26.	d
3.	d	9.	b	15.	a	21.	c	27.	e
4.	a	10.	d	16.	c	22.	a	28.	b
5.	e	11.	c	17.	b	23.	d	29.	c
6.	c	12.	e	18.	d	24.	e		

Chapter 11

1.	b	8.	e	15.	b	22.	c	29.	b
2.	b	9.	c	16.	d	23.	a	30.	c
3.	d	10.	c	17.	b	24.	a	31.	a
4.	a	11.	c	18.	c	25.	e		
5.	a	12.	d	19.	e	26.	b		
6.	a	13.	e	20.	b	27.	d		
7.	e	14.	a	21.	c	28.	c		

Chapter 12

1.	a	8.	d	15.	b	22.	c	29.	e
2.	a	9.	a	16.	c	23.	a	30.	d
3.	e	10.	b	17.	b	24.	b	31.	e
4.	e	11.	d	18.	a	25.	c		
5.	d	12.	e	19.	a	26.	a		
6.	c	13.	e	20.	a	27.	b		
7.	c	14.	d	21.	b	28.	d		

Chapter 13

1.	a	6.	a	11.	d	16.	a	21.	c
2.	c	7.	c	12.	e	17.	b	22.	e
3.	b	8.	b	13.	c	18.	d	23.	b
4.	a	9.	d	14.	c	19.	e	24.	d
5.	d	10.	b	15.	d	20.	d		

Chapter 14

1.	b	7.	d	13.	c	19.	b	25.	c
2.	d	8.	a	14.	d	20.	d	26.	a
3.	c	9.	a	15.	b	21.	e	27.	a
4.	b	10.	e	16.	c	22.	d	28.	e
5.	e	11.	a	17.	c	23.	b		
6.	a	12.	e	18.	d	24.	b		

Chapter 15

1.	e	9.	d	17.	e	25.	a	33.	d
2.	e	10.	e	18.	d	26.	b	34.	b
3.	d	11.	b	19.	b	27.	c	35.	e
4.	e	12.	c	20.	d	28.	a	36.	c
5.	d	13.	a	21.	e	29.	a		
6.	e	14.	a	22.	b	30.	e		
7.	c	15.	c	23.	a	31.	e		
8.	a	16.	c	24.	d	32.	e		

Chapter 16

1.	d	7.	d	13.	b	19.	d	25.	a
2.	b	8.	a	14.	a	20.	d	26.	e
3.	e	9.	d	15.	c	21.	b	27.	c
4.	d	10.	d	16.	d	22.	e	28.	e
5.	b	11.	e	17.	b	23.	b	29.	b
6.	a	12.	e	18.	d	24.	e	30.	d

Chapter 17

1.	d	8.	c	15.	e	22.	d	29.	d
2.	b	9.	c	16.	c	23.	d	30.	b
3.	e	10.	e	17.	c	24.	d	31.	a
4.	e	11.	e	18.	b	25.	d	32.	d
5.	c	12.	e	19.	d	26.	c		
6.	d	13.	a	20.	d	27.	c		
7.	e	14.	e	21.	d	28.	a		

Chapter 18

1.	b	8.	b	15.	b	22.	b	29.	e
2.	a	9.	d	16.	c	23.	c	30.	e
3.	c	10.	d	17.	b	24.	c	31.	e
4.	a	11.	c	18.	d	25.	e	32.	e
5.	d	12.	b	19.	d	26.	d	33.	b
6.	e	13.	c	20.	d	27.	e		
7.	a	14.	c	21.	c	28.	b		

Chapter 19

1.	b	8.	c	15.	e	22.	d	29.	d
2.	b	9.	b	16.	c	23.	d	30.	e
3.	b	10.	b	17.	e	24.	d	31.	e
4.	c	11.	e	18.	e	25.	c	32.	e
5.	c	12.	e	19.	e	26.	a		
6.	b	13.	d	20.	c	27.	c		
7.	d	14.	a	21.	a	28.	c		

Chapter 20

1.	b	8.	d	15.	c	22.	d	29.	a
2.	d	9.	e	16.	c	23.	c	30.	a
3.	d	10.	a	17.	a	24.	b	31.	e
4.	c	11.	d	18.	d	25.	b	32.	a
5.	e	12.	e	19.	e	26.	e	33.	d
6.	b	13.	e	20.	c	27.	b	34.	a
7.	e	14.	d	21.	c	28.	d	35.	b

Appendix

1. b	4. b	7. e	10. c	13. e
2. e	5. d	8. c	11. e	14. e
3. b	6. d	9. e	12. b	15. a

Final Examination

1. e	23. a	45. c	67. d	89. d
2. b	24. e	46. d	68. b	90. d
3. b	25. b	47. a	69. b	91. c
4. a	26. c	48. a	70. c	92. d
5. a	27. b	49. a	71. b	93. b
6. d	28. d	50. b	72. b	94. c
7. c	29. e	51. d	73. c	95. e
8. c	30. c	52. b	74. a	96. e
9. c	31. b	53. c	75. d	97. c
10. b	32. c	54. b	76. b	98. c
11. e	33. e	55. c	77. d	99. e
12. c	34. e	56. e	78. b	100. e
13. c	35. b	57. a	79. e	101. b
14. e	36. d	58. c	80. b	102. e
15. e	37. a	59. d	81. c	103. a
16. e	38. e	60. b	82. b	104. e
17. d	39. c	61. d	83. c	105. b
18. b	40. d	62. a	84. e	106. e
19. c	41. a	63. d	85. c	107. c
20. e	42. b	64. e	86. c	108. d
21. b	43. b	65. d	87. e	109. d
22. e	44. a	66. c	88. a	110. e

Name Index

Subject Index